English Literature, Theolo

CW00420281

Theology in Dialogue Series
Series Editor: Ian Markham

The Theology in Dialogue series is an internationally supported response to a pressing need to explore the relationship between theology and the different, ostensibly secular, academic disciplines which appear within the degree programmes of colleges and universities. It has been developed by The Council of Church and Associated Colleges (CCAC), a network of UK-based colleges and universities which have Church foundations.

Each volume begins with a chapter and a reply, providing a thoughtful justification for the interaction of theology and each subject. This is followed by a theoretical analysis of this interaction, and a range of case studies illustrating the difference this makes in the classroom. All volumes contain contributions from the most highly respected scholars in their field.

Other books in the series:

Spirituality and the Curriculum edited by Adrian Thatcher
'Spirituality' and 'spiritual development' are increasingly widespread concepts, particularly within the pastoral profession of education. In this volume, leading theologians and educationalists discuss spirituality from the point of view of theology, its home discipline, and apply the results of their enquiries to the curriculum in colleges and schools.

Sociology, Theology and the Curriculum edited by Leslie J. Francis
The innovative essays in this dialogue demonstrate how sociology can be enriched by the scrutiny and insights of theology, and how the proper subject matter of theology can be illuminated by the theories and empirical methodologies of sociology. A focus is placed on the particular case of the church college, as an institution which teaches sociology, but which is also of sociological interest itself.

Theology in Dialogue Series
Series Editor: Ian Markham

English Literature, Theology and the Curriculum

Edited by Liam Gearon

CASSELL
London and New York

Cassell

Wellington House, 125 Strand, London WC2R 0BB
370 Lexington Avenue, New York, NY 10017-6550

© Liam Gearon and the contributors 1999

All rights reserved. No part of this publication may be reproduced or
transmitted in any form or by any means, electronic or mechanical including
photocopying, recording or any information storage or retrieval system,
without prior permission in writing from the publishers.

First published 1999

Bible quotations in Chapter 1 are the author's translation; others are from the
Authorized version, Crown copyright.

British Library Cataloguing-in-Publication Data
A catalogue record for this book is available from the British Library.

ISBN 0-304-70486-5

Typeset by BookEns Ltd, Royston, Herts.
Printed and bound in Great Britain by Biddles Ltd,
Guildford and King's Lynn

Contents

Contents

Contents

vii

Series Editor's Foreword

One of the central questions facing theological discourse must be its relationship with other discourses in the academy. For the academy this issue is acute. The twin pressures of secularization and plurality have inhibited theological reflection; theology has been confined to a 'department'; the result being that students on different degree programmes do not explore the overall framework and assumptions of their study. Certain fundamental value questions are entirely neglected.

This series is a challenge to the confinement of theological reflection to a single department. We believe that a full and rounded education ought to provide the space for wide-ranging reflection. Education is not value-free: all students ought to be encouraged to confront questions of value.

Each volume examines both questions of approach and questions of content. Some contributors argue that an overtly Christian or religious framework for higher education actually affects the way we approach our study; a religious framework supports faith, while the secular framework is opposed to faith. Other contributors insist that a religious framework simply makes the curriculum wider. The approach will be the same as our secular counterparts; however, where the content of a course has a religious implication this will be included. Each volume brings out the diversity of positions held within the academy.

We have attracted the best writers to reflect on these questions. Each volume concludes by reflecting on the curriculum implications – the precise implications for educators in our schools and higher education colleges.

Ian Markham

The Contributors

David N. Beauregard is Dean of Studies, Our Lady of Grace Seminary, Boston, Massachusetts, USA.

Beverley Clack is Senior Lecturer in the Department of Theology and Religious Studies at Roehampton Institute London.

Gavin D'Costa is Senior Lecturer in the Department of Theology and Religious Studies at the University of Bristol.

Philip Davis is Reader in English at the University of Liverpool.

Liam Gearon is Senior Lecturer in the Faculty of Education at the Roehampton Institute London, where he has also lectured in the Department of Theology and Religious Studies.

William Gray is Senior Lecturer in the School of English at University College Chichester, where he also lectures in the School of Religion and Theology.

Susanne Greenhalgh is Senior Lecturer in the Department of Drama: Theatre, Film and Television Studies at Roehampton Institute London.

Suman Gupta is Lecturer in Contemporary English Literature in the Department of English at Roehampton Institute, London.

J. Mark Halstead is Reader in the School of Humanities and Cultural Interpretation at the University of Plymouth.

Graham Holderness is Professor of English and Dean, Faculty of Humanities, Languages and Education at the University of Hertfordshire, and a Research Associate of the Centre for Advanced Theological Research, Roehampton Institute London.

The Contributors

David Jasper is Professor of Literature and Theology and Dean in the Faculty of Divinity at the University of Glasgow.

Elisabeth Jay is Head of Humanities at Westminster College, Oxford.

Norman Klassen lectures in the Department of English and Modern Languages at Trinity Western University, British Columbia, Canada.

Colin Lyas is Senior Lecturer in Philosophy at the University of Lancaster.

Kevin McCarron is Senior Lecturer in the Department of English at Roehampton Institute, London.

Kevin Mills was formerly Lecturer in Philosophy at the University of Wales and is now Research Fellow at Westminster College, Oxford.

Nike Kocijancic Pokorn lectures in the Department of English at the University of Ljubljana, Slovenia.

Stephen Prickett is Regius Professor of English Language and Literature at the University of Glasgow.

Christopher Southgate is Lecturer in the School of Classics and Theology at the University of Exeter.

Heather Walton, until recently Lecturer in Applied Theology at Westminster College, Oxford, now lectures at the University of Glasgow in the Faculty of Divinity.

Graham Ward is Professor of Contextual Theology and Ethics at the University of Manchester.

Michael Wheeler is Professor of English Literature and Director of the Ruskin Programme at the University of Lancaster.

Thomas Woodman is Senior Lecturer in the Department of English at the University of Reading.

Terence R. Wright is Professor of English Literature at the University of Newcastle.

Introduction

Liam Gearon

Writing Worlds[1] and Writing Communities

The world, it seems, is continually being rewritten; and writing, as readers of this volume may readily acknowledge, is central, obviously to the processes of literary creation and criticism, but equally to the processes of theology, and especially since language itself has achieved priority in so much contemporary thinking. What is notable here is the far from marginal presence of theological grandnarrative (to borrow ironically from Lyotard) as a metatext for reading the world, even if theology becomes its antithesis, that is, an atheology.[2]

The world then, is written and rewritten. Thus, if scripture (the Bible, say, as the 'Great Code'[3]) rooted 'pre-modern' theological reflection in the written word, the post-Enlightenment world of 'modernity' was a world which was literally rewritten by certain key texts, seminal *writings*. 'Postmodern' thinkers have themselves rewritten the text of 'modernity': morally, the world is rewritten as a product of cultural contingency where the ironist is called to human solidarity; but it is a world in which there are no non-circular reasons to ground the ironist's call not to be cruel (Rorty, 1989); epistemologically, the world is rewritten as a shifting 'narrative' where knowledge is a product of dialogic understanding (Gadamer, 1979) or the construct of 'paradigm shift' (Kuhn, 1970), and so forth; and for each newly accepted reading of the world there is generally a community of readers.[4]

The writing of worlds and the writing of communities are

1

therefore interrelated. Thus, when Wilfred Cantwell Smith (1993) attempted to privilege sacred texts (scripture) over other forms of writing by stressing the investment of social value in scripture, he was perhaps neglecting the fact that secular texts too can be marked by special community use, as this present volume on literature and theology itself illustrates.[5] Conflicting readings of texts between communities of text-users are evident in religious *and* secular contexts: for example, Catholic and Protestant communities disagreeing on the canon of the Bible[6] or university 'communities' of theologians and literary critics engaging in interdisciplinary dispute. As Kuhn has famously, if contentiously, pointed out within the philosophy of science, there is only a paradigm shift in the scientific reading of the world when an alternative 'script', a revolution in scientific hermeneutics, is accepted by the scientific *community*.

Indeed, the many implications of the foregoing for both literary and theological studies have been impressively addressed elsewhere by some of the contributors to this volume. Graham Ward's (1996) outstanding work, *Theology and Contemporary Critical Theory*, for instance, is part of the general series, Studies in Literature and Religion, whose series editor is another key contributor to this volume, David Jasper. A number of the European editors of the international journal *Literature and Theology*, in addition to Ward and Jasper, are represented here too with the contributions of Elisabeth Jay and Terence Wright. Wright's (1988) book, *Theology and Literature*, of course, is itself a significant contribution to the field. And what greater expert commentary on theology and literature could one wish for than that of Stephen Prickett, also included in this volume, whose recent achievements have included a new commentary (1997) on the King James Version of the Bible.

The considerable number of issues around the ('premodern', 'modern', 'postmodern') ways of reading the world must, though, be set aside here in this introduction. The uninitiated reader could do worse than read the chapters in this volume since this present work is itself attempting to further discussions of theory. Distinctive, though, is the manner in which *English Literature, Theology and the Curriculum* combines both theory and case study in a single text, a single collection of writings; and what comes across is the extraordinarily complex but also culturally enriching interaction between theology and literature over so many centuries of writing.

Models of Writing as Theological Activity

Thus, the underlying historical and contemporary relations which constitute a major focus for literature and theology are presented vigorously in the keynote chapters by Jasper and Wright. Also addressing important issues of theory, Stephen Prickett's 'Orality, Literacy and the Idea of the Spiritual' dwells on the central notions of writing and religious experience and provides a brilliantly expansive historical examination of how we have come to associate spirituality with textuality and the written word. The other chapter in this section highlights one of the most influential figures in Western religious thinking, Saint Augustine, and the latter's reading of the world in the fourth and fifth centuries. In Ward's analysis, Augustine, as a writer and imposing theological intellect, achieves a new directness.

The main body of the volume presents a range of case studies in English literature and theology from Anglo-Saxon verse to the twentieth-century novel. Graham Holderness's chapter opens with an insightful commentary on the reciprocal relations between Anglo-Saxon poetry and early Christian theology. Norman Klassen explores 'that ambiguous space between medieval and modern' and the relationship between moral and geographical space in Chaucer's *Canterbury Tales*. Nike Pokorn's chapter looks at the influential fourteenth-century mystical text of *The Cloud of Unknowing* and draws parallels between its content and style and that of postmodern readings of the world. '"How It Might Have Been To Believe": Re-imaging the Social Body in Contemporary Productions of the English Mystery Plays' by Susanne Greenhalgh provides a thorough analysis of a distinctive literary and specifically theatrical form of the medieval period. Remaining with drama, David Beauregard's case study on *Much Ado About Nothing* presents important commentary on the development of Shakespeare's moral as well as more strictly theological outlook.

Late sixteenth- and seventeenth-century poetry is the focus

3

for Mark Halstead's 'John Donne and the Theology of Incarnation', a painstaking and most successful attempt to review modes of interpretation for John Donne's religious verse in theological terms. Philip Davis's chapter provides a brilliant analysis of the mind and eighteenth-century life of Samuel Johnson and his 'tacit theological cosmology'.

Michael Wheeler's international renown as a scholar of the Victorian period is evident in 'Ruskin's Christian Theory of Art', an analysis of Ruskin's important nineteenth-century writings on the visual arts which provides a view of a theological world through Ruskin's words on painting. Wheeler considerably extends the aesthetic scope of this volume in a way which is also evident in a later chapter by Colin Lyas.

Kevin Mills's chapter provides an analysis of *The Time Machine*, H. G. Wells's first novel, published in the last years of the nineteenth century. This period is important for the growing influence of science as a world-view in late Victorian society. The apocalyptic themes of *The Time Machine* are shown to be both historically significant and, theologically, thoroughly contemporary. Christopher Southgate's 'Re-Considering Phlebas' presents us with a twentieth-century poet without whom any volume such as this might be deemed poorer – even though many other important twentieth-century poets may for reasons of space be absent – and provides a good case for 'the importance of studying the hermeneutics of Eliot criticism' as theology and for the way in which Eliot's poetry points to 'spiritual realities'.

The twentieth-century novel is represented in five chapters. Thomas Woodman, an acknowledged expert on the British Catholic novel, presents an engaging reading of the detective genre of 'Chesterton and Father Brown: Demystification and Deconstruction'. William Gray's chapter on C. S. Lewis, 'Spirituality and the Pleasure of the Text', draws on many themes which are central to this volume, in particular the act of reading itself. Gray's contribution, like C. S. Lewis's own priorities in reading, highlights a refreshing approach to reader-response, emphasizing reading as fundamentally transformative; centrally, the reader's pleasurable engagement with literature. Kevin McCarron's ' "Gentle Jesus Meek and Mild" ' presents a powerful portrayal of the religious themes in the novels of William Golding. Gavin D'Costa's chapter on

Rushdie shows just *how* powerful the modern novel can be in its effects beyond the pages of the narrative itself. His analysis of *The Satanic Verses* also provides crucial commentary on the literary, as well as socio-cultural and political, influence of Islam on literary form and content. My own chapter looks at the pre- and post-Vatican II portrayal of Catholicism in the novels of Brian Moore and the latter's development of a 'spiritual geography'.

The last five chapters present possibilities for extending curriculum considerations into areas of new challenge and insight for literature and theology, often involving an expanded understanding of what may be meant by both. Beverley Clack opens with a religiously 'anti-realist' perspective, 'The Theologian As Artist: Exploring the Future of Religion', focusing upon Graham Greene and Iris Murdoch as justification for her thesis. Elisabeth Jay's 'The Liberal in Crisis: or, Teaching Queer Theory in a Methodist College' gives practical examples of teaching situations in higher education and raises important issues about the assumptions which underlie both literary and theological curricula. Both personal *and* curriculum considerations in women's writing and theology are explored in Heather Walton's 'Love Relations', with many highly useful exemplars. Suman Gupta's 'Post-colonial Literature and Metaphysics' is an authoritative overview of that area of 'conceptual, critical and creative flux rather than the *terra firma* that is already mapped by literary cartographers' and with great skill draws those co-ordinates which extend the map of this volume's literary and theological concerns. The philosopher Colin Lyas concludes with his usual clarity of insight in the field of aesthetics. 'Getting Someone to See' establishes invaluable links between writing, world-view and ethics, a reminder that what is involved here is at heart a moral process, in which, educationally, 'literature might be essential to bringing about religious understanding'.

Notes

1. This useful expression was derived and adapted from Barnes and Duncan (1992) *Writing Worlds: Discourse, Text and Metaphor in the Representation of Landscape*. There is a growing geographical literature on the representation of social space which has largely untapped implications for theology and literature, see Benko and Strohmayer (1997) *Space and Social Theory: Interpreting Modernity and Postmodernity*; but see my (1997) article, 'Exploring the landscape of spiritual

geography'. Also, see the emphasis upon place in contributions by Holderness and Klassen in this volume.

2. Thus, for instance, Rorty (1989) comments: 'A postmetaphysical culture seems to me no more impossible than a postreligious one, and equally desirable' (p. xvi). Rorty (1989) uses the term 'ironist' to define 'the sort of person who faces up to the contingency of his or her own central beliefs'. In areas such as moral choice Rorty argues that anyone who believes there is an order, 'well grounded theoretical answers' to such questions, 'is still, in his heart, a theologian or a metaphysician. He believes in an order beyond time and change which both determines and establishes a hierarchy of responsibilities.' Nevertheless, Rorty acknowledges that 'The ironist intellectuals who do not believe that there is such an order are far outnumbered (even in the lucky, rich, literate democracies) by people who believe there *must* be one. Most nonintellectuals are still committed either to some form of religious faith or to some form of Enlightenment rationalism' (1989: xv). Mark C. Taylor (1984) gave currency to the term "atheology", for which see his *Erring: A Postmodern A/ theology* (Chicago: Chicago University Press). For a theological response to the postmodern critique of metaphysics and postmodern atheology see Milbank's (1993) *Theology and Social Theory: Beyond Secular Reason*, especially pp. 278–325. For a commentary on the relation between philosophy, deconstruction and theology see Hart's (1991) *The Trespass of the Sign*. Also relevant is Ward's (1996) overview of *Theology and Critical Contemporary Theory*. More recently still, see Ward's (1997) *The Postmodern God: A Theological Reader*, and Klassen's reference to Ward on the problem of periodicity below (pp. 100–1). For an analysis of this notion of writing and modes of thinking, see Wood's (1990) *Philosophy at the Limit: Problems of Modern European Thought*. More recently, see Porter's (1996) *The Nature of Religious Language*, Ingraffia's (1995) *Postmodern Theory and Biblical Theology* and Milbank's (1997) *The World Made Strange: Theology, Language and Culture*. See also Pickstock's (1998) acclaimed *After Writing: On the Liturgical Consummation of Philosophy*.

3. Frye (1982).

4. This itself has considerable educational implications; see my (1997a) article, 'What's the story?: spirituality and writing'.

5. Smith (1993) comments: 'Fundamental, we suggest, to a new understanding of scripture is the recognition that no text is a scripture in itself and as such. People – a given community – make a text into scripture, or keep it scripture: by treating it in a certain way. I suggest: *scripture is a human activity*.' (Emphasis in original.) He goes on to exclaim: 'Scriptures are not texts!' (pp. 18–19).

6. See J. H. Hayes in (M.) Hayes and Gearon (1998), *Contemporary Catholic Theology: A Reader*, pp. 62–86.

References

Barnes, T. J. and Duncan, J. S. (eds) (1992), *Writing Worlds: Discourse, Text and Metaphor in the Representation of Landscape* (London: Routledge)

Benko, G. and Strohmayer, U. (eds) (1997), *Space and Social Theory: Interpreting Modernity and Postmodernity* (Oxford: Blackwell)

Derrida, J. (1978), *Writing and Difference*, trans. Alan Bass (London: Routledge)

Derrida, J. (1982), *Margins of Philosophy*, trans. Alan Bass (Hemel Hempstead: Harvester Wheatsheaf)

Frye, N. (1983), *The Great Code: The Bible and Literature* (London: Ark Paperbacks)

Gadamer, H.-G. (1979), *Truth and Method*, 2nd edn (London: Sheed and Ward)

Gearon, L. (1997), Exploring the landscape of spiritual geography', *Journal of Beliefs and Values*, 18, 1, pp. 69–82

Gearon, L. (1997a), 'What's the story?: spirituality and writing', *The International Journal of Children's Spirituality*, 2, 2, pp. 41–52

Hayes, J.H. (1998), 'The canon of the Old Testament' in Hayes and Gearon (1998)

Hayes, M.A. and Gearon, L. (eds) (1998), *Contemporary Catholic Theology: A Reader* (Leominster: Gracewing)

Ingraffia, Brian D. (1995), *Postmodern Theory and Biblical Theology* (Cambridge: Cambridge University Press)

Hart, K. (1991), *The Trespass of the Sign: Deconstruction, Philosophy and Theology* (Cambridge: Cambridge University Press)

Kuhn, T. (1970), *The Structure of Scientific Revolutions*, 2nd edn (London: University of Chicago Press)

Lyotard, J.-F. (1984), *The Postmodern Condition: A Report on Knowledge* (Manchester: Manchester University Press)

Milbank, J. (1993), *Theology and Social Theory: Against Secular Reason* (Oxford: Blackwell)

Milbank, J. (1997), *The Word Made Strange: Theology, Language and Culture* (Oxford: Blackwell)

Pickstock, C. (1998), *After Writing: On the Liturgical Consummation of Philosophy* (Oxford: Blackwell)

Porter, S. (ed.) (1996), *The Nature of Religious Language* (Sheffield: Sheffield Academic Press)

Prickett, S. and Carroll, R. (eds) (1997), *Introduction to the King James Version of the Bible* (Oxford: Oxford University Press)

Rorty, R. (1989), *Contingency, Irony and Solidarity* (Cambridge: Cambridge University Press)

Smith, W.C. (1993), *What is Scripture?* (London: SCM)

Taylor, M.C. (1984) *Erring: A Postmodern A/theology* (Chicago: Chicago University Press)

Ward, G. (1996), *Theology and Contemporary Critical Theory* (Basingstoke: Macmillan)

Ward, G. (1997), *The Postmodern God: A Theological Reader* (Oxford: Blackwell)

Wood, D. (1990) *Philosophy at the Limit: Problems of Modern European Thought* (London: Unwin Hyman)

Wright, T. (1988), *Theology and Literature* (Oxford: Blackwell)

Part I Interdisciplinary Dialogue

1

How Can We Read the Bible?

David Jasper

M y opening contention is that the Bible, that 'basic book of our civilisation',[1] is not *read*, and rarely has, in fact, been read, for two fundamentally opposed reasons in the Western tradition. First, it has not been read *within* the religious traditions of Jews and Christians because those traditions have preferred to confine the majority of believers to a condition of being read to. Thus the priest and prophetic scribe Ezra, in the apocryphal book 2 Esdras, is given 94 inspired books from the mouth of God, of which only the first 24 are to be given directly to the people. The remaining 70 'are to be kept back and given to none but the wise among your people' (14.46). These books, in other words, are to come to the people only through the interpretative medium of the theologically competent and privileged few. In the same way, in Margaret Atwood's dystopic novel *The Handmaid's Tale* (1985), the captive handmaids are not allowed to read the Bible, but only to have it read to them by the male 'commander', the one in control.

Second, the Bible has not been read *outside* the religious traditions precisely because its privileged and powerful status has been a matter of deep suspicion. Non-believers suspect the peculiar claims of theology and the use of the Bible as an instrument of oppression, coercion and the sustaining of privilege and power. Meanwhile, around the canon of Scripture believers set a *cordon sanitaire*, protecting it from the kind of attention given to almost all other forms of literature and text.

It is not, therefore, surprising that from time to time critical voices are raised of those who feel themselves to be excluded or coerced for many reasons – of race, gender, or any other ground of subjection to exclusive structures of power and authority. So, for example, in 1895, Elizabeth Cady Stanton, author of *The Woman's Bible* in the United States of America began her Introduction:

> From the inauguration of the movement for woman's emancipation, the Bible has been used to hold her in the 'divinely ordained sphere', prescribed in the Old and New Testaments. The canon and civil law; church and state; priests and legislators; all political parties and religious denominations have alike taught that woman was made after man, of man, and for man, an inferior being, subject to man. Creeds, codes, Scriptures and statutes, are all based on this idea. The fashions, forms, ceremonies and customs of society, church ordinances and discipline all grow out of this idea.[2]

Later in her Introduction, Cady Stanton explicitly denies the divine inspiration of Scripture, and elsewhere, in an article in the *North American Review*, she observed that the Bible 'has been interpreted to favor intemperance, slavery, capital punishment and the subjection of women'.

In other words, the problem may lie not so much *in* Scripture itself as in those who claim responsibility for its interpretation, and it is certainly my explicit contention that biblical critics, at least in the Christian tradition, have, from the earliest times to the present, tended to work within a theological agenda which regards the Bible as specifically the Church's inspired book, and its learned readers also as properly appropriately privileged and inspired.[3] The consequences of this religious racket are not limited to the question of the Bible itself, but have gone far also to define and limit the canonical boundaries of our contemporary culture and educational procedures. Within the broad area of my own concern with the relationship between both the practice and study of literature and religion, what this demands of us is a return to the question of the nature of a *sacred text* (and its place within textuality broadly understood), and the recovery of the practice of *religious reading*, that is a practice of reading which allows us to return to the Bible, not to speak of a great number of other literary texts, in a mutually sustaining exchange. This is not simply a reprise of Benjamin Jowett's notorious, yet deeply reverent essay of 1860 in which he claims that when interpreted like any other book the Bible will be found to be quite different and unique,[4] but something far more radical than this.

But lest we move too hastily, let us consider the ancient tradition in Western art and literature of what has been termed 'Christian iconoclasm'.[5] The early Christian Church took over the Jewish prohibition of idolatry more or less wholesale, and has sustained through the centuries a highly ambiguous attitude towards art and creative literature. Paradoxically, the Protestant Reformation was responsible for a fierce attack on art and images at a time in Europe when secular art was flourishing, not least as a result of the Protestant spirit itself. It was precisely in his conflict with the Reformed Church in Amsterdam that the greatest of all artists of the Bible, Rembrandt, found his most spiritual expression in painting. In poetry, John Milton struggled to justify the ways of God to humankind, and succeeded only at the price of orthodox Christian theology (so that it is legitimate to ask whether *Paradise Lost* is even a Christian poem at all), and in magnificent verse, within the *poetics* of which 'God is justified, in a way that might perhaps have surprised him'.[6] Or, in the nineteenth century within the Roman Catholic Scotist tradition, Gerard Manley Hopkins struggled tragically between his vocation as a priest and his calling as a poet, finding both his most profound poetry and his deepest Christian theology in moments of anguish and despair of both.

The assumption underlying a great deal of study in literature and the arts, and their relationship with religion, seems to be that there is a basic harmony flowing between the two – and this I believe to be profoundly untrue. Rather, there is and always has been a deep, painful and yet finally creative tension, and it is that with which I am here concerned. On the one hand we find a dangerous and self-serving critical attitude summed up in the demand for

> the characteristics and insights of a specifically Christian criticism. Such a criticism must have a theological grounding. That is, it must attempt not the inferring of Christian belief or theme in writers who will in most cases be non-Christian; but

rather the exploring of the creative laws, under which writers operate, as they might be understood both by a critic and a Christian theologian.[7]

Despite disclaimers, the assumptions of Christian supremacy here are unavoidable. On the other hand, however, there is the widespread practice in academic departments of literature to dismiss the 'religious' and 'theological' as dangerously narrow and evangelistic (in practice, sadly, all too often true). Neither position will encourage us to return to the Bible as the most formative influence on Western literature (even while that literature is being profoundly influenced also by other religious traditions in our increasingly multicultural society) as well as the central text of the Judaeo-Christian tradition, and attempt to find *legitimate* ways of reading it. Nor do they recognize an astonishing and persistent theme in so-called postmodern critical theory, that to read is itself a religious act, and that in teaching students to read we simply cannot avoid the question of reading *religiously*, and that finally the most important collection of texts in our tradition is, not by accident and certainly not because of the Church or Synagogue, that most scandalous and exciting of all books – the Bible.

It is not by accident that, quite apart, indeed, quite separate from the tradition of biblical interpretation in the Christian West, is the tradition of literary and artistic intertextuality which perceives the Bible saturating our whole experience of word and image. This continues unabated in the most apparently god-forsaken corners of contemporary culture. The popular Hollywood cinema feeds off the Bible, so that it is virtually impossible to go to the cinema or watch a video without encountering some kind of scriptural reference. Blockbuster Hollywood films like *Terminator Two* draw immediately from the biblical tradition of apocalyptic, quite apart from the continuing fascination with overt retellings of biblical narratives in the epic tradition of cinema – films which tell us a great deal more about the culture of twentieth-century North America than anything else. The central images of the Bible, in particular the cross, remain as potent symbols in our society to interpret our experience of the world even while the intellectual current apparently flows strongly against the belief systems within which those images were born. I do not think it is necessarily the case that this suggests that we live in a world which continues to hunger for a redeeming faith which it has somehow lost. That is a naive argument put forward by the pious who continue to be sustained by narrow and unreflective notions of what is 'true'. Literature and art have always returned to the world of biblical and religious symbol though with their own various agendas, suggesting that the relationship between the 'sacred' world of the Bible and their 'profane' worlds is much more complex than most of us are prepared to admit. Thus we have the odd result in our educational programmes that departments of literature generally neglect to read to Bible because it represents a dangerous and exclusive tradition, while departments of theology and religious studies develop hermeneutical strategies which actually *prevent* us from reading it as protective measures to maintain that tradition. Meanwhile, the Bible remains as the single most fertile resource for reflection upon our culture and experience.

I suggest that what we need to begin to do is distinguish between the terms *text* and *reading*. On the whole most of us are deeply neurotic readers and spend a great deal of time training our students to be the same. From the earliest stages of education we refuse theoretical reflection and work with the assumption that a text contains meaning which, with a good dictionary and a proper sense of grammar, we can excavate.[8] Texts, we assume, mean something and we learn, obediently, to search for that meaning. That is what reading is about, we think. A much better model would be to employ the activity of reading as an opportunity to engage in self-reflection (a much more difficult and possibly threatening process) in the interaction between text and reader. This need by no means degenerate into an exercise in pure subjectivity. The critic Stanley Fish reflects in his now famous essay *Is There a Text in This Class?*[9] on the *status* of the literary text in the process of reading, and whether the abandonment of a stable sense of meaning need imply simply indeterminacy and undecidability. I certainly do not think that this is the case, although it does provoke a healthy reflection on the contexts, both personal and communal, in which meaning is developed. In short, we have to begin to *think* as we read.

The Bible has become a very powerful text – and the more powerful a text becomes, the less we actually read it. What we do instead is employ strategies to implement its power, or else ignore it altogether if we prefer to play other power games. For example, the modern emphasis on the objective recovery of the ancient meaning and contexts of biblical literature[10] is part of an ancient tradition which ensures that the Bible is maintained as a political and social control – a whip to beat us when we are naughty, and a carrot to encourage us to be good. Not by accident has the Christian Church maintained a relentless political interest – sometimes blatant, sometimes more embarrassed. Or again, since *The Woman's Bible*, the increasing crescendo of feminist critics of the Bible have exposed the patriarchal impositions upon the text which have done so much to establish in our society the so-called 'natural' structures of family and human sexuality. Not by accident, a great many of the best *readers* of the Bible are within this feminist tradition.[11]

I see it as a great problem that while there are movements in the academy to 'rescue' the Bible (and therefore literature) at the so-called 'research' level, there is almost nothing happening at the probably much more important level of the schools. Despite the huge impact of literary theory during the past two decades, the teaching of literature and the traditional canon of texts remain resolutely unchanged, and the business of real critical thought almost entirely neglected. Turning our attention from text to reading is a crucial educational move. Most specifically, turning our attention from sacred text to religious reading is not a matter simply for departments of religious studies or theology. Rather, it is a business which lies at the sharp end of schooling, where matters of power, self-identity, gender, race and all questions of the greatest importance in our social and political lives are to be found. Whether or not we believe in the theological claims made in and for Scripture, freeing it to be read will involve us in a unique exercise in the deconstruction of power and the realization of freedom. Such things, I suggest, are not unimportant in the processes of education and will affect all our reading and encounters with texts within the 'canons' of our secular literature and art.

What does it mean precisely to speak of a sacred text? It has, I suggest, a number of characteristics.[12] Regarded as in some sense inspired, it reveals something which is otherwise veiled or hidden, and requires some sort of decoding. Attracting a community of believers, the sacred text will claim to be able to change lives, often through specific ceremonies or 'liturgical' acts. Such a text will often be regarded as a substitute for the divine presence itself. Now, if these are characteristics of the Bible in the Judaeo-Christian tradition, they apply also, though to a much lesser extent, to other texts in our literature as well. I would not want to suggest that the notion of a sacred text is necessarily a bad thing – it is simply, like religion and its handmaid theology, powerful and two-edged, and we need therefore to be wary and know what we are doing when we deal with it. This process of 'deconstruction' is quite different from Rudolf Bultmann's programme in his biblical studies of 'demythologizing', which involves a moving through the text to the 'truth' which lies within and beyond it. Rather, warily and with playful respect we need to learn to encounter the text – a respect which abandons all bibliolatrous tendencies. Perhaps paradoxically, some may think, such wariness will be engendered by a healthy practice of reading *religiously*, primarily a literary act which stands in creative, nervous tension with the strong text. The practice of religious reading[13] entails an abandonment of those aggressive and confrontational attitudes which we breed into our children from the earliest days of reading, with their demands for *the* correct interpretation and for conclusion. Rather, reading becomes an opportunity for human expression and self-knowledge in a dialogue with the text. The 'space' offered by this act of reading will become a garden of serious play, where profound and creative games can be played which do not demand or seek anything beyond self-realization and the development of a genuine and responsible sense of community. Rather than violating the text (or being subjected to the imposition of the text upon us), we become members of a 'religious' community of readers characterized not by definition and specificity of meaning, but a surplus of meaning,[14] a celebration of awareness in the festivities of reading.

Religious reading can offer us insight into what Robert Detweiler has called 'the great ineffability of existence in the face of its richness of meaning'. Properly this is nowhere better exercised than in the literature of the Bible, could we but once learn to read it, and it is the reason why the Bible has endured, in spite of all the attacks of priest and critic, sacred and secular, as the great living centre of our Western tradition. As D. H. Lawrence (no believer he) put it, 'The novel is the book of life. In this sense, the Bible is a great confused novel.'[15] Nevertheless, though this is true for most of us, at the same time we live in a society increasingly composed of people for whom other texts are sacred. This is all the more reason to emphasize the need for a religious reading of literature, as the idea of a sacred text becomes at once more difficult to define and also more embattled.

All of this has profound implications for education, and for our structures of teaching and learning. First, it implies a far more *interdisciplinary* approach to study. The assumption that we are experts in particular fields and that different canons pertain to different subjects must be loosened, and as teachers we need to be much more attentive to the legitimate demands of both texts and young readers. The practice of interdisciplinarity has far wider and more important significance than a shift in the curriculum and our self-understanding as teachers in different disciplines. It is, I believe, crucial in our addressing of our increasingly multicultural society, which pays a heavy price for the unthinking defence of cultural specificity, and whose laws are still incredibly biased towards the myth, now utterly obscene and probably never true (despite T. S. Eliot's ominous 1939 lectures on *The Idea of a Christian Society*), that we live in Britain in a fundamentally Christian society.

Take, for example, the furore in Britain following the publication of Salman Rushdie's *The Satanic Verses* in 1988. Here is not the place to enter into a discussion of the *fatwa*. More domestically we were reminded that our laws of blasphemy in England simply exclude the literature of anyone outside the Anglican tradition: that blasphemy was a concept none of us really understood anyway: that regarding the novel as a powerful *text* tended to prevent most people from actually reading it, though they still seemed prepared to say a great deal about it – not unlike the Bible in this sense: that the argument emerged out of a deeply culturally specific reaction (understandable at one level, but finally terrifying) against a book which is in fact a celebration of cultural unspecificity. Rushdie is, after all, like many of his critics, an immigrant with close connections to at least three countries (India, Pakistan, Britain) – the term he himself uses is 'mongrel' – seeking a new self-definition in a context which continually requires *translation*.[16]

16

The Satanic Verses is a wholesale denial of the possibility of culturally specific reading. Yet we see in this novel a text becoming immensely powerful and then ceasing to be read. In a curious way it has become almost scriptural itself. It is in no-one's interest, and certainly among those involved in the cultural and religious argument, to read the book. What Rushdie is calling for, dangerously perhaps, to an often unwilling audience, is a celebration of reading in a difficult, challenging, healthy comedy. Here are some of the last words of the book.

> He stood at the window of his childhood and looked out at the Arabian Sea. The moon was almost full; moonlight, stretching from the rocks of Scandal Point out to the far horizon, created the illusion of a silver pathway, like the parting in the water's shining hair, like a road to miraculous lands. He shook his head; could no longer believe in fairy-tales. Childhood was over, and the view from this window was no more than an old and sentimental echo. To the devil with it! Let the bulldozers come. If the old refused to die, the new could not be born.
> ... 'Let's get the hell out of here'...[17]

Rushdie turns a huge responsibility onto his reader, and his readership has largely refused to accept the challenge. Literature has made its intertextual demands upon religion and culture, which quickly retreat to their fastnesses of prejudice and incipient violence. In many ways, we do the same with the Bible – and forget the celebration of religious reading for the supposed security, cultural specificity and the dogmatic violence of guarding the 'sacred text'. As educators, therefore, we must address the task of teaching students to read, and have the courage to 'translate' their responses (just as the Bible has always been a translated book) into new and challenging contexts which expose new questions rather than offer tired answers to irrelevant ones.

As teachers I suggest that we generally prefer not to lose our grip on the traditional model of the single teacher as the fount of wisdom for the class, rarely if ever exposed to the critique implied in, say, joint teaching of classes, in which one teacher actually critiques the other, leaving the class to work out a response for themselves. Such forms of teaching can be dangerous – indicating how factions can form, how prejudices can deafen us to certain things, how we prefer certainty – but can also lead to a process of self-reflection, reflection on the experience of listening and reading, and the realization that we can celebrate diversity and that tension can be creative, not simply divisive.

We return, then, to where we began, with the recognition of the creative tension between literature and religion, and the need to learn to read, and for most of us, to read in particular the Bible, or, perhaps, other 'sacred' literature. Giving students the courage to believe in themselves as readers – which is precisely what our traditional curricula and examination systems generally fail to do – will begin to allow them to relate to words both intellectually and emotionally, which words then become themselves contexts for adult relationships with traditionally powerful texts that, as Rushdie has so vividly demonstrated, can whip back at us unless we learn to 'get the hell out'. What we seek to restore is a legitimacy to our own reading, and thereby recover legitimate ways of reading the Bible and sacred texts – ways which allow us to be offended and angry, even, or perhaps especially, at God, as part of our response and celebration.

What is supremely true of the canon of Scripture has become true also of the canon of secular literature from Chaucer to Shakespeare and Milton and up to the present day. They become texts which we learn to read only fearfully, without that joyous sense of 'overliving' which truly characterizes poetry and the creative arts. Rules, it is often said, are only made to be broken – and certainly this is true of the rules of religion. Breaking down the rules which hem us in, protect us perhaps – though from what? – allows reading to become an arena for ethical and social reconstruction, and for self-construction in an age which has notoriously lost its sense of the self and subject, and that honesty which is perhaps the beginning of a recovery of the sacred in and as part of our lives.

Students of literature are often introduced too quickly to James Joyce's *A Portrait of the Artist as a Young Man* (1916). In my experience, few are ever encouraged to reflect what it means *for them* to read the hell-fire sermon and to turn that against our 'readings' of Scripture.

> Every word of it was for him. Against his sin, foul and secret, the whole wrath of God was aimed. The preacher's knife had

18

probed deeply into his disclosed conscience and he felt now that his soul was festering in sin. Yes, the preacher was right.[18]

Students of the Bible are familiar with the parable of the Prodigal Son (Luke 15.11–32). While the boy is among the pigs we are told (to translate directly from the Greek) that 'he came back into himself', and turned back to his father for forgiveness. That is, he comes to 'metanoia' – a self-recovery which enables him to act to give an opportunity of repairing the social and familial tear which his self-indulgence had brought about. He begins to test words which will bring freedom and salvation on his return home. For James Joyce, listening to the sermon, words become a burden, an imposition, intimidating without intimacy. For the Prodigal, who has begun to 'read' again, words become liberating as he breaks the rules and invites others to break the rules in a celebration of awareness and joyous excess that changes the deathly and deadly into the lively and life-inspiring.

As I look back now on this attempt to address some of the issues that first struck me as I was introduced to this forum of *Engaging the Curriculum* I can see why some of those who proposed the project were rather puzzled or disappointed. Nevertheless, it has been a necessary road to travel as these issues began to clarify in debate and discussion. The experience has, at least, made me more aware of some of the initial, necessary, though perhaps quite simple questions. It is sometimes easy to miss the obvious.

And so now, with what has already been said in mind, allow me to try and address directly the central question of 'engaging the curriculum'. Presumably what is expected of the literature forum is that it should offer a way forward for some kind of legitimation of the role of religion, and specifically Christianity, within departments of literature. Since for most of my professional life I have been concerned with the interdisciplinary study of literature and theology, it was presumably assumed that I would have some ready answers to this question. But what sort of answers were expected? Clearly what I have said about the Bible and our failure to read it did not go down well with those who invited me to be involved. Perhaps engaging the curriculum means articulating, in some way, a Christian approach to English studies, or at least legitimating such an approach. It might presuppose the notion that 'literature and religion' is a naturally harmonious study – a view which I have vigorously opposed – or at least yield a viable hermeneutic useful for students of literature, perhaps based upon a confessional attitude.

Such a hermeneutic might be expected to 'engage' the curriculum of English studies. In spite of endless revisions of the school and college curricula, and the deluge of 'literary theory' since the 1960s, as we have seen, this curriculum and ways of teaching it have remained largely unshaken, and probably for most teachers of English (though not all), 'religion and literature' suggests either a 'Christian' reading of the literary canon, or a 'Christianizing' of authors who would deeply resist such a move. One still encounters endless projects to establish 'Christ figures' in literature, or versions of doctrines of atonement embedded in the narratives of fiction and drama.[19]

I deeply resist all such moves, harking back as they do to the days of Lord David Cecil or T. S. Eliot. For I really do not think that it is possible now – if it ever has been – to impose a confessional framework upon our reponse to literature and art and expect to find anything other than what we began with. On the other hand, as I find continually in exchanges with critics who come from other religious and cultural backgrounds, all of us carry, largely unconsciously, an enormous freight of presuppostions which, even if we cannot shed them, need to be exposed and acknowledged if our sympathies are to be enlarged.

I suggest that one of the consequences of studying 'literature and religion' is that it becomes increasingly difficult for someone like myself to define what it means to be 'Christian', yet at the same time, increasingly impossible to escape that which one no longer surely knows. The reason for this lies in the fact that, although the *agenda* continues to be set by theology, literature having in itself no particular agenda, the *medium* is literature rather than formal theology as such. Yet literature, which so readily prompts theological reflection, generally resists to the 'nth degree any transformation into the demands of 'a theology'.

And so, I return at last to the question of reading. In the first part of this essay I argued that before we even begin to tackle the question of how, for example, a formal adherence (however loose) to the confession of Christianity has a bearing upon the teaching of English literature, we need to address the basic questions raised by this mysterious act which lies at the heart of the whole business – that is the act of reading. Not only are these questions very largely neglected, but in addition, the vast majority of people teaching English literature appear to profess a profound lack of interest in religion except as a curious archaic left-over indulged in by the few. Institutionally speaking that is not an unreasonable attitude, were it not that it is still largely supported by that curious inheritance from the nineteenth century, fed in the twentieth by influences as diverse as F. R. Leavis and Sixties Marxist criticism, that literature with its culture is a replacement for the decayed doctrines and metaphysics of Western Christianity. But when we reflect upon that central activity of our trade it quickly becomes painfully clear that everything we do is wrapped up the presuppositions of a culture formulated not so much upon the orthodox rectitudes of Christian doctrine, but upon its consequences in a society which has never been (and least of all today) monologic or universal.

All we have are our prejudices and the neuroses that emerge from them. At least learning to read – which will probably be the most painful and disorientating thing in the world – may take us back to the fundamental questions involved in engaging with the curriculum ethically, aesthetically and even religiously. It will probably have a profound effect upon our notions of canon, which texts are acceptable and which are not; it will certainly make us take literature more seriously; and it may shock us into recognizing that we are far more religious than we had ever dared to acknowledge. If what has been lost in our postmodern condition is a sense of the self – so successfully construed in different ways in the West through the biblical traditions until Descartes, and then through the Enlightenment, the engagement I am now suggesting may be a possible way of recovering our sense of self through a re-enlivened sense of textuality. Only then, I believe, can we truly return to the Bible and read it, as if for the first time.

But, of course, there is always that catch, the 'as if'. However much we succeed in recovering the excitement of the text, it comes to us with its history for good and ill. Harold Bloom, in his attempt to recreate the Book of J in the Pentateuchal literature, says that he 'wants the varnish off', believing that he can reveal a writer in the first books of the Bible of the literary stature of Shakespeare or Dante, a 'writer [who] is worth more than many creeds, many churches, many scholarly certainties'.[20] Meanwhile, Gabriel Josipovici reads the Bible again and finds it 'far fresher and more "modern" than any of the prize-winning novels rolling off the presses'.[21] A great deal of the academic literary assault on biblical criticism in the past couple of decades has, I suppose, brought the Bible back into canon of books which are read 'as literature'. But then I find myself, for once, agreeing with T. S. Eliot when he claims that

> the Bible has had a *literary* influence upon English literature *not* because it has been considered as literature, but because it has been considered as the report of the Word of God. And the fact that men of letters now discuss it as 'literature' probably indicates the end of its 'literary' influence.[22]

I suspect that that is probably the case, and therein lies the catch. For Spinoza, long ago, wrote the *Tractatus Theologico-Politicus* precisely because he saw that people in traditions which profess the religion of the Bible misunderstand it by taking it for granted – that is, they have a vested interest in not reading it in order that the tradition might be sustained. Meanwhile, in English, with its difficulty in reading the Bible compounded by the lasting literary power of the King James Bible (and behind that the translations of William Tyndale and Miles Coverdale absorbed by Shakespeare and others into the literary canon), the Bible is not read both because it is regarded in some mysterious way as the Word of God and at the same time because it is regarded as literature, with the consequent end of its 'literary' influence. Either way you lose.

Although I have devoted myself for many years to the study and teaching of literature and religion, I still find it almost impossible to give advice on how new courses and degrees should be set up in this field. Yet, for some reason, we persist in Britain in trying to do so. They gave up long ago in the USA, and got themselves lost in the swamp of cultural studies in which nobody reads anything at all, but they simply observe literature and culture from the outside in timid and self-congratulatory acts of political correctness. When I make my demands for 'reading', I do so fully well aware that all reading claims commitment, and is ultimately both costly and dangerous. This is never more so than when we try to come back to that most dangerous book of all, the Bible, with all its history and its ghostly authority, even (perhaps especially) for those for whom its religions are no longer tenable or relevant.

The Bible simply swamps us. When we come to read it and teach it the problem is that it is on the one hand everywhere, and yet on the other it is distinct and peculiar, exclusive and making enormous claims of privilege. It saturates our literature and culture so that, after the King James Bible, we cannot distinguish which comes first – the Bible or Shakespeare, Bunyan, Milton. Either way it remains impossible to read – it is everywhere and ubiquitous, and as Qoheleth reminds us, of the making of many books there is no end, implying, as Michael Edwards has argued,[23] that this is a necessary fact of the human condition. There is, no doubt, much vanity in writing and danger in rhetorics of reading and interpretation, and nowhere more so than when it comes to the Bible.

As I reflect upon that phrase in Ecclesiastes, I think also of the terrible last verse of St John's Gospel:

> And there were also many other things which Jesus did, the which, if they should be written every one, I suppose that even the world itself could not contain the books that should be written. Amen.

This stands in sharp contrast to the opening verse of the Gospel: 'In the beginning was the Word.' From that solitary Word we move through the Gospel to a world threatened with extinction through the sheer weight of words and books, most of which must be utterly trivial: sacrality of word and deed taken to the absurd limit. And in the huge and unknowable accumulation of texts we (perhaps necessarily) develop strategies of reading to protect ourselves from the flood of words and their power – and end up reading nothing. The Bible overreaches itself, and we do not read it at all – it is too dangerous, too much, impossible to engage with.

I return in conclusion to Stanley Fish. In the essay already referred to, *Is There a Text in This Class?*, Fish wrote about interpretative communities and their authority, affirming that 'the condition required for someone to be a solipsist or relativist, the condition of being independent of institutional assumptions and free to originate one's own purposes and goals, could never be realised'.[24] Those who teach and those who are taught are already members of interpretative communities with varying institutional assumptions and constraints. Escape is no easy thing, and perhaps impossible. But learning to 'read', as I have explored this activity, is possibly the major, perhaps the only pursuit which may draw those communities together by drawing them out of themselves, making them more self-aware and more aware of others. So much of our teaching is already the victim of our consumer society. As the poet and professor of literature, Peter Meinke, puts it in his poem 'Supermarket':

> Everywhere there are lies, I lie to my classes, I say,
> Eat this poem. Eat that poem. *Good* for you.
> I say, Sonnets have more vitamins than villanelles,
> I give green stamps for the most vivid images.[25]

But supermarkets, we know, destroy communities, and so we must return to Fish's notion of the interpretative community and also to our earlier theme of 'religious reading'. In *Breaking the Fall*, Detweiler suggests that

> A religious reading might be one that finds a group of persons engaged in gestures of friendship with each other across the erotic space of the text that draws them out of their privacy and its stress in meaning and power.[26]

In the context of trying to read the Bible this raises a number of issues. Who would this group of persons be? What would keep them together? What would be the nature of their friendship realized across the space of the text? Would this simply end up within another church or Christian Union? How do we deal with the term 'erotic' here, and in what sense, positively, can the Bible become an erotic space? Finally, how do most of us overcome the sense of reading as essentially private, or else as a coercion and an excavation of meaning somehow resident within the text?

When he became Director of the *Engaging the Curriculum* project, Ian Markham wrote:

> The whole programme is dedicated to recovering the religious, ethical and spiritual dimensions of all study. The secularisation

of education diminished the task of education ... It reduced education to the reporting of supposed 'facts' in a supposedly neutral manner, and lost sight of the need to locate those 'facts' in a value framework.[27]

In the same issue of the *Bulletin*, Shannon Ledbetter wrote:

The mission statement of *Engaging the Curriculum* is a direct challenge to those individuals who would desire a complete withdrawal of religion from higher education institutions in the UK.[28]

It is at least arguable that the 'rise of English' as described by critics like Terry Eagleton[29] lies at the heart of the secularization of education. It is arguable also that the emergence of a sense of 'literature' not only diminished the role of the Bible, but exposed the limitations of how it is read and whether it is actually 'read' at all. My whole chapter has rested on the assumption that we are at best highly corrupt readers, and that our education system is deeply subjected to this corruption. 'Reading', it seems to me, is finally a religious activity within community – and thus to learn to read the Bible, lying as it does at the heart of Western culture, may be to recover in the study of literature a religious freedom which is entirely undogmatic, completely unevangelistic, and close to the heart of the mission of this programme. Whether, going back to the original embarrassment with which my contribution was first received, this is possible, with all its implications, remains to be seen. At least, as this volume attests, the debate is open and lively.

Notes

1. Stephen Prickett and Robert Carroll, Introduction to *The King James Version of the Bible*, Oxford World Classics (Oxford: Oxford University Press 1997), p. xi.
2. *The Woman's Bible* (New York: European Publishing Company, 1898), p. 7.
3. See further, Terence J. Keegan, *Interpreting the Bible: A Popular Introduction to Biblical Hermeneutics* (New York: Paulist Press, 1985), pp. 146–55.
4. 'The interpretation of Scripture' in *Essays and Reviews* (1860).
5. See, George Pattison, *Art, Modernity and Faith: Restoring the Image* (London: Macmillan, 1991), pp. 10–29.
6. David Daiches, *God and the Poets* (Oxford: Oxford University Press, 1984), p. 49.
7. Ruth Etchells, *A Model of Making: Literary Criticism and its Theology* (Basingstoke: Marshall, Morgan & Scott, 1983), Prologue.
8. 'Virtually all this activity [biblical criticism] has been what we might call "excavative" – either literally, with the archeologist's spade and reference to its findings, or with a variety of analytic tools intended to uncover the original

meanings of biblical words, the life situations in which specific texts were used, the sundry sources from which longer texts were assembled.' Robert Alter, *The Art of Biblical Narrative* (London: George Allen & Urwin, 1981), p. 13.

9. Stanley Fish, *Is There a Text in This Class? The Authority of Interpretive Communities* (Cambridge, Mass.: Harvard University Press, 1980), pp. 303–21.

10. See, The Bible and Culture Collective, in R.M. Schwartz, S. Moore, C.A. Castellie and G.A. Phillips, *The Postmodern Bible* (New Haven: Yale University Press, 1995), pp. 1ff.

11. For example, Mieke Bal, Elizabeth Schussler Fiorenza, Phyllis Trible.

12. See also, Robert Detweiler, 'What is a sacred text?' *Semeia* 31 (1985), pp. 213–30.

13. See further, Robert Detweiler, *Breaking the Fall* (London: Macmillan, 1989), ch. 2, 'What is reading religiously?'.

14. See further, Paul Ricoeur, *Interpretation Theory: Discourse and the Surplus of Meaning* (Fort Worth: Texas Christian University Press, 1976).

15. D. H. Lawrence, 'Why the novel matters' in Anthony Beal (ed.), *Selected Literary Criticism* (London: Heinemann, 1967), p. 105.

16. On the Bible as a translated book, see Stephen Prickett, 'The changing of the host: translation and linguistic history' in David Jasper (ed.), *Translating Religious Texts* (London: Macmillan, 1993), pp. 4–20.

17. Salman Rushdie, *The Satanic Verses* (London: Viking, 1988), pp. 546–7.

18. James Joyce, *A Portrait of the Artist as a Young Man* (1916) (Harmondsworth: Penguin, 1969), p. 115.

19. Classic examples of this are F. W. Dillistone's *The Novelist and the Passion Story* (London: Collins, 1960), and Roy W. Battenhouse's *Shakespearean Tragedy: Its Art and Christian Premises* (Bloomington: Indiana University Press, 1969). Such works, worthy in themselves, have spawned a number of later books, such as David Anderson's *The Passion of Man in Gospel and Literature* (The Bible Reading Fellowship, 1980).

20. Harold Bloom, *The Book of J* (London: Faber and Faber, 1991), p. 44.

21. Gabriel Josipovici, *The Book of God: A Response to the Bible* (New Haven: and London: Yale University Press, 1988), p. x.

22. T. S. Eliot, 'Religion and literature' (1935) in *Selected Essays*, 3rd edn (London: Faber and Faber, 1951), p. 390.

23. Michael Edwards, *Of Making Many Books: Essays on the Endlessness of Writing* (Basingstoke: Macmillan, 1990).

24. Fish, *Is There a Text?*, p. 321.

25. Peter Meinke, 'Supermarket' in *Liquid Paper: New and Selected Poems* (Pittsburgh: University of Pittsburgh Press 1991), p. 65.

26. *Breaking the Fall*, pp. 34–5.

27. *Bulletin of Engaging the Curriculum* 5 (Spring 1997), p. 3.

28. Ibid., p. 11.

29. Terry Eagleton, *Literary Theory: An Introduction* (Oxford: Blackwell, 1983), ch. 1.

2

'Get Thee Behind Me, Satan': On Resisting Fishy Models of Reading

Terence R. Wright

As a professor of English literature, it is clearly in my interests to believe that my discipline has a future; I am bound to defend my discipline both as a body of knowledge and as a set of skills, the two aspects of all subjects as they are defined in the National Curriculum. I would like, therefore, to arrest Professor Jasper's question in mid-sentence and ask first 'What, then, is reading?' before proceeding to the particular problems which arise when one brings a set of skills honed on the reading of 'secular' literature to this 'sacred' collection of texts. I am sufficiently postmodern to place these terms (sacred and secular) in scare quotes, recognizing their problematic status, and I share Professor Jasper's concern that too many people in too many 'academic departments of literature' do dismiss the Bible as not worth reading with the same care and attention which they lavish upon other literature.

One of the difficulties I have with Professor Jasper's model of reading, however, which he presents as a metaphorical return to paradise, 'a garden of serious play' in which we can indulge in eternal 'festivities of reading' in 'lively and life-inspiring ... joyous excess', is that it is dangerously self-indulgent, postmodern in the worst sense of that much-abused term. I remain sufficiently 'modern' to believe that we (teachers of literature) have a serious responsibility to train our students to uncover the 'truths' about texts (notice the plural and lower-case status of these 'truths') and their contexts (also plural and subject to interpretation). I should also admit at the outset that the old-fashioned sense of the phrase 'literary criticism', as it was used by biblical critics to refer to the process of identifying separate documentary strands of the final text, has more legitimacy in many respects than much of what now passes among biblical critics as 'literary criticism', a term now too often used to refer to a naive belief in the value of an immediate personal response to a supposedly whole and harmonious text which is quite evidently a concoction of contradictory fragments.

First, however, let me clarify what I mean by teaching people to read, a process which I consider to be the primary function of teachers of English. Reading, as Stanley Fish and many other literary theorists have argued, is neither a simple nor a natural process; it is only *Doing What Comes Naturally*, the title of one of his many books, in the sense of being so embedded in our ideological, cultural and historical formation, that we often do it unreflectively. It is so familiar as to seem natural (Fish 1989: ix). The opening essay of his best-known book, *Is There a Text in This Class?* attempts to explain how one becomes an 'informed' or 'competent' reader, familiar with a range of literary repertoires and conventions, skilled in genre recognition and able consequently to decide how to read a particular piece of writing:

> The reader of whose responses I speak, then, is this informed reader, neither an abstraction nor an actual living reader, but a hybrid – a real reader (me) who does everything in his power to make himself informed ..., by making my mind the repository of the (potential) responses a given text might call out and ... the suppressing, in so far as that is possible, of what is personal and idiosyncratic and 1970ish in my response.
>
> (Fish 1980: 49)

The least one can expect of an informed, competent or disciplined reader, one who has successfully completed a degree in English literature, is that he or she will have reflected upon the process of reading, including what he or she brings to the text in terms of ideology, implicit assumptions, previous

28

experience (both of life and of literature) and commitments. Fish does not, like Richards, the theorist of an earlier generation, expect his readers to abandon all beliefs and commitment, but they should at least be aware of them.

'Everyone who has seriously studied literature,' as Northrop Frye claimed in his magisterial *Anatomy of Criticism*, 'knows that the mental process involved is as coherent and progressive as the study of science. A precisely similar training of the mind takes place, and a similar sense of the unity of the subject is built up' (Frye 1949: 10–11). His claims perhaps reflect an over-confidence in the scientific status of the humanities character-istic of early structuralism, but Jonathan Culler elaborates on what Frye means by 'coherent', 'progressive' and scientific:

> it is clear that study of one poem or novel facilitates the study of the next: one gains not only points of comparison but a sense of how to read. One develops a set of questions which experience shows to be appropriate and productive . . .; one acquires a sense of the possibilities of literature and how these possibilities may be distinguished. (Culler 1975: 121)

This is what Culler means by 'Literary competence', the title of a chapter in his extremely influential exposition of *Structuralist Poetics*.

Both Culler and Fish, of course, have moved on from the mid-1970s, when these essays were written. Culler has shown himself to be so much of a modernist, so confident in the principles of rationalism and the enlightenment, that he complains bitterly of the continuing interest his colleagues show in the Bible, serving 'to legitimize religious discourse and strengthen its political power rather than to foster a critique of religion and religious authoritarianism', which he sees as a prime function of literary criticism (Culler 1988: 71). Fish, from a different standpoint, has expressed dismay at the unasham-edly committed political agenda of some of his radical colleagues. *Professional Correctness* (1995) pleads for teachers of literature to retain their professionalism, not to abandon the distinctive ways of proceeding, their long-established (but evolving) rules. Literary criticism, he argues, means producing readings of texts 'in the sense of extended and coherent interpretations' (Fish 1995: 27). He makes a department of English sound rather like a combination of monastery and mystery religion when he celebrates 'the conventional and obligatory routines that are the content of literary work for those who have been initiated into its practice' (p. 41). But in a profession which has shown a distressing tendency to despise itself (Fish 1989: 197) it is refreshing to find a strong defence of what we (teachers of literature) do for a living.

What I find problematic in Fish (as in Jasper) is his failure to recognize the power of the text, the possibility of readers learning something, even being changed by the act of reading. In contrast to continental reception theorists such as Iser, who attempt to explain the capacity of texts to determine what count as appropriate responses to them, Fish displays an alarming tendency, which I find reflected in Jasper's chapter, to give all power to the interpretive community and none at all to the text. This utterly undermines the point of reading, reducing it to a therapeutic exercise, a celebration of already existing beliefs. In the case of the Bible, this seriously underestimates its power to shape our faith, its capacity (in Herbert Schneider's phrase) to demythologize us, to weigh us in its balance and find us wanting.

There are, of course, genuine problems about defining what constitutes a text, about deciding what is actually *in* a text. One of Fish's most famous examples is that of *Samson Agonistes*, Milton's verse dramatization of the heroic account in the Book of Judges of Samson's heroic self-sacrifice for his people. Most interpreters would agree that Samson's saving death typologically anticipates Christ's but since this is a play, no-one can actually say this without anachronism. All has to be implicit, nothing explicit in the text (Fish 1980: 272–4). Less convincing (although very funny) is Fish's reading of Blake's 'The Tyger' as the first-person lament of someone suffering from indigestion as a result of eating tiger meat. Agreed, it is possible to imagine this alternative context for the line 'Did he who made the Lamb make thee?' but it is hardly a convincing reading of the poem (pp. 348–9). Nor have any of *my* students been gullible enough to believe, as Fish claims of some students of his, that a list of prominent names in linguistics scribbled on a blackboard could be a seventeenth-century concrete devotional poem. It can (with ingenuity and tongue firmly in cheek) be read as one (pp. 323–4). But no-one in their right mind would genuinely fall for this, even in the sense of Fish's early model of reading, outlined in *Surprised by Sin*, where the whole point is that Milton has so structured *Paradise Lost* as to cause his readers continually to fall. In those days, notice, Fish still believed in the power of the text, its capacity to elicit certain responses from its readers.

All texts, then, I believe, wield some power over their readers and none more so than the Bible, that extraordinary collection of vastly differing texts, ranging from epic to chronicle, history to fiction, pious psalm to erotic poem, letter to apocalypse. David Jasper is quite right to complain of the way churches have homologized these texts, insisting on splitting them into pre-packaged soundbites, discouraging the kind of genre-recognition essential for all intelligent reading. One of the services that literary critics such as Alter and Kermode have rendered to biblical criticism, both separately and in their collective *Literary Guide to the Bible*, is to have fostered a more subtle awareness of the wide range of genres represented in the Bible. This, *pace* Jasper, is one element of the literary agenda: alerting students to the complexity of interesting texts (and the Bible is at least interesting).

It is, therefore, entirely legitimate for Jasper to celebrate these developments in reading the Bible and also to draw attention to the difference between Derridean deconstruction and Bultmannian demythologizing. At its best (and I have carefully to qualify all references to Derrida, given the variety of ways in which he has been interpreted) deconstruction continues to respect the *otherness* of texts, their resistance to homologizing interpretation. This is what deconstructive critics such as Hillis Miller and Simon Critchley meant by *The Ethics of Reading* and *The Ethics of Deconstruction* respectively (and notice how biblical critics were quick to pick up on these titles, Daniel Patte producing his *Ethics of Biblical Interpretation* in the wake of the earlier two volumes). The ethics with which Patte is concerned may be broader than those of the earlier titles; he is aware of the extent to which his own earlier practice of 'modernist', objective, 'scientific' criticism neglected both his own embeddedness in ideological contexts and the effect of his readings upon others (Patte 1995: 1–2), whereas the primary concern for Hillis Miller and Simon Critchley is to be aware of the otherness of the text itself, its irreducibility to their own views of life. Derrida and deconstruction begin with a recognition of the limits of knowledge as appropriation, the dangers of 'seizing something and making it one's own, ... an activity which *appropriates* and *grasps* the otherness of the known' (Levinas 1989: 76).

Reading, however, as all these critics stress, is a dialogue, a two-way process, not just a recognition of the other but a struggle for power. The first moment of deconstructive double-reading may require a recognition of what the text 'wants to say' (*veut dire*) but the second involves 'leaving the order of commentary and opening a text up to the blind spots or ellipses within the dominant interpretation' (Critchley 1992: 23). Texts may resist the appropriations readers attempt to make while readers learn to resist the designs texts have upon them. Women readers in particular have learnt to follow Judith Fetterly and become resisting readers, refusing the embraces of much classic American fiction which constitutes 'a series of designs upon the female reader' (Fetterly 1978: xii).

This is one of the aspects of Jasper's model of reading that I find refreshing: his recognition of the power-struggle involved in the Church's reading of the Bible, in particular its continuing subjection of women. I welcome too his acknowledgement of the 'creative tension' between literature and theology (the opening section of my own study of *Theology and Literature* was, in fact, entitled: 'Theology and literature: a creative tension' (Wright 1988: 1–13)). Jasper, following Detweiler, describes reading religiously as 'a literary *act* which stands in creative tension with the strong text', displaying at least some awareness of the power of the text itself. All these aspects of his contribution are to be welcomed.

I am more suspicious, however, of his setting the 'celebration of reading' against 'the supposed security' and 'cultural specificity' of the 'sacred text'. For cultural specificity, in my view, is what all reading should recognize: all texts are both produced and consumed in specific cultural conditions which *must* be respected. That is another part of the agenda for literary studies: the necessity for contextualization. If we lose sight of the specific cultural conditions in which the Gospels, for example, were produced, our readings will become hopelessly unhistorical, so far removed from the origins of Christianity as to render them no longer part of that tradition. To do anything like justice to the richness of the Bible requires close attention to all relevant detail: historical, cultural, formal, literary and more. For too long, Jasper argues, we have read its pages 'fearfully' and in awe. He may be right, but I have my fears too about his utopian community of self-confident readers, all too full of 'the courage to believe in themselves', happily abandoning all concern with historical accuracy and cultural specificity, producing creative readings which overflow with 'joyous excess' and 'surplus of meaning'. This may not be the return to paradise which he envisages. In fact, I feel a need to warn the angels at the gates of Eden that there are some fishy models of reading around which need closer inspection before being allowed to enter the groves of academe. Just as Peter found it hard to accept what Jesus, in St Mark's Gospel, warned him was in store both for him and his disciples, Jasper is in danger of making reading appear too easy. Hence the warning of my title, issued, of course, in a spirit of friendship and love. Remember, Peter, like Fish, went on to be very successful (gaining perhaps *the* most influential chair) but not before he was told of the duty to discriminate, to accept some readings and not others, for not anything goes (especially, it appears, in heaven).

In order to understand all these allusions, of course, even in as uninteresting a piece of prose as the previous paragraph, a reader needs to be well-informed, competent in literary conventions and familiar with the Bible, with the history of the early Church, and with Milton. And that is precisely the point. Reading is not an easy activity, something that comes 'naturally'. It is an acquired skill, something that needs to be learnt. This competence, which is only acquired through an engagement with a reasonably wide range of texts (the body of knowledge, or canon, broadly understood) is the goal of literature as a discipline, whether in English or in any other language. Before that competence can be applied to a text of such extraordinary difficulty as the Bible, an exercise involving particularly complex linguistic and contextual skills, it needs to be acquired, I would suggest, in the reading of more straightforward texts in one's native tongue.

Interdisciplinary study, in other words, if it is not to be shallow and worthless, must be founded on the basic skills of single disciplines. Theological engagement with literature will only be welcomed by literary critics (always anxious to defend their 'patch' and to resist the suggestion that there is nothing to it) if it recognizes and respects the values and skills of that discipline. The same principle, of course, applies in reverse, so that literary critics who barge in upon the Bible with no respect for its theological dimension, its status within believing communities, deserve the scorn heaped upon them by T. S. Eliot (cited by Jasper). Engagement in interdisciplinary study, like the act of reading itself, requires genuine dialogue, which depends upon mutual respect. Both disciplines must believe that they have something to learn, otherwise the engagement is unlikely to develop into a fruitful marriage.

References

Critchley, Simon (1992), *The Ethics of Deconstruction: Derrida and Levinas* (Oxford: Blackwell)

Culler, Jonathan (1975), *Structuralist Poetics: Structuralism, Linguistics and the Study of Literature* (London: Routledge)

Culler, Jonathan (1983), *On Deconstruction: Theory and Criticism after Structuralism* (London: Routledge)

Culler, Jonathan (1988), *Framing the Sign: Criticism and its Institutions* (Oxford: Blackwell)

Fetterly, Judith (1978), *The Resisting Reader: A Feminist Approach to American Fiction* (Bloomington: Indiana University Press)

Fish, Stanley (1967), *Surprised by Sin: The Reader in 'Paradise Lost'* (London: Macmillan)

Fish, Stanley (1980), *Is There a Text in This Class? The Authority of Interpretive Communities* (Cambridge, Mass.: Harvard University Press)

Fish, Stanley (1989), *Doing What Comes Naturally: Change, Rhetoric, and the Practice of Theory in Literary and Legal Studies* (Oxford: Clarendon)

Fish, Stanley (1995), *Professional Correctness: Literary Studies and Political Change* (Oxford: Clarendon)

Frye, Northrop (1949), *Anatomy of Criticism* (Princeton: Princeton University Press)

Levinas, Emmanuel (1989), *The Levinas Reader*, ed. Sean Hand (Oxford: Blackwell)

Miller, J. Hillis (1987), *The Ethics of Reading* (New York: Columbia University Press)

Patte, Daniel (1995), *Ethics of Biblical Interpretation* (Louisville, Ky.: Westminster John Knox Press)

Wright, T. R. (1988), *Theology and Literature* (Oxford: Blackwell)

3

Orality, Literacy and the Idea of the Spiritual

Stephen Prickett

Of the making of books there is no end.

Though it is right that it should be so, it is worth calling attention to the degree to which the current debate about the nature and content of the curriculum is focused on questions of *reading*. In a literate society we take it so much for granted that the transmission of our culture, knowledge and methods of innovation – not to mention the basic processes of socialization that underlie it – are done by means of writing and reading that we scarcely consider the wider implications of this assumption. Even in an era of radio, television and the telephone, for all but an increasingly marginalized minority of unfortunates, most of the business and even the collective awareness of our society is conducted through a highly stylized system of written symbols.

One reason why we tend to ignore this very obvious point is a matter of 'levels' of consciousness. As anyone who has done proofreading knows very well, in so far as we are conscious of the actual marks on the paper or screen in front of us, we cannot concentrate on the meaning; in so far as we concentrate on what is being communicated, we are largely unaware of the letters themselves. Similarly, working with the written word we are very rarely aware of being 'literate'; indeed, to be conscious of reading is very likely to inhibit our understanding of the meaning of what is being read! Yet once we do become aware of our basic dependence on literacy, we suddenly become aware of certain very important corollaries.

Again, this is a matter of levels – and their largely unconscious interaction. Literacy itself is dependent upon a further process of symbolism: that of language. The written word is thus at two removes from immediate experience: a symbolization of a symbolization. But, as we all know, such symbolization is always a two-way process. If, in one sense, language describes and mediates the basic impressions of our senses, in another – and perhaps more important sense – it also so organizes our senses that it is very difficult to think of what non-linguistic perception might feel like. Thus when we see a tree, or a house, a jet airliner, or some animal, the visual perception is virtually indistinguishable from the (unconscious) verbalization. Only occasionally, when we see something that we do not recognize or cannot label, do we realize what non-verbal perception involves. Even the question '*is* that a house?' or 'a tree?' confers verbal meaning of a kind on the sense impression. An object for which we can find no label at all, whether descriptive, collective, functional or even interrogative, is oddly unsettling – and we go to great lengths to avoid it. It seems to be a psychological truth that there is no perception without interpretation. Indeed, Gombrich has pointed out, there is a sense in which we do not 'see' things we cannot identify; we see in 'wholes' even if they are mistaken wholes which subsequently must be corrected.[1]

I am not arguing that all interpretation is verbal – though much of it undoubtedly is. But just as interpretation influences or, more positively, controls perception, so verbalization clearly influences and often controls interpretation. If we need illustration of this, we only have to consider how differently different languages symbolize the world. If, as Stephen Pinker has claimed, the story that the Eskimos have forty different words for 'snow' is a myth,[2] on the other hand they do, it seems, perceive and articulate the qualities of snow with an accuracy that leaves other cultures illiterate in such 'readings' – as Stephen Høeg, for instance, shows so dramatically in his prize-winning novel, *Miss Smilla's Feeling for Snow*.[3]

Similarly, and this is the point I am driving at, this 'top-down' process is a normal (though, of course, not invariable) part of our discovery of the world. Though my observations of my own children's language acquisitions were (in the process described above) no doubt influenced by my prior reading of

Piaget, it seems to me that children are natural Platonists. They begin with Platonic 'forms' ('house', 'tree', 'ball', etc.) and move from there to more subtle sub-divisions. At the next level of symbolism, for instance, adult verbalization is more often influenced and controlled by the processes of writing than *vice versa*. What we say, and the words we use, are more likely to come from our reading than from our sense experience. Just as our vocabulary and syntax shape our apprehension of the world about us, so our vocabulary and syntax are themselves shaped by our reading.

This leads me to my main thesis in this chapter: that what we mean by the 'spiritual' is essentially a written and literary concept in precisely this sense, and that any meaningful discussion of what we mean by spirituality in our present age must therefore engage with the implications of this. The best way to explain what I mean by this is to turn to Walter J. Ong's ground-breaking book, *Orality and Literacy*.[4] In it Ong makes a number of crucial distinctions between an oral and a literate culture.

Oral cultures are essentially *static*. This does not mean, of course, that they do not change at all – all literate cultures were once oral ones, after all. What it means is that oral cultures find it very difficult to *think* about change. When change comes it is either so gradual as to be unnoticeable over living memory, or unplanned, contingent and bewildering – often with randomly Darwinian consequences, that can involve the decimation or extinction of the village, group or tribe. The primary task in such a society is not innovation but remembering. Bruce Chatwin's *The Songlines*, vividly portrays the way in which Australian aboriginal peoples must learn their tribal songs in order to survive in the harsh desert conditions of the outback. Encoded in the songs for each area is vital information concerning the location of water-holes, food or possible dangers. If you have to travel over the territory of another tribe, it is not just a matter of courtesy but of survival to learn their songs first. In other areas of the world specific elders are charged with the task of acting as the tribal memory-bank, recalling vital genealogies, medicines, emergency diets in times of famine, etc. In West Africa the collective knowledge of the tribe can be stored not so much in songs as in proverbs. To be a respected elder means to know the proverbs of the village, clan or tribe. In such cases the whole structure and syntax of the language can be essentially proverbial. Among the Mende of Sierra Leone, the English words 'I'm hungry' are translated 'An empty sack can't stand by itself.' Moreover the phrase 'I have eaten' refers only to the staple diet of rice and palm-oil. Someone who tells you he has 'not eaten for three days' may (or may not) have been eating something else. Rather than being poetic, such linguistic structures are, by definition, time-tested and functional, but they do not necessarily facilitate accurate dietary discussions.

In such a context the idea of 'tradition' is profoundly different from that of Judaeo-Christian culture. Where oral tradition represents the collected wisdom of all time – the equivalent of all the contents of all our libraries combined – the idea of 'change' makes no sense at all: indeed, it is suicidally dangerous. A mistake in the songlines could kill. Accuracy of repetition is paramount. This concept of tradition can, of course, persist even in semi-literate societies, and for very similar reasons: one thinks of Qur'anic schools in the Near East where students are obliged to learn by heart (though in written form) passages of the seventh-century Arabic of the Qur'an. Rabbinic schools teaching Hebrew to Jews who may speak anything from first-century Aramaic to modern American, or the mediaeval memorizing of the Vulgate by peoples who had never spoken Latin, present very similar concepts of tradition as blind repetition. Alongside such activities, however, a very different concept of tradition has existed for thousands of years, where *midrash*, or an ongoing tradition of exegesis and comment, has always accompanied the teaching of the sacred texts. 'What is the Torah?' runs one Jewish catechism, with its answer, 'It is midrash Torah' – it is the Law *and* its associated tradition.[5] The Law, sacred as it is, is incomplete without its ongoing tradition of comment and discussion. Here, of course, is the origin of what T. S. Eliot was to see as the distinctive quality of the great European literary tradition: its capacity for innovation and change. For him, only the new could truly be traditional.[6] But such a notion of tradition as change presupposes a firm grasp on what is being changed. A commentary on the Jewish dietary prescriptions – even the progressive rejections of it in the New Testament by Jesus, Peter and Paul – would be without meaning or use if we did not have the original texts themselves. Such a record of debate and change is only possible in a literate and textually based society.

Associated with this new meaning of tradition made possible by writing are two other key innovations. The first is the movement from 'outer' to 'inner'. Reading was once quite as noisy a process as consulting the tribal memory-man. To read, was to read aloud. In some early English manuscripts the injunction to the reader to 'rede' can mean either to read for one's own personal edification, or to recite for the benefit of all present. The difference between the two interpretations is not so much one of vocalization as of volume. At what point people started reading silently, to themselves, and therefore, in that sense at least, 'internalizing' what they were reading is unclear, but we do know that it was associated with devotional and religious exercises. St Augustine records his astonishment as a young man when, on paying an unexpected visit to St Ambrose studying in his cell, he found the holy bishop of Milan poring over a book *without moving his lips*. The fact that Augustine, who had moved in literate and educated circles all his life, had never seen such a phenomenon before tells us much – as does his immediate conviction that this was a product of the most advanced spirituality.[7] At what point such internalizing became the norm is difficult to determine, but we have sufficient records of the noise created by hard-working school classes to suggest that is persisted well into the eighteenth century, and we have records of so-called 'blab schools' in the United States still going strong in the early nineteenth.

In the meantime, a second source of internalization had transformed both author and readership: the invention of the movable-type printing-press. Protestantism was the product of advanced technology: not for nothing was the first book published by Gutenberg in Mainz a Bible. Whilst one should not exaggerate the spread of either printing or literacy across Europe, within two hundred years – by the middle of the seventeenth century – it was possible to assume that the Protestant faithful could, and did, read the Bible in the privacy of their own homes even if, as so often, they read virtually nothing else. By becoming a commercial artefact, the Bible had passed for ever beyond the institutional control of the Church (whether Protestant or Catholic) and just as readers were free to read it directly in terms of their own contexts and circumstances, so too were they free, and even encouraged, to internalize its message as speaking directly to them.

It is with this distinction in mind between orality and literacy – however crudely sketched here – that I want to distinguish between the 'sacred' and the 'spiritual'. Though the former is common to societies the world over, whether oral or literate, it is essentially pre-literate in form; while the latter may indeed exist, and has no doubt existed, in oral societies, the mere fact that we have, by definition, no record of it until we come to written textual records means that it was, more often than not, isolated, sporadic and unable to constitute the kind of tradition across time and space that we now almost invariably associate with it. If we take the 'sacred' in Rudolf Otto's classic sense of the 'holy'[8] it involves fear of a semi-magical, numinous, even ghostly quality that is probably common to us all at some level, but is often below, or beyond, the threshold of articulation. It adheres to places, to rituals, even sometimes to beliefs that cannot be challenged. To dismiss it as 'primitive' begs the question; it is almost certainly universal; but to the cry of the modern conservative, 'is nothing sacred?' the answer is probably, and perhaps regretfully, 'less and less' – at least in a literal sense: if it is to survive it may be that its explicitly metaphorical form, as in bonds of friendship, love, honour, etc., may serve to remind us that it was always a metaphor for something 'other' than ourselves, and our immediate self-interest.

If the 'sacred' has always had about it something of an encounter with the alien and the other, the 'spiritual' was, by contrast, always something to be internalized and made our own. It adheres less to particular places and rituals than to people, ideas and written texts. A tradition of spirituality is at once communal and personal, commonly associated with the reading of particular holy books, whether Zoroastrian, Buddhist, Jewish, Christian or Islamic, and often within the kind of discipline provided by a religious movement or monastic order – one thinks of Essenes, of Tibetan mystics, and Christian organizations as diverse as the Benedictines, the Jesuits, the Quakers and the Confessing Church of Dietrich Bonhoeffer. To the degree that it is psychological, internal and literary, it is also essentially dynamic. Spirituality is usually described by initiates not in terms of objects, nor even of states of mind, but as a 'way', a 'path', and as a 'journey'.

Though the word 'spirit' is, of course, a very ancient one, with roots in both Greek and Hebrew thought, 'spirituality', as we now use it, is a comparatively modern word. Apart from one, slightly odd, use by the Scottish poet, William Dunbar, in the early sixteenth century, the earliest uses of the word cited by the OED come from the mid-seventeenth century. Such a meaning is itself the product of a long evolutionary process. In his fascinating and seminal article. 'The meaning of *literal*',[9] Owen Barfield has pointed out that most of our words for inward and especially moral qualities were originally derived, as metaphors, from material things. Thus, for instance, the word 'scruple' is a metaphor from the Latin *scrupulus*, a small sharp stone that might get into your sandal and so prevent you walking uprightly and evenly. 'Noble' was originally a coin of high value; we now speak of 'feelings' almost exclusively in terms of emotions – and so on. Since the root words from which our modern idea of 'spirit' evolved, the Hebrew *ruach*, the Greek *pneumos*, or the Latin *spiritus*, all originally referred to wind, it would be easy to conclude that the word spirit was similarly originally a metaphorical construction of this kind. However, Barfield continues, to say that 'spirit' is a metaphor in this sense would imply that there was an idea of what it meant already present in the language, and this, of course, is not so. We have, therefore, to think of the wind as *always* having had a ghostly, numinous and magical quality about it, and it was only when the notions of wind and spirit had finally been separated that the literal (and scientific) meaning of 'wind' could finally emerge sometime around the seventeenth century. Similarly, it was only then that the idea of the 'spirit' as a purely abstract, moral and inward phenomenon, purged of all material associations, could finally make its appearance – which coincides with the coming into use of derivative terms such as 'spirituality'.

Whether in this process of what Coleridge called 'desynonymy' other qualities may have been lost is beside the point – though if we were to have clear evidence that this was so, there would be nothing to stop those who wished to retrieve such a lost meaning coining (or desynonymizing) yet another term that would cover it. What is clear is that such an evolution of meaning was only possible in a literate and textually orientated society. Desynonymy doubtless occured thousands of times in oral societies, and, incidentally, we also know a little of some oral societies where the reverse seems to have happened, and a once-rich and complex language 'degenerated' into a much cruder and more simplistic one.[10] There is no law of inevitable linguistic progress. My point is rather that, except in very rare (and usually highly debatable) instances, there is, by definition, no record of the process, and therefore no sense of it as constituting an ongoing and dynamic tradition. It is in this power to hold past and present in simultaneous focus that a literate society possesses, at least potentially, powers of spirituality and a sense of unfolding tradition almost impossible for an oral one.

My conclusion should, I think, be obvious – and deeply relevant to this particular enquiry. Not merely are writing and spirituality so historically intertwined that separation of the two is virtually impossible, but it is to literature (in its broadest, post-romantic sense[11]) that we must look for the exploration and future development of this encounter between the human and whatever we may mean by the divine in the twenty-first century. Indeed, such a quest is vital, too, for the future of literature itself.

Notes

1. E. H. Gombrich, *Art and Illusion* (London: Phaidon, 1960).
2. Stephen Pinker, *The Language Instinct* (Harmondsworth: Penguin, 1995).
3. Trans. F. David (London: Flamingo, 1993).
4. Walter J. Ong, *Orality and Literacy: The Technologizing of the Word* (London: Methuen, 1982).
5. See Michael Wadsworth, 'Making and interpreting Scripture' in Michael Wadsworth (ed.), *Ways of Reading the Bible* (Brighton: Harvester, 1981).
6. T. S. Eliot, 'Tradition and the individual talent' in *Selected Essays*, (London: Faber, 1933).
7. 'When he read, his eyes scanned the page and his heart sought out the meaning, but his voice was silent and his tongue was still. Anyone could approach him freely and guests were not commonly announced, so that often, when we came to visit him, we found him reading like this in silence, for he never read aloud' (*Confessions*, VI. 3). See also Alberto Manguel, *A History of Reading* (London: HarperCollins, 1996), p. 42.
8. Rudolf Otto, *The Idea of the Holy*, trans. John W. Harvey (Harmondsworth: Penguin, 1958).
9. Owen Barfield, 'The meaning of *literal*' in Basil Cottle and L. C. Knights (eds), *Metaphor and Symbol* (Bristol: Butterfield, 1960) reprinted in *The Rediscovery of Meaning* (Middletown, Conn.: Wesleyan University Press, 1977).
10. The Mayan language and mathematical notation, a written system that was unknown to the later people living in the area, who may, or may not be their descendants, has been cited as one example; another possible example has been the loss of vocabulary and technology among the Tasmanians prior to white settlement – who had apparently lost the art of both navigation and fishing which archaeology confirms they once possessed.

11. There is an extensive body of work available on this history of the word 'literature'. Apart from my own *Words and the Word: Language, Poetics and Biblical Interpretation* (Cambridge: Cambridge University Press, 1986) and *Origins of Narrative: The Romantic Appropriation of the Bible* (Cambridge: Cambridge University Press. 1996), I would call attention to *The Literary Absolute: the Theory of Literature in German Romanticism*, by Philippe Lacoue-Labarthe and Jean-Luc Nancy, trans. Philip Barnard and Cheryl Lester (Albany: State University of New York Press, 1988) and *From Romanticism to Critical Theory: The Philosophy of German Literary Theory*, by Andrew Bowie (London: Routledge, 1997).

4

Reading as Doxology in St Augustine

Graham Ward

Written texts have always been recognized as possessing a power. Calligraphy – literally meaning beautiful writing in Greek – is one of the oldest art forms. The early illuminated manuscripts of the fifth to the fifteenth centuries show a fascinating respect for the written. The scribe's work was a form of prayer, a meditation upon Scripture in which the concentration of mind and the discipline of hand were fused. The beauty that manifested itself was a sign of grace. The communication of mysteries, the maintenance of the enigmatic and secret, has always been the province of hieroglyphics, codes, arcane symbols. To the illiterate, to write and to read were the offices of priests; for these activities were closely related to the sacred powers, to transcendent and transformative forces. In the Jewish Kabbalistic tradition God was himself a writer, creating the world by means of specific letters. Only the circumcised – those marked by the Yod on the penis, those whose bodies had been inscribed upon by God – could read and interpret the Torah. For the conversion of the heart implied by circumcision was believed to effect 'a change in the very substance of the individual – and not only in his ethicoreligious stature – which prepares him for the visionary experience'.[1]

In the early years of post-exilic Israel, when the Temple of Solomon once more stood grand and imposing on the mountain of Zion and the walls of Jerusalem had been rebuilt, crowds gathered in the Temple courtyard to hear a Levite read from the Mosaic law, the book of books. The event and effect of this reading is recorded in the Book of Nehemiah:

> And Ezra the scribe stood upon a pulpit of wood, which they had made for the purpose; and beside him stood Mattithiah, and Shema, and Anaiah, and Urijah, and Hilkiah, and Maaseiah, on his right hand; and on his left hand, Pedaiah, and Mishael, and Malchiah, and Hashum, and Hashbadana, Zechariah, and Meshullam. And Ezra opened the book in the sight of all the people; (for he was above all the people;) and when he opened it, all the people stood up: And Ezra blessed the Lord, the great God. And all the people answered, Amen, Amen, with lifting up their hands: and they bowed their heads, and worshipped the Lord with their faces to the ground. Also Jeshua, and Bani, and Sherebiah, Jamin, Akkub, Shabbethai, Hodijah, Maaseiah, Kelita, Azariah, Jozabad, Hanan, Pelaiah, and the Levites, caused the people to understand the law: and the people stood in their place. So they read in the book of the law of God distinctly, and gave the sense, and caused them to understand the reading. (Nehemiah 8.4–8)

The power, institutional and sacred, described in this passage, invested in that occasion, is immense. The ranks of priests, the liturgy before the reading – one can almost smell the incense and see the great swathes of white and gold vestments. Of the effect we read that 'all the people wept, when they heard the words of the law' (v. 9). And although Ezra bids them to turn their sorrow into celebration, the day is considered holy because the reading brought about a change, a repentance, in the hearts of the people.

In Luke's Gospel we have a similar account of the power of reading. This time the reading comes not from the Law but the prophets (the Book of Isaiah). Once again the reading is part of a liturgy and placed within the context of the sacred – a synagogue in Nazareth. Jesus reads the famous passage about the Spirit of the Lord anointing him to preach the good news, heal the broken-hearted, preach deliverance, restore sight to the blind and set at liberty those who are bruised. The atmosphere is tense with expectation. For as with the reading by Ezra, the liturgical context had turned this event into a public performance. Every gesture, every movement, every word is rendered significant. In an awesome silence, Jesus closes the book, gives it again to the minister, walks back to his seat, sits down and, we are informed, 'the eyes of all them that were in the synagogue were fastened upon him'(Luke 4.20). Then he makes his announcement: 'This day in your hearing the Scripture is fulfilled.' The reading has become the realization. The tension breaks, violently: 'And all they in the synagogue, when they heard these things, were filled with wrath, and rose up, and thrust him out of the city' (Luke 4.28).

The power of the written text, realized in and through its reading (its verbalization) – a power to affect the hearts of those who hear – is significantly emphasized in both Judaism and Christianity. Reading, as such, becomes the vehicle for revelation, and in the wake of the revelation there is healing and redemption. Reading, or the orchestration of language, affects our desires, and it does so by means of engaging our imaginations. Our imaginations are sensitive and forceful motivational centres, linked closely with our emotions, our moods and our memories. They are constituted by the accumulation of our imaged experience and by the motile forces of demand and desire which permeate our conscious and unconscious life. Contemporary psychologists like Jacques Lacan, speak not of our imagination but of our imaginaries. The imaginary, for him, is that dimension of images, conscious or unconscious, perceived or imagined. It is never the opposite of what is real because it is always the impress of what is experienced – whether that experience has an empirical form or not. As such, for Lacan, the imaginary operates at the border between that which is internal to us (the chaotic real) and that which is externally constitutive of *our* experience (the symbolic). It is that dimension from which we draw our representations of the real, which subtends all our abilities to represent. It is closely linked then to language.

The experiential aspect of representation, the reading of or the listening to what is written and verbalized has been fundamental in Christianity as one element in the mechanism of repentance and conversion (the means whereby the atonement wrought by Christ is personally appropriated through the Spirit). The experience of reading or listening to the sacred text, a necessary part of any doctrine of Scripture, also bears upon the Church's commission to preach the Word. Words and signs having causal effect is, furthermore, linked to teaching on the sacraments and the donation of grace. The subsequent experience transforms personal identity and, as such, becomes both a dynamic and an event of spiritual biography. We will come to Saint Augustine in a moment and the divine command to take and read, *Tolle, Lege*. But here is John Bunyan in the seventeenth century, in his *Grace Abounding to the Chief of Sinners*, journeying into a paranoia which is fuelled by the power of reading the Scriptures: 'I was followed by this Scripture, ''Simon, Simon, behold Satan hath desired to have you'' (Luke xxii.31). And sometimes it would sound so loud within me, yea, and as it were call so strongly after me, that once above all the rest, I turned my head over my shoulders, thinking verily that some man had, behind me, called to me.'[2]

For Bunyan, the lack of an interpretive space between himself and the living Word of God in the Scriptures invokes a dreadful, haunting paranoia; a paranoia that has its social analogue in the English Civil War and Protestant sectarianism of the seventeenth century. He only is able to stabilize the trauma of reading the Scriptures by establishing a space between his own identity and the meaning of the text.[3] Reading, like the imaginary, operates at a boundary between interiority and exteriority. It performs a mediation or transaction between what we give to the text – in recreating the text through our reading of it – and what the text gives to us. It operates through the activation of signs. As such reading is a dangerous act, for the power of reading comes both from the reader and the text; there are no controls on the potential effects of the intercourse. St Ignatius Loyola recognized the resources of reading for the formation and disciplining of the soul. To read was to pray. By meditating upon scriptural events the one undergoing the Ignatian exercises interweaves his or her life with the biblical events through the imagination.[4] But where he differed from Bunyan was that all such reading took place under spiritual guidance. Such guidance directed the concurrence of energies of the reader's imagination and the activation of the written. It is significant that in the two scriptural accounts we have been looking at reading is a liturgical activity; it is staged within the framework of a community practising its faith.

But prior to that activation of the signs there has to be a recognition that these markings on the page are indeed intelligible signs, are indeed significant. Only in the wake of such a recognition can we ask what these are signs of; can we ask the question about their meaning. And it is in this way that Biblical semiology – the study of signs – becomes part of a larger philosophical and hermeneutical enquiry. For the practice of reading and the activation of the power of signs is not simply a Scriptural phenomenon. And although much that has developed in the history of hermeneutics, the science of interpreting signs, has been the product of a history of biblical interpretation and the writing of commentaries, the earliest theories and practices of interpretation were with reference to a literary corpus – namely the work of Hesiod and Homer. Let me illustrate the problem here with reference to two experiences of reading which have neither liturgical context nor religious content.

In the second circle of Dante's inferno, a troop of lovers pass by the poet and his ancient guide. The last of these lovers are blown like doves through the whirlwind of their desire. The passage is full of tenderness, compassion and a sense of there-but-for-the-grace-of-God-go-I. The lovers are identified as Francesca da Polenta and Paolo da Rimini. Weeping, Francesca narrates the story of their downfall. For it was while reading about Lancelot and Guinevere that she, married ten years and with one daughter, and Paolo, married with two children, felt the powers of mutual attraction. Francesca speaks as Dante writes: 'Many times that reading drew our eyes together and changed the colour in our faces.'[5] Reading turns to kissing, and kissing to adultery. The book becomes the pander who mediates between them and draws them down into the circles of hell. Reading here occasions a second fall, another Adam and another Eve surrender to a desire greater than that sanctioned by the will of God.

With Keats's sonnet *On first looking into Chapman's Homer*, the experience of reading is also one of self-transcending passion. Here we have described an experience of the Romantic sublime – an experience akin to Wordsworth's account of the view from the top of Snowdon on a moonlit night in *The Prelude* or the depiction of the Wanderer in Casper David Friedrich's painting standing on an Alpine precipice gazing into the misty abyss below. The Romantic sublime was an ineffable experience that seemed to transcend one's ability to understand and assimilate it. Reading

Chapman's Homer opens, for Keats, a space for infinite exploration and discovery: 'Then felt I like some watcher of the skies / When a new planet swims into his ken'. It leads to the rapture of comparing himself to Cortez standing above the vast stretch of the Pacific ocean in speechless admiration: 'Silent, upon a peak in Darien'.[6]

The experience of reading both these passages opens again that question of revelation and mediation, but the experiences described and the reading experiences encountered are not religious. And yet there is a transcendent quality about these experiences, particularly that of Keats's sonnet. Recently, in an analysis of the experience of reading Marcel Proust's *Remembrance of Things Past*, the American moral philosopher Martha Craven Nussbaum has used the word 'catalepsis' to describe those accounts in Proust's narrative when a knowledge emerges which is more profound and prior to rationality.[7] Catalepsis is characterized by surprise, a vivid particularity, a qualitative intensity about a memory in which, with blinding certainty, we gain self-knowledge or awareness of our finitude. Catalepsis is the experience described and reperformed in both the passage from Dante and the sonnet by Keats. As such, catalepsis shares certain characteristics with mystical intuition. To draw this out a little more, and develop the problematic relationship between aesthetics, imagination and religious experience, let me compare Keats's experience of the ineffable and infinite with St John of the Cross's experience of the last degree of love.

> In this state the soul is like a crystal that is clear and pure; the more degrees of light it receives, the greater the concentration of light there is in it, and the enlightenment continues to such a degree that at last it attains a point at which the light is centred in it with such copiousness that it comes to appear to be wholly light, and cannot be distinguished from the light ... and thus appears to be light itself.[8]

In both the Keats and the St John of the Cross passages, the experience itself is one where the self and the infinite (space in Keats, light in St John of the Cross) blur; where distinctions become impossible; where participation, even union, necessitates silence. The experience can only be observed by others (Cortez' men with their wild surmise) or observed by ourselves after the event. The experience, then, requires representation in order to be. The representation re-enacts the moment of ultimate encounter. As the passage from St John of the Cross in *The Flame of Living Love* illustrates, in trying to explain, representation attempts to persuade, to perform, to communicate something of the religious experience. In doing this how different is it from, and to what extent can it be distinguished from, aesthetic experience? In both passages, the world of the text confronts the world of the reader; an experience of transcendence offers the reader possibilities for transformation. One's view of the world and of oneself within that world is transfigured. Impressions from outside have synthesized with, challenged and modified that internal store of images and memories which we, following Jacques Lacan, have called the imaginary. The philosopher Paul Ricoeur, whose work is concerned with hermeneutics and linguistic analysis, has done much to expound and examine this transformative relationship between reader and the text, and to place such a relationship in the context of revelation and religious experience. '*Aisthesis* [*sic*] itself already reveals and transforms' he writes. 'Aesthetic experience draws power from the contrast it establishes from the outset in relation to everyday experience.' He emphasizes that 'the wholly original relation between knowledge and enjoyment that ensures the aesthetic quality of literary hermeneutics ... parallels that between the call and promise, committing a whole life, characterising theological understanding'.[9]

Ricoeur only just stops short of saying that aesthetic experience *is* religious experience. What he does announce is that the experience of reading is the experience of encountering the other, the stranger, the unfamiliar, allowing that exterior to engage with that interior world of the imagination. Imaginative reading, then, draws the world, its books, other people into us, challenging and transforming us by reorientating our desires and intentions towards understanding what is outside and beyond us. By reading we are stretched out towards a universe where numbers lose their meanings, towards the infinity and enigma of other worlds (real or imagined, for recall there is no distinction made between these at the level of the imaginary) which reflects the infinity and enigma of our own. By reading we encounter and engage in what I have called elsewhere the textual sublime.[10]

Let me illustrate and develop the nature and the theological consequences of this encounter and engagement by turning now to the work of St Augustine of Hippo. And let me leave a question hanging, which issues directly from what we have come to understand (I hope) so far. That is: Is there any qualitative difference between reading Proust and reading John's Gospel or are all imaginative encounters and engagements equivalent?

Towards the close of the fourth century, sitting isolated and defensive on the North African coast, having just been made a bishop by unorthodox and contentious means, St Augustine thrashed out the question of how we know God by means of prayer and confession. As an erstwhile distinguished rhetorician in Carthage, Rome and Milan and then an ardent preacher of the Word, we should not be surprised at Augustine's interest in language and its effects upon our desires. Several major works have significant discussions on the nature of language or signs.[11] And concurrent with that interest was a curiosity concerning human psychology: the role of the will, intentionality and desire. As one recent scholar has said, 'the will and love ... inspires man's search for knowledge. This desire underlies everything Augustine writes.'[12] We will look chiefly at his *Confessions*, written between AD 397 and 400, and the way he comes to learn the theology of language, rhetoric and desire.

We will begin at the end, with Augustine's reading of Scripture, in particular his interpretation of Genesis 1.28, and the command to human beings to 'increase and multiply and fill the earth'. For he reads this verse as indicating 'the capacity and ability to articulate in many ways what we hold to be a single concept, and to give a plurality of meanings to a single obscure expression in the text we have read'. Our human fertility then is related to what Augustine calls 'the fertility of reason' and 'the variety of significations'.[13] In paradise, Augustine pictures Adam and Eve living in a state of ease and plenty in a world where the 'natural working of Providence [could] be seen in God's hidden governance'.[14] They dwelt, therefore, in a world as an allegory in which every aspect of creation was a manifestation of God's plenitude and the multiple meanings that issued from the words God spoke in order for the worlds to come into being. Creation itself is an extension of God's

Logos and Adam and Eve lived in this land of signs which all clearly signified God's goodness. Polysemy, or what Augustine calls 'plurality of meanings', constituted the very abundance and ineffability of God's grace. In paradise God's desire and human desire, God's revealed Word and the fertility of human thought, were in harmony. And they will be again, Augustine prophesies, in the City of God.

In such a world there is no need for speech or writing for all things communicate themselves directly, and Augustine is in some perplexity as to how communication between God and human beings differs from that between human beings themselves. It might have been 'in a special interior manner (and how could it be described in human words?)' or 'with the aid of a creature, either in an ecstasy of spirit with corporeal images or in the bodily senses with some objects'.[15] It is with the Fall from grace that the need arose for syllables and the exchange of signs – signs which no longer clearly manifest the provenance of God. The thought, will and desire of the primal couple, between themselves and with their God, splintered and pluralized. Where one, holy desire ruled, through one Word, with one will, polysemy illustrated the abundance of God's meaningfulness. There was no room in polysemy for mis-understanding. But as a consequence of the Fall, human beings passed as Augustine tells us 'from eternal good to temporal good, from spiritual to carnal good, from intelligible to sensible good, from the highest to the lowest good'.[16] They leave off dwelling in the Word and take up occupancy in words. Nevertheless, words are not evil. They are still a part of creation, still a means of communication, and therefore good. Only they are a lower good, a good that needs disciplining in order that the signs might come to signify something of God's grace. And so, following the Fall, Augustine's 'variety of signification' requires acts of reading and interpretation. Signs need to be related back to the Word, reunited with it, rather than continue to be multiplied endlessly by the inventive, but now darkened, human mind. The very displacement of the literal by the allegorical or spiritual sense in the exegesis of Genesis 1.28 illustrates Augustine's sense that we are each called upon to read the world around us that we might understand the provenance of God. As Rowan Williams has pointed out, for Augustine 'the incarnation manifests the essential quality of the world as "sign".[17] Where the Word presses close to the edge of our words, where God's own desire is expressed in a flow of polysemic signs, each human being is called upon to learn from God how the texts of Scripture, creation and time are interwoven. We have to learn how to read, imaginatively.

This reading of the world and concern with human representations is central to the events and narrative movement of the *Confessions*. The book can be appreciated as a celebration of rhetoric through which time, self and society are swept back into a participation in God's creative goodness. The book itself takes the form of an act of prayer, a liturgical performance. Language is being put to holy use, its proper use; all signs are being drawn back into a relationship with the Word of God. The ineffability of God, the silence in which all language bows before the divine, stands in dialectical tension with the recognition that 'If what I said were ineffable, it would not be said. And for this reason God should not be said to be ineffable, for when this is said something is said.'[18] Nevertheless, language is part of God's grace for our redemption. 'For God, although nothing worthy may be spoken of Him, has accepted the tribute of the human voice and wished us to take joy in praising Him.'[19] The very unity of the *Confessions* issues from an interweaving of internal and external dialogues. The external dialogues constitute the conversation throughout with God (in the role of Father confessor) and the internal dialogues constitute a series of relationships – with his mother Monica, with his friends, with his teachers, with other texts (like the writings of Cicero and the biography of St Antony) – which form the content of the autobiography and develop the plot. Language is pivotal here, and Augustine's thoughts on representation, memory, time, narrative, signification and exegesis present moments, somewhat like those mirrors found in early seventeenth-century Dutch paintings, when the act of writing and the role of language examines itself, theologically.

It is Augustine's understanding of the Scriptures as the Word of God which governs his understanding of authorship, and those several concerns which we might place under the categories of textuality and interpretation. Williams writes that for Augustine, 'the difficulty of Scripture is a kind of parable of our condition'.[20] Augustine reads his life as he reads his Bible, and this is the point of significant development over and above the relationships between reading and experience (aesthetic and religious) which we looked at earlier. I want to develop this with respect to the imaginative reading of the Scriptures and that question which still is hanging and drawing: Is there any qualitative difference between reading Proust and reading John's Gospel or are all imaginative encounters and engagements equivalent? But first a word that may sound like the worst instance of postmodern jargon – intratextuality – and an elucidation.

Intratextuality describes the way our experience of the world, in order to be communicated, has to draw upon established social networks of current signs. Our experience of the world is not only translated by the signs that are available to us in any specific time and culture, it is interpreted or produced by these symbolic systems. These signs can be words, but we also communicate through many other signs – gestures, pictures, music, architecture. The very clothes we wear, the food we eat, the way we furnish our house and the very house we choose to live in, all bespeak the kind of people we are because they provide opportunities for personal choice and selection, and they say something too about the culture we inhabit. They are forms of language, social discourses, to those – like anthropologists and ethnographers – who wish to read them.[21] Signs, then, are everywhere. The world is a vast web of human significations. Intratextuality describes this and de-scribes also how we occupy certain places within this web, mapping ourselves onto other textual webs when, for example, we read a book, or join a community (a church, a political party, a club for trainspotters) or simply speak to friends. In each of these other textual webs signs are being given to us and create a context for us which modifies our own use of signs.

Now Augustine moves through several different sign-systems in the *Confessions* – home life with Monica, the schools of rhetoric, the Manichean sect, the church of St Ambrose, etc. – but the key to interpreting the significance of any of these sign-systems and their interrelationship, that which enables him to interpret how the sign-systems have constituted his life-story, is the Bible. On a simple level this can be seen from the way the autobiography is littered with quotations from the Scriptures which, say, draw parallels between the Psalmist's experience and Augustine's. But there are more complex levels. Let me draw out three of the most important. The first concerns the very nature of authorship, the writer who is composing the Scriptures and the autobiography. Augustine writes: 'Your divine Scripture has more sublime authority since the death of the mortal authors through whom you provided it for us.'[22] Therefore interpretation does not need to refer continually back to questions concerning what these 'mortal authors' intended. God is the final author, as he is the final authority. Interpretation then is governed by God's mercy and love, evidenced in and through the Spirit of Christ. So 'these texts contain various truths',[23] Augustine tells us. A great 'mass of entirely correct interpretations can be elicited',[24] he concludes. He can even see how two interpretations of the Scriptures, independent and contrary to each other, can still be valid, because it is God's use and intention behind them which is more important than the literal surface of the words themselves. In the same way, the autobiographical 'I' in the *Confessions* is not entirely in command either of his own life or his own text and what future generations of readers will understand by his text. He tells his story out of love for God's love, 'not doing this merely by physical words and sounds, but by words from my soul'.[25] His intention then is to arouse those who will read his account; to draw them by their reading or hearing into an identification with his condition. That is the role of a rhetor. His text is then to perform within and upon his readers so that the 'I' becomes what linguists call a shifter, a sign empty in itself through which the readers might articulate themselves and understand the love of God. 'The heart is aroused in the love of your mercy and the sweetness of your grace',[26] we are told. Beyond his own intention, then, because Augustine's life is authored by God in the same way as the Scriptures are authored by God, his words will resonate and a greater authority than himself will be heard in and through them. For 'I carry out your command by actions and words.'[27]

Second, and consequently, like Scripture, events in the autobiography have an allegorical or spiritual sense as well as an historical and concrete one. When temporality is an endless chain of signs governed by God's Providence, history is always His story and the narrative of an individual 'I' becomes a text woven into the Godhead. 'For you yourself are a book,'[28]

Augustine tells us. The composition and nature of representation in God's book determines the composition and nature of representation in any autobiography. Biographical events, then, are refracted through biblical events. Let me give you an example. Towards the end of the strictly autobiographical section of the book, Augustine and his mother Monica stand at a window in the Roman town of Ostia overlooking a garden. There both of them experience an ascension into the eternal 'by internal reflection and dialogue'[29] we are told. This is the high point in the spiritual development of both figures. A cameo is framed: two people, a man and a woman, looking out over a garden, bound by a spiritual intimacy into the Godhead like one flesh and yet without sexual desire. This is Augustine's picture of a paradise regained, the uncomplicated sociality of Adam, Eve and God before the Fall as depicted in Augustine's large thesis *The City of God* and in his *Literal Commentary on Genesis*.

Thirdly, in his work *On Christian Doctrine* Augustine outlines the scriptural principle of composition: the principle of contraries and similarities. So, for example, there is Eve and Mary. The Fall Eve helps bring about, Mary will help to salve. Here they are contraries. But they are drawn into a similarity through Christ – for just as Christ was born of a woman so he 'freed those deceived by a woman'.[30] In Christ they are both similar in that, allegorically, they depict the flesh from which humankind need liberation. This principle of analogy follows from the order and beauty Augustine sees both in God and in his Word as Scripture. What is established by this rule of faith is a vision of the Scriptures as controlled by the principles of irony and allegory. These principles are also evident in the structure of the *Confessions*. Monica, the mother, stands in a relationship of contrast to and similarity with Augustine's concubine; the Manichean Faustus is poised in such a relationship with the Catholic Bishop St Ambrose; the stealing of the pears from a vineyard in Carthage stands in such a relationship to the call to pick up and read the Scripture (the contents of the passage to be read being the giving of all things to the poor) in the garden at Milan; the death of the unnamed friend in Book Four is related likewise to the death of his mother in Book Nine. The representation of any event in the autobiography, then, is caught up in a cavernous semiotic echo chamber from which issue meanings both ironic and allegoric. Or, to employ one of Augustine's own metaphors, representation causes each of us (authors and readers) to enter the 'vast palace of memory, where are the treasures of innumerable images of all kinds of objects brought in by sense-perception'.[31] Representations conduct us into imaginaries – our own and other people's, other people's and God's (if we read Augustine through Lacan). Through representation there is a re-presentation, a re-remembering, a re-cognizing. Augustine writes that 'the mind perceives through the experience of its passions and entrusts them to memory'.[32] To read imaginatively, for Augustine, is to experience, to have one's passions aroused and to enter the memory, in order to add to and modify the arrangement of its images. Representation through reading inflames and transforms our desire. Our experience of the world and the stories of ourselves within that world as an allegory, are read through other stories which change us. But what direction does the change in us take and who controls it?

We are now approaching a way of answering that question: Is there any qualitative difference between reading Proust and reading John's Gospel or are all imaginative encounters and engagements equivalent? Throughout the *Confessions* Augustine is aware of the mimetic effects of representation and how they can be used and abused. In Book One he narrates how he was moved to tears by Virgil's account of Dido and Aeneas. There is, in Book Three, his visits to the theatre: 'I was captivated by theatrical shows. They were full of representations of my own miseries and fuelled my fire. Why is it that a person should wish to experience suffering by watching grievous and tragic events which he himself would not wish to endure? Nevertheless he wants to suffer the pain given by being a spectator of these sufferings, and the pain itself is his pleasure. What is this but amazing folly?'[33] In this Book he also inveighs against the deceptive powers of persuasion summoned by rhetoric – a rhetoric he taught and still employs to good effect (where 'good' is defined also with respect to the Good, that is, the nature of God). But the power of language is not all bad, for it aids his spiritual growth. Reading Cicero's *Hortensius* inspires him and changes his life. In fact between Books Four and Eight it is reading that has the power to effect a personal transformation and an intellectual renewal. This culminates in the scene in the garden at Milan where he hears a voice from a nearby house repeating over and over again 'Pick up and read, pick up and read' with reference to the Scriptures.

The last Books of the *Confessions*, as I pointed out earlier, are a commentary on the story of creation itself – God as a writer, the world as his book, a world now Augustine has learnt how to read. Reading the Scriptures, this time, brings about his conversion and deepens his spiritual understanding. But it nevertheless remains significant that other forms of literature, sacred and secular, have their place in the pilgrimage. Each textual form develops, supplements and modifies the imagination, a faculty Augustine relates closely to memory.[34] A qualitative difference does remain in both the imaginative and spiritual effects of different types of reading, and this is associated with the nature of scriptural language itself as a language which draws more closely to the Word of God. Scripture, like all discourse, 'speaks in a time-conditioned language', Augustine notes.[35] That is, Scripture employs the language and ideas of a specific time, place and community. Because of the gap this opens up between the present reader and the past expression, there is hermeneutics or a science of interpretation. We have all these signs before us but we are unsure how they are being used. The reader enters this gap opened up by time and begins to interpret. Augustine is aware this gap is the origin of differences and arguments between exegetes, but he suggests, in his book *On Christian Doctrine*, that the hermeneutic governing any reading of the Scripture is the hermeneutic of love: 'what is read should be subjected to diligent scrutiny until an interpretation contributing to the reign of charity is produced'.[36] Earlier, he explicitly states that 'I call "charity" the motion of the soul toward the enjoyment of God for His own sake, and the enjoyment of oneself and of one's neighbour for the sake of God.'[37] The hermeneutic of love which governs reading the Scriptures is not just an intellectual rule, it involves our emotions, our desires, our wills. In reading the Scripture, for Augustine, a dialogue opens up akin to the dialogue of prayer and confession which shapes Augustine's own book. Through the time-conditioned language, the eternal Word draws us with strings of love. It is this power to draw us that Augustine calls Scripture's eloquence. It is an eloquence which differs from the rhetorical persuasiveness of other

literary forms because it entices us, as readers, into a dialogue
of love between ourselves and God, an echo of the dialogue of
love between the persons of the Trinity. In such reading we are
caught up into the eternal while being stirred in the very
physical and emotional roots of our beings. We are changed by
the Word made flesh. Augustine exclaims, 'What wonderful
profundity there is in your utterances! The surface meaning lies
open before us and charms beginners.' And notice that word
'charms'. He goes on: 'Yet the depth is amazing, my God, the
depth is amazing. To concentrate on it is to experience awe –
awe and adoration before its transcendence and the trembling
of love.'[38] Signs, which we exchange in order to communicate
one with another, and define ourselves and our perceptions of
the world, seem to float here on a vast and extensive ocean of
meaning. Other forms of reading can become sacramental
because of this – other books may have their impact and draw
us deeper into God. But the linguistic signs which compose
Scripture have, for Augustine, a more powerful effect – an
effect, furthermore that we know is good and beautiful because
the one we come to know through them is God himself. Later
in the *Confessions* he even seems to suggest that these linguistic
counters only become signs through their relation to the Word
– 'through your Word those signs emerged'.[39] And so without
God's Word the world is simply composed of atomized things
without meaning.

We are readers, then, that we might be redeemed. The world
has been written that we might interpret it. In the play between
the reader and the text – and with Augustine a text is not just a
book: it is his very life and the cosmos he indwells – in the play
between the reader and the text the desire to understand
circulates. This is never just an intellectual desire – people
engrossed forget to eat, refuse to sleep, grow hungry with
excitement as their hearts beat faster and their metabolism
changes. Psychoanalysis informs us that desire is the most
profound motivator of our intention; for Augustine we only
have intention through desire. Reading then can effect what we
do and hence what we become. When we read we engage with
dynamics far more powerful than we are aware, enter and
extend the rich store-houses of our imagination, open ourselves
to an exterior, an other which can injure as well as heal us. For
Augustine, a theology of reading – inextricably linked with his

theology of the sacraments, his understanding of incarnation, and his doctrine of Trinitarian participation – takes place in this play between the reader and the text. There is a spirituality of reading, most evident in reading the Scriptures. Through reading God draws us to an understanding of himself, a participation in his Godhead, a realization in our lives of truth, love, beauty and goodness. Reading, for Augustine, is doxology.

I think of those scribes in the seventh century on the islands of Iona and Lindisfarne laying down their lives in hours and weeks and months and years in an act of love as an act of writing which is also an act of reading and an act of prayer.

Notes

1. See Elliot R. Wolfson, *The Circle in the Square: Studies in the Use of Gender in Kabbalistic Symbolism* (New York: State University of New York Press, 1995), p. 33.
2. *Grace Abounding to the Chief of Sinners*, ed. Roger Sharrock (Oxford: Oxford University Press, 1960), p. 30.
3. See my 'To be a reader: Bunyan's struggle with the language of Scripture', *Literature and Theology*, 4/1 (March 1990), pp. 29–49.
4. *The Spiritual Exercises of St Ignatius Loyola*, trans. Thomas Corbishley SJ (Wheathampstead: Anthony Clarke, 1973).
5. *Inferno*, tr. John Sinclair (Oxford: Oxford University Press, 1971), p. 79.
6. *The Poetical Works of John Keats*, ed. H. W. Garrod (Oxford: Oxford University Press, 1958).
7. See 'Love's knowledge' in her collection of essays *Love's Knowledge: Essays on Philosophy and Literature* (Oxford: Oxford University Press, 1990).
8. Stanza 1 of *Living Flame of Love*, trans. E. Allison Peers (New York: Doubleday, 1962), p. 41.
9. *Time and Narrative* vol. 3, trans. Kathleen Blamey and David Pellauer (Chicago: University of Chicago Press, 1988), pp. 174–6.
10. See the final section of my book *Theology and Contemporary Critical Theory* (London: Macmillan, 1996), pp. 102–31.
11. The major texts in which Augustine discusses the nature of language and its relation to a general theory of signs would include: *De Magistro, De Doctrina Christiana, Confessions* and *De Trinitate*.
12. Carol Harrison, *Beauty and Revelation in the Thought of St Augustine* (Oxford: Oxford University Press, 1992), p. 148.
13. *Confessions*, trans. Henry Chadwick (Oxford: Oxford University Press, 1991), p. 296.
14. See *The City of God*, trans. Henry Bettenson (Harmondsworth: Penguin, 1984), xiv.26, and *De Genesis ad Litteram*, vii. 9.17.
15. *De Genesis ad Litteram*, xi.33.43.
16. *De Vera Religione*, 38.
17. 'Language, reality and desire in Augustine's *De Doctrina*', *Literature and Theology*, 3/2 (July 1989), p. 14/1.
18. *On Christian Doctrine*, trans. D. W. Robinson, Jr (New York: Macmillan, 1958), I.vi, p. 11.

19. Ibid.
20. 'Language, reality and desire', p. 142.
21. See here Clifford Geertz, *The Interpretation of Cultures* (London: Fontana, 1973), pp. 3–30, for a more detailed account of social semiotics.
22. *Confessions*, p. 282.
23. Ibid., p. 270.
24. Ibid., p. 265.
25. Ibid., p. 179.
26. Ibid., p. 180.
27. Ibid., p. 182.
28. Ibid., p. 283.
29. Ibid., p. 171.
30. *On Christian Doctrine* I.xiv.13, p. 15.
31. *Confessions*, p. 185.
32. Ibid., p. 192.
33. Ibid., pp. 35–6.
34. For a good analysis of the relationship between desire, will and memory as all doxologically ordered, see Michael Hanby, 'Desire: Augustine beyond Western subjectivity' in John Milbank, Catherine Pickstock and Graham Ward (eds) *Radical Orthodoxy* (London: Routledge, 1998), pp. 109–26.
35. Ibid., p. 300.
36. *On Christian Doctrine*, III.xv.23, p. 93.
37. Ibid., III.x.16, p. 88.
38. *Confessions*, p. 254.
39. Ibid., p. 289.

Part II Case Studies

5

From Exile to Pilgrim: Christian and Pagan Values in Anglo-Saxon Elegiac Verse

Graham Holderness

We wish to inform [Bishop Augustine] that we have been giving careful thought to the affairs of the English, and have come to the conclusion that the temples of the idols among that people should on no account be destroyed. The idols are to be destroyed, but the temples themselves are to be aspersed with holy water, altars set up in them, and relics deposited there.

Pope Gregory the Great, letter to Mellitus (601)[1]

Yee cannot drinke the cup of the Lord, and the cup of deuils: ye cannot be partakers of the Lords Table, and of the table of deuils.

St Paul, 1 Corinthians 10.21[2]

I

There has been much debate about the relationships between the Christianity brought to England in the sixth century, and whatever pre-existing pagan cults it may have confronted and eventually supplanted.[3] Historians and archaeologists admit that, since our direct knowledge of pre-Christian Anglo-Saxon religions is sketchy, it is all but impossible to gain access to them through the Christian explanations of Bede and others, which naturally interpret the evidence from a single ideological perspective. A literate culture taking over an oral one has even more advantages than usual when it comes to writing history, in Walter Benjamin's terminology, from the point of view of the victors.[4] Since Christianity, wherever it was established, had to distinguish itself sharply from existing religions, and yet negotiate some, at least temporary, co-existence with them, the Christian missionaries of the sixth century must in practice have operated carefully in that difficult territory between the pragmatic assimilationism recommended by Pope Gregory (as reflected in his letter to another missionary to England, Abbot Mellitus), and the fiercely rigorous denunciation of pagan idol-worship provided in 1 Corinthians by St Paul, and formulated in, for example, Tertullian's *De Idolatria*.[5] And while, on the one hand, it is obvious that, both evangelistically and organizationally, the Christian Church provided a much more robust and powerful religious institution than anything that had preceded it, it is much more difficult to guess at the exact spiritual condition of the converted English populace. After all, since survivals of pagan ritual were still troubling church and civic authorities as late as the seventeenth century,[6] it would be easy to agree with what Rosalind Hill says of the newly converted English a millennium earlier:

> Where Christianity in seventh-century England went deep, as in the case of St Hilda ... it went very deep indeed. In other places it seems merely to have scratched the surface of an essentially pagan society.[7]

Another way of looking at the problem would be to consider in what ways English Christianity developed under the influence of the native religious culture. 'To what extent', asks Gerald Bonner, 'did Christian converts bring relics of their old religion into their new faith?'[8] 'Conversion', the turning-around to face a new future, still leaves the values and imperatives of an old belief-system at the convert's back: a past that can certainly be transcended, but perhaps never entirely repudiated. The many examples of 'syncretism' in art of the period, such as the famous 'Franks Casket', which combines scenes from Roman history, biblical narrative, and Nordic mythology – collocating depictions of the hero Welund the Smith with a tableau of the Nativity – suggest some such process of assimilation and continuing co-existence.[9] One can imagine the Christian convert, accustomed to sacrificing oxen to a heathen deity, readily accepting, perhaps (under Gregory's instructions) in the same already sanctified place,[10] the sacrifice of the Eucharist; though such opportunistic continuities, while facilitating the ease of conversion, obviously ran the risk of preserving elements of a pagan heritage which could remain a tempting fall-back position for any Christian disenchanted with the promised benefits of the new faith. The high-profile cases of apostasy documented by Bede, such as that of King Sighere of the East-Saxons, probably indicate the more widespread incidence of relapses into the security of the old beliefs;[11] and of course paganism was reintroduced, generations after Bede's death, by successive waves of Viking invaders.

For the laity there seems to have been little difficulty, as had been the case with Rome, in reconciling Christian faith with what remained, at least culturally and ideologically, the main masculine preoccupation of Germanic society – warfare. Anglo-Saxon warriors fought as valiantly under the banner of Christ as did Constantine's legionaries. Even a very late heroic poem like *The Battle of Maldon* combines Christian orthodoxy with some of the Germanic values noted from the first century AD by Tacitus;[12] while the Old English biblical epic *Judith* echoes motifs from the Scandinavian mythology of warfare.[13] Thus Anglo-Saxon heroic poems, from *Beowulf* to *The Battle of Maldon*, are frankly syncretistic, knitting together the values of pagan militarism with the principles of the new faith.[14]

Since it was Christian missionaries from Rome and Gaul who brought literacy into the oral culture of the Germanic English peoples, all Anglo-Saxon literature was, by definition, written down within the environment of a Christian culture. So one would hardly expect to find, among the Anglo-Saxon literary corpus (all preserved by Christian, and quite probably monastic, scribes) any hymns to Woden, or liturgies in praise of Thor. Yet the Christian feast of Passiontide took its English name from the Teutonic spring-goddess Eostre; and Woden himself appears in the *Anglo-Saxon Chronicle*, neatly inserted between biblical antiquity and tribal ancestry: on the one hand descended from the patriarch Noah, and on the other credited as an ancestor of the West Saxon kings.[15]

Even thus safely 'euhemerized' into legendary human characters and folk-tale culture heroes, the old Nordic characters still retained, for some practitioners of the new faith, an element of threat and danger. 'What has Ingeld to do with Christ?', asked Bishop Alcuin, scorning the popular hero of Germanic legend. 'The eternal king reigns in Heaven, the lost pagan laments in Hell.'[16] Alcuin was complaining about monks who had evidently been listening to the recital of heathen poetry, where they should have been hearing the Scriptures. If even monks enjoyed reciting stories from the pagan past, it is natural to assume that a stronger and more general attachment to traditional culture may have been dispersed throughout the English population as a whole. Whatever its manifest attractions, Christianity could also be seen as threatening to deprive the English of much they had valued and cherished in their traditional culture, as indicated by the Tyneside peasants who complained to St Cuthbert about the monks: 'They have robbed men of their old ways of worship and how the new worship is to be conducted, nobody knows.'[17]

Certainly there is much evidence from the literature, that while Anglo-Saxon Christians may have cheerfully surrendered their polytheistic and anthropomorphic Germanic beliefs, they remained strongly attached to cultural traditions embodying values and attitudes that proved to some extent difficult to square with Christianity. 'Insofar as Anglo-Saxon paganism was not only a religion but also a major heritage encompassing the values, ethics, hopes, fears and collective memories of a people,' suggests John D. Niles, 'it did not die with the Conversion, but rather lived on in the form of both odd pagan survivals and, more importantly, deep-set patterns of belief.'[18]

If such 'deep-set patterns of belief' can survive – in the form of 'values, ethics, hopes, fears and collective memories' – the overthrow of the belief-system that underpinned them, then we should be able to find evidence of them in poetry, where most cultures are likely to encode their deepest anxieties and longings. Although all the Anglo-Saxon verse was written down by Christians within the environment of a Christian culture, Christian poetry was made by adapting language and verse forms that had previously been used for composing, within a Germanic oral tradition, heroic lays, elegies and love songs. The story of Caedmon, as Bede tells it, provides a 'myth of origin' for English Christian poetry: visited by an angel, Caedmon suddenly finds himself able to sing, and composes a Song of Creation, based on that in Genesis, and using, not the standard Latin of the Vulgate (since he was illiterate), but traditional oral-formulaic Anglo-Saxon verse.[19] Christian culture therefore not only adapted the language in which the old gods had been worshipped and the old values celebrated, but took over, for purposes of Christian expression, poetic forms previously employed only to articulate the experience of pagan life and living, and therefore, it is reasonable to assume, imbued with the 'deep-set patterns' of the older culture.

While the confrontation and synthesis of pagan and Christian elements is necessarily foregrounded in the heroic and devotional poetry of the period,[20] it seems to me that some of the 'deep-set patterns of belief' transmitted from the past into the consciousness of English Christians can also be traced in the elegies, poems regarded as quintessentially expressive of the spirit of the age, yet not formally or explicitly concerned with matters militaristic or theological. It is there, it seems to me, in poems that articulate with the greatest clarity and power some of the deepest desires and anxieties of Anglo-Saxon culture, that the complex interrelations of pagan and Christian values may most clearly be discerned.

II

The Wanderer,[21] like its companion piece *The Seafarer*, is a dramatic monologue with an intensive focus on the psychological suffering and existential anguish of an exile, narrated within an elegiac space of memory that separates a radiant lost past from a painful and despairing present. The climatic extremities of ice and frost, hail and snow, a northern sky perpetually threatening thunderous darkness, are polarized against the vividly recalled happiness of social relationships, the painfully remembered pleasures of communal joy. The poem sites its expressions of psychological anguish, and its meditation on the emptiness of all human hope, in two adjacent landscapes: one is the sea, always in Anglo-Saxon poetry the exile's surrogate home; the other a demolished building that provokes general reflections on the transience of worldly achievement.

The speaker of the poem has been forced into exile, certainly by the death of his lord, and probably by the annihilation of his community. We don't know exactly why he's an outcast, since he is careful not to reveal his 'secret' even to the reader –

It's only too true that a man is wise
To trap his thoughts tight in his head,
And fasten his feelings firm in his breast.
A spent spirit can't fight fate.
Hard thoughts don't help. A secret is safe
If you keep the key secure in your skull.

He may, perhaps, have shamefully have survived his lord and his kin in a battle in which he would rather have died. The poet's imagination is not, however, concerned with the antecedent causes of exile; rather with depicting the exile's world of rejection and isolation, and his psychological land-scape of loneliness and despair.

Near and far
Through the world I searched, sick for a home,
Hungry for a hall: wanting only one
To befriend me, friendless, one wistful to wind me
In welcoming arms.

In this poem the present is always cold, dark, fast in the grip of some enormous northern winter; the past is warm, bright, filled with generosity and affection. There is also a future of tenuous hope, which in the course of the poem shifts from a desire to find another worldly home, to a yearning for the more permanent home of God's eternal love. The polarities of past and present alternate, the one modulating into the other like a musical sequence of harmonies and discords.

You have to have known
How bitter it is – when care's your companion,
Forlornness your friend – to open your eyes
On no green field, or forge-bright gold;
But on foreign faces, and hostile hearts.
Cruel memory calls then to mind,
In the milling mead-hall, the granting of gifts
From the gold-giver's grace; how in years of his youth
His loving lord embraced his loyalty,
And joyed him with gems. But that glee's all gone.

Thus the wanderer wakes each day from luminous and brightly coloured dreams of green fields and shining gold, back to the monochrome and inhospitable environment of his present exile; and the sight of that landscape of deprivation, in turn, provokes memories of its opposite, that past in which he participated fully in the reciprocal social relationships of his community, receiving gifts from his lord in exchange for the loyal services he had rendered.

The poem then repeats the same movement, describing the vividly deceptive dreams in which the exile thinks himself once again back in his vanished past, again embedded in the physical intimacies and social rituals that formed the infrastructure of social cohesion:

> He kens that he kisses
> His loved liege-lord; with head and hands
> Caresses his knee; remembers the rites
> Of gift and service, the endless exchanges
> Of loyalty for love.

Awaking to the discomfort and privation of the empty sea, he sees, in place of the presences that filled his dream – the hall, the hall-companions, his loved lord and the gifts of his generosity – only the dreary emblems of a perpetual winter:

> But when he awakes
> To the yellow waves, and glimpses the gulls,
> Fanning their feathers in baths of brine,
> It's snow he sees, and hostile hail.

Eventually the poet begins to broaden his vision out from the focus on individual suffering, and to extend the perspective of his own misery from dramatized personal pain, to a larger, existential despair. The individual bereavement, the loss of a lord, has widened into an elegiac reflection on the inevitable loss, by death, of all such leaders, and the perpetual process of mortal transience. All men, in this sense, are destined to become wanderers, since no lord lives for ever, no community can guarantee perpetual security and protection:

> So why in the world should I not
> Despair, and my heart grow
> Dark with the northern night sky's
> Annunciation of snow, when I see
> Peerless princes, royal retainers,
> Such valiant men so suddenly vanish,
> The homesteads vacated, voided the halls?
> Between heaven and hell, this whole middle-earth
> Moults and moulders, withers and wanes.

The wanderer's own particularity of suffering has become the condition of the whole human world, this *middangeard* (Leslie, l. 62), this 'middle-earth'. The poem then dwells on the kinds of moral strength and stoic endurance required to sustain life and hope in the midst of such universal decadence and despair.

> You have to have had your fair share of winters
> In this whitening world, before you can call yourself
> Worldly wise. Wisdom is patient, long-suffering,
> Keeps control of its speech, bears and believes
> And endures all things. Wisdom is neither
> Recklessly rash, nor faltering in fight;
> Not avid for glory nor greedy for gold;
> Neither too careless, nor too concerned.
> With wisdom the wise see the world
> As it is.

The passage is interesting, since it recommends certain values that would have been perfectly at home within a pre-Christian context of Germanic culture: maturity; patience; thoughtful and considerate speech; clarity and determination of purpose. These are also however merged with principles that seem to belong more naturally to Christian ethics – courage, but carefully checked by prudence; restraint or even renunciation in the appetite for glory and gold.[22] '... the wise see the world / As it is.' But is that 'wisdom' to be understood primarily as pagan stoicism, or as Christian patience? Is the world a place which is simply likely to provide more sorrow than joy; or a place which cannot be trusted to deliver any lasting satisfaction or reward?

So far I have discussed the poem as addressing the situation of the individual exile, who has lost his lord, and has possibly seen his kin slaughtered; for whom all happiness and pleasure lie in an irrevocably lost past; and who sees the world as a topography of desolate seas, ruined buildings, a landscape coloured by a permanent winter of the mind. But in the poem the individual predicament becomes a universal condition. We are no longer looking at one man who happens to have encountered misfortune and unhappiness: but at a world in which loss, the death of aspiration, the decay of all hope, is the normal condition. The vestigial ruins of Roman occupation are extrapolated into a universal vision of the Last Judgement, when the whole earth will be destroyed to make way for a new (as the first created world was destroyed in the Great Flood).

>   Wisdom knows well
> What a dreadful place this world will be
> When all of its wealth stands waste;
> As we see every day, everywhere,
> Such ruinous remnants of spent splendour
> As the windswept wall of a broken
> Building, tattered by tempests
> And fringed with frost ...
>
> ... So in the past, the ancient Architect
> Annihilated this earth, till the inhabitants
> Lay drowned and deep, the edifices of elders
> Destroyed, desolate and destitute of revelry.

Under the pressure of deep-rooted Christian doctrines, the poem essays a radical questioning of the pagan inheritance of Anglo-Saxon culture. For if all human achievement comes to nothing, then what lasting value can finally be attributed to such activities? Similarly, the image of the warriors, valiantly and courageously defending the wall -

> And though, by that wall,
> Daring defenders, vaunting in valour,
> Protected their prince, in their pride they perished
> And fell at its foot. Deprived of delight,
> Now they lie with their liege-lord, while the mead-hall
> Quietly moulders in the rubble of its ruin ...

– is seen in the perspective of their heroic death; but also of the ultimate destruction of the defensive bulwark they symbolically died for. The poem continues to pay its respects to the past, both its impressive monuments and its heroic achievements. But the conclusion it ultimately draws is that all such achievements are destined to an ultimate oblivion. The importance, in pagan culture, of a man's securing an enduring memory after his death, achieved by notable action and transmitted from generation to generation, almost a type of after-life, is here fundamentally questioned, since no-one now remembers who those defenders were, or even what they were defending.

This gives us an insight into another aspect of the Anglo-Saxon elegiac form, which laments not just the loss of security, love and pleasure, but the passing of the very historical culture within which such experiences were formulated, recorded and

memorialized. There is a chilling finality about the poem's final
vision of a world over which a remorseless destiny is inexorably
tightening its grip, as the cold and darkness of winter inevitably
overwhelm the earth, seemingly adumbrating some great final
cataclysm. What the poet derives from an honest facing of that
harsh reality is not, however, despair, but wisdom and a gift of
song. That which is lost, the pagan world itself, can be
appropriately and movingly lamented in a formal elegy, which
is marked off from the narrative by an introductory statement,
'My heart has the wisdom to sing this song':[23]

> 'Alas! for the day
>   Of the horse and the hero,
> Alas! for the lord's
>   Hospitable hall;
> Alas! for the bright cup
>   With wine overflowing
> Alas! for the loss of it all.
>
> Where now can we find
>   The joys of the mead-hall?
> The splendour of princes,
>   The glory of kings?
> To darkness departed,
>   And under night's helmet
> Vanished, as if
>   There were never such things.'

But that is not the end of the story, for this is not the only
poetic medium the poet is able to command. For he has also
learned, from experience and meditation, another poetic
language, derived from another belief-system, and with it
another basis for hope. Hence the poem ends with a Christian
prayer, again differentiated as a formal 'poem-within-a-poem'.
The wanderer has at last found another lord, another
allegiance, another home:[24]

> Blessed the man
> Who keeps his faith firm, and never reveals
> Tormenting thoughts, till a certain remedy's
> Ready to hand. Blessed the man
> Who hungers for grace; who longs
> For the love, and craves for the comfort
> Of the Father in heaven. All succour,

All safety, all certainty, all love
Lie only with Him, our only
Assurance. He is our haven; He
Is our home.

III

Although *The Seafarer*[25] displays so many similarities with *The Wanderer*, its structure is substantially different: so much so that editors have been reluctant to accept it as a consistent and continuous dramatic monologue, and have attempted to identify within the poem the presence of more than one speaker.[26] My view is that the poem is, in this respect, no different from *The Wanderer*; and that the apparently contradictory impulses and incompatible ideas we find in it are all part of a single, complex account of a deep spiritual crisis.

The difficulty the poem presents (and in this respect it can be differentiated from *The Wanderer*) is that the situation of exile is regarded from two almost opposite points of view. The poem begins in almost the same way as *The Wanderer*, with a description of the privations and psychological suffering of an exile; and it employs the same polarities as the other poem, comparing a miserable present with a bright regretted past.

> Hammered by hail,
> Savaged by snow, my ears heard only
> The sound of the sea, splash of the surge
> And the swan's song.

But *The Seafarer* reaches the point of Christian resignation, the recognition that mortal life can offer nothing of any enduring value by comparison with the eternal promise implicit in the love of God, much more quickly than does *The Wanderer*; and then it goes on to formulate, in poetic and imaginative terms, a spiritual aspiration which offers to lift the soul free from the tangling complexities of a miserable and unpromising world.

> And so my heart heaves to wander the waves,
> The unplumbed oceans, and taste of the tang
> Of the salt-sea's spray; to seek the deep streams
> And their restless rolling.

The spiritual hunger for an eternal world is symbolized, however, by the same metaphor as is the experience of exile:

that of a sea-voyage. It is possible to see here why editors, in search of consistency of character or ideas, have found some difficulty in reconciling the poem's different elements, and have sought to attribute different sentiments to different speakers. For at one moment the poem is emphasizing exile on the sea as the characteristic location of human suffering; the next, expressing an urgent longing to undertake a sea voyage that will ultimately restore the seafarer to his true and only home.

As in *The Wanderer*, the sea is the scene of the seafarer's ordeal. We know even less about the causes of this man's exile than we know of the wanderer's; his situation of dispossession is simply stated and described. The piercing 'desire' that strikes inwards towards the narrator's heart or spirit (*hungor innan slat* – 'Keen as a knife, desire drew inwards / To stab at my soul'[27]), is at first unspecified, suggesting the various possibilities of regret for the past, envy of others' present happiness, or an unappeasable yearning for the hoped-for future. Nostalgic longing for a lost past is the common preoccupation of all the elegies. But *The Seafarer* introduces a different concern, by focusing on the exile's awareness that there are others who, unlike him, still enjoy present pleasure. The emphasis here is on the ignorance and lack of sympathetic awareness he assumes in such fortunate people.

> A life of luxury's made for that man
> Who sojourns in cities, caressed with comforts
> And warmed with wine. He feels not a fraction
> Of the seafarer's sorrow, the hateful hardships
> An exile endures. He'll never know,
> That creature of comfort, how some of us suffer
> On this vast voyage.

This suggests to me that, already, a Christian concern with the limitations of worldly advantages is beginning to make itself felt in the poem – the kind of secure and pleasurable life the exile regrets is to some degree compromised by the observation that such beneficiaries of good fortune are likely to remain insensitive to the miserable plight of the dispossessed and wretched of the earth.

The polarity between past pleasure and present pain is reinforced by a series of ironic comparisons, corresponding to a similar rhetorical device used in *The Wanderer*: in place of the happiness, mirth and feasting of the mead-hall, the exile hears only the harsh and raucous cries of sea-birds, which reinforce his loneliness by mocking the sounds of human company.

> The clamour of gulls
> My only glee; the call of the curlew,
> No man's mirth; the mew's plaint
> In place of mead.

The seafarer is a typical Anglo-Saxon exile in that he has apparently lost his lord, and presumably also his other friends; and he feels keenly the deprivation of a life without comfort or luxury. But the lack of any explanation of his predicament, and the profound sense of difference and otherness from those who still occupy and enjoy 'normal life', bring into focus the idea of the exile as a universally representative figure, eloquent of a general existential condition of isolation and deprivation.

The deepening winter of the poem's tragic landscape seems to presage some ultimate climactic catastrophe, some global and glacial disaster, some ice-age of the soul.

> Darkness deepens
> With drifts of snow, shadows of night
> Bring sleet from the north. Hail falls hard.
> Frost grips the ground.

It is from the hardship and unhappiness of this doomed world that the seafarer is determined to escape. His aspiration is formulated, as I have indicated above, as another sea-voyage. But either this is a journey across a very different sea – an ocean of the spirit, rather than the literal waters that encircle the globe – or it is simply a comparable voyage, conceived in terms of a very different sense of purpose and meaning, and approached from a completely different perspective. For this voyage is not a voyage of exile and escape, not a negatively conceived flight from unhappiness to even greater misery; but a voyage of discovery, a journey of value and purpose. It may even be legitimate to define the journey as a sort of pilgrimage, since the poet begins here to use formal Christian vocabulary. Though he speaks of the new journey's object as the discovery of another home, and of the friendship of new companions, this is no ordinary journey from one land to another; nor is its destination a restoration, in another form, of the community to which the seafarer has bidden a final farewell. This is a journey into uncharted waters, towards an undiscovered country, in search of a destination unknown. The seafarer knows full well that the home he is seeking is to be found in alien territory, on a distant and foreign shore, beyond the limits of his present society, or even beyond the boundaries of mortal existence.

There is certainly anxiety entailed in this embarkation: not because the direction or destination of the voyage is in any doubt, but because no man can ever be absolutely certain as to how his soul will be judged by the Lord.

> No-one in this world is so haughty in heart,
> So generously gifted, nor so peerless in pride,
> So daring in deeds, nor so loved of his lord
> That he feels no fear before he embarks,
> Of what will befall him on the far seas:
> What seafarer's lot the Lord holds in store.

Even one who, by the worldly standards of his society, may be regarded as pre-eminently noble and successful – one who is gifted with wealth, confident in his pride, famed for courageous deeds and strongly protected by a loving lord – can derive no particular confidence from those achievements, since they may have little or no value when brought under the terrible judgement of the Christian God. For this reason, the familiar worldly desires and aspirations for the joys of the hall necessarily fall away from the pilgrim's imagination:

> He hears no harping, sees no bright hall,
> No place of pleasure. Hollow his heart,
> And drained of desire; vacant and void
> Is the spirit that's set on the traveller's trail,
> The mind that's fixed on the whelming waves.

In this remarkable passage we find a virtually complete reversal of the 'normal' priorities of Anglo-Saxon elegiac poetry: for instead of expressing regret for the loss of worldly pleasures, and arriving, in a mood of disenchantment, at the need for an other-worldly religious faith; here the paramount importance of spiritual aspiration leads to a voluntary dispossession of conventional worldly longings and desires. Not only does the seafarer cease to regret the loss of such earthly pleasure; he also renounces any wish to regain them. Earthly pleasures and benefits are ascetically subordinated to the fostering of a spirit ready for withdrawal from the world.

In the space cleared by this renunciation of traditional Anglo-Saxon society's principal values, a new spiritual evolution is enabled to develop, beautifully expressed in images of springtime growth and development:

> Blossoms burst, fields grow fair,
> Forests flourish, the country quickens.
> All motions move the stirring spirit
> To prepare for departure, and fathom the flood.

Such uses of natural imagery to express spiritual awakening became widespread in mediaeval literature (a particularly well-known example is the opening of Chaucer's *Canterbury Tales*). The Anglo-Saxon poem, however, still remains to some extent poised between two worlds: there is regret in this renunciation as well as hope; a painful sense of loss, coexisting with a joyful expectation of the future. The song of the cuckoo, herald of spring, paradoxically sounds a note of sadness, since, for the Christian, springtime means departure from the land that is manifesting these signs of abundance and fertility, and the seafarer is bidding a sad farewell to the natural world from which his metaphors of spiritual regeneration are derived.

His spirit, symbolized in the metaphor of a falcon, is already ahead of him, driven by a keen migratory impulse from its confinement in his breast (the Latin word *peregrinus*, used to identify a species of hawk – peregrine falcon – means literally 'wanderer' or 'pilgrim').

> So, stirring, my spirit raps at my ribs,
> Flutters her feathers, then quits her cage
> To soar on the wing, to fathom the flood-ways,
> The earth's expanses, the haunts of the whale.
> Wheeling and hovering, my heart's hawk yells,
> Eagerly inciting the unappeased spirit
> To seek the sea's stretches, where the dead lie deep.
> Then circling, homing, my falcon stoops,
> Repossesses her perch, full of fierce feelings
> Of desperate desire: longing for Love she is,
> Greedy for Grace.

Through the eyes of that disembodied spirit, as in a 'near-death experience', the narrator is able to secure a lofty aerial perspective on both his present life, clinging timidly to the edge of the land, and the vast seas of infinity that roll perpetually ahead of him and draw him onwards towards them. Death is inevitable: and the fear of death undermines human happiness. Nothing in life, then, can equal the 'joy unspeakeable' (1 Peter 1.8) that the Christian can find in God's eternal love.

Moreover, since death can arrive with arbitrary and unexpected suddenness, a man must at every moment look to the condition of his soul. Interestingly, this is expressed initially in terms of the traditional pagan conception of a good and enduring memory. A memory, carefully preserved and transmitted by affectionate family, or by respectful warrior companions and enemies, was of the first importance to the Germanic pagan. Christianity accepted this deep-rooted premise, and simply encouraged men to leave behind them a reputation for piety, saintliness and deeds of charity rather than the heroic nobility of a proud and noble name.[28]

> What's said after
> By still-speaking tongues is a man's memorial:
> It's memory that matters.

The poet of *The Seafarer* subtly merges the pagan conception of a good posthumous reputation, with the kind of fame attaching to saints and martyrs, likely therefore to be celebrated not only by surviving men and women, but by the angels of God's heavenly host.

> So strive to accomplish
> Actions of worth, do down the devil
> And confound your foes, that your meed may be sung
> By the sons of men, and echoed by angels
> As high as the heavens. For ever and ever,
> As life eternal, your fame will be found
> In the heavenly host.

In this context, active resistance to the devil becomes more heroic than the slaughter of mere human enemies. The poem then temporarily returns to that traditional pagan world the poet is explicitly determined to renounce and leave for ever, for one of its most moving and beautiful passages, a formal elegiac lament for the passing of such magnificence, the great kings and emperors of the past, their wealth and their glory.

> Dead are the days
> Of ancient magnificence, the glories are gone
> That once were on earth. No more do we see
> Caesars and kings, those givers of gold
> Who were hailed as heroes, and loved as lords.
> They depart into darkness, earth knows them no more.
> The great men have gone, their empire on earth
> The weak have inherited: men insignificant
> Cling in their comfort to the world's wealth.
> Gone is all glory, all splendour spent,
> All empire interred.

Thus when the image of the lost lord returns towards the end of this passage, it is the entire glory of Germanic pagan culture that is being interred and mourned.

> A man ages:
> Gaunt and grey-haired, he dreams of departed
> Days when his loved lord graced him with gifts;
> He remembers the royalty of that peerless patron,
> Given to ground now, enveloped in earth.

Clearly, however, there is no going back. The poet explicitly comments on the continuing practice of burying useful or precious objects together with an inhumed corpse:

> A man may hoard
> In hidden heaps, a trove of treasure
> To safeguard his soul; bereaved, a brother,
> Broken with grief, will bury bright gold
> In his brother's grave, hoping to light him
> On his shadowy way.

Where, in Germanic tradition, it was believed that the body and spirit continued in some mysterious way to survive together, so that the various implements, articles of currency and vehicles of transport that were inhumed with the dead would remain somehow useful, Christian teaching showed clearly that in death the spirit leaves its *flaesche-hama* (Gordon, l. 94 – 'covering of flesh', 'body') and takes its departure from the shores of this mortal world. An Anglo-Saxon man, devastated by the death of his brother, in a desperate attempt to assist his passage to the other-world, deposits grave-goods with his body, against the Church's teaching. But his brother, like all men and women, is on his way to appear as a naked soul before the terrible Judgement-seat of God, where worldly wealth will avail him not at all.

> But what good's gold
> To the sinful soul, when empty-handed
> It goes before God? The wealth of the world's
> Too poor a price, to placate and pacify
> That awful power.

IV

Before conversion, we can assume, the English preserved a traditional religious culture brought by their ancestors from the European mainland, entailing worship of the Nordic pantheon (gods such as Woden and Thor) or of more localized divinities of field and spring, worshipped in forests and groves. Here and there other local cults, featuring Celtic and Roman divinities, may have survived from the days of Roman Britain. All these belief-systems would have displayed the characteristics of 'primitive religion': animistic, anthropomorphic, strongly focused on sexual fertility, full of magical rituals and charms, centred around human or animal sacrifice. The religious environment provided a framework for the culture of everyday life; hence our weekdays are named from the Teutonic gods, and the English map still littered with sacred Old English place-names.[29]

From their ancestry among the Germanic tribes, and from the violent conditions of their existence, the Anglo-Saxons continued to place a high priority on warfare and its associated values, such as heroic fellowship and military camaraderie, the *comitatus* code of loyalty and courage. These values of fellowship between men extended into very strong bonds of community, reflected in the depressing fears of exile and isolation expressed in the elegiac poems. Clearly English communities were tightly knit in bonds of family affection and loyalty: but when the 'wanderer' figure of the elegies laments his lost past, it is always in terms of masculine relationships, the solidarity of comrades, the intimacy between generous lord and loyal retainer. Though this 'pattern of relationships' could obviously be Christianized, it was by no means in itself a model of Christian community or common-wealth.

Lastly characteristic of this pagan culture was a strong attachment to the body, to its appetites, and to the weapons, tools and implements it needed for survival and for civilized intercourse. This is strongly reflected in burial customs, especially in the careful equipping of a corpse for its mysterious journey to a world beyond mortality, where it would still need cooking-utensils, keys and money, sword, spear and shield. Magnificent pagan burials like that at Sutton Hoo could yet contain Christian artefacts;[30] and the provision of grave-goods in Christian burials like that of St Cuthbert indicate a survival of pagan practice, albeit assimilated to a Christian symbolic register.[31]

Clearly the poems we have examined here show no nostalgia for the old religions *per se*. Even though, we might suggest, *The Wanderer* is more equivocal, less secure in its command of Christian doctrine, than is *The Seafarer*, neither poem displays any radical doubt as to the unique and irresistible majesty and might of the Christian God. And though the service He requires, in the harsh and inhospitable world inherited by His children, may be arduous and apparently thankless, it provides, in the end, the only promise of perfect freedom. Both poems, despite the differences of emphasis detailed above, could be described as 'second-order' elegies, in that they initially express regret for the loss of a temporal world of comfort and security, then move on, again regretfully, to renounce the fundamental values of that world in favour of the greater promise of eternal salvation.

It is at this point, where the poems bid a sad but resigned farewell to their pagan ancestry, that we can glimpse the signs of strong attachment to a traditional pre-Christian culture. The exile in each poem is simultaneously a pagan exile yearning for a lost lord and a vanished community; and a Christian pilgrim, mournfully paying his last respects to a loved past that can now be seen as limited and inadequate in the benefits it can provide. The pilgrim-exile still laments the secular lord he loved, even though that loyalty has now been supplanted by allegiance to a greater king. The physical culture of paganism, which entailed a tender care of the body (evident both in the physical intimacy of the social relationships now foregone, such as the ceremonies of gold-giving, and in the careful preparation of a corpse for the after-life) is still looked back on with some affection, although it has now become alien to the rigorous asceticism of early monastic Christianity. The material possessions that assumed a high priority in the culture as well as the economy of Anglo-Saxon society are also regretted in a double loss, deprived from the exile, renounced by the pilgrim. The importance of a good and enduring reputation, initially achieved by heroic actions, remains an imperative, but has changed its nature in acknowledgement of the temporary nature of human memory, and the newly predominant importance of divine judgement.

It is in *The Seafarer* that the Christian vision emerges most certainly and strongly; and it is worth noting that in this poem we find, superimposed on the traditional view of the natural world as forbidding and inhospitable compared with the warmth and security of human settlement, a proto-mediaeval expression of the seasons as a grammar of Christian death and resurrection, with springtime awakening a natural metaphor for the process of dying to sin, and being born again to Christ. Here, where the poem is at its closest to the heart of the Christian mystery, the Anglo-Saxon imagination returns to the sacred groves previously sanctified by worship of the old heathen divinities. The idols have been destroyed, but the temples aspersed and re-consecrated.

Notes

1. Bede, *Ecclesiastical History of the English People*, trans. Leo Sherley-Price, rev. R. E. Latham (Harmondsworth: Penguin, 1955; rev. 1990), p. 92.
2. Quoted from *The Authorised Version of the English Bible, 1611*, ed. William Aldis Wright (Cambridge: Cambridge University Press, 1909), vol. IV, p. 380.
3. See, e.g., Brian Branston, *The Lost Gods of England* (London: Thames and Hudson, 1974); and Gale R. Owen, *Rites and Religions of the Anglo-Saxons* (1981; New York: Barnes and Noble, 1996).
4. 'Whoever has emerged victorious participates to this day in the triumphal procession in which the present rulers step over those who are lying prostrate.' Walter Benjamin, 'Theses on the philosophy of history' in *Illuminations*, ed. Hannah Arendt, trans. Harry Zohn (London: Fontana/Collins, 1973), p. 258.
5. See Timothy David Barnes, *Tertullian: A Historical and Literary Study* (Oxford: Clarendon, 1971), pp. 93–100.
6. See, e.g., Keith Wrightson, *English Society 1580–1680* (London: Hutchinson, 1982), pp. 200–1.
7. Rosalind Hill, 'Bede and the Boors' in G. Bonner (ed.), *Famulus Christi: Essays in Commemoration of the Thirteenth Centenary of the Birth of the Venerable Bede*, (London: SPCK, 1976), p. 104.
8. Gerald Bonner, 'Some factors in the conversion of the English', *Tufton Review* 1/1 (May 1997), p. 20.
9. See Owen, *Rites and Religions*, p. 54; James Campbell (ed.), *The Anglo-Saxons*

(London: Book Club Associates, 1982), pp. 93, 196; Lloyd and Jennifer Laing, *Anglo-Saxon England* (1979; London: Granada, 1982), pp. 75, 133, 152.

10. The excavated heathen temple at Yeavering in Northumberland seems to provide evidence of ritual animal sacrifice involving oxen: see Owen, *Rites and Religions*, pp. 43–5. 'Since they have a custom of sacrificing many oxen to demons', wrote Bede, 'let some other solemnity be substituted in its place, such as a day of Dedication or the Festivals of the holy martyrs.' Bede, *Ecclesiastical History*, p. 92.

11. 'During a plague the East Saxons lapse into idolatry'. Bede, *Ecclesiastical History*, p. 200.

12. See *The Battle of Maldon*, ed. E. V. Gordon (London: Methuen, 1937), p. 26; Tacitus, *Germania*, trans. S. A. Handford (Harmondsworth: Penguin, 1948; rev. 1970), p. 113.

13. Owen, *Rites and Religions*, p. 15.

14. See Katherine O'Brien O'Keeffe, 'Heroic values and Christian ethics' in *The Cambridge Companion to Old English Literature*, ed. Malcolm Godden and Michael Lapidge (Cambridge: Cambridge University Press, 1991).

15. See Roberta Frank, 'Germanic legend in Old English literature' in Godden and Lapidge, *Cambridge Companion*, p. 95.

16. See S. Allott, *Alcuin of York c. AD 732 to 804: His Life and Letters* (York: William Sessions, 1974), pp. 165–6.

17. Bede, *Vita Sancti Cuthberti Prosaica*, ed. B. Colgrave as *Two Lives of St Cuthbert* (Cambridge: Cambridge University Press, 1940), p. 164.

18. John D. Niles, 'Pagan survival and popular belief' in Godden and Lapidge, *Cambridge Companion*, p. 140.

19. Bede, *Ecclesiastical History*, pp. 248–51.

20. I have discussed these issues in relation to devotional poetry in 'The sign of the cross: culture and belief in *The Dream of the Rood*', *Literature and Theology* 11/4 (December 1997); and in relation to heroic poetry in my book *Anglo-Saxon Verse* (London: Northcote House, 1999).

21. *The Wanderer*, ed. R. F. Leslie (Manchester: Manchester University Press, 1966). My translation, from which all the quotations in this essay are taken, appears in *English*, 47/188 (Summer 1998), pp. 99–102.

22. The reader should note that the language of the translation here is strongly influenced (substituting 'wisdom' for 'charity'), by the King James Bible's version of 1 Corinthians 13, composed some five centuries after the Anglo-Saxon poem was written down.

23. The song is marked off from the narrative by an introduction, '*thas word acwith*' (Leslie, l. 91), and by a clear rhetorical and metrical structure that marks it off from the rest of the poem: '*Hwaer cwom mearg? Hwaer cwom mago? / Hwaer cwom mattumgyfa? / Hwaer cwom symbla gesetu? Hwaer sindon seledreamas? / Eala beorht bune! Eala byrnwiga! / Eala theodnes thrym!* (Leslie, ll. 92–5). The quotations supplied here convert two Anglo-Saxon characters 'thorn' and 'eth', each signifying a different pronunciation of 'th', indiscriminately into English 'th'.

24. Again the closing prayer is delineated from the rest of the monologue by a narrative marker: '*Swa cwaeth snottor on mode ...*' (Leslie, l. 111).

25. *The Seafarer*, ed. I. L. Gordon (London: Methuen, 1960). My translation, from which all quotations are derived, appears in *Literature and Theology* 11/4 (December 1997), pp. 371–5.

26. See Gordon, pp. 2–4. J. C. Pope actually divides the poem between '1st Seaf.' and '2nd Seaf.' See his *Seven Old English Poems* (New York: Bobbs-Merrill, 1966; rev. edn, New York: Norton, 1981).

27. Gordon, l. 11. *hungor* literally means 'hunger'; but I agree with Gordon (note on l. 11) that '*hungor* may imply more than the literal meaning here, and include figuratively the pangs of loneliness and suffering that gnaw at the seafarer's heart'.

28. Ealdorman Byrhtnoth, real-life hero of *The Battle of Maldon*, achieved both kinds

of fame: celebrated in monastic chronicles as a great patron of the Church, he was also memorialized as a chivalric hero, not only in the poem, but in a tapestry woven after his death by his wife Aelflad, to commemorate his deeds (*cortinam gestis viri sui intextam atque depictam in memoram probitatis ejus*). See Gordon, pp. 9 and 16–21.

29. See Bonner, 'Some factors in the conversion of the English', p. 18.
30. In 1939 a burial-ship, apparently the tomb of a seventh-century king, was excavated at Sutton Hoo, near Woodbridge in Suffolk. The tomb contained an astonishing collection of treasures, weapons of war and domestic utensils, objects of value and of religious significance. See Campbell, *The Anglo-Saxons*, pp. 32–3.
31. See Laing and Laing, *Anglo-Saxon England*, pp. 145–8; and Campbell, *The Anglo-Saxons*, pp. 80–1.

6

Chaucerian Ethics: The Spaces of Dialogue

Norman Klassen

Introduction

To introduce readers to a question in which theology and Chaucer studies could engage and benefit from greater dialogue, I want to discuss in some depth a particular development in Chaucer criticism. Within the context of what can still be called, albeit loosely, literary studies in English, Chaucer studies occupy a unique position, at once participating in familiar notions of a literary canon and in a rather different organizing principle known as medieval studies; the concept of cultural studies does not surprise most Chaucerians. The possibilities for dialogue with theology might in some ways seem obvious: one might suppose that Chaucer belongs to a medieval world obviously and thoroughly Christian, heavily influenced by scholastic theology and quiet hierarchies, free from dissent. In fact, Chaucer and medieval studies, with the help of a vast array of theoretical tools, have revealed a much more complex environment, the result of persistently challenging assumptions with a call for a more detailed enquiry. Questions of ideology, dissent, pluralism, and so on turn out to be as interesting here as elsewhere. In some ways, more so, because Chaucer studies are also constituted in an ambiguous space between medieval and modern, and because Chaucer's and his nation's relationship with continental Europe is particularly complicated. This complexity represents a stimulating challenge:

dialogue between theology and literature here necessarily involves questions regarding such labels as humanism and modernity, and such practices as periodization.[1]

With this awareness as a starting point, I want to foster dialogue of Chaucerian ethics. In some ways, we cannot know Chaucer's values.[2] Yet it does not follow either that we should not discuss the problem of ethics in connection with Chaucer's poetry or that we can only blandly restate what is now the default position of ethical pluralism. Chaucer was clearly interested in the problem of ethics and his approach to moral questions was anything but bland. I want to suggest that we need briefly to reconsider a particular aspect of the development of Chaucer criticism, and that we can enrich this discussion by considering ethics in terms of the relationship between the self and the other as articulated recently by Paul Ricoeur. My aim here is not to attempt to provide a solution but to foster dialogue in a new direction. Dialogue along the lines of this volume is not without influential opponents. Jill Mann entitled her presidential address at the 1994 Chaucer congress 'Chaucer and Atheism'.[3] She is interested in dialogue too, including dialogue between contemporary atheism and medieval belief, but not, it seems, with contemporary theology. For those for whom biblical theology today provides an important impetus for dialogue, the challenge offered recently by Richard Hays is relevant. In his study of New Testament ethics, he invites the reader to consider how 'to live in imaginative obedience' to the moral vision of the New Testament.[4] Hays's use of the term *imaginative* would seem to provide at least one possible point of contact between those who take seriously both biblical theology (including ethics) and literature; his interest in narrative theology, particularly the role of metaphor-making, indicates another.

Plurality and Incommensurability

We would all readily agree upon the value of reading the General Prologue to the *Canterbury Tales* with reference to medieval estates satire. We have grown accustomed, particularly since the appearance of Jill Mann's standard study on the topic,[5] to reflecting on Chaucer's presentation of the classes and various professions of society, acknowledging both a simple division between those who work, those who fight, and those who pray, and women as a separate estate, and Chaucer's masterful ability to draw highly individualized portraits that outstrip and in many ways work against the expectations of the genre. In the past decade or so, Chaucer studies have expanded dramatically in the areas of social and cultural studies. Mann's pioneering work has served no small role in effecting this development: she acknowledged the latent complexity of the term 'estates' and drew fresh attention to Chaucer's emphasis upon a professional world.

Recent studies of social Chaucer, the social contest, and absolutist lineages and associational forms, to give just three examples, have encouraged us to layer competing and contrasting social grids upon one another so as to reveal the diversity of social interactions in the late fourteenth century. Usually these studies acknowledge the importance of the estates structure but look for complementary and conflicting structures as well. Paul Strohm effectively shows the value of examining forms of social coherence that are horizontal, involving flux among people at a similar rank, as well as ones that are hierarchical, or vertical;[6] Peggy Knapp similarly avows interest 'in the discontinuities, the consciously articulated struggles and the unconscious, inarticulate unease engendered when a set of ideologies no longer adequately accounts for people's experienced lives'.[7] David Wallace explores Chaucer's attraction to associative polity, as in guild structures for example, but considers him to see 'associational governance as a difficult, precarious, practical affair', threatened by absolutism.[8] We have become more aware of the complex forces involved in social interaction and the competing ways in which a fourteenth-century writer such as Chaucer perceived his society. One effect of these developments has been a greater emphasis on social interaction. Another has been the emphasis of those in the middle strata in Chaucer's vision, particularly those who may have shared his position of what Strohm describes as 'gentlepersons "en service"'.[9] Studies that have explored alternatives to the hierarchical structure of estates have emphasized the plurality of conceptualizations regarding societal structure and the incommensurability of these visions. For Knapp, the *Canterbury Tales* is a 'boundary text', by which she means 'one whose environment holds more than one configuration of power contending for preeminence as the fundamental way for its society to see life'.[10] In the *Tales* are multiple discourses 'which make their claims in opposition to one another' and reflect the social reality of the late fourteenth century.[11] In this assessment she echoes Strohm, who sees in Chaucer's 'commonwealth of styles' the poet's recognition of 'diversity and conflict among ranks, interests, and styles as inherent in the nature of ordinary social existence'.[12] David Aers similarly argues that 'late medieval England was a heterogeneous society confronting greatly changed circumstances in the post-plague period'.[13]

In his overview of approaches to Chaucer, S. H. Rigby divides readings into 'Monologic versus dialogic Chaucer', borrowing terminology from Mikhail Bakhtin.[14] Those critics offer a monologic view who present Chaucer as committed to an understanding of society as a divinely ordained hierarchy, whether they argue that medieval society was relatively free from social conflict or see such relations as dysfunctional and the *Tales* as a form of dominant ideology.[15] In fact, as he later admits, most critics view the *Tales* dialogically;[16] that is, they consider Chaucer's works to challenge the claims of dominant ideologies and the *Tales* as a text 'which, in its insistence on the clash of different world-views embodied in the pilgrims' tales, undermines the claims to authority of any single dominant discourse'.[17]

The orientation of this work has had implications for our understanding of ethical discourse, truncating it. In this regard too Mann's study of estates satire established a precedent. Writing in her preface she argues that 'Chaucer is ironically substituting for the traditional moral view of social structure a vision of a world where morality becomes as specialised to the individual as his life-work.'[18] Recent study of estates literature has highlighted a strong connection between the category of morality and narrow self-interest in the traditional paradigm of social stratification;[19] the failure of those interested in maintaining hierarchical structures to satisfy dissenters is becoming very clear.[20] The study of the estates has produced notions of moral fragmentation that have been underscored by recent emphasis upon competition and market-place exchange.[21]

While an interest in ethical discourse in Chaucer and other

medieval works has been severely circumscribed in studies that emphasize heterogeneity, a desire to be able to discuss these works in ethical terms nevertheless persists. Strohm's discussion of pluralism points to a discourse of virtue in that it stresses both the acceptance of the Aristotelian dictum that polity is natural and the importance of a social agreement. What binds society together is a common awareness of the need for a *pactum*: 'The pilgrimage thus necessarily confronts an issue that besets any heterogeneous social body: the quest for *coherentia* or the coherent relationship of parts, for *concordia* or agreement among them.'[22] David Aers alludes to Alasdair MacIntyre's influential *After Virtue* to suggest the relevance of the topic for his examination of community, gender and individual identity. He argues that 'the continuation of the human species, let alone the practice of what may count as vices and virtues, is inextricably bound up with the existence of particular communities, a fact as axiomatic to Aristotle as to Thomas Aquinas and much pre-enlightenment moral thought – no Robinsonades here'.[23] For Aers, the discourse of virtue is nonetheless attenuated and problematic: 'The competition, the mobility, the reorganisations of opportunities, disadvantages, and social divisions sponsored by a market economy, all these are likely to undermine public roles prescribed by traditional moral and social theory. In these circumstances the relations between individual identity and community are likely to become problematic.'[24] He proceeds to focus on issues of identity but to hold the topic of virtue in abeyance. In his recent *Chaucerian Polity*, Wallace highlights a problem arising out of the approach to ethical questions that accentuates a disjunction between each individual and all others. Citing Mann at length, Wallace writes that 'The ethical imperative in such a world is to negotiate, to live with or within, this abiding sense of isolation.'[25] Wallace goes on to point out the potentially disastrous consequences of such an attitude with a brilliantly illuminating reference to Heinz Schirk's film *The Wannsee Conference*, in which the participants, or *compagnye*, members of the Third Reich, work towards the Final Solution. Almost in passing, Wallace draws attention to the need for carefully developed ethical engagement.[26] Significantly, the experience of the Holocaust contributed to Emmanual Lévinas's radical insistence on ' "ethics as first philosophy" ', 'where the ethical and the theoretical cannot yet be opposed'.[27] Chaucer studies still requires greater engagement with such an approach to both ethics and theory.

Selfhood and Ethics

In the face of the problems cultural heterogeneity poses for moral discourse, and whilst acknowledging the sensibility of a refusal like Knapp's to seek 'the one final thematic key which will encompass and explain all the details of the *Canterbury Tales*',[28] I want to explore other possibilities for enlarging our consideration of ethical discourse in Chaucer, particularly in terms of dialogue. Tzvetan Todorov has recently observed that Bakhtinian dialogism indeed opposes any form of dogmatism, but he goes on to argue that 'one should not adopt the facile solution of supposing that it therefore implies an affirmation of subjectivism and radical relativism ... Bakhtin's Russian readers are especially sensitive to this misinterpretation, because they know that, as Orwell had already observed, there is a secret form of complicity between this form of relativism (or, as it is called nowadays, 'postmodernism') and totalitarian ideology ... Intersubjectivity is not reducible to subjectivity any more than to pseudo-objectivity.'[29] The dialogical approach is amenable to theology, as the writings of Martin Buber, John Macmurray and others attest. For Todorov, Bakhtin's status as a religious thinker is somewhat paradoxical: it 'might be that Bakhtin's thought is not religious but that, in many respects, it remains Christian'.[30] For the remainder of this discussion, I wish to focus on the recent work of Paul Ricoeur, particularly his *Oneself as Another*,[31] which derives from his 'philosophy that refuses the absolute' rather than the biblical faith he confesses.[32] In doing so, I perhaps situate this chapter near the edge of the stated area of interest of the volume as a whole, though I believe that dialogism inherently provides sufficient points of contact; an ambiguous position relative to theology also appears to me to do most justice to the ambiguity of Chaucer's theological concerns.

Discussing selfhood in the context of the 'shattered' Cartesian *cogito*, Ricoeur stresses in *Oneself as Another* that 'the selfhood of oneself implies otherness to such an intimate degree that one cannot be thought of without the other'.[33]

Working intensively with linguistic, practical and narrative dimensions of selfhood, he posits a series of oppositions that are at the same time dialectical relations, involving various aporias. These become increasingly rich, culminating in the ethical and moral dimension of selfhood. Ricoeur offers us a definition of ethical intention with three aspects: 'aiming at the "good life" with and for others, in just institutions'.[34] The dialectical structures he posits throughout incorporate the other as 'the "thou" of interpersonal relations and the "each one" of life in the context of institutions', allowing for the passage from ethics to politics.[35] This formulation allows for a clear distinction between the related fields of ethics and politics. Ricoeur is also careful to distinguish between ethics, thus defined, and morality, 'with its imperatives and its prohibitions'.[36] The dialectic between ethics and morality gives rise to a third requirement in the ethical domain, practical wisdom, 'required by the singular nature of cases, by conflicts among duties, by the complexity of life in society where choice is more often between grey and grey than between black and white'.[37] For Ricoeur, practical wisdom has no option but to return to the initial intuition of ethics. It is powerfully shaped by tragedy and suffering, by the 'inevitable place of conflict in moral life'.[38] In fact, the dialectic formed by tragic wisdom and practical wisdom 'can shelter moral conviction from the ruinous alternatives of univocity or arbitrariness'.[39] We return, in Ricoeur, to the intersubjectivity stressed by Todorov, though now with a more detailed understanding of ethical discourse in connection with selfhood.

Much of Chaucer criticism has been content, it seems to me, to accentuate arbitrariness and to isolate the ludic, without sufficient interest in the possibilities arising from what Ricoeur calls a dialectic formed by tragic and practical wisdom. With an emphasis upon intersubjectivity and a three-part understanding of ethics to guide the enquiry, I want to return to the General Prologue to the *Canterbury Tales to* explore the concept of virtue there. In the General Prologue, virtue is intimately associated with the notion of space. In what follows I will be drawing upon space in three converging senses: in the sense of Ricoeur's understanding of the aporetic nature of intersubjectivity; in the sense of the imagined physical loci associated with characters in the descriptions of the General Prologue, spaces that virtue and virtues are invited to fill; and the space in which Chaucer's narrator positions himself as observer and interlocutor, with strongly implied self-reflexivity.

Ethical Spaces in the General Prologue

Chaucer was influenced by Stoic conceptions of virtue. Stoic writings such as Cicero's *De inventione* and *De officiis*, the latter known through the *Moralium dogma philosophorum* and Guillaume de Peyraut's *Summa virtutum et vitiorum*, and the *Formula vitae honestae*, which provided Seneca's theory of the virtues, influenced Chaucer's presentation of specific virtues.[40] One general feature of Stoic ethical thought that can enlarge our understanding of this category in Chaucer's poetic is its spatiality. Quentin Skinner has drawn attention to this feature of Stoic political theory in his analysis of the influences upon Italian pre-humanist thought.[41] Italian pre-humanists drew upon Stoic conceptions of virtue to inculcate in civic leaders the understanding that they were bound to act in whatever way seemed most beneficial to the common good of the *commune*. This stress upon collectivity in pursuing the common good was combined in pre-humanist thinking with the feature that individuals hold power only for a short time. The focus, in this theory of government deriving from the Stoics, is on the virtues themselves. As Skinner puts it, 'The effect of this system . . . is that the laws themselves rule.'[42] Not only does this system emphasize principles as opposed to individuals, but Stoic thought introduces an important spatial quality. Values of particular significance ought to be brought *in medio*, into our midst. Skinner calls this 'a distinctive idiom', one which the Stoics and the Italian pre-humanists employ quite literally as opposed to thinking of the virtues as the possession of individual rulers.[43] There are important ways in which this needs to be qualified. This conception accompanies a communal form of government: the community is defined by the people living in equality, and they give definition to the space into which the virtues are to come *in medio*. Furthermore, the virtues particularly emphasized would therefore be public ones, like peace. Even still, the virtues are distinct from the equal citizens, and the public virtues were compatible for the pre-humanists with the theological virtues of faith, hope and love.

The General Prologue reveals a similar recurring suggestion of the importance of a discourse of virtue *per se*, accompanying a twofold emphasis on individuals and associational forms. Indeed, following Ricoeur, there is a space created by this dialectic: the notion of a discourse of virtue associated with space (impersonal) is not incompatible with the dialogism of oneself as another. Ethical discourse, far from being able to be marginalized as being collocated with individuals and their specializations, or potentially being lost in political discourse and the recovery of detailed political understanding,[44] occupies a similar space to narrativity. It provides the dialectical strategies otherwise observable in Chaucer's *oeuvre* with much of their richness, and in turn can contribute to our detailed understanding of the poetry.[45] My aim in the remainder of this chapter is to illustrate the possibilities for recognizing the implied presence of a discourse of virtue *in medio* in the General Prologue as the equivalent of the desired presence of the virtues in Stoic and Italian pre-humanist thought.

My emphasis will be upon virtue as a concept increasingly intimating a rich ethical discourse also bound up with authorial self-reflexivity, rather than individual virtues.[46] Self-reflexivity is an ethical gesture. It draws attention to and furthers an engagement between meanings of virtue.[47] The author is distinct from the subject matter he describes – such as the moral dilemmas to which he draws attention on either a horizontal or vertical plane, with reference to the individual or to social interactions – yet cannot absent himself, a phenomenon of which Chaucer is well aware and which gives rise to his self-reflexivity. In ethical terms, the particular dilemma presented may be undecidable, but the subject of ethics is more poignantly associated with the author, who cannot absent himself. In terms of the construction of spatiality, this self-reflexivity fits well with Charles Taylor's notion of 'the self in moral space'.[48] Chaucerian self-reflexivity in the General Prologue involves both spatiality and ethics.

Chaucer's vision of society in the General Prologue is rooted in the land. Even as Chaucer establishes the temporal setting, the Prologue establishes and sustains an emphasis upon geography and location that serves as a recurring marker for a significant number of the personages assembled in it:

Whan that Aprill with his shoures soote
The droghte of March hath perced to the roote,
And bathed every veyne in swich licour
Of which vertu engendred is the flour ...   (1–4)[49]

The opening scene is shot through with virtue, which we understand initially to be raw, natural power. In this season, according to the rhythms of the land, virtue courses through the land. Pilgrims, as such belonging to a category defined largely in terms of space – movement through the land and arrival at a sacred place – seek strange 'strondes' (l. 13) or, especially, Canterbury. They leave from strange places too. Southwark, with its ambiguous relationship to the city of London as a place difficult to assign or to comprehend legally, a disreputable place to live as well as to work, serves as an enigmatic starting point.[50] It is in some ways a comprehensive locus of the anxieties of late-fourteenth-century life, a place in need of virtue. The relationship to places that Chaucer immediately establishes does not provide us with any real clues as to the degree of the pilgrims' desire to do a good work and to be better people, though we do know that pilgrimages had such a goal at least as their ostensible focus. Yet Chaucer immediately fuses, without yet having drawn attention to anyone in particular, the discourse of virtue and physical locations. The motif of pilgrimage underlines this collocation.

Physical location is a recurring theme in the descriptions of many of the characters, contributing at once to their construction and to their qualitative character evaluation. The identity of the knight unfolds from the introductory phrase, 'That fro the tyme that he first bigan | To riden out ...' (ll. 44–5) and goes on to enumerate the many places where he has fought. Terry Jones has attempted to denigrate the knight because of his association with these places; he usefully draws attention to their relevance for his characterization and an analysis of his virtue.[51] The knight's status as an ideal character and the notion of perfection relevant in his case are bound up with his identification in spatially localizing terms. The situation is similar with two other characters commonly classified as ideal figures, the parson and the ploughman. Four times in the first eighteen lines of his description of the 'persoun of a toun' (l. 478), Chaucer refers to his 'parisshens' or his 'parisshe'. In spite of the fact that 'Wyd was his parisshe, and houses fer asonder' (l. 491), the parson is 'a good man' (l. 477) partly because he visits 'the ferreste' (farthest) (l. 494). For the narrator, the parson's chief virtue consists in his dwelling 'at hoom' (l. 512) and keeping his fold (l. 512), rather than leaving his sheep 'encombred in the myre' (l. 508) while he runs off 'to Londoun unto Seinte Poules' (l. 509) to seek a retainer. By inference, his brother has a similar virtue in that he diligently works the land, either for himself or for others:

> He wolde thresshe, and therto dyke and delve,
> For Christes sake, for every povre wight,
> Withouten hire, if it lay in his myght. (ll. 536–8)

The innocuous 'therto' takes on particular significance as it underscores his laudable devotion to working the land. As has often been observed, these three characters represent those who fight, those who pray and those who work; their virtue has a common denominator in that Chaucer demonstrates it in spatially localizing terms, a conception of virtue at once reinforced by and reinforcing the ideals associated with physical pilgrimage.

The conception of virtue in these terms applies to other pilgrims as well. Much of the poignancy of the monk's portrait derives from the narrator's description of him as an 'outridere' (l. 166), someone who leaves a specific space with which he is associated. Echoing the description of the knight, this epithet does not so well fit the monk since it draws attention (and Chaucer makes sure we notice this) to the association of monks with the cloistered life. Just beneath the surface of his explanation of the monk's habits and opinions are very complex questions: how should the world best be served? at what point and how easily ought one 'leet olde thynges pace' (l. 175) and hold 'after the newe world the space' (l. 176)? If these should perhaps be settled issues for someone who has become a monk, they need not be settled questions for Chaucer. He accesses these fundamental questions of moral philosophy in his own late-fourteenth-century 'newe world' by raising questions of the monk's convictions in terms of his willingness to leave the enclosed world of the cloister and to ride out to hunt. The description of the monk raises two general problems that impinge upon fourteenth-century ethics: the Christian's relationship to the world, to which the monastic tradition had supplied a supposedly unambiguous answer; and the thorny problem of how to define 'the world', a category bequeathed to Christendom by the Apostle John as one of three enemies the Christian faces. These are of course overlaid with spiritual meanings, yet in the medieval world of physical attempts to express separateness, Chaucer's details provide reminders of this orientation.

If the portrait of the monk raises questions of such import, then the description of the friar, which follows, adds fuel to the fire of anxieties based on the relationship between physical sites and virtue with allusions to a pertinent contemporary problem. The problem of the friars, in ubiquitous satires on this walk of life, attends their independence from bishops and status as wanderers in the world. This one has been licensed as a 'lymytour' (l. 209), licensed by his order to beg in a specific district, in an effort at containment. What at one moment appears to be a straightforward issue of jurisdiction spills over into other issues of containment. Of this friar the narrator relates,

> Ful wel biloved and famulier was he
> With frankeleyns over al in his contree,
> And eek with worthy wommen of the toun.
> (ll. 215–17)

The suspicions of him that the narrator plants stem from a statement that begins as approbation of his character – if he is 'ful wel biloved' he is probably a good fellow well met – then degenerates through the loaded word 'famulier' to an emphasis upon his relationships in two realms: with franklins 'in his contree' and with worthy women 'of the toun'. With these two localizing descriptions Chaucer flags moral concerns regarding the worldliness and the sexual licentiousness of the friars, two faults they cannot seem to contain, and accentuates the relationship between a question of virtue and categories of location.[52]

In other descriptions seemingly anodyne localizing details are also bound up with possibilities for moral readings, ironic or otherwise. The franklin occupies an ambiguous position in the lower nobility; his status is difficult to pin down in large measure because of his tenuous claim to land as a country gentleman. He has a claim to a reputation for virtue in that 'Seint Julian he was in his contree' (l. 340). Julian is the patron saint of hospitality, a highly prized courtly virtue as well as a gift of the Holy Spirit. It is, of course, a virtue of place and a certain attitude towards the space over which one has control. Chaucer suggests two degrees of localization, the franklin's house and the 'contree' in which he has this vaunted reputation. Later in the description we learn too that 'Ful ofte tyme he was knyght of the shire' (l. 356), and as general as this term might have been it here further establishes the franklin's identity and praiseworthy ways territorially. Another character whose livelihood is bound up with the land is that of the reeve; in spite of the logic of emphasizing the reeve's connection with the land, Chaucer's narrator goes to extraordinary lengths to locate his reeve geographically, telling us first 'His wonyng was ful faire upon an heeth; | With grene trees yshadwed was his place' (ll. 606–7) and a dozen lines later that 'Of Northfolk was this Reve of which I telle, | Biside a toun men clepen Baldeswelle' (ll. 619–20). This precise localization takes on added significance when he tells us finally that 'evere he rood the hyndreste of oure route' (l. 622). The reeve watches, and on pilgrimage does so from the ideal location; at home he would undoubtedly have watched and been watched.[53] Chaucer locates the reeve with a high degree of specificity, and the reeve thus construed serves as the site of another question of virtue. Significant individualizing characteristics about such figures as the franklin and the reeve in fact reveal a concerted effort on Chaucer's part to isolate moral discourse from the binary of individuals and types.

Chaucer consistently puts the specialisms of the characters in the common context of place; for Chaucer ethical considerations keep impinging themselves. In the case of the shipman, there is none like him 'from Hulle to Cartage' (l. 404) who knows so well his craft, a profession that conjures up geographical categories, as highlighted by the shipman's knowledge of

> all the havenes, as they were,
> Fro Gootlond to the cape of Fynystere,
> And every cryke in Britaigne and in Spayne.
> (ll. 407–9)

This is commonplace phrasing, yet Chaucer gets our attention when the narrator uses a shipman's turn of phrase to indicate that he murders his prisoners: 'If that he faught and hadde the hyer hond | By water he sente hem hoom to every lond' (ll. 399–400). We perceive the shipman exerting his will territorially. The sweeping superlatives in geographical terms find an odd echo in the description of the pardoner, whose dubious abilities Chaucer tells us are similarly without their match 'fro Berwyk into Ware' (l. 692). The apparently innocuous appeal to geography in the case of the shipman resonates here in a discourse where the pardoner is more explicitly unsavoury and where the land is invested with moral relevance. While on the one hand Chaucer presents a uniquely individualized portrait of a pardoner, he is a figure of such dimensions as to cast a moral pall from one end of England to the other. So industrious as to travel to Rome for papal indulgences, and belonging, like the friar, to another religious group dangerous in part because of their ability to travel around, the pardoner's lack of virtue is meaningful as a threat to his society considered in terms of the land and spatial environment.

Details of Chaucer's descriptions such as these draw attention to an aspect of moral discourse that emphasizes neither individuals nor social groups in their specificity or social relations. They suggest a discourse of virtue made present another way, and perhaps a subtly expressed longing for a republican form of government. The Prologue offers an attenuated social vision in the context of the larger project of the *Canterbury Tales*. This attenuation is itself instructive for, apart from signalling the narrator's own gregariousness and concluding the Prologue with the host's plan, Chaucer holds in abeyance the drama of social interaction. The lack of social interaction in the General Prologue haunts it. Discussion of a certain ambiguity where the nature of social relationships and moral judgements are concerned obscures the fact that Chaucer seems more interested in vivifying the concept of virtue (and virtues) as *in medio*.

The presence of virtue is directly related to the foregrounding of the narrator and through him the absent presence of the author. Although apart from the narrator the group of pilgrims already constitutes a fellowship, he can speak 'with hem everichon' (l. 31), seemingly conducting personal interviews.

The emphasis is on their separateness, reinforced by the individual portraits that follow. Even though Wallace is right that the Prologue includes a notion of community through-out,[54] we cannot ignore the sense of atomization (however provisional) as well. The space created in the General Prologue is pre-eminently the space the narrator occupies:

> But nathelees, whil I have tyme and space,
> Er that I ferther in this tale pace,
> Me thynketh it acordaunt to resoun
> To telle yow al the condicioun
> Of ech of hem, so as it semed me ... (ll. 35–9)

The place of the 'Chaucerian I' as both the seemingly detached observer of the others at the Tabard Inn, and the individual who mingles with all of them and inveigles his way into their 'felaweshipe' (l. 32), draws attention to Chaucerian self-reflexivity. That he seems to offer 'the view from nowhere' merely enriches the Chaucerian irony and the sense of instability we feel when the narrator declares that a character is 'worthy' or his opinion 'good'. We are not in an objective world; the work draws attention to the situatedness of the author.

For Ricoeur, reflexivity has inherent dangers but cannot be avoided. On the one hand, he observes that 'Reflexivity seems indeed to carry with it the danger of turning in upon oneself, of closing up, and moving in the opposite direction from openness, from the *horizon* of the "good life".'[55] Yet his entire project is based upon the notion that to say the self is to say the other, that one implies the other, as we have noted. On the ethical plane, self-esteem implies 'solicitude', or 'benevolent spontaneity' towards the other 'within the framework of the aim of the "good" life'.[56] Chaucerian self-reflexivity implies the other, a phenomenon we recognize as readers. Our engagement with Chaucer's poetic on an ethical plane occurs in our awareness of his self-reflexivity: he is aware of himself as an ethical being; the trace of the author entails the trace of ethics. Taylor has argued that 'Moral argument and exploration go on only within a world shaped by our deepest moral responses ...; just as natural science supposes that we focus on a world where all our responses have been neutralized.'[57] Part of the attractiveness of Taylor's approach lies in his suspicion of the concept of scientific objectivity and his desire to shift discussion of ethics away from the umbrella of epistemology.[58] Such observations do not disable moral enquiry but rather put it on a different footing. The ethics of engagement are not easily truncated by the acknowledgement of plurality and the inevitability of conflict. I would argue that Chaucer's self-reflexive awareness of his own presence on the ethical plane is an acknowledgement of this challenge as a starting point rather than the ludic end point, though laughter will always be present, along with suffering. Iris Murdoch's vision of the 'endless aspiration to perfection which is characteristic of moral activity' comes into view here.[59]

I have positioned Chaucer's ethical discourse in the aporia between the dialectics of the individual and political forms, and between the poles represented by vertical and horizontal political structures. In doing so I have followed the dialectical strategy of Paul Ricoeur. The ethical can be seen to occupy a definite place in Chaucer's poetry, one not restricted to identification with individuals and their own life's work, with the exception of himself and the life's work of the poet. The current emphasis on plurality in Chaucer studies has begun to produce the effect of drawing attention to the need for an ethical discourse beyond that of the imperative to negotiate, with an abiding sense of isolation. Such pluralism has accentuated horizontal forms of polity. The role of ethics in a dialectical environment, related to but distinct from politics, can more overtly be applied to Chaucerian poetics. We read, and write, not for answers, but to be reminded that we cannot escape the questions; and that our engagement with others and understanding of ourselves occurs fundamentally in ethical terms.

Notes

1. These questions have not always been adequately addressed in philosophical works that nonetheless can make an important contribution to dialogue between theology and literature, such as Alasdair MacIntyre, *After Virtue: A Study in Moral Theory*, 2nd edn (London: Duckworth, 1985); Charles Taylor, *Sources of the Self: The Making of Modern Identity* (Cambridge: Cambridge University Press, 1989). Graham Ward's introduction to a recent theological reader reflects on the importance of the medieval Christianization of Averroism, hinting at the complexity of the medieval intellectual environment. The relationship between developments in the thirteenth century and present theological challenges indicate

the need for careful consideration of the pre- and post-modern; both are constituted by what we mean by 'modernity', and both constitute 'modernity'. Graham Ward, 'Introduction, or, A guide to theological thinking in cyberspace' in Graham Ward (ed.), *The Postmodern God: A Theological Reader* (Oxford: Blackwell, 1997), pp. xv–xlvii.

2. Chaucerians were recently reminded of this at their biennial congress. Mary Carruthers, 'Micrological aggregates: is the New Chaucer Society speaking in tongues?' Presidential address of the Eleventh International Congress of the New Chaucer Society, to be published in *Studies in the Age of Chaucer* 21 (1999) (forthcoming).

3. Jill Mann, 'Chaucer and atheism', *Studies in the Age of Chaucer* 17 (1995), pp. 5–19. This theme was taken up in the following presidential address. V. A. Kolve, 'God-denying fools and the medieval "religion of love"', *Studies in the Age of Chaucer* 19 (1997), pp. 3–59.

4. Richard B. Hays, *The Moral Vision of the New Testament: A Contemporary Introduction to New Testament Ethics* (New York: HarperCollins, 1996), p. xi.

5. Jill Mann, *Chaucer and the Medieval Estates Satire: The Literature of Social Classes and the General Prologue to the 'Canterbury Tales'* (Cambridge: Cambridge University Press, 1973).

6. Paul Strohm, *Social Chaucer* (Cambridge, Mass. and London: Harvard University Press, 1989), esp. ch. 1, 'Chaucer and the structure of social relations' pp. 1–23.

7. Peggy Knapp, *Chaucer and the Social Contest* (New York and London: Routledge, 1990), p. 1.

8. David Wallace, *Chaucerian Polity: Absolutist Lineages and Associational Forms in England and Italy* (Stanford: Stanford University Press, 1997), p. 79.

9. Strohm, *Social Chaucer*, p. 13. Strohm points out the tendency to make increasingly fine distinctions to clarify relations of groups within the middle strata (p. 7).

10. Knapp, *Chaucer and the Social Contest*, p. 8.

11. Ibid.

12. Strohm, *Social Chaucer*, p. 151.

13. David Aers, *Community, Gender, and Individual Identity: English Writing 1360–1430* (London: Routledge, 1988), p. 9.

14. S. H. Rigby, *Chaucer in Context: Society, Allegory and Gender* (Manchester: Manchester University Press, 1996), pp. 18–77. This work provides an excellent summary of recent scholarship on the *Canterbury Tales*.

15. The most famous example of this approach is D. W. Robertson, alluded to above by Aers, discussed in Rigby, *Chaucer in Context*, pp. 26, 79–81. Rigby also devotes considerable space to Paul Olson's *The 'Canterbury Tales' and the Good Society* (Princeton: Princeton University Press, 1986) esp. pp. 29–33.

16. Rigby, *Chaucer in Context*, p. 174.

17. Ibid., p. 42.

18. Mann, *Chaucer and the Medieval Estates*, p. 11.

19. Aers, *Community*, pp. 6–8.

20. The literature on the topic of dissent continues to grow. For a ranging recent volume on the subject, see Rita Copeland (ed.), *Criticism and Dissent in the Middle Ages* (Cambridge: Cambridge University Press, 1996), esp. Copeland's 'Introduction: dissenting critical practices', pp. 1–23.

21. The situation described in medieval studies conforms remarkably well to the vision of contemporary society Alasdair MacIntyre outlines at the beginning of *After Virtue*, where he argues that modern society has only fragments or a simulacrum of a coherent moral discourse. This influential study calls attention to the need for revaluations of the discourse of virtue not only in philosophy but throughout the disciplines of the humanities and cultural studies.

Norman Klassen

22. Strohm, *Social Chaucer*, p. 145. Strohm also devotes a chapter to 'Selflessness and selfishness' (pp. 84–109). This discussion offers a dualism verging on gnosticism between 'the relative selflessness of characters oriented to transcendent ideals and the selfishness of characters who find their objects of aspiration in this world' (p. 91). Such a sharp distinction dismisses a tension Chaucer arguably wishes to preserve and express in the experience of his characters, fourteenth-century society as he finds it, and his ideals for that society.
23. Aers, *Community*, p. 2. It is sadly telling of the effect Robertsonianism still has when a leading medievalist should have to worry about being branded Robertsonian simply because he has tried to discuss ideas of virtue.
24. Ibid., p. 16.
25. Wallace, *Chaucerian Polity*, p. 78.
26. Wallace's own emphasis is largely descriptive as he draws attention to the importance of 'wifely eloquence' to Chaucer. See especially the important chapter, 'Household rhetoric: violence and eloquence in the *Tale of Melibee*', pp. 212–46.
27. Adriaan T. Peperzak (ed.), *Ethics as First Philosophy: The Significance of Emmanuel Levinas for Philosophy, Literature and Religion* (New York and London: Routledge, 1995), p. xi.
28. Knapp, *Chaucer and the Social Contest*, p. 8.
29. Tzvetan Todorov, 'I, thou, Russia,' *TLS*, 13 March 1998, p. 7.
30. Ibid.
31. Paul Ricoeur, *Oneself as Another*, trans. Kathleen Blamey (Chicago and London: University of Chicago Press, 1992).
32. Paul Ricoeur, 'Intellectual autobiography', Lewis Edwin Hahn (ed.), *The Philosophy of Paul Ricoeur* (Chicago and La Salle: Open Court, 1995), p. 53. In his autobiography he writes that, seeing a basic conflict of interpretations arising in hermeneutics, although he discovered moments of mediation between them, he realized 'the ambition to totalize them into a Hegelian-style system appeared to me ever more vain and suspect. What was becoming evident was not only the indirect and mediate side of reflection, but its nontotalizable and ultimately fragmentary side as well' (p. 23).
33. Ricoeur, *Oneself as Another*, p. 3.
34. Ibid., p. 172.
35. Ricoeur, 'Intellectual autobiography', p. 52.
36. Ibid.
37. Ibid.
38. Ricoeur, *Oneself as Another*, p. 247.
39. Ibid., p. 249.
40. Denise Baker has shown, for example, that Chaucer drew upon a range of Stoic texts in his presentation of four women associated with the four cardinal virtues. Denise Baker, 'Chaucer and moral philosophy: the virtuous women of *The Canterbury Tales*', *Medium Aevum* 60 (1991), pp. 241–56, esp. 242.
41. Quentin Skinner, 'Ambrogio Lorenzetti: the artist as political philosopher', *Proceedings of the British Academy* 72 (1986), pp. 1–56.
42. Ibid., p. 23.
43. Ibid., p. 32.
44. Again, Ricoeur's strategy for distinguishing ethics and politics is significant.
45. In this regard I am suggesting that a three-part understanding of ethics could have similar implications as for Ricoeur, who admitted that with the 'three-cornered' ethics in place, 'the entire architecture [of *Oneself as Another*] had to be reworked bit by bit' ('Intellectual autobiography', p. 52).
46. Though as Baker has shown, specific virtues as understood along Ciceronian lines are clearly detectable in the *Tales*.
47. As a point of comparison, Dante uses this term in a variety of ways in the

102

Commedia. Broadly speaking, *virtù* denotes a natural capacity to act. It can refer to the life-giving power of plants and animals, as well as the power that infuses the heavenly bodies. In the *Commedia*, it variously connotes moral excellence, scientific knowledge and power, artistry, the capacity to propagate, and the power to move. Philippe Delhaye and Giorgio Stabile, 'Virtù', *Enciclopedia Dantesca* (Rome, 1976), p. 1050.

48. Taylor, *Sources of the Self*, pp. 25–52.
49. All references to Chaucer's poetry are from Geoffrey Chaucer, *The Riverside Chaucer*, 3rd edn, ed. Larry D. Benson et al. (Boston, 1987). Citations are all from Fragment I.
50. On the significance of Southwark in the project of the *Tales* see Wallace, *Chaucerian Polity*, esp. pp. 157–8.
51. Terry Jones, *Chaucer's Knight: The Portrait of a Medieval Mercenary* (London: Weidenfeld & Nicolson, 1980). In his counterargument, Maurice Keen similarly focuses on the importance of location. 'Chaucer's knight, the English aristocracy and the crusade', V. J. Scattergood and J. W. Sherborne (eds), *English Court Culture in the Later Middle Ages* (London: St Martins, 1983), pp. 45–61.
52. Jean de Meun adopts a similar strategy in the *Roman de la Rose*, where Faus Semblant, illuminated in MS Morgan 324 as a preaching friar, must first tell the god of love where he lives.
53. J. A. W. Bennett, *Chaucer at Oxford and at Cambridge* (Oxford: Clarendon, 1974), p. 89.
54. Wallace, *Chaucerian Polity*, pp. 66–8.
55. Ricoeur, *Oneself as Another*, p. 180, emphasis his.
56. Ibid., p. 190.
57. Taylor, *Sources of the Self*, p. 8.
58. Charles Taylor, 'Overcoming Epistemology', in *Philosophical Arguments* (Cambridge: Cambridge University Press, 1995), pp. 1–17.
59. Iris Murdoch, *The Sovereignty of Good* (London and New York: Routledge, 1970), p. 31.

7

'How It Might Have Been To Believe': Re-imaging the Social Body in Contemporary Productions of the English Mystery Plays

Susanne Greenhalgh

> With any production of the mysteries, the audience is
> confronted with the question: in Britain, in the nineties, what
> possible relevance can there be in a medieval retelling of the
> Bible?
>
> Hanks, 1997

Prompted by Bill Bryden's production of Dennis Potter's passion play *Son of Man* for the Royal Shakespeare Company in 1995, the drama critic Michael Billington suggested that

> something significant and scarcely noticed seems to be
> happening in our culture which is that, as a counter to the
> materialism of the age, we increasingly look to art, and
> specifically to theatre, to provide a substitute religion. God we
> are told, is dead; I would argue He is currently very much alive
> in the British theatre.   (Billington 1995)

If Billington is right, such tendencies are also expressed in the growing attention given to the English medieval Corpus Christi plays as texts and pretexts for political, as well as spiritual and ethical, exploration. The guild drama of the English midland

and northern towns has enjoyed increasing theatrical popularity since the York cycle was first revived as part of the Festival of Britain in 1951. During the last four decades a number of amateur and professional productions of the various surviving versions of the mystery cycles[1] have taken place in Britain, at the metropolitan heart of the nation, within the hegemonic institutions of the National Theatre and Royal Shakespeare Company, as well as at the regional peripheries, in the north and west of England and in Scotland. A number of these versions have also been broadcast on national television or radio.[2] At Easter 1997, in the professional theatre, one could have seen Katie Mitchell and Edward Kemp's *The Mysteries* at the Royal Shakespeare Company's Other Place at Stratford-upon-Avon; at Greenwich the Italian socialist Dario Fo's *Mistero Buffo* (*The Comic Mysteries*), which used carnivalesque traditions of comic, even grotesque performance to foreground the Gospels' concern with social justice,[3] and a gospel music version for children at the Arts Theatre. Numerous amateur versions, such as those at Spitalfields or Long Crendon in Buckinghamshire, are also regularly performed.

If, for Christian participants, such productions are, in a sense, theology in performance, linking the beliefs of the past with those of the present, they can also pose troubling questions about the nature and continuing validity of religious faith in contemporary society. According to Derrida theatre dominated by an 'author-creator' (who may be a director or actor as well as a playwright) is intrinsically theological and logocentric (Derrida 1978: 235; Auslander 1997: 29) but the mysteries, which survive only in multiple-authored fragments, may provide the occasion for a *deconstruction* of theology. The rewriting and restaging of medieval Christianity for a modern audience also inevitably throws into sharp relief the complex issues involved in performing any religious subject matter in a secular society. In fifteenth- and sixteenth-century England the mysteries arguably presented a unifying image of the social body to a community increasingly fractured by class and economic difference. In contemporary versions this ideal of Christian community, often regarded as central to the drama's emotional power, can be tested, sometimes to breaking point, by tensions between amateurs and professionals, or believers and agnostics. Whereas the medieval cycles brought a community together in celebration and civic pride, in contemporary production they are as likely to articulate radical visions of a social body that is fragmented, alienated or plural. The vibrant popular idioms of language, humour and gesture to be found in many parts of the surviving texts may be co-opted in the service of a celebration of 'Englishness' verging on nationalism, or made to mirror the continuing class and regional divisions of British society. In post-Holocaust, post-feminist times the plays' representation of women and Jews are minefields for those casting and editing them, and theological controversy about the nature of God, the Son of Man, or the mother of Jesus must be played out in public within a multicultural and multi-faith society. In this brief examination of how productions of the cycles have responded to theological debates and theories as well as to changing religious attitudes the main focus will be on the portrayal of Jesus and what this might reveal about the ways in which the social body has been imaged in late twentieth-century Britain.

Who's Afraid of Jesus Christ? The Body of Christ on Stage and in Society

In the theatre, of course, images of Christ are always offered through the body of the actor, who in the words of the Polish theatre practitioner Jerzy Grotowski, is one 'who works in public with his body' (Grotowski 1968: 33). In performance the physicality of the actor is inseparable from his (almost never her) representation of the spiritual, and if, as Billington suggests, theatre does in some way present a 'substitute religion' to a secular audience, it is essential to ask what kind of theatricality is employed to provide that substitute religion, and precisely how the actor's body encodes that of Christ. Whereas, for Brecht, the actor's body 'suggests' the character so that 'his performance becomes a discussion [about social conditions] with the audience he's addressing' (Brecht 1964: 139), Grotowski outlines another possible performance mode:

> As social groupings are less and less defined by religion, traditional mythic forms are in flux, disappearing and being reincarnated. The spectators are more and more individuated in

their relation to the myth as corporate truth or group model, and belief is often a matter of intellectual conviction. ... Group identification with myth – the equation of personal, individual truth with universal truth – is virtually impossible.

What is possible? *Confrontation* with myth rather than identification. ... while retaining our private experiences, we can attempt to incarnate myth, putting on its ill-fitting skin to perceive the relativity of our problems. (Grotowski 1968: 23)

Whichever mode of performance is chosen, casting decisions as to the race, gender or professional status of the actor, as well as the encoding of the performance through costume, gesture and delivery, are the means by which a particular interpretation of the religious content will be offered to an audience assumed to be largely secularized and agnostic.

Scholars of the medieval mysteries have also emphasized that, however important their audience's perception of plays as images or live paintings, equally significant was their reading of the materiality of Christ's body, which could be represented by more than twenty different actors at one performance. Opinions differ as to the type of acting performance that was offered. Preconceptions of naive and even ludicrous acting have largely given way to emphasis on skilled 'cunning' performers, some of them perhaps virtually professional. Arguments remain, however, whether such performance, within its own conventions, was largely mimetic, aimed at making it possible for his audience 'to imagine that he really *was* the character he was playing and to move the audience's emotions accordingly' (Elliott 1989b: 243) or whether, as Meg Twycross has claimed, the effect of such multiple portrayals was to reduce identification with any one star performer, creating rather 'an exremely strong sense of the role itself', in which the 'actor, as image, does not become but represents' the person he plays echoing medieval views on the relationships between 'images' (pictures or statues) and the sacred persons and truths they represent (Twycross 1994: 43). Such performances require 'acts of presentation rather than identification' (Marshall 1994: 304), in which the actor 'must make himself first and foremost a communicator of his own material, not a medium of his own personality and feelings' (Twycross 1994: 54); a theatrical mode which is often discussed in terms of Brecht's theory and practice of 'making strange' or distanciation.

This recent consideration of the semiotics of performance has been accompanied by reappraisal of the significance of Christ's body in medieval society. Peter Travis has argued that 'medieval drama is preoccupied with the body of Christ', which provided the means of both celebrating and questioning the social fabric of the cities in which it was performed (Travis 1990: 67). Such representations, staged by the craft or religious guilds, could offer an image of 'the city's mythic wholeness ... unified, harmonious, healthy and sacred' (p. 71) in its images of a body triumphing over death, but also, through its imaging of a body in pain, wounded and tortured, could form a radical sermon 'speaking of the body itself, unallegorized, uniting with things marginal, profaned and disordered' (Travis 1987: 33–4). As Mervyn James has shown in his study of the relations between ritual drama and social body, the guild Corpus Christi productions provided medieval urban society with a symbolic space, mapped out on the familiar streets and buildings of their city, in which potentially competing ideologies of 'social wholeness' and 'social differentiation' could be be put into 'creative tension' through play (James: 1986). Sarah Beckwith, though with reference to devotional writing rather than to drama, has also stressed the significance of Christ's body as a highly contested area in medieval thought. It is a body which can be emblematic of both resistance, *acting*, but also of submission, humble, that which is *acted on* (Beckwith 1993: 23). Either way Christ's body provides 'a basic metaphor for pre-modern thinking about the social order, one nuanced ... to consider the urgent questions of who was to be included in that social order and on what terms' (p. 27).

It was therefore both the implicit blasphemy threatened by theatrical replay of the Incarnation and its potential for veiled political comment that contributed to the banning of portrayals of Christ on the English stage from the sixteenth century to the abolition of the censorship powers of the Lord Chamberlain in 1968. One of the first breaks with this convention came in 1941 when the detective novelist Dorothy L. Sayers was commissioned by the BBC to write what turned out to be a controversial play-cycle on the life of Jesus, *The Man Born to be King*, for children's radio. Sayers looked first to the mysteries for inspiration, but her own twelve-part cycle concentrated on the events of Jesus's life and aimed to present complex theological ideas about the Incarnation accessibly as well as with complete historical accuracy, her portrayal of life in Judea given edge and authenticity by the contemporary wartime context of a nation fighting off the danger of military occupation. Although there were some protests from the Sunday Observance Society the fact that Jesus (played by Robert Speight) existed as a voice rather than an image undoubtedly helped the audience accept the representation as reverent and moving, and when the plays were later adapted for the theatre public opinion continued to find nothing shocking or blasphemous in such performances. Despite occasional flurries of public concern, especially when the figure of Christ was linked with homosexuality, productions such as the Tim Rice and Andrew Lloyd Webber hit rock-musical *Jesus Christ Superstar* could construct a counter-cultural Jesus without risk of censure, as long as he continued to be cast physically as male, white, blond and blue-eyed, as in the 1997 London revival. Nowadays productions of the mysteries are as likely to draw their images from films such as Pasolini's *The Gospel According to Saint Matthew*, Scorsese's *The Last Temptation of Jesus Christ* or Denys Arcand's *Jesus of Montreal* as from the religious art of the past. Nevertheless the image of Christ retains a potential for controversy in contemporary English culture. The public interest surrounding the 1997 painting of the footballer Eric Cantona, which drew on the iconography of sacred and secular triumph associated with paintings of Christ and Julius Caesar by the renaissance artists Della Francesca and Mantegna to celebrate a contemporary sports hero, is just one example.

Acting on Faith: The Mysteries in Performance 1951–1998

Although as early as 1946 *The Second Shepherd's Play* was incorporated by the left-wing Merseyside Unity Theatre into a political review, *Unity Fare*, it was E. Martin Browne's 1951 Festival staging of the York cycle which began the modern theatrical rediscovery of medieval drama, and formed the basis for what could be termed the heritage version of the cycles. Most of the northern or midland cities and towns associated with cycle drama have staged productions of these plays over the last three decades. York has maintained a cycle of productions every three years, and with it a tradition of casting mainly professional actors in the main roles, for instance the Indian actor Victor Bannerjee (best known for his performance as the victimized Dr Aziz in the film of *Passage to India*) as Christ in 1988. The casting of God in the 1996 production was doubly controversial, being played by a woman *and* an amateur. In 1988 the poet Adrian Henri's updated version was staged at Wakefield as part of the Wakefield 100 centenary celebrations. Condensed into two plays, each two hours long, it was performed in promenade mode in the ruins of Pontefract Castle, with God played as a child. Chester is another city which has regularly staged its cycle, most recently in 1997, its various 'pageants' acted by different groups in a variety of theatrical modes, all showcasing the well-preserved medieval streets and buildings for which it is famous. In such productions tradition and tourism are comfortably allied, in a way probably not very different from medieval times. Apparent innovations in casting confirm the image of the community as open and hospitable to difference but are never allowed to overshadow the mood of local participation and communal celebration.

Even cities whose cycles survive only in a few mentions in civic records have attempted to make community drama out of the Christian myth. The discovery of a fifteenth-century props list for a Corpus Christi procession was sufficient to inspire Dundee to stage a version of the mysteries as part of its 1989 arts festival, scripted by a workshop of local writers and staged by volunteer groups within the city. The performance was completely contemporary and colloquial in style, and although co-ordinated by the Dundee Playhouse, used only a minimum of professional personnel. Its most consistent and successful theatrical strategy was the reclaiming of civic and national space. The production began inside the Town Hall, incorporating dance displays by local schoolchildren and comic turns from God and Satan, both played in broad Scots as argumentative housewives, and moved into the main square for the later parts. Sir Nigel Herd (a combined Herod and Pilate), who was played as a parody of the then Secretary of State for Scotland, Malcolm Rifkind, arrived in the Mayor's limousine, escorted by police outriders. Overall the production avoided any engagement with theology, converting the story

110

into a Scottish Nationalist fantasy in which Josh Mann (Jesus) was shot by police during an anti-Poll Tax demonstration. Although the resurrection, on the roof of the Town Hall accompanied by 'Amazing Grace' and a firework display, effectively combined a mood of religious and civic celebration, the only moral message discernible was that 'every human being is worth something ... and without compassion ... we might as well piss in the wind'.[4]

This production, like most of the others, owed much to the rise of regionally based community theatre movements in the 1960s and '70s.

> The distinctive features of the community play – the sheer numbers, the complicated real mobilization of bodies and objects, the appropriation of non-theatrical space, the multiple playing configurations which place actors and audience in unpredictable relationships – combine to give the drama the weight and rootedness of an *event* (as opposed to the representation of an event). Within this event, the energies and skills and gestures of ordinary social living suddenly become theatrically significant; this is a peculiarly defined space where many people turn out to be 'cunning, discreet and able players': it is not a play about the community, but the community playing itself.   (Shepherd and Womack 1996: 12)

The medieval cycles are often claimed as prototype community drama, localized, historical documents which in performance today can provide the means for a reassertion of regional or civic identity, and express pride in place and solidarity. But like their originals they can also be used to negotiate a sense of otherness, whether manifested in terms of race, gender or class, which demands a constantly shifting redefinition of what constitutes community in the late twentieth century, through such moves as, for instance, casting women or Asians in roles traditionally hallowed as male and white. As Simon Shepherd argues, such performances do not simply celebrate but also implicitly *critique* the community, with a promise of 'access to something more transcendent, something less frivolous, than what is available in contemporary culture ... not just a contrast with, but a challenge to, a debased present' (Shepherd and Womack 1996: 35). Victor Bannerjee, viewing the 1988 York performances through eyes neither English nor Christian, perceived the cycle as 'an epic which takes pride in the very roots of a society and its future ... in performing these plays more and more, you are – although you do not admit it to yourselves – really in search of roots and stability' (Bannerjee 1988). Such observations construct these materials as more than pretexts for the community to play, or even play itself. Rather they are envisaged as attempts to make contact with 'the yearnings of raw spirituality', modern quests for a lost Eden, reaching back to a mythical pre-capitalist 'organic community', for which 'medieval drama' becomes the focus (Shepherd and Womack 1996: 34, 37).

Bill Bryden's epic staging of *The Mysteries* at the National Theatre in the late Seventies and early Eighties explicitly sought to bring the values of community theatre into the professional theatre as a way of renewing the larger community of the nation. According to the Yorkshire poet Tony Harrison the concept began with a heated dinner party argument about the image of Christ (Jones 1985: unpaginated). Harrison had been angered by seeing the cycle at York where 'God and Jesus were played by very posh-speaking actors from the South, and the local people again played the comic parts' (Harrison, in Hoggart 1991: 44), and wanted to restore a homogeneous, levelling 'public speech' in which God, Christ and everybody else speak the same colloquial and forceful language: 'If it's Christ on the Cross with a northern accent, I'll do it,' he promised. In the event an important dimension of the production was the *multiplicity* of accents – Scottish, Tyneside, Devon, Yorkshire, West Indian, Ulster – that spoke Harrison's translation, mapping an imaginary territory, or nation, that stretched far beyond narrow Northern regionality.

The trilogy was developed between 1977 and 1985, years which saw the end of the Labour government, union unrest, the first of four Conservative electoral victories, and the miners' strike. To many 'the ethos of social responsibility and mutual aid' seemed be be unravelling under the influence of newly dominant market values of individualism and entrepreneurial acquisitiveness (Quart 1993: 20, 33). Within the Church of England a growing realization that many of the population were as disaffected by religion as by their growing economic and job insecurity led to the *Faith in the City* initiative. If cultural and social structures formerly at the heart of nation and community, such as trade unions and the churches, were under attack or in crisis, the Cottesloe company sought to transform theatre into a substitute communal meeting place 'a space of moving light and quiet and originality, where the audience who had spent the day in the office and rushed to the theatre ... could find *peace*' in place of strife (William Dudley, in Jones 1985).

Like Harrison, and many socialists before him, Bryden found at the heart of the Christian narrative a resonant myth of the quest for social justice and a utopian vision of how the world might be transformed. Himself the author of a passion play set in contemporary Glasgow,[5] Bryden set out to create 'a celebration of the simple faith of the common people played in modern dress for a lot of people who have lost belief in anything at all', using show business rather than preaching to remind its audience of what it was like to believe in something (Bryden, in Jones 1985). Unable to take the mysteries out to the people as the original productions had done, he and his designer Bill Dudley created a promenade format which allowed the audience to pass in front of a play designed and performed as if by present-day trade-unionists rather than by medieval guildsmen, with every prop and object turned into a piece of modern technology, which by another act of imagination became the fourteenth-century world of the play, a forklift-truck the stairway to heaven, a giant Ferris wheel an emblem of Doomsday (J. Shepherd 1991: 424).

Within this kind of production the figure of Christ, however dramaturgically and theatrically central, is part of the ensemble of performances, arrived at via Bryden's open rehearsal methods, the company work on devising the text acknowledged in the theatre programmes, and the power of the myth of community represented by the plays themselves. The role was played by several actors during the eight years in which the production evolved, from the York 'Crucifixion' played on the Terrace of the National Theatre at Easter 1977 to the Lyceum productions in 1985, most notably, at the beginning, by Mark McManus (best known for his performance as the television detective Taggart) and in the complete trilogy by Karl Johnson. Just as the production evolved from the human drama of the York passion, often labelled as more 'realist' than other medieval cycle plays, to include the Nativity and Doomsday, derived equally from the Chester and Wakefield or Townley plays, the figure of Christ evolved from a predominantly human figure to a divine solution to humanity's failings. Along with Brian Glover, who played God, and unlike the rest of the cast, Johnson doubled only one role, that of Abel in *The Nativity*, where the typological links between the two sacrificial victims were made in accessible theatrical terms.

Johnson has said that he based his concept of the role on the childhood prayer 'Gentle Jesus meek and mild' but also sought to suggest an inner certainty and strength that would fit the judge of Doomsday. As Peter Travis has noted modern productions tend to sanitize and civilize the semiotics of nakedness and torture so significant in medieval performance (Travis 1987: 26–7). This Christ was crucified in his white joiner's overalls, and his presentation of Christ's suffering was delicately balanced between emotional intensity and demonstration. If the identification of actor with role became complete at any point, the end of *The Passion*, when he was helped down from the cross and comforted by his fellow actors, foregrounded a Brechtian perception that this acting was work rather than magic. Buried (in a magician's cabinet rather than a grave) in his best black suit and tie, this Jesus was a young evangelical preacher when he opened the gates of hell, and a working man, gardener or fisherman when he appeared to his friends in Galilee, evident as the Son of God only when dressed in the traditional biblical white gown in which he rose, surrounded by parachute silk, to heaven. The multiplicity of actors in medieval performances was replaced by a succession of 'takes' on Christ by a single actor, each bringing different religious nuances through gesture, costume and delivery – a Son of Man for all seasons.

Harrison has written angrily and movingly about the vandalizing of his parents' grave in his poem 'v', presenting society's lack of care for the dead as a symptom of its moral decline. His reordering of his texts, especially in *Doomsday*, grappled with the implications of mortality. Many of the characters were now dead, dressed in grave clothes, and the mining imagery which had such political resonance in the mid-Eighties as events such as Orgreave unfolded, became theatrically dominant. Much of the second half was taken up with the death and funeral of Mary, played as a sharp-tongued pensioner by Edna Doré. This Jesus, even when ascended to his father, remained a mother's boy, crowning her with flowers like a May Queen and on Judgement Day elevating her to magistrate status at his side. The play ended with reminders of the need for human and worldly response to material suffering, on the basis of which God would

> doom folk far and near,
> After their working, wrong or right
> (Harrison 1985: 221)

Bryden's proud claim that the audience 'took the actors for workers' (Jones 1985), was thus itself almost a political slogan in the aftermath of the Conservative Party's election campaign which accompanied images of dole queues with the headline 'Labour isn't working'. As Karl Dallas concluded after watching the Channel 4 production, this made *The Mysteries*, in its social and political context and through its emphasis on the actors and characters as workers, 'almost an act of defiance', in which 'the players of *The Mysteries* have managed to restore the revolutionary content to the Christian message' (Dallas 1985). Through the appeal to traditions of popular entertainment and community theatre, the production implicitly sought to remind their audience of their ability to act *outside* the theatre as well as within it, to be as transformed by the quest for social justice as the actors were by the experience of playing their roles in the divine comedy.

However 'spurious' the production's appeal to a romanticized nineteenth-century trade union iconography,[6] the implicit message to take thought of others, rather than simply of the individual, and to reject the redefinition of 'community' proposed by Conservative policies such as the Community Charge or 'care in the community', had undoubted popular resonance. It also offered prescient theatrical images of the kind of 'organic communitarianism' which was subsequently to influence New Labour policy in the late Nineties. The production's loving recreation of social rituals, especially communal mourning, was to find its public apotheosis more than ten years later in the 'people's grief' expressed at the funeral of Diana, Princess of Wales, interpreted by many as the final rejection of 'Thatcherite' values and harbinger of a newly caring Britain (and indeed as another kind of substitute religion).[7] Although Martin Hoyle identified three drawbacks for a modern audience: 'a basic religious scepticism; a popular culture drawn from a technological and lay society; and a range of reference, and moral awareness, both wider and more complex than was ever dreamed of by the original (literally) parochial performers' (Hoyle 1985), Bryden and Harrison's goal was a *restoration* of faith, if not in religion then in society itself. *The Mysteries* juxtaposed seemingly irrelevant or even anti-religious modern attitudes with the original language 'as a way of feeling how it might have been to believe' (Harrison, in Dallas 1985). By reviving this 'folk memory' of faith, an audience of agnostics might come to believe, however temporarily, that their society had a future as well as a past, and that social justice was still possible.

The adaptation of the mysteries which opened at Stratford in January 1997 began almost as an act of homage to this vision. Katie Mitchell, a director whose experiences of Polish folk theatre at Gardzienice had sparked an interest in pre-Reformation culture, planned her entire first season as artistic director of the Other Place around medieval drama, including an *Everyman* by Simon MacBurney and Kathryn Hunter in Théâtre de Complicité's mode of intensely physicalized, intercultural performance. Her writer and dramaturge, Edward Kemp, son of the Bishop of Chichester, wanted to explore Englishness and the possibilities for a vigorous poetic speech in a way reminiscent of Harrison. Jointly they were interested in what lessons for living these materials might provide.

> Perhaps if one could begin to understand the ties that bound a medieval community together ... then maybe one could come to a wider understanding of how communities can be built and labour valued in our own age when patterns of both are changing fast. What might a pre-industrial age teach us about living in a post-industrial age? (Kemp 1997a: vii)

After months of research into all available versions and the biblical and apocryphal sources that lay behind them the production team concluded that the political climate no longer existed for the kind of evocation of community that had such political appeal in the Eighties.

> It seemed that we were in danger of building some quaint medieval time-capsule at the end of the millennium, inevitably compromised by lack of knowledge, indubitably coloured by

twentieth-century prejudice. A piece of heritage theatre ... devoid of any attempt fully to engage either with the material or with our audience. (Kemp 1997a: x)

They also found the 'Catholic propaganda' of the plays, with their 'ideologically unsavoury baggage' of anti-Semitism and sexism, increasingly hard to take. With influences from films like Wim Wender's *Wings of Desire* and Denys Arcand's *Jesus of Montreal*, Jack Miles's *God: A Biography*, feminist revisions of biblical studies, and the evolutionary theories of scientists such as Stephen Hawking and Richard Dawkins, they found a new starting point in the life and teaching of Jesus.

> We were interested in certain aspects of his message, as we saw it, and drew up a list of oppositions – altruism vs selfishness, responsibility vs irresponsibility, community vs individualism, spiritual vs material, nature/harmony vs technology/dissonance ... That a man needed to say these things, that a society felt it necessary to kill him for saying them, but other members of that society felt his message to be sufficiently important to promote it, even at the cost of their own lives: this seemed like a story worth telling, independent of whether we could commit to particular beliefs about the man's divinity. (Kemp 1997a: xi)

Although they linked their work to liberation theology what excited Mitchell and her cast most at this stage was not the social revolution implicit in the gospel's message, but the experience of tapping into one of the great story-webs of world culture. They set out to peel away all the Christian accretions from the stories and 're-Judaicize' them. Out therefore went the fall of the angels, Satan and hell, and in came material from the Middle-Eastern cultures, Jewish and Aramaic, from which the fragments of legend, history and mysticism that became the Bible first emerged, together with stories from the Koran and apocryphal medieval sources that gave more scope to the expanded and sympathetic representation of women, all 'middle-Englished' into a framework derived primarily from the 'N-Town' version, the Cornish *Ordinalia* and *The Play of Creacion*. The driving intention behind the telling was to reinterpret the stories to suit our own times, acknowledging their poetic power but also their *fictiveness*, stories, as John Peter points out, for an audience who might be 'Buddhists, Muslims, Hindus and non-believing Jews and Christians' (Peter 1997: 10).

The result was an almost minimalist version, played in two parts. With an economy which verged on asceticism, many of the dramatic high-points of the medieval versions – Mak the Shepherd, Mrs Noah's transgressive rebellion, the massacre of the innocents, the grotesque comedy of the York crucifixion – were omitted. In place of Bryden and Dudley's celebration of everyday objects, technology and the material world, the Other Place was virtually bare of set, costumes were simple bleached robes, music and spectacle were kept to a minimum, and character was sketched with almost child-like simplicity and physicality combined at times with a Stanislavskian interrogation of motives and emotional truth which treated God (David Ryall), too, as a character in an unfolding drama the outcome of which was still unknown. This Jesus (Paul Hilton) was very much more the Son of Man than of God, (or God-in-Man, GIM for short, as the cast termed him), expressing himself in headstands as readily as parables. The play ended not with Doomsday but with the sending of the disciples (two of whom were women) into the world to bear the message and create the texts out of which this version had been created. In place of 'folk memory' these were 'folk-tale versions', 'a wonderful, unsettling mix of the curious and spurious' (Nightingale 1997), parallels for which could be found in any culture of the world. With its quixotic God and central image of the Tree of Mercy, flowering and withering with the fortunes of humanity, critics unsurprisingly detected an almost Beckettian quality in the production. Mitchell and her company sought to distil the essence of the myth, to reach, quite literally the *spirit* of the stories, but found a simple message at its heart: 'personal faith, God within you, and a sense of responsibility locally, to just one other person, that's enough' (Mitchell, in Normington 1998: 108). Inevitably this focus on the plays as religious drama rather than community theatre removed any sense of society and *communitas* (see Normington 1998: 18, 110). Gestures such as the casting of a black actress as Eve and Mary, which in a community version might address local tensions, seemed more myth-making than political discourse, their moral message adrift from any realized social context.

This vague 'altruistic individualism' (Normington 1998: 110) finally wasn't enough. The radical reworking of the play for its 1998 transfer to the Pit, in the London Barbican, was an attempt to ground its moral probings in a more concrete social world, but this in turn led further away from the medieval mysteries and closer to the 'theatre of atrocity' of writers such as Howard Barker or Sarah Kane. Whereas Kemp's authorial voice had been deliberately subsumed into an overall 'middle-Englishness' in the first version, the Barbican script, together with the shortened adaptation broadcast on Radio 3 at Easter 1998, contains much more of his own writing (as well as extracts from Rilke, Bulgakov's *The Master and Margarita* and Dostoyevsky's *The Brothers Karamazov*).[8] Indeed the play's language is deliberately made to evolve as the world's story progresses, from the medieval pastiche of the creation, retained from the first version, through an archaic heightened prose drawn from Shakespeare and the King James Bible, to a clipped, charged dialogue that would be at home in a play by Pinter or Edward Bond. The two-part structure of the first script, in which the Old Testament material of 'The Creation' provided a context of belief for Jesus's teaching in 'The Passion', was replaced by a six-hour epic, which found room for the brutal stories of Saul, Holofernes and Ephraim, as well those of Job, Lot and Noah, in order to trace the disastrous failure of human beings to respect creation and themselves, or control their murderous violence. Jesus represented a second chance for the world, but in a war-torn landscape that was half-Bosnian, half a future Middle-Eastern armageddon, an increasingly dark atmosphere enveloped the narrative. As a raped Mary gave birth she groaned out her hatred of both God and her child, and in the torture cells John the Baptist could only save Jesus from being forced to execute him by killing himself first. Peter's call came as he attempted a violent mugging and Judas was assassinated on Pilate's orders. Whereas the first version ended with St Paul's epistle of love, at the Barbican there was no resurrection and Mary Magdalen's vigil at the deathpits after the crucifixion left her alone to make sense of a world from which God had departed.

> You know the old story. God made the world in seven days. He looked at everything he made and it was good. If it is not good now, who is to blame for that? It can only be us. But he made us in his own image. He made us like him. Isn't that the lesson? Of course Jesus died, of course the man had to die, we all have to

die, but that doesn't mean we have to live in the shadow, on the edge of the deathpits, it doesn't mean we can't be free while we live, that we cannot live like God, that we cannot be like God and make something that is good.   (Kemp 1998: 71)

The play ended with Peter's suicide – in this version the Christian Church would never be founded.[9] The garden of Eden remained a wasteland whose restoration required that humanity outgrow its need for either a god or a saviour.[10]

If, as John Elliott has argued, 'virtually all twentieth century performances of the mystery plays have been adaptations to "the requirements and necessities of the present"' (Elliott 1989a: vii) they also show us, as in a glass darkly, the distance between what our society has been and what it might become, between what belief once was and how far it is evolving into something new. Bryden's and Harrison's version of the mysteries substituted faith in the power of theatre as communal event for religious faith in the service of a socialist vision that acknowledged its own historical roots in Christian teaching. They aimed at provoking a 'direct', 'authentic' emotionally charged exhilaration – 'how it might have been to believe' – which fused past and present as part of the historical continuity of English culture. In Mitchell's and Kemp's initial reading of the Bible and of medieval drama the Christian myth (and Western culture) was just one vehicle for a spiritual quest with no clear goal. The mood was more of meditation than militancy. In their second version they confronted the myth in a Grotowskian manner:

> the theatre must attack what might be called the collective complexes of society, the core of the collective consciousness . . . the myths which are not an invention of the mind but are, so to speak, inherited through one's blood, religion, culture and climate.   (Grotowski 1968: 42)

The figure of Jesus carried the burden of the world's suffering without any certainty of redemption, and was finally abandoned. In place of a community on- and off-stage there was one disciple – significantly a woman – left alone to carry a tentative message of hope for the human species.

Reviewing the Royal Shakespeare Company production, John Peter asked 'Why mount a medieval play if all we see in it is ourselves? Who's afraid of Jesus Christ?' (Peter 1997). As I have argued, we will inevitably see ourselves in *any* version of medieval drama, but if that drama, in both the distant and recent past, once offered a distinct and powerful way for society to image itself through its imaging of the Son of Man, on the verge of the twenty-first century perhaps the body of Christ, as emblem of the social body, has finally been written out of the story. However, one last dramatic project, not yet performed at the time of writing, may point in another direction. There are proposals for a celebratory millennium event, 'JC2000', in which schools all over the nation would devise their own dramatic enactments of the Bible story as films or websites as well as theatrical performances. Such a project conjures up the prospect of hundreds, if not thousands of interpretations of Jesus: male, female, black, white, young, old, theologically radical or conservative, reverent or blasphemous, influenced by many cultures and religious traditions, speaking in all the accents of a kingdom no longer united. Whether this venture will produce visions of Babel or of a new Jerusalem only time and the twenty-first century will reveal.

Notes

1. There are records of some thirty mystery cycles, in London, Cornwall and Scotland, as well as the north and east of England but only four versions have survived in more than fragmentary form; York, Chester, Townley (Wakefield), and the 'N-Town' cycle, once thought to originate from Coventry or Lincoln but now more strongly linked with Norfolk. Most productions draw on one or more of these texts, which have been published in a number of scholarly editions and acting adaptations over the years.

2. The National Theatre's *Mysteries* was filmed in part for *The South Bank Show* (London Weekend Television) in 1980 and in its entirety by Limehouse Productions for Channel 4 in 1985. See Greenhalgh 1998. The 1997 Chester plays were broadcast on BBC2 in 1997 and the RSC production was adapted for Radio 3 and transmitted on Easter Sunday, 1998.

3. For further discussion of this production see Normington 1998: 108

4. This account is based on my recollections of the performance of 9 July 1989, together with information drawn from the programme and an interview with Cliff Burnett, the artistic co-ordinator of the production, on the same day.

5. *The Holy City* (BBC2, 1986).

6. See Twycross 1994: 38.

7. See my article 'Our Lady of Flowers: the ambiguous politics of Diana's floral revolution' in A. Kear and D. Steinberg (eds), *Mourning Diana* (London: Routledge, 1999).

8. References are to the author's unpublished manuscripts prepared for the Barbican production and Radio 3 Broadcast. I am grateful to Edward Kemp for granting me access to these versions.

9. It should be noted, however, that in the Radio 3 version Mary Magdalen speaks the final lines, which imply a rejection of Peter's suicidal despair.
10. Marion O'Connor presented a paper on both the Stratford and London versions of *The Mysteries* at the quinquenial meeting of the International Federation of Theatre Research, University of Kent at Canterbury, July 1998, to be published in *Medieval and Renaissance Drama in England* 11 (1999). This chapter was completed without the opportunity of reading her discussion.

References

Auslander, P. (1997), *From Acting to Performance: Essays in Modernism and Postmodernism* (London: Routledge)

Bannerjee, V. (1988), *The Guardian*, 8 June

Beckwith, S. (1993), *Christ's Body: Identity, Culture and Society in Late Medieval Writing* (London: Routledge)

Billington, M. (1995), *The Guardian*, 20 October

Brecht, B. (1964), *Brecht on Theatre: The Development of an Aesthetic*, trans. J. Willett (London: Methuen)

Dallas, K. (1985), *The Morning Star*, 21 December

Derrida, J. (1978), *Writing and Difference*, trans. A. Bass (Chicago: University of Chicago Press)

Elliott, Jr, J. R. (1989a), *Playing God: Medieval Mysteries on the Modern Stage* (Toronto and London: University of Toronto Press)

Elliott, Jr, J. R. (1989b), 'Medieval acting' in M. Briscoe and J. Coldeway (eds), *Contexts for Early English Drama* (Bloomington and Indianapolis: Indiana University Press)

Greenhalgh, S. (1998), 'The Mysteries at the National Theatre and Channel Four: popular theatre into popular television' in J. Ridgman (ed.), *Boxed Sets: Television Representations of Theatre* (Luton: John Libbey and the Arts Council of England)

Grotowski, Jerzy (1968), *Towards a Poor Theatre* (New York: Simon & Schuster)

Hanks, Robert (1998), *Independent on Sunday*, 25 January

Harrison, T. (1985), *The Mysteries* (London: Faber)

Hoggart, Richard (1991), 'In conversation with Tony Harrison' in N. Astley (ed.), *Tony Harrison* (Newcastle: Bloodaxe)

Hoyle, M. (1985), *Financial Times*, 20 May

James, M. (1986), 'Ritual drama and social body in the late medieval English town' in *Society, Politics and Culture: Studies in Early Modern England* (Cambridge: Cambridge University Press)

Jones, D. (1985), *The Making of the Mysteries* (London: Channel 4 Broadcasting Support Services)

Kemp, Edward (1998), *The Mysteries* (unpublished manuscript)

Kemp, Edward, with Mitchell, Katie, (1997a), *The Mysteries*, Part One: *The Creation* (London: Nick Hern)

Kemp, Edward, with Mitchell, Katie, (1997b), *The Mysteries*, Part Two: *The Passion* (London: Nick Hern)

Marshall, John (1994), 'Modern productions of medieval English plays' in R. Beadle (ed.), *The Cambridge Companion to Medieval English Theatre* (Cambridge: Cambridge University Press)

Nightingale, B. (1997), *The Times*, 10 March

Normington, Katie (1998), 'Little acts of faith: Katie Mitchell's 'The Mysteries' in *New Theatre Quarterly* 13/2, 99–110

Peter, John (1997), 'Acting in the best of faith' in *The Guardian*, 16 March, p. 10

Quart, L. (1993), 'The religion of the market place: Thatcherite politics and the British film of the 1980s' in L. Friedman (ed.), *Fires Were Started: British Cinema and Thatcherism* (Minneapolis: University of Minnesota Press)

Shepherd, J. (1991), 'The "scholar" me: an actor's view' in N. Astley (ed.), *Tony Harrison* (Newcastle: Bloodaxe)

Shepherd, S. and Womack, P. (1996), *English Drama: A Cultural History* (Oxford: Blackwell)

Travis, P. (1987), 'The social body of the dramatic Christ in medieval England' in A. Tricomi (ed.), *Early Drama to 1600* (Binghampton: Centre for Medieval and Early Renaissance Studies, State University of New York at Binghampton)

Travis, P. (1990), 'The semiotics of Christ's body in the English cycles' in R. Emmerson (ed.), *Approaches to Teaching Medieval English Drama* (New York: Modern Language Association of America)

Twycross, Meg 1988), 'Beyond the picture theory: image and activity in medieval drama' *Word and Image* 4/3–4 (July–December), pp. 589–617.

Twycross, Meg (1994), 'The theatricality of English medieval drama' in R. Beadle (ed.), *The Cambridge Companion to Medieval English Theatre* (Cambridge: Cambridge University Press)

8

The Cloud of Unknowing in Dialogue with Postmodernism

Nike Kocijancic Pokorn

T*he Cloud of Unknowing*, a fourteenth-century English
mystical text, is a work of spiritual guidance. It consists
of 75 chapters, in which the author teaches his disciple the art
of contemplation and thus helps his reader to experience
mystical union with God.

The teaching of the *Cloud* successfully joins two Christian
traditions of spiritual thought in an orthodox marriage of the
East and the West; the author primarily follows the teaching
belonging to the so-called *via negativa* as understood in the
Latin tradition, i.e. the mystical theology developed by the
great representatives of apophatic thought, such as Origen,
Gregory of Nyssa and Dionysius Areopagite; and adds to this
grounding the interpretations and innovations made by later
scholastic teachers like Hugh and Richard of St Victor, the
representatives of Augustinian, kataphatic mysticism.

The text belongs to the so-called *Cloud* corpus, which
consists of four treatises: *The Cloud of Unknowing*, *The Book
of Privy Counselling*, *The Epistle of Prayer* and *The Epistle of
Discretion of Stirrings*; and three translations: *Deonise Hid
Diuinite* (the translation of Dionysius' *De Mystica Theologia*),
The Study of Wisdom or *Benjamin Minor* (the translation of
Richard of St Victor's *Benjamin Minor*) and *The Treatise of
Discerning of Spirits* (the translation of two of St Bernard's
sermons).

Neither the *Cloud* nor any of the other six treatises attributed to the same author are signed; therefore, since the beginning of the twentieth century, traditional research of medieval texts has tried to reveal the identity of its author. However, all the attempts to find the author have failed, so that in the last few years the anonymity of the author of the *Cloud* has been almost unanimously accepted. The vocation of the author also remains unknown; however, the author is nowadays most often associated with the Carthusian order, since this monastic order was the most likely environment in which the *Cloud*'s author might have come into contact with Dionysian theology.[1]

The name and vocation of the author of the *Cloud* thus evade every attempt at precise identification – the anonymity then apparently leaves the text open, not fixed by the authority of its author's name, which could define its meaning. Thus the monastic practice of leaving a text unsigned might at first sight be considered as a reflection of the post-structuralist insistence on the necessity of authorial disappearance in the critical act; however, as we shall see, it appears that the removal of auctorial authority is caused in these two cases by the different realities from which the two lines of thought sprang.

The post-structuralist attack on the cult of the author is directed against a known and established author and not against the hidden creator of a text. And it is against this position of strength that Roland Barthes in his essay 'The death of the author'[2] fights, expressing the need to displace the author from the central position the author has held in critical art since the Renaissance and pleading for the reader and the writing to be placed in the focus of our critical attention instead. Contrary to the traditional concept, according to which the authority of the author gave the impression that the text can be ultimately explained, i.e. that we can reach and define the 'real' meaning of the text through the identification and determination of the author,[3] Barthes claims that the text should stand on its own and the authority of the auctorial intentions should be disregarded.

And indeed, in the fourteenth century scholars considered the determination of the author of a text as one of the most important issues when approaching a particular piece of writing.[4] The author, i.e. the name of the 'efficient cause', was considered the guarantee that the writing is worthy of the reader's attention. Since works of unknown and uncertain authorship were believed to possess an authority far inferior to that of works which circulated under the names of *auctores*,[5] it is not surprising, therefore, that even today many scholars try to attribute the *Cloud* to Walter Hilton[6] – Hilton as an *auctor* would represent the source of *auctoritas* needed for the *Cloud* and ensure the orthodoxy and truthfulness of the work.

Against this false security, Barthes argues for a different position of the author caused by the new concept of a text, which was granted an independent life not defined by its environment and its creator. According to Barthes, no author can guarantee the 'right' meaning of his/her writing, since no text can be finally deciphered; in fact, each text reveals the eternal play of signifieds, the elusiveness of the presence of meaning. The concept of 'the death of the author' was thus used to indicate metaphorically the displacement of the author from the centre of the critical act – the author had to disappear, since s/he provided an illusion of imposing a limit on the text, closing the writing,[7] and thus constraining the plurality of its meanings.

The anonymity of the author of the *Cloud* (an anonymity which was not unusual in the Carthusian environment), however, does not manifest the post-structuralist wish to leave the text open to endless readings. In fact, the *Cloud* did not need the critic to remove the auctorial authority, to tear the author from the text, since the author himself most probably deliberately removed his name from his works. But although the *Cloud* author refused to be an *auctor*, i.e. he refused to influence the reader with the authority of his person as a righteous man, perhaps a recluse, he did not deny his writing's *auctoritas* – he rather tried to define it by other means.

First, in *The Book of Privy Counselling* and in *Deonise Hid Diuinite* the author referred to three of his other texts belonging to the *Cloud* corpus,[8] and by connecting them, he broadened the horizon of understanding shared by his readers. The works complemented each other by approaching a similar problem from more than one direction, and thus lessened the possibility of misinterpretation. Second, he mentioned some authoritative authors: among them Dionysius Areopagite in the 70th chapter, St Gregory the Great and St Augustine in the 75th chapter of the *Cloud*,[9] and derived *auctoritas* from their names. Then, the *Cloud* author insisted on defining the readership of his text.

The book begins and ends with the definition of the audience that is to be given the book.[10] He demanded that the work be read only by those who had decided for the contemplative life, i.e. by the most radical Christians, and that it be read from the beginning to the end and not only in fragments which might leave certain issues vague and prone to misinterpretation. The author of the *Cloud* was convinced that his text did not remain open to endless interpretation, if his intended message was accessible only to those who shared with him a sincere wish for the experience of mystical union. And finally, the *Cloud*'s author expressed his belief in the existence of the final, transcendental truth, which ensures the meaning of the text. The 'right' understanding of the message of the text is thus guaranteed by the faith shared by the author and his readers, by their common faith in the hyper-essential God, who revealed himself in the person of Jesus Christ. And if in the post-structuralist world 'the absence of the transcendental signified extends the domain and the play of signification infinitely',[11] in the world of our fourteenth-century mystic the presence of the transcendental God, of the divine *auctor*, the source of *auctoritas*, ensures the meaning, if the author and the reader of the text share the same horizon of understanding and faith.

The reasons for the authorial disappearance are then essentially different in the two cases; while Roland Barthes proclaims the death of the author because he wants to announce the birth of the reader and above all that of the critic with his/her own interpretation of the text, the medieval author of the *Cloud* conceals his name because he thinks that his authority is not needed, and that the shared experience with the reader of his book will grant access to the divine transcendental authority, which bestows meaning on the text.

Besides authorial disappearance, the *Cloud*'s negative discourse could also at first sight find an echo in the discourse of deconstruction as developed by Jacques Derrida. In spite of the fact that it might seem unusual to find any parallels between the *Cloud*'s mysterious description of the ascent to God and Derrida's rigorous attempts to undermine traditional notions of thinking, it is, however, not at all impossible.

In fact, both thoughts might be seen as showing the limitation of metaphysical affirmations;[12] while the *Cloud*'s author uses the basic principles of negative theology to fight against the oversimplification of the basic tenets of Christian religion, Derrida fights against a 'logocentric bias' in Western metaphysics which rejects all meaning that does not conform to a centralizing rationalistic logic of identity and non-contradiction. On the other hand some of the differences between the two are obvious: for example, while the *Cloud*'s author wrote one of the most skilful syntheses of medieval spiritual currents, supplementing the apophatic grounding with kataphatic elements and succeeded in creating a work that reveals a sincere and trustworthy guide to the reader's ascent to God, Jacques Derrida, on the other hand, developed a thought that best reflects the sceptical and fragmented state of a postmodern subject. Both authors were also influential beyond their own fields: the *Cloud*'s influence could be found in comparative theology,[13] medicine,[14] psychology,[15] philosophy[16] and law[17] as well as in Christian theology and English literature; while Derrida's writings echo not only in philosophy itself, but also in literary criticism, sociology, political theory, psychology, anthropology, theology and many more. But despite their large influence, deconstruction, like negative theology, resists a clearcut definition: they both deliberately avoid every attempt at classification. Deconstruction aims to disrupt all univocal classifications and definitions typical of the logocentric bias of Western philosophy, and rejects every attempt at limitation; negative theology, on the other hand, tries to preserve the sacredness of its faith in keeping the basic tenets beyond intellectual grasp.

Because of this essential insistence on the 'undecidability' which could be detected in both, critics as well as supporters of Derrida's deconstruction have persistently attempted to find parallels between his critical strategies and apophatic thought.[18] And indeed, Derrida himself has expressed his fascination for mystical theology:

> Negative theology, we have said this enough, is also the most economical and most powerful formalization, the greatest reserve of language possible in so few words. Inexhaustible literature, literature for the desert, for the exile, always saying too much and too little, it holds desire in suspense. It always leaves you without ever going away from you.[19]

The parallels between Derridean deconstruction and mystical

theology are not drawn only from the fact that Derrida in his own way admires apophatic thought, but also from the truth that Derrida's thought and negative theology at first glance reveal numerous points of contact.

> I have nothing to say in addition or afresh. I found these [apophatic] texts lucid and rigorous, and in any case, I believe I have no objection to make to them ... in effect I believe that what is called 'negative theology' (a rich and very diverse corpus) does not let itself be easily assembled under the general category 'onto-theology-to-be-deconstructed'.[20]

In fact, Derrida himself never ignored the resemblance and even admitted that there exist similarities between the discourse of deconstruction and that of negative theology. However, while deconstruction insists on the eternal position, or rather non-position, experiencing 'the impossible possibility of the impossible'[21] – the impossible possibility of the proper death of being-there (*Dasein*) that speaks, and that speaks of what carries away, interrupts, denies, or annihilates its speaking as well as its own *Dasein*[22] – a contemplative speaks of the death of the self, the self that attempts to utter the ineffable, revealing the inability to express the hyper-essentiality, proclaiming the death of language and reason, and celebrating the unknowable silence. The passage in which Derrida attempts to describe *différance*, one of the basic tenets of his thought, does not hide the affinities of his discourse with that of negative theology.

> So much so that the detours, locutions, and syntax in which I will often have to take recourse will resemble those of negative theology, occasionally even to the point of being indistinguishable from negative theology. Already we have had to delineate that *différance* is not, does not exist, is not a present-being (*ón*) in any form; and we will be led to delineate also everything that it is not, that is, everything; and consequently that it has neither existence nor essence. It derives from no category of being, whether present or absent.[23]

When negative theologians try to 'describe' and capture God in their words, they also use expressions that could in many ways remind us of the deconstructive discourse. Thus this impossibility of any definition is most clearly expressed in the *Cloud* author's translation of Dionysius Areopagite's *De Mystica Theologia*:

... he is neither soule, ne aungel ... ne he is liif, ne he is substaunce, ne eelde, ne tyme, ne ther is any vnderstondable touching of hym, ne he is kunnyng, ne trewthe, ne kyngdom, ne wisdom, ne on, ne vnitee, ne Godheed, or goodnes; ne he is spirit after that we vnderstonde spirit; ne sonheed, ne faderheed, ne any other thing knowen of us, or of any that ben; ne he is anything of not-beyng thinges, ne anything of beyng thinges; ... ne (knittyngly to sey) ther is of hym no settyng, ne doyng awey ...[24]

This fundamental hesitation and undecidability is also reflected in the *Cloud*: the cloud – the dwelling of God – is described in paradoxical language: the place is compared to 'nothing' and 'nowhere', which is 'all' at the same time:

This nought may betir be felt then seen; for it is ful blynde & ful derk to hem that han bot lityl while lokid ther-apon. Neuertheles, yif I schal sothlier sey, a soule is more bleendid in felyng of it for abundaunce of goostly light, then for any derknes or wantyng of bodely lightte. What is he that clepith it nought? Sekirly it is oure vtter man, & not oure inner. Oure inner man clepith it Al ...[25]

However, despite the similarities in discourse, Derrida insists on a fundamental difference between his thought and mystical theology and therefore continues the above quoted thought in the following way:

And yet those aspects of *différance* which are thereby delineated are not theological, not even in the order of the most negative of negative theologies, which are always concerned with disengaging a superessentiality beyond the finite categories of essence and existence, that is, of presence, and always hastening to recall that superior, inconceivable, and ineffable mode of being.[26]

The same wording obviously conveys radically different meaning to a deconstructionist and a negative theologian. Although they both discuss the subject which is ineffable, escaping the possibility of determination and total description, that does not mean that their subject is the same nor that they share their horizons of understanding. While the mystic uses this language to unveil the unrevealable mystery, which, according to him, nevertheless exists beyond reality, the deconstructionist uses this discourse as the reflection of the only existing reality, revealed in an unstable and free play of language, eternally deferring meaning. There is no certainty, no rest for the deconstructionist, while for the negative theologian there exists beyond reason the ultimate harmony in union with the hyper-essential God, who revealed himself in the person of Jesus Christ. In fact, Derrida explicitly stresses that the *différance* which is neither a word nor a concept,[27] which is unthinkable, 'the mirage and illogicalness',[28] is radically different from the concept of God in the Christian tradition:

> *Différance* is not. It is not a present being, however excellent, unique, principal, or transcendent. It governs nothing, reigns over nothing, and nowhere exercises any authority. It is not announced by any capital letter. Not only is there no kingdom of *différance*, but *différance* instigates the subversion of every kingdom.[29]

Différance is not divine, it is not God.[30] 'No, what I write is not "negative theology",'[31] claims Derrida and thus openly rejects negative theology, which, according to him, always turns out to be implicitly affirmative. Deconstructivists are convinced that Christian apophatic thought at the end of all negation reveals itself as 'a reversal that merely repeats, by inverting, the ontological and epistemological principles that lie at the foundation of Western thought and culture',[32] and as such remains ontotheological, which is the basic characteristic of Western theology and philosophy. However, since Derrida cannot deconstruct this 'negativity without negativity',[33] since he cannot spot the fissure in the elusive paradoxical definitions of mystical theology, he has to 'define' his position. And thus this position of eternal instability, of saying 'neither one nor the other',[34] is forced to be fixed. Although he claims that 'I never repudiate anything, through either strength or weakness, I don't know which; but, whether it's my luck or my naiveté, I don't think I have ever repudiated anything,'[35] he feels that he has to reject negative theology, he has to explicitly renounce any connection between this thought and his position: 'No, what I write is not "negative theology".'

And indeed, negative theology essentially differs from deconstruction, since it eventually transcends its own negativity. Contrary to deconstructive claims, it does not become 'negativity without negativity', but negativity *beyond* negativity. Negative theology has no need to be reminded that at the end it turns out to belong to Christian spirituality, it has never forgotten that, in fact, all its negativity stems from its fundamental faith in mysterious transcendental reality. Since *via negativa* never renounced the revealed message, the opposition between affirmative theology and negative (mystical) theology is denied within the cessation of all discourse. If God is ineffable, he is nevertheless worshipped and praised. Thus the *Cloud* opens with a prayer, and, as every apophatic text, 'recognizes, assigns or assures its destination'[36]:

> God, unto whom alle hertes ben open, & unto whom alle wille spekith, & unto whom no priue thing is hid: I beseche thee so for to clense the entent of myn hert with the unspekable ȝift of thi grace, that I may parfiteliche loue thee & worthilich preise thee. Amen.[37]

This is what Derrida calls the 'language of promise',[38] i.e. the language that openly expresses a promise of and faith in God. Contrary to this transcendental certainty, Derrida tries to prolong his play of deconstruction infinitely, to continue discrediting every affirmation, to negate without cessation. He attempts to leave all possibilities open, never to take the final decision, never to mark his position, trying to remain in the place of eternal oscillation. Derrida chooses a position which is, according to him, that of a philosopher 'emancipated from every external power (not lay, not secular), for example from dogmatism, orthodoxy or religious authority'.[39]

The question arises, though, whether Derrida's openness to all possibilities is in fact neutral and innocent; or is this 'emancipation' an ideological decision similar to the one taken by a negative theologian? In fact, sometimes it seems that Derrida not only insists on remaining 'in the place of infinite resistance'[40] but that he appears to deny legitimacy to every other standpoint which is not as 'resistant' as his:

> There is no secret as such: I deny it. And this is what I confide in secret to whomever allies himself to me. This is the secret of alliance. If the theo-logical necessarily insinuates itself there, this does not mean that the secret itself is theological.[41]

Derrida tries to persuade his readers that his thought is emancipated from every external authority, infinitely resisting every attempt at limitation, but at the same time he imposes limits to his position by renouncing the possibility of divine intervention. Even though he is convinced that he has never repudiated anything, he repudiates the negative theologian's answer to the mystery:

> However, I don't believe in the inimitable any more than I believe in the secret and absolutely pure proper name.[42]

By insisting in this 'place of infinite resistance' and rejecting the possibility of a theological answer, deconstruction seems to have lost its aura of eternal elusiveness. Repudiating the possibility of the intervention of supernatural grace, which could pierce the cloud of unknowing, deconstruction does not just remain 'on the threshold'[43] but makes this threshold its chosen position, ornamenting it with the myth of philosophical objectivity and 'emancipation'. It appears that by its rigidity, in denying any other truth than the one it expresses, by prescribing this openness and 'emancipation' as the only legitimate position, deconstruction turns out to be the opposite of what it claims to be – it becomes an authoritative system of thought.

Even though both the *Cloud* and Derrida's deconstruction seem to be using the same discourse and to talk about the same place, or rather non-place of undecidability that cannot be defined, they, in fact, do not have anything in common. Every similarity is just superficial, since the same words convey completely different meanings in the two thoughts. If their readers want to understand any of those two currents, they have to share the horizon of understanding of a particular author; they either affirm the groundlessness and the anti-theological scepticism of Derrida's deconstruction or accept the Christian mysterious promise of the negative theology of the *Cloud*.

Notes

1. It was a Carthusian, Richard Methley, who first translated the *Cloud* into Latin in the fifteenth century, and two fifteenth-century Carthusian manuscripts (BM Add. 37049 (ff. 87b-89b) and BM. Add. 37790 (ff. 234a–236a)) give evidence that the Carthusians in the fifteenth century read and studied Hugh of Balma in conjunction with *The Cloud of Unknowing*; it was the Carthusian commentator James Grenehalgh who ascribed the *Cloud* to Hilton. See Rosemary Ann Lees, *Negative Language of the Dionysian School of Mystical Theology: An Approach to The Cloud of Unknowing*, Analecta Cartusiana 107 (Salzburg: Institut für Anglistik und Amerikanistik, Universität Salzburg, 1983), pp. 433, 443.
2. R. Barthes, 'The death of the author' in *Image–Music–Text: Essays Selected and Translated by Stephen Heath* (Glasgow: William Collins Sons & Co., 1977).
3. Barthes, 'The death of the author', p. 144.
4. A. J. Minnis, *Medieval Theory of Authorship: Scholastic Literary Attitudes in the Later Middle Ages* (Aldershot: Scolar Press, 1988), p. 9.

5. Minnis, *Medieval Theory of Authorship*, p. 11.
6. W. Riehle, 'The problem of Walter Hilton's possible authorship of *The Cloud of Unknowing* and its related tracts', *Neuphilologische Mitteilungen* 77 (1977), pp. 31–44.
7. See Barthes, 'Death of the author', p. 147.
8. *The Book of Privy Counselling*, Early English Text Society, Original Series (= EETS OS) 218, p. 154; *Deonise Hid Diuinite* in *The Cloud of Unknowing and Related Treatises*, ed. P. Hodgson, Analecta Cartusiana 3 (Salzburg: Institut für Anglistik und Amerikanistik, Universität Salzburg, 1982), p. 119.
9. In *The Book of Privy Counselling* he mentions St Bernard, in *Deonise Hid Diuinite* Thomas Gallus and in *The Epistle of Prayer* St Thomas Aquinas.
10. *The Cloud of Unknowing*, EETS OS 218, pp. 1–3, 129–30.
11. J. Derrida, 'Structure, sign and play in the discourse of the human sciences' in *Writing and Difference* (London: Routledge & Kegan Paul, 1981), p. 280.
12. See K. Hart, *The Trespass of the Sign: Deconstruction, Theology and Philosophy* (Cambridge: Cambridge University Press, 1989).
13. See G. W. Tuma, *The Fourteenth Century English Mystics: A Comparative Analysis* (Salzburg: Institut für Englische Sprache und Literatur, Universität Salzburg; K. Watson, '*The Cloud of Unknowing* and Vedanta' in M. Glasscoe (ed.), *The Medieval Mystical Tradition in England: Dartington 1982* (Exeter: University of Exeter, 1982), pp. 76–101; N. Smart, 'What would Buddhaghosa have made of *The Cloud of Unknowing*?' in S. T. Katz (ed.), *Mysticism and Language* (Oxford: Oxford University Press, 1983), pp. 103–20; R. Corless, 'From ignorance to unknowing in *The Cloud of Unknowing* and the *Guide to the Bodhisattva's Way of Life*' in V. M. Lagorio (ed.), *Mysticism: Medieval and Modern* (Salzburg: Institut für Anglistik und Amerikanistik, Universität Salzburg, 1986), pp. 118–34; W. Johnston, *The Mysticism of The Cloud of Unknowing*, 2nd edn (Hertfordshire: Antony Clarke, 1992).
14. See D. J. Rogers, 'Psychotechnological approaches to the teaching of *The Cloud*-author and to *The Showings* of Julian of Norwich' in M. Glasscoe (ed.), *The Medieval Mystical Tradition in England*, Dartington Hall 1982 (Exeter: University of Exeter, 1982), pp. 144–57.
15. See F. Wohrer, 'An approach to the mystographical treatises of the *Cloud*-author through Carl Albrecht's psychology of mystical consciousness' in M. Glasscoe (ed.), *The Medieval Mystical Tradition in England*, Dartington Hall 1984 (Cambridge: D. S. Brewer, 1984), pp. 123–34.
16. See S. Sikka, 'Transcendence in death: a Heideggerian approach to *via negativa* in *The Cloud of Unknowing*' in M. Glasscoe (ed.), *The Medieval Mystical Tradition in England*, Dartington Hall 1992 (Exeter: University of Exeter, 1992); N. Kocijancic Pokorn, 'The language and discourse of *The Cloud of Unknowing*', *Literature and Theology* 11/4 (1997), pp. 408–21.
17. See R. E. Ball, *The Law and The Cloud of Unknowing* (Devon: Arthur H. Stockwell, 1976).
18. M. C. Taylor, *Nots* (Chicago and London: University of Chicago Press, 1993), p. 3; Hart, *Trespass*, p. 189.
19. J. Derrida, 'Post-scriptum: aporias, ways and voices' in H. Coward and T. Foshay (eds), *Derrida and Negative Theology* (Albany: State University of New York Press, 1992), pp. 321–2. See also J. Derrida, *Sauf le nom* (Paris: Editions Galilée, 1993), pp. 113–14.
20. J. Derrida, 'On an apocalyptic tone recently adopted in philosophy', *Semeia* 23 (1983), p. 61.
21. See Derrida, 'Post-scriptum', p. 290; *Sauf le nom*, p. 32.
22. See Derrida, 'Post-scriptum, p. 291; *Sauf le nom*, p. 34.
23. J. Derrida, *Margins of Philosophy* (Brighton: Harvester, 1982), p. 6.

24. In all Middle English quotations *thorn* is transliterated as *th*, and *yogh* as *3*.
Deonise Hid Diuinite in *The Cloud of Unknowing and Related Treatises*, pp. 127–8.
... God is neither soul nor angel; ... he is not life or substance or age or time; we can understand nothing about him, nor is he knowledge or truth or kingdom or wisdom or singularity or unity or Godhead or goodness. Nor in the sense that we understand "spirit" is he spirit; there is no sonship or fatherhood, nor anything else that is known by us or by anyone else. He is none of the things that have no being, none of the things that have being.... Speaking generally there is no affirmation we can make of him, nothing we can deny of him.' ('Dionysius' mystical teaching' in *The Cloud of Unknowing and Other Works*, ed. C. Wolters (London: Penguin, 1978), pp. 217–18.

25. All Middle English quotations from *The Cloud of Unknowing* are taken from *The Cloud of Unknowing and The Book of Privy Counselling*, EETS OS 218 (London: Oxford University Press, 1944); all modern English translations are taken from *The Cloud of Unknowing and Other Works* ed. C. Wolters (London: Penguin, 1978).
The Cloud of Unknowing, EETS 218, p. 122.
'One can feel this nothing more easily than see it, for it is completely dark and hidden to those who have only just begun to look at it. Yet, to speak more accurately, it is overwhelming spiritual light that blinds the soul that is experiencing it, rather than actual darkness or the absence of physical light. Who is it then who is calling it "nothing"? Our outer self, to be sure, not our inner. Our inner self calls it "All" ... (*The Cloud of Unknowing*, ed. Wolters, p. 143.)

26. Derrida, *Margins of Philosophy*, p. 6.

27. See Derrida, *Margins*, p. 7.

28. See Derrida, *Margins*, p. 19.

29. Derrida, *Margins*, pp. 21–2.

30. See also G. Ward, *Barth, Derrida and the Language of Theology*, (Cambridge: Cambridge University Press, 1995, p. 226 n. 20, where he says that 'there is an important distinction between the openness of *différance* and the openness of negative theology'.

31. J. Derrida, 'How to avoid speaking: denials' in S. Budick and W. Iser (eds), *Languages of the Unsayable: The Play of Negativity in Literature and Literary Theory* (New York: Columbia University Press, 1989). p. 7.

32. Taylor, *Nots*, p. 3.

33. Derrida, 'How to avoid speaking', p. 44.

34. J. Derrida, *The Ear of the Other: Otobiography, Transference, Translation* (Lincoln and London: University of Nebraska Press, 1985), p. 140.

35. Ibid., pp. 141–42.

36. Derrida, *The Ear of the Other*, 'How to avoid speaking', p. 29.

37. *The Cloud of Unknowing*, The Prayer on the Prologue, EETS OS 218, p. 1.
'God, unto whom all hearts are open, unto whom all wills do speak, from whom no secret thing is hidden, I beseech thee so to cleanse the purpose of my heart with the unutterable gift of thy grace that I may perfectly love thee, and worthily praise thee.' (*The Cloud of Unknowing*, ed. Wolters, p. 50.)

38. Derrida, 'How to avoid speaking', p. 23.

39. J. Derrida, 'Foi et savoir' in J. Derrida and G. Vattimo (eds), *La religion* (Paris: Éditions du Seuil, 1996), p. 16.

40. '... *khôra* ne se présente jamais comme telle. Elle n'est ni l'Être, ni le Bien, ni Dieu, ni l'Homme, ni l'Histoire. Elle leur résistera toujours, elle aura toujours été /.../ le *lieu* même d'une résistance infinie, d'une résistance infiniment impassible: un tout autre sans visage' (ibid., p. 31).

41. Derrida, 'How to avoid speaking', p. 26.

42. Derrida, *The Ear of the Other*, p. 110.

43. Cf. Ward, *Barth, Derrida and the Language of Theology*, p. 256.

9

'Slanderous Tongues': Shakespearean Mimesis and Virtue Ethics in *Much Ado About Nothing*

David N. Beauregard

By virtue of the dexterity and intricacy of its wit, *Much Ado About Nothing* impresses us as a very complex play. Yet its plot and cast of characters are balanced in a remarkably clear and symmetrical design. The two plot lines involving the romantic lovers Hero and Claudio on the one hand, and the contentious Beatrice and Benedick on the other – together with the two brothers Don Pedro and Don John – provide the structural basis for the representation of certain images of virtue and vice. What I shall argue in this essay is that Shakespeare in *Much Ado* represents a cluster of Aristotelian-Thomistic virtues and vices having to do with 'verbal injustice'. Such a *mimesis* or representation has deep roots in Renaissance humanism with its emphasis on 'the centrality of the virtues' (Caspari 1968: 1–2; Skinner 1978, I: 213–43), an emphasis clearly apparent in Elizabethan poetics. Thus, in three of the foremost poets of the age, we find a poetics intimately linked with 'virtue ethics', the Aristotelian-Thomistic form of ethics that in the seventeenth century was reduced to an ethics of law and obligation (Pinckaers 1995: 216–79). In his *Apology for Poetry* Sir Philip Sidney formulates a poetic which 'figures forth' the virtues and vices (Smith 1964, I: 158–66). In his

'Letter to Ralegh' Edmund Spenser similarly shows a concern with 'expressing' the virtues in the main figures of his *Faerie Queene*. And in *Hamlet* (3.2.18–23) Shakespeare conceives of poetry as holding 'the mirror up to nature, to show virtue her own feature, scorn her own image'. In each case the objects of poetical *mimesis* or representation are the virtues and vices. The central importance in Renaissance literature of what is currently called 'virtue ethics' is thus clearly evident (Beauregard 1995).

Thanks to the pioneering work of Paul O. Kristeller and the extensive labours of Charles B. Schmitt, Charles Lohr and Jill Kraye, we now have a better sense of Renaissance moral philosophy in general, and of the Aristotelian tradition in particular. What is usually overlooked, however, is the theological tradition of Thomistic 'moral theology', a significant and extensive development of Aristotelian virtue ethics, which had a major influence on 'ethics'. It influenced Catholic and Protestant alike in the Renaissance, and in England it was used by figures such as William Perkins, Richard Hooker and the Caroline theologians. Let me hasten to add that we can find sources of characterization in Shakespeare other than virtue ethics or moral theology, e.g. typology – scriptural figures are used to shape character (Portia in *The Merchant of Venice* is called 'a second Daniel'; Iago in *Othello* has a certain resemblance to Satan; King Lear suffers like Job) – and allegory (Malvolio seems to embody 'bad will' as his name suggests, Caliban the deformity of original sin). But this latter method has been much abused in the quest for Christ figures in Shakespeare, and discretion must be used in its employment (Vickers 1993: 372–84). It would seem abundantly clear, however, that Shakespeare's representations have been affected by theology, whether in the form of moral theology, doctrine, or Scripture. In the main, Shakespeare holds the mirror up to nature, but what the mirror shows is significantly affected by 'saving grace' as we can sense from the notions of sin, grace, penitence and providence at work in the plays. Shakespeare's personal faith is, of course, another question altogether, but there is increasing evidence that he was a 'church papist' who kept a low profile (Beauregard 1997). Thus, his theology is not aggressively explicit: in *Much Ado* the 'holy friar' and the imposition of penance agreed to by Claudio (5.1.260) are

137

clearly Catholic elements, but Shakespeare shows great reserve and discretion by virtue of their not obtruding upon his main concern with representing the forms of slander.

In any event, the unity of Shakespeare's arrangement of plot and character in *Much Ado* has been defended in aesthetic terms as springing from the 'interplay of formality and naturalism' (Leggatt 1973: 152) and the interlocking of 'courtly love conventions and natural passion, affectation and spontaneity, romance and realism, or style and substance, saying and believing, simulation and dissimulation' (Nevo 1980: 162). From a different quarter more concerned with the meaning of the play, commentators have described various unifying themes, such as the difference between appearance and reality (Lewalski 1968), the action of misprision and misapprehension (Rossiter 1965: 54), the limits and methods of knowledge, rational love as a mean between idealization and contempt (Parker 1987: 67–80), and death and redemption. But these 'themes', which intellectualize if they do not quite allegorize the play, can be more profitably understood against the more fundamental, if somewhat more obvious, moral concerns of the play with 'slander' (Sexton 1975), or more precisely with false accusation and derisive mockery. Even if we concede the relevance of the aforementioned themes, it is difficult to overlook the heavy emphasis on the latter vices in the language and action of the play. The basic actions, after all, consist of the 'skirmish of wit' between Beatrice and Benedick and the false accusation brought against Hero, at first by Don John in private and then by Claudio in public. Significantly, the words 'accuse' and 'slander' are declaimed over ten times in the course of the fourth and fifth acts. Against the backdrop of hearsay, misprision and deception, the war of wit in the play, then, operates not as a mere competitive exercise or as an intellectual 'attempt to come to terms with the world' but as one form of verbal abuse taking place between lovers.

It is important, therefore, to consider what the Aristotelian-Thomistic tradition says about the vice of 'slander', a term that had a very complex designation in the sixteenth century. In the Latin–English dictionary *Biblioteca scholastica* (1589), for example, John Rider translates 'to Sclaunder or backbite' as 'Vitilitigo, obtrecto, obloquor, calumnior' and as 'Maledico, allatro, laedo, detraho, infector, sugillo, traduco'. All these

Latin shades of distinction are lost in the English word 'slander'.

Aristotle has very little to say about slander, except to allude to it as legally forbidden in the course of describing the virtue of *eutrapelia*, a kind of tactful wittiness in social intercourse whose extremes are buffoonery and boorishness (*Ethics* 4.8). St Thomas Aquinas, however, develops the matter with some complexity (see 2a2ae qq. 68; 72–6). Among the vices opposed to commutative justice, or justice between private individuals, he makes a basic distinction between injuries done by deed and by word. Injuries by deed occur in such actions as homicide and theft. Injuries by word take place either in a judicial or extra-judicial setting, and they cover, on the one hand, such injustices as unjust judgment on the part of a judge, false accusation on the part of a plaintiff, false witness, improper conduct of defence, and so on; or they cover, on the other hand, the sins of contumely, detraction, *susurratio*, derision and malediction, all forms of evil-speaking outside a courtroom setting. Since in an Elizabethan context the word 'slander' might be applied to false accusation as well as detraction and other of these sins, it is necessary to define each of them with some precision.

According to Aquinas, *accusation* must be first of all distinguished from *denunciation* in that the object of the former is the punishment of a crime while the object of the latter is the reform of a brother. In order to assure accuracy and certainty with respect to the facts for the benefit of the judge, an accusation should be put in writing, but a denunciation need not be put in writing since it suffices to make a denunciation to the Church, which then will proceed to the brother's correction. Obviously, in an accusation it is necessary for the accuser to be sure of the facts; otherwise we have calumny or false accusation, which may proceed from either rashness or simple error. If a false accusation occurs, then the balance of justice requires that the accuser himself should suffer a similar penalty.

But formal public accusation or denunciation is one thing, and private evil-speaking in an extra-judicial sense is another. This latter can assume a variety of forms. Defamation (*contumelia*) consists in the taking away of someone's honour by injurious words. It differs from detraction (*detractio* or *obtrectatio*) in being open and originating from anger.

Detraction, which is the injury of someone's reputation rather than their honour, proceeds secretly and originates from envy. While it is sometimes fitting to passively endure defamation, it is necessary to actively oppose detraction. As for Aristotle's virtue of *eutrapelia*, or wittiness, St Thomas allows it as a virtue provided the intention is not to dishonour or cause pain but rather to please and amuse (2a2ae q. 72.2).

Susurratio may be translated as either tale-bearing or whispering. Essentially it is the attempt to separate friends by speaking evil of one to the other. Thus it is similar to detraction but different in aim, intending not only to blacken another's name but to deprive him of a friend as well. Hence it is a more serious sin since it inflicts greater harm, a friend being a more precious good than any external possession.

Derision (*derisio*) is the ridicule or mockery of another's defect in an attempt to upset his conscience or to make him blush in confusion or shame, a minor form of dishonour differentiating derision from detraction. If it is about a serious matter or spoken in contempt, it is a serious sin. If about a minor defect or spoken in fun, it is less serious.

Finally, malediction (*maledictio*) is the actual ordering or commanding of an evil against another, so that one is not content with simply declaring an evil but causing it as well.

To sum up, then, 'slander' is a blanket term that can carry the general meaning of speaking evil of another, or it can carry several very specific meanings depending on the object and manner of the one who speaks evil of another. In Shakespeare's play, it seems to be both. The characters use the term in a blanket sense, but they themselves represent various specific forms of the vice. It is not surprising that the word 'slander' and its variants is used fifteen times throughout the play, and 'accuse' and its variants fourteen times (see Spevack 1973). Here we must add a word of caution: in representing the various species of 'slander' Shakespeare is not attempting to illustrate the forms of the vice point for point, but rather he is representing their general contours insofar as they can be fitted to the characters and the plot. The schematic analyses of moral theology are one thing, dramatic representations another.

One of the two main lines of 'slanderous' action occurs with the mutual 'skirmish of wit' that takes place between Beatrice and Benedick. Several scholars have aptly described the contrast between the Hero–Claudio and Beatrice–Benedick plots, delineating them in terms of various oppositions. Against the silence of Hero and the formalized and conventional romantic courtship of Claudio, Shakespeare counterposes the 'naturalistic' comic war of wit and derision between Beatrice and Benedick (Leggatt 1973: 182). The former plot is generally more serious and public, even solemn in its latter stages, the latter more light-hearted and private. The settings serve to reinforce this impression, and in fact serve also to focus attention on the nature of the representation. In the opening scene, Claudio and Benedick have just returned from 'these wars', and there is an immediate shift from the serious world of war and military deeds to the 'merry war' of words:

> You must not, sir, mistake my niece. There is a kind of merry war betwixt Signior Benedick and her. They never meet but there's a skirmish of wit between them.   (ll. 53–6)

We are brought thus into the proper environment for a study in the peacetime war of verbal contention and injury. As the action of the play unfolds, the basic Thomistic distinction between 'judicial' and 'extra-judicial' verbal injury finds expression in the contrast between ceremonial and more casual settings. The conventional courtship of Hero and Claudio takes place in large part in formal circumstances. It begins at a formal celebration or 'reveling', moves to a climax in the wedding scene in Church, and concludes in the tomb and restoration scenes. The 'extra-judicial' verbal contention between Beatrice and Benedick, by contrast, occurs in a courtly setting or in the orchard scenes, and it develops in a more intimate, relaxed and informal atmosphere.

What becomes rapidly prominent is the verbal 'skirmish of wit' between Beatrice and her lover, conducted as it is with continual jabs of verbal derision. At various times, Beatrice is called 'Lady Disdain' and 'my Lady Tongue'. She 'mocks all her wooers out of suit', and 'Disdain and scorn ride sparkling in her eyes' (1.1.105; 2.1.247, 311; 3.1.51). Her extraordinary wit provides full, indeed obvious, confirmation of these characterizations, its chief object being to shame and humiliate Benedick. From the very beginning, she merrily attacks his reputation as soldier:

> I pray you, how many hath he killed and eaten in these wars? But how many hath he killed? For indeed I promise to eat all of his killing. (1.1.37–9)

Her intention of course is hardly to destroy Benedick's reputation, but rather, in keeping with the Thomistic definition of derision, to embarrass him and bring him to confusion through merry raillery and banter. So Benedick is led to say of her effect on him:

> ... She speaks poniards and every word stabs... You shall find her the infernal Ate in good apparel. I would to God some scholar would conjure her, for certainly, while she is here, a man may live as quiet in hell as in a sanctuary; and people sin upon purpose, because they would go thither; so indeed all disquiet, horror, and perturbation follows her. (2.1.222–35)

And Don Pedro also remarks on the humiliation to which Benedick comes through Beatrice's sharp wit: 'You have put him down, lady; you have put him down' (2.1.253).

The final humorous paradox is that the mutual scorn that separates these two dissolves into love through the benevolent deception of Don Pedro in the orchard scenes. Again, the power of words is emphasized, as both Benedick and Beatrice in turn overhear their pride and scorn 'slandered' and their virtuous excellence praised. The motifs of detraction, slander, reputation and mockery run through both orchard scenes, so that with the parallel actions of 'overhearing' we have an ironic counter-demonstration of the power of praise and good report, as opposed to the various vices that go by the name of slander. Benedick himself, having overheard the 'false report' of Beatrice's love for him, registers the effect of good words spoken in secret:

> Happy are they that hear their detractions and can put them to mending. They say the lady is fair – 'tis a truth, I can bear them witness; and virtuous – 'tis so, I cannot reprove it; and wise, but for loving me – by my troth, it is no addition to her wit, nor no great argument of her folly, for I will be horribly in love with her. (2.3.210–15)

Still, both orchard scenes implicitly play on the essential elements of secrecy in detraction and the separation of friends in *susurratio* or tale-bearing. With a delightful irony, the secrecy is knowingly and laughingly feigned, and the tale-bearing is benevolently intended to unite rather than separate.

As critics have observed, the action involving Hero and Claudio stands in serious, almost solemn, counterpoint to the comic war of wit between Beatrice and Benedick. To begin with, there are clear similarities between the two plots. Both men have returned from the recent wars victorious and with honour. Both sets of lovers are brought together through the offices of Don Pedro, who is the architect of harmony following the pattern of Petruchio, Portia, and Prospero in other comedies. Both couples have an initial difficulty with love that is resolved through the 'practice' of the same guiding figure. Both are deceived. And of course both are finally united in marriage. But there are obvious differences as well in that Claudio and Hero have no initial aversion to love and marriage, pursue a more conventional line of courtship, and are brought to a state of separation and near tragedy by the evil and 'slanderous' machinations of Don John.

Thus, the two brothers, one benevolent and successful, the other malignant and ultimately defeated, serve in the play as the guiding forces working toward good and evil, exercising virtue and vice. Don John in particular stands out as a complex representation of 'slander', in his case *susurratio* or tale-bearing. As such he is the central generalized source of evil in the play (Leggatt 1973: 156). Both a defeated rebel and a bastard, he appears in a state of sadness and discontent. His motives are left somewhat unclear, but he seems especially envious of Claudio. To Borachio's revelation that Claudio intends to marry, he replies:

> Who? the most exquisite Claudio? ... That young upstart hath all the glory of my overthrow. If I can cross him any way, I bless myself every way. (1.3.43, 58–60)

The fact that he has 'stood out' in rebellion against his brother suggests a possible motive of anger and revenge, but it seems clear that the establishment of a coherent motive does not overly concern Shakespeare (Sexton 1975: 423–4; Anderson 1987: 83). In any case, the figure of Don John captures the essence of the various species of 'slander', that is, the verbal injury of another's honour. Whether he carries out his slander openly or secretly, out of envy or anger, may be open to interpretation, but in his basic mode of procedure most probably he is meant to represent the envious secrecy of tale-bearing. Thus, he pursues an intention of dividing two friends, in this case two lovers, the specific distinguishing mark of *susurratio*:

> Any bar, any cross, any impediment will be medicinable to me. I am sick in displeasure to him, and whatsoever comes athwart his affection ranges evenly with mine. How canst thou cross this marriage? (2.2.4–7)

And he tells Don Pedro and Claudio of Hero's supposed dishonour in private (3.2.72–97), again a mark of the tale-bearer. In this he provides a contrast with the open and merry derision practised by Beatrice and Benedick.

If Don John represents the essentials of the form of 'extra-judicial' slander called *susurratio*, Claudio represents the more formal and 'judicial' vices of unjust accusation and denunciation. What Don John begins in private, Claudio completes in public. And it is thus appropriate that he makes his false accusation during a formal and public ceremony, that is, in the course of his own wedding in church before a friar. While Shakespeare does not follow Aquinas to the letter in having Claudio deliver his false accusation in writing to a judge or in giving us a courtroom trial, an action rather inappropriate for a sin of fornication, he does portray Claudio as denouncing Hero to the Church in the person of the friar. He seems thus to conflate the technical sense of false accusation with denunciation, both of which Aquinas discusses in the same question (2a2ae q. 68). In any event, he creates a truly extraordinary scene which underlines the gravity of Claudio's charge and resonates with the shock of outrageous impropriety, violating both religious decorum and bridal feelings.

In consequence, several critics of the play have found Claudio a problem. He has been called a 'pitiful fellow', a 'hateful young cub', a 'miserable specimen', and the 'least amiable lover in Shakespeare', whose final reconciliation with Hero is something of an outrage (Humphreys 1981: 54). But what he clearly represents is all too apparent in the church scene, and that is false accusation springing from rashness and error. Thus the extreme language in his charge of infidelity against the innocent Hero, a charge delivered at a formal ceremony and discomforting to all his auditors, including the audience who know the falsity of his accusation:

144

Give not this rotten orange to your friend.
She's but the sign and semblance of her honor.
Behold how like a maid she blushes here!
...
You seem to me as Dian in her orb,
As chaste as is the bud ere it be blown;
But you are more intemperate in your blood
Than Venus, or those pamp'red animals
That rage in savage sensuality.   (4.1.30–2, 55–9)

St Thomas's observations on the matter are very much to the
point: he remarks that sometimes a man makes a false
accusation rashly in believing too easily what he hears or,
again, accuses someone on account of an error for which he is
not responsible (2a2ae q. 68.3.1). In either case, he is not guilty
of calumny. Claudio's case fits this description exactly in that
his accusation is mistakenly based on the slanderous deception
set up by Don John. It is pointless, then, to blame him, because
he is essentially an innocent dupe.

In any event, following this dramatic scene, the word
'slander' is used eight times and 'accusation' seven times in
relation to Claudio's action. Beatrice, for example, explodes in
malediction, ordering Benedick to 'kill Claudio' and wishing
herself a man so that she could revenge her friend:

Is he not approved in the height a villain, that hath slandered,
scorned, dishonoured my kinswoman? O, that I were a man!
What? bear her in hand until they come to take hands, and then
with public accusation, uncovered slander, unmitigated rancour
– O God, that I were a man! I would eat his heart in the
marketplace.   (4.1.297–302)

And Borachio confesses to Don Pedro that he and Don John, in
their intrigue and deception of Claudio, have been guilty of
slander and 'false accusation' (5.1.224, 230). The nature of
Claudio's action, therefore, seems more than sufficiently
established in the text.

Into the midst of this world of verbal injustice, the great
comic figure of Dogberry steps – or rather stumbles – as the
'angel of salvation', to use Leggatt's phrase (1973: 162),
bringing a resolution to the action. As constable and keeper
of the watch, he suggests once again the play's concern with
justice in Messina, and his malapropisms wittily underscore its

concentration on the abuse of language and report. He is of course the quintessence of judicial ineptitude, indeed a brilliant parody of justice in word, as he brings Conrade and Borachio before the Sexton for examination and accusation – just accusation in this instance by the watch that has overheard and uncovered the plot against Hero. Accordingly, these clowns make hilariously malappropriate and inaccurate charges against the accused – they first suspect treason; then they level confused charges of 'lechery' (i.e. treachery), 'perjury', and 'burglary'; next they deliver a volley of generalized denunciations – 'arrant knaves', 'aspicious persons', 'false knaves' and 'villains'; and finally they hit on the correct accusation (3.3.99, 154; 4.2.19, 20, 26, 38, 44–5). Thus Dogberry is instrumental in bringing about an ultimately just accusation while at the same time subjecting himself to derision:

> SEXTON: Master constable, you go not the way to examine. You must call forth the watch that are their accusers.
> DOGBERRY: Yea, marry, that's the eftest way. Let the watch come forth. Masters, I charge you in the Prince's name accuse these men.
> . . .
> CONRADE: Away! you are an ass, you are an ass.
> DOGBERRY: Dost thou not suspect my place? Dost thou not suspect my years? O that he were to write me down an ass! But, masters, remember that I am an ass. Though it be not written down, yet forget not that I am an ass.
>
> (4.2.31–4, 67–72)

In its structural function, the Dogberry episode, like that involving Don John, makes us aware beforehand of the injustice of the accusation against Hero. The innocence of Hero then becomes super-apparent, and the evil of Claudio's rash accusation that much more outrageous. And, as several scholars have observed, there is a certain providential resonance in the very ineptitude of Dogberry and the watch. The words of Borachio, in the course of his summary of Don John's plot as intending slander and false accusation, bring home the point: 'What your wisdoms could not discover, these shallow fools have brought to light' (5.1.221–2), an allusion to 1 Corinthians 1.18–19, 27: 'But God hath chosen the foolish things of the worlde to confounde the wise' (Lewalski 1968: 250–1; Kirsch 1981: 60–1; Anderson 1987: 90–2).

Much Ado essentially represents, then, the two-fold complex of vices having to do with judicial and extra-judicial verbal injuries – on the one hand with denunciation and false accusation, and on the other with slanderous tale-bearing, derision and malediction. Its two plots, in their basic thematic unity, turn on this distinction, and its dexterous wit and its various settings reinforce it. Indeed, with the final wonder of Hero's resurrection, we are made aware of the power of words, both to injure – even in a sense to 'kill', in that it is slander that has 'killed' Hero (e.g. 5.1.68, 88; 5.3.3) – and to restore, for it is with the restoration of Hero's good name that she finally comes back before us – 'She died, my lord, but whiles her slander lived' (5.4.66).

References

All quotations of Shakespeare's works are from *William Shakespeare: The Complete Works*, ed. Alfred Harbage (Baltimore: Penguin, 1969).

Anderson, L. (1987), *A Kind of Wild Justice: Revenge in Shakespeare's Comedies* (Newark: University of Delaware Press)

Aquinas, T. (1963–81), *Summa Theologiae*, ed. T. Gilby et al., 61 vols. (New York: McGraw). Latin text and English translation are on facing pages.

Aristotle. (1976), *The Ethics of Aristotle: The Nicomachean Ethics*, trans. J. A. K. Thomson, rev. H. Tredennick, intro. J. Barnes (New York: Penguin)

Beauregard, D. (1995), *Virtue's Own Feature: Shakespeare and the Virtue Ethics Tradition* (Newark: University of Delaware Press)

Beauregard, D. (1997), 'New light on Shakespeare's Catholicism: Prospero's epilogue in *The Tempest*', *Renascence* 49 (Spring), pp. 159–74

Caspari, F. (1968), *Humanism and the Social Order in Tudor England* (Chicago: University of Chicago Press)

Humphreys, A. R. (ed.) (1981), *Much Ado About Nothing* (London: Methuen)

Kirsch, A. (1981), *Shakespeare and the Experience of Love* (Cambridge: Cambridge University Press)

Kraye, J. (1988), 'Moral philosophy' in *The Cambridge History of Renaissance Philosophy* (Cambridge: Cambridge University Press)

Kristeller, P. O. (1990), 'The moral thought of Renaissance humanism' in *Renaissance Thought and the Arts*, expanded edn (Princeton: Princeton University Press)

Leggatt, A. (1973), *Shakespeare's Comedy of Love* (London: Methuen)

Lewalski, B. K. (1968), 'Love, appearance and reality: much ado about something' *Studies in English Literature* 8, pp. 235–51

Lohr, C. H. (1988), *Latin Aristotle Commentaries, vol. II: Renaissance Authors* (Florence: Olschki)

Nevo, R. (1980), *Comic Transformations in Shakespeare* (London: Methuen)

Parker, B. (1987), *A Precious Seeing: Love and Reason in Shakespeare's Plays* (New York: New York University Press)

Pinckaers, S., OP (1995), *The Sources of Christian Ethics*, trans. Sr. M. T. Noble, OP (Washington, D.C.: Catholic University of America Press)

Rider, J. (1612), *Riders Dictionarie*, 3rd edn (Oxford)

Rossiter, A. P. (1965), 'Much Ado About Nothing' in Kenneth Muir (ed.), *Shakespeare: The Comedies* (Englewood Cliffs, N.J.: Prentice-Hall)

Schmitt, C. B. (1983), *John Case and Aristotelianism in Renaissance England* (Montreal: McGill-Queen's University Press)

Schmitt, C. B. (1984), 'Aristotle's ethics in the sixteenth century: some preliminary considerations' in *The Aristotelian Tradition and Renaissance Universities* (Brookfield, Vt.: Gower)

Schmitt, C. B. (1988), *The Cambridge History of Renaissance Philosophy* (Cambridge: Cambridge University Press)

Sexton, J. (1975) 'The theme of slander in *Much Ado about Nothing*', *Philological Quarterly* 54 pp. 419–33, reprinted in *The Slandered Woman in Shakespeare* (Victoria, B.C.: University of Victoria Press, 1978)

Skinner, Q. (1978), *The Foundations of Modern Political Thought*, 2 vols (Cambridge: Cambridge University Press)

Smith, G. G. (ed.) (1964), *Elizabethan Critical Essays*, 2 vols (Oxford: Oxford University Press)

Spevack, M. (1973), *The Harvard Concordance to Shakespeare* (Cambridge, Mass.: Harvard University Press)

Vickers, B. (1993), *Appropriating Shakespeare: Contemporary Critical Quarrels* (New Haven: Yale University Press)

10

John Donne and the Theology of Incarnation[1]

J. Mark Halstead

Donne's Religious Verse

How are we to read Donne's religious verse? One way of answering this question is to see how far it fits into the main traditions of religious poetry (and religious writing generally) that are found in the seventeenth century. These traditions fall into five main categories:

1 poetry which is concerned with the adoration and praise of God (e.g. Herbert's 'Praise' and 'Antiphon');
2 poetry whose subject is either the doctrines of religion, or religious or sectarian debate (e.g. Milton's 'Paradise Lost');
3 poetry whose subject is the personal spiritual experience of the individual believer, which may extend from an overwhelming sense of unworthiness at one extreme, through repentance and continuing spiritual conflicts, to the serenity of worship and prayerful devotion at the other (e.g. Herbert's 'Love III' and Marvell's 'The Coronet');
4 mystical poetry (e.g. Crashaw's 'A Hymn to the Name and Honor of the Admirable Sainte Teresa' and Traherne's 'Wonder' and 'The Anticipation');
5 poetry which is designed to strengthen the reader's faith (e.g. Vaughan's 'Peace' and Herbert's 'Vertue' – and Bunyan's prose work The Pilgrim's Progress).

At first glance, Donne's religious poetry does not fall neatly into any of these categories, and this has led some critics to be rather disappointed with it (cf. Gardner 1952: xvii), comparing it unfavourably to Herbert's devotional poetry, and has led others to dismiss it as 'feigned devotion' (Oliver 1997). In this chapter I shall propose an alternative approach to the poems which draws on insights taken from theology and particularly the theology of incarnation. Before attempting this, however, I intend to look a bit more closely at Donne's religious poems in the light of each of the above categories.

First, there is some evidence that Donne *is* interested in reflecting on the nature of God, and not only on the power of God which Carey dwells on with such relish (1981: 122–3). In 'Upon the Translation of the Psalmes by Sir Philip Sydney', for example, he suggests that it is perhaps too daring a task to seek for new ways of describing God and that any attempt to do so would be like squaring a circle (the emblem of perfection and eternity), or reducing the infinite to the finite (cf. Wilcox 1994). We can also find the same image in 'Devotions upon Emergent Occasions: Prayer': 'O Eternal, and most gracious God, who, considered in thy selfe, art a Circle, first and last, and altogether' (Simpson 1967a: 93). However, it does seem that Donne is much less concerned in his religious poetry with the praise and adoration of God than are Herbert, Crashaw or Vaughan, and much more concerned with what God will or will not do for him. There is little direct worship, but a repeated tendency for him to tell God what to do ('Impute me righteous ...'; 'Batter my heart ...'; 'Take me to you, imprison me ...'). He is interested in God because God in turn has an interest in him ('Thou hast made me, and shall thy work decay?'). Yet just as there is often a pronounced absence of the 'other' in the love poems (Herz 1994: 139), so in the religious poems there is generally not much sense of the 'divine other', as Oliver points out (1997: 9). God's voice is never heard (as it so often is in Herbert: see, for example, 'Dialogue', 'Redemption', 'Love III', 'The Collar' and above all 'The Sacrifice'). Donne often appears to focus on himself[2] so strongly that he treats God with arrogance. In the last three lines of 'Holy Sonnet II' he seems to be warning God that there are limits to his patience:

Oh I shall soon despaire, when I doe see
That thou lov'st mankind well, yet wilt'not chuse me.
And Satan hates mee, yet is loth to lose mee.

The poet's relationship with Christ may be an intimate one, as is shown in the sexual imagery of 'Holy Sonnet XVIII', but even here he is most concerned with what Christ can do for him ('Show me, deare Christ ...'; 'Betray, kind husband ...').

Second, to a certain extent, Donne does seem to be concerned with Christian doctrine and with religious and sectarian debate in his religious poetry. For example, in 'Satire III' and 'Holy Sonnet XVIII' he asks which is the true Church; he explores a variety of views on election and predestination in the holy sonnets; and in numerous poems he shows a continuing fascination with the nature of angels. But these issues do not generally manifest themselves in a sustained argument or discussion about doctrinal disagreements, and the pace is much less intense than one might expect. Often Donne prefers to abstain from doctrinal controversy altogether, and in his sermons usually tells his congregation not 'to enquire too curiously into such matters' (Gardner 1952: xliii). In fact in both poetry and sermons he often tries to bring together differing religious views; in the true spirit of Anglicanism, 'The Litanie' attempts a synthesis of Catholicism and Calvinism, and in a sermon preached in 1630 he calls himself both a Papist and a Puritan in his attempt to stress the point that the worship of God transcends religious difference (Simpson 1967a: 364). Oliver (1997: 243) comments on Donne's habit of 'simultaneously entertaining a multiplicity of viewpoints' in his sermons – a habit which is by no means limited to his religious views. Some have seen this as inconsistency or indecisiveness in his religious ideas, others as even-handedness (*ibid.*: 92).

Third, Donne's poetry is not spiritual in the normal seventeenth-century sense of devotion, worship or meditation on the vicissitudes of personal faith (Martz 1954 and 1970). It is true that there is an implicit sense of his personal unworthiness in his poems, but even here his main interest seems to be his own emotions, whether of guilt, fear, insecurity, grief, arrogance, rebellion, remorse, inconstancy, doubt or despair. His poetry is more self-absorbed than most other religious verse, more marked out by theatricality and self-dramatization.

151

He seems to concentrate much more on his own feelings than on his experience of worship or his relationship with God. Gardner describes him as 'not remarkable for any spiritual gifts and graces', and as 'by nature arrogant, egotistical, irreverent', with a mind that is 'naturally sceptical and curious, holding little sacred' (1952: xvii).

Fourth, Donne's religious poetry lacks many of the features most commonly associated with mystical poetry. There is no compelling sense of the loss of self, of the presence of the divine, of union with the transcendent or of the exultation which this sense of union brings. In fact, there is more mysticism in the love poetry than in the religious poetry (for example, in the ecstatic out-of-body experience described in 'The Exstasie'), and I shall argue later that the sexuality of the love poetry is often, as in Islamic mystical verse, a tangible, physical representation of spiritual truth. But what prevents Donne's religious poetry from being interpreted as traditional Christian mystical verse is the absence of the divine 'other' which has already been noted, the dominance of intellectual speculation in his poetry, the absence of a suffused joy and spiritual certainty, and above all the consuming fascination with, and projection of, self in his verse.

Fifth, in contrast to Herbert's poetry, there appears to be no intention of setting an example to believers of true faith and devotion. Indeed, in his self-absorption, his arrogance, his wit and his shocking imagery he seems to be consciously avoiding setting an example of holiness to others. Donne's most widely admired poem of devotion is 'A Hymn to God the Father', but even this continues the tendency already mentioned of telling God what to do ('Sweare by thy selfe'). But for the sheer capacity to shock, there is little to surpass the Holy Sonnets. The reference to 'profane mistresses' in the context of religion in 'Holy Sonnet XIII' is shocking enough, but the desire to shock the reader seems to take complete control in Holy Sonnets XIV and XVIII. As Carey says, 'we cringe from the blasphemy' (1981: 47).

We are bound to conclude that none of these five traditions of religious poetry provides an adequate characterization of Donne's own verse. His primary interests seem to lie elsewhere. His poetry is at the same time too intellectual and too self-absorbed, too witty and full of emotion, and too arrogant, even though generally orthodox in its religious content, to be categorized in any of these ways. If these five approaches to religious poetry are the only ones possible, then perhaps Gardner and Oliver are correct in their judgement. They may at least be closer to the truth than those less discriminating critics who have seen in Donne's religious poetry a fine example of meditative and devotional verse. However, I want to suggest an alternative approach which seeks to reconcile some of the difficulties and apparent contradictions in Donne's religious poetry. The starting point for this approach is Christian theology, and the next section will therefore be concerned with a brief explanation of what theology is and how a theological perspective helps to draw together the disparate elements in Donne's poetry. Thereafter the focus narrows to one particular branch of theology – the theology of the incarnation – and argues that this is the theology which sheds most light on Donne's concerns in his religious writing and in his poetry generally because it is in many ways closest to his own thinking. The remaining sections offer a more detailed examination of the spiritual and the physical and the soul and body in Donne's poetry in the light of the illuminations offered by the theology of incarnation.

The Nature of Theology

Hull (1984) offers us a number of helpful starting points in thinking about the nature of theology. First, he points out that the subject matter of theology is

> the contents of the religious consciousness, that is, the characteristics of the self-awareness in so far as these are knowingly influenced or formed by participation within a religious tradition. (p. 252)

Thus the subject matter of theology is not the New Testament, but the Christian experience of understanding and interpreting the New Testament; it is not the critical study of the Bible but the way in which the Bible impinges on the religious consciousness; it is not God, but the religious apprehension of God. Theology thus differs from both philosophy and religious studies. It deals with the revelation of God, Hull suggests, 'in so far as that revelation is subjectively ... realized within consciousness'. And the task of theology is 'to articulate, to clarify and to conceptualize that consciousness' (p. 253).

Second, though theology has a distinctive subject matter, Hull claims, its manner of discourse is shared with other disciplines. Theology is 'a form of thinking' (p. 251) characterized by rational judgement, a critical spirit, openness, coherent and systematic thought. This characteristic distinguishes theology from the practice of religion; the believer who engages in the practice of prayful intercession is doing something quite different from the theologian who critically examines the concept of intercession as an aspect of religious consciousness. Theology is the 'critical, systematic conceptualization of the religious consciousness' (p. 253).

Third, Hull distinguishes between *studying* theology and *doing* theology – in other words, between the more objective approach to theology which goes on in schools and universities and the more personally significant activity of systematically investigating one's own religious consciousness. Unlike studying theology, doing theology is an existential activity which 'demands commitment' (p. 254) because it emanates from the participant's own religious consciousness and self-awareness.

Already we can see how this resonates with some of the key characteristics of Donne's religious poetry. First, as we have already seen, his poetry is not concerned with religious teaching as objective truth but with the way it is subjectively realized within his own consciousness and the way it affects his own self-awareness. Second, his poetry is marked out by rational argument, a critical spirit, systematic thought. Third, the exploration of his own consciousness is a personally significant activity for him which involves both his cognitions and his emotions, and the function of the activity is to integrate the various elements of his consciousness into a unified whole.

Let us be more specific. There are a number of key concepts in Christian theology, and in contemporary terminology each of them may potentially generate its own 'theology'. Thus following Karl Barth (1962) we hear a lot these days of 'trinitarian theology', suggesting that relationships are part of the inner structure of God's own being and that this sheds new light on the Christian understanding of relationships. Though it may be true that Donne has a variety of theological interests, I shall argue that it is incarnation theology which resonates most closely with Donne's thinking and which provides most insight into his religious poetry, and I shall therefore focus exclusively on this aspect of theology for the remainder of this chapter.

Incarnation Theology and Donne's Poetry

So what is incarnation theology? It can usefully be analysed on two planes. Wiles (1977: 1) distinguishes between a narrower and a broader sense of incarnation, whereas Brunner (1952: 322) distinguishes a downward or deductive approach to incarnation from an upwards or inductive approach. In the narrower sense, incarnation refers to the belief that the second person of the Godhead became flesh in the person of Jesus of Nazareth; as Donne himself succinctly puts it in one of his sermons, 'He that was God the Lord became Christ, a man' (Simpson 1967a: 204). On this view, the incarnation refers to a specific historical event, namely, the birth and life of Jesus. In the broader sense, what is important about the incarnation from a theological point of view is not whether this event actually happened in the course of human history (cf. Hick 1977) but what this event symbolizes: that what we understand of God comes 'through the physical world rather than by escape from it' (Wiles 1977: 1), or, more generally still, that the incarnation unites the human and the divine, the physical world and the spiritual world, and thus promotes what Wiles calls the 'anti-dualist emphasis in Christianity' (*ibid.*: 7). In the New Testament the human body is described as the temple of the Holy Spirit (1 Corinthians 6:19), an idea which Donne expands on in one of his sermons when he compares the Holy Spirit to a high priest who 'inhabits and consecrates' the body (Simpson 1967a: 256). In another New Testament image the Church is described as the 'body of Christ' (Ephesians 5:29–30), thus representing a further extension of the incarnation principle of the fusion of the human and the divine (Macquarrie 1966: 348–9; Osmond 1990: 154–7).

Ultimately, incarnation theology maintains that God is present in the neighbour, so that Jesus, speaking of charitable acts said, 'inasmuch as ye have done it unto one of the least of these my brethren ye have done it unto me' (Matthew 25:40). Such a theology has a potentially profound influence on human behaviour. It is clear that Christianity without belief in the incarnation in the narrow sense would still be an incarnational faith in the broader sense, and this is precisely the position adopted by the contributors to *The Myth of God Incarnate* (Hick 1977). In the seventeenth century, however, the doctrine of the incarnation in the narrow sense and the symbolic value of the broader understanding of the incarnation are inter-dependent and mutually supportive, though, as I shall argue shortly, Donne's interest in the incarnation is very much at the symbolic end of the spectrum, and he stresses the importance of the physical as a visible manifestation of the spiritual.

The second plane is the distinction between a downward or deductive approach to incarnation and an upward or inductive approach. The former approach celebrates God's initiative in the incarnation (Barth 1936: 177), emphasizing his desire to share our grief and suffering, to become involved in the reality of human existence, to reveal his nature to humankind by becoming human himself. The inductive approach, on the other hand, suggests that incarnational theology leads our under-standing upwards from the familiar, the human, to the divine, so that understanding and loving God (whom we cannot see) must begin by understanding and loving our fellow human beings (whom we can see, and who show in tangible form something of God's nature). Thus the spiritual world is approached through the physical, since the physical world is a more accessible mirror which reflects and symbolizes spiritual reality. This approach is captured precisely in Raphael's words to Adam and Eve in Book V of Milton's *Paradise Lost*:

> ... And what surmounts the reach
> Of human sense, I shall delineate so,
> By lik'ning spiritual to corporeal forms,
> As may express them best; though what if Earth
> Be but the shadow of Heaven ...?   (ll. 571–5)

It is this latter, inductive approach which is most in line with Donne's religious poetry. This movement from the human to the divine, or from the physical to the spiritual, is precisely the idea at the heart of Holy Sonnet XVII, in which the poet shows how his love for his wife Ann led him to seek God, and how God's love has filled the vacuum left by her death:

> Since she whom I lov'd hath payd her last debt
> To Nature, and to hers, and my good is dead

And her Soule early into heaven ravished
Wholly in heavenly things my mind is sett.
Here th' admyring her my mind did whett
To seeke thee God; so streames do shew their head;
But though I have found thee, and thou my thirst hast fed,
A holy thirsty dropsy melts me yett.
But why should I begg more Love, when as thou
Dost wooe my soule, for hers offring all thine:
And dost not only fear least I allow
My love to Saints and Angels things divine
But in thy tender jealosy dost doubt
Least the Worlde, Fleshe, yea Devill putt thee out.

The first four lines are much more than the conventional
platitude that after the death of a beloved spouse one turns to
heaven for comfort. 'Ravished' is a term used much more
frequently for the carrying away of bodies than of souls, and
conveys the poet's unwillingness to see his wife wrested from him
and the physical wrench he feels at her loss. Yet since the early
arrival of her soul in heaven ('early' conveys not only the sense
of a premature death but also the sense that as one of the elect
she received her heavenly reward without delay), his mind is
now fixed 'wholly in heavenly things'. It is as if his mind has
followed her from earth (where all the 'good' he can gain from
her is over) to heaven; she is perhaps the first of the 'heavenly
things' on which his mind is set, though by leading his thoughts
to heaven she helps him to think of other heavenly things as
well, indeed, to seek God himself. It is his admiration for his
wife while she was on earth which now stimulates his desire to
seek God; the earthly love he had for his wife leads him to the
divine love. The image in line six of streams being traceable
back to their source suggests two things: first, since the stream
is essentially the same as its source, the physical love he
experienced with his wife is a direct parallel with the divine
love which now feeds his thirst; and second, it is his admiration
for his wife which leads him to seek God as the most
appropriate object of his ultimate admiration.

While he highly values the experience of God's love, there is
a sense at first that this love leaves his physical appetite
unsatisfied (the 'dropsy' of line eight). But this is only a
momentary glance back at the physical world that has been left
behind, not a fatal attraction like Lot's wife's. For he quickly

realizes that God's love is all he needs, and that when God offers all his own love (which lasts for eternity) in exchange for the love of the poet's wife (which has been brought to a premature end), the poet has indeed got a good bargain.[3] Grenander (1975) fancifully suggests that 'God woos the speaker's soul in order to unite it with the woman's, even to the extent of offering all his own soul in exchange', but this is not only doctrinally dubious but also internally inconsistent with the rest of the poem. The movement of the poem's argument is clearly from earthly love to heavenly love: earthly love is good in itself, though it comes to an end, but it points symbolically to the eternal love of God. The last four lines describe God's love in a clever combination of the Old Testament picture of a jealous God and the New Testament picture of a God of love and self-sacrifice: the image is of a tenderly jealous lover willing to give everything for the one he loves but worried that in the end he may lose out to a rival. In a sermon preached the same year that this poem was written (1617), Donne provides a very similar picture of God as lover: 'Dost thou not feele that He seeks thee now, offering His love and desiring thine?' (Simpson 1967a: 180).

The Spiritual and the Physical

The central theme of incarnation theology, namely, the impossibility of approaching and understanding the spiritual world except through the physical, is a recurrent idea in the poetry of Donne. It is seen, for example, in the first verse of 'Aire and Angels':

> Twice or thrice had I loved thee,
> Before I knew thy face or name;
> So in a voice, so in a shapelesse flame
> Angells affect us oft, and worship'd bee;
>   Still when, to where thou wert, I came
> Some lovely glorious nothing I did see.
>   But since my soule, whose child love is,
> Takes limmes of flesh, and else could nothing doe,
>   More subtile then the parent is,
> Love must not be, but take a body too,
>   And therefore what thou wert, and who,
>   I bid Love aske, and now

That it assume thy body, I allow,
And fixe it selfe in thy lip, eye, and brow.

The first experience of love described in this poem is immaterial, spiritual. The narrator feels he has already loved his mistress before he has even seen her or knows her name (just as angels can be sensed and worshipped when still invisible), and even when he comes into her presence, the first impression he gets is of a delightful spiritual (loss of?) consciousness. 'Nothing' implies the absence of anything physical or tangible, but also implies zero, naught, the circle, the symbol of eternity; it may thus perhaps allude to the Platonic eternal world of true realities, of which the familiar everyday world is an imperfect reflection. However, just as the soul of a human being is incomplete without a body and must therefore 'take limmes of flesh', so love (which is the 'child' of the soul) cannot be more spiritual ('subtile') than its parent, but must itself become incarnate. His love therefore comes to focus on her body and its various physical charms. Like angels, women have to 'put on' corporeality in their relations with men. Clearly, important theological ideas are lurking beneath the surface of this love poem. God's love, like human love, needs to 'take a body too' if it is to be understood and appreciated; because of the way that humans themselves are made (as a combination of body and soul), love, whether human or divine, is incomplete if it is purely spiritual. The Word must become flesh, and dwell among us.

Thus for Donne the physical world is more than a symbol of the spiritual world, and sexual relationships are more than symbols of spiritual relationships: incarnation – the embodied world – is the *only way* in which the spiritual dimension to life can be understood. We can detect two major influences at work on Donne's thinking here. The first is biblical language itself: the language and imagery of sexual love are accepted ways in the Bible of talking about divine love. As Donne himself points out in one of his sermons delivered in 1619, Christ's 'greatest work, when he was come, which was his union and marriage with the Church, and with our souls, he hath also delivered in a piece of a curious frame, Solomon's Song of Songs' (Simpson 1967a: 183). But this is not only a biblical tradition. In linking sexual and divine love, Donne comes close to that form of

J. Mark Halstead

Islamic mysticism in which the soul's longing for union with its Maker is invariably described in terms of physical human love. The seventeenth-century English poet who reflects this most closely is Crashaw (cf. his 'Hymn to Saint Teresa'), and he may have been influenced by Islamic mysticism via Italy; but Donne himself was not without knowledge of Islamic teaching, as 'Elegy XIX' makes clear.

The second influence is one which has already been touched on – Platonic ideas, especially the contrast between the unseen world of true realities and the familiar world of everyday things. This is a significant influence on several metaphysical poets: Vaughan's 'The World (1)' contrasts the great ring of eternity with the temporal world, and Marvell's 'A Dialogue between the Soul and Body' contrasts the soul which longs to return to the spiritual reality of heaven with the body which is tied to this world. In 'Elegy XIX' Donne wittily compares the 'full nakedness' of his mistress once she has stripped off her last remaining garment to a soul free at last from the encumbrance of the body. Elsewhere, however, Donne is more concerned to explore the growth from the physical love of an individual to the Platonic idea of the abstract, spiritual union of souls. Sometimes he describes platonic love as a miraculous achievement ('The Relic'), at other times he is cynical about it ('Love's Alchemy'). In 'A Valediction: Forbidding Mourning' he strikes more of a balance: on the one hand, his love is more refined than that of 'dull sublunary lovers' love (whose soul is sense)', but on the other, he is not totally oblivious to the charms of 'eyes, lips and hands'. Spiritual love is a mystery and can only be explained (perhaps even experienced) through physical images and symbols, but nonetheless this kind of love is real and eternal, and elixir-like it transforms the commonplace into the divine (cf. Osmond 1990: ch. 6).

The emphasis in incarnation theology on understanding spiritual truths through the mediation of the physical is made explicit in verse four of 'A Valediction: of the booke':

> For, though minde be the heaven, where love doth sit,
> Beauty a convenient type may be to figure it.

This does not mean that *all* of Donne's sexual poetry has spiritual undertones (as is often argued about the erotic poetry of the Islamic mystics; cf. Gibb n.d.: 8–11); it is hard to find such undertones in 'Loves Usury', for example. It simply means that we need to be alert to both dimensions when reading either the love poetry or the religious poetry. At the very least, we can be certain that spirituality is not incompatible with the vigorous sexual awareness that is found in much of Donne's love poetry. The love poetry has many parallels with the religious poetry in imagery, style and theme, as Carey points out (1981: 11–12) and indeed the one helps us to understand the other. Love is described in religious language, whether for comic or serious effect; in 'Elegy III', for example, he puns on the phrase 'fall back' (he calls it 'apostacy', but obviously intends the same meaning as Juliet's nurse when she uses the same phrase), and in 'Elegy VIII' he compares his own tender love-making to the 'devoutly nice' manner of 'priests in handling reverent sacrifice' (cf. Davies 1994: 38–9). Similarly, religious experiences are described in terms of sexuality, most famously in 'Holy Sonnet XIV' where he asks God to ravish him and in 'Holy Sonnet XVIII' where he suggests that Christ's spouse (the Church) is most pleasing to her husband 'when she is embraced and open to most men'. He does not hold back from using his own physical love affairs when developing a religious argument, as in 'Holy Sonnet XIII' (it seems that it was only towards the end of his life that he became an advocate of chastity: cf. Carey 1981: 11). Perhaps the most extreme example of incarnational imagery comes in 'The Relic'; just as Jesus reveals God in human form, so the poet and his mistress become tangible representations of Mary Magdalene and ... Jesus himself (though for once we see the poet shying away from this near-blasphemous idea and hiding behind the euphemism 'a something else thereby'). But this is of course precisely what a holy relic is, a tangible representation of saintliness and spirituality.

To understand this more fully, we need to explore Donne's understanding of the relationship between soul and body.

Soul and Body

Donne's fascination with both body and soul and their interrelationship, which has been noted by many critics in the last half century, lies at the heart of incarnation theology. In a sermon in 1629, Donne claims that 'the soule of man is part of the Essence of God' (Simpson 1967a: 352). In another sermon, preached at the funeral of Sir William Cokayne Knight in 1626, Donne points out that

> God made the first Marriage, and man made the first Divorce; God married the Body and Soule in the Creation, and man divorced the Body and Soule by death through sinne. (Simpson 1967b: 219)

It is in this fusion of body and soul more than anywhere else that we see the union of the physical and the spiritual, of the human and the divine. As we shall see, Donne inclines less to Plato (who sees the soul as separate and distinct from, and often in conflict with, the inferior body), and more to Aristotle (who argues that it is only their fusion and equal involvement in life that constitutes the essence of human nature). For Donne, as for Aristotle, the soul only becomes meaningful when incorporated into and expressed through the body (cf. Osmond 1990: chs 1 and 2).

By selective quotation particularly from the sermons, Carey (1981: ch. 5) paints a lurid and rather one-sided picture of Donne's view of the body: it is 'wet mud', 'dust held together by plaisters'; 'there is not so noysome, so putrid a thing in nature'; women's bodies exude sweat either in fear ('bathed in a cold quicksilver sweat' – 'The Apparition') or in lust (the woman's brow in Elegy VIII is covered with 'ranke sweaty froth … like spermatique issue of ripe menstruous boils'). But this is only part of the story as far as Donne's thoughts on the body are concerned. In a sermon preached in 1625, Donne argues that although 'God is a Spirit' and the human 'soul is a spirit', this does not mean that the life of the body is unimportant in God's eyes. On the contrary, the body is dignified by the whole Trinity:

> The Father was pleased to breathe into this body, at first, in the Creation; the Son was pleased to assume this body himself, after, in the Redemption; the Holy Ghost is pleased to consecrate this body, and make it his Temple, by his sanctification. (Simpson 1967a: 255)

In the Eleventh Paradox, Donne argues wrily but not unseriously that the

> soule it seemes is enabled by our body, not this by it. My body licenseth my soule to see the Worlds beauties through mine

eyes; to heare pleasant things through mine eares; and affords it
apt Organs for the conveiance of all perceivable delight.
(*ibid.*: 17)

This emphasis on the importance of the body is a recurrent
theme in both poetry and sermons. Though Donne never
doubts the doctrine of the immortality of the soul (Simpson
1967a: 326), he seems to devote much more attention to the
resurrection of the body (see Carey 1981: 219–26). At one stage
he seems to have held the heretical view that both soul and
body die at the same time ('Holy Sonnet V', line 4) and will be
raised together at the last day ('Holy Sonnet VII', lines 3–4).[4]
Later, however, he accepted the orthodox belief that at death
the souls of the faithful went straight to heaven, to be reunited
with the glorified body at the day of resurrection (Gardner
1952: Appendix A). In a sermon in 1620 on the text 'Yet in my
flesh shall I see God', Donne says that when the soul and body
are reunited, the soul will no longer call the body 'her prison,
nor her tempter, but her friend, her companion, her wife'
(Simpson 1967a: 203). It is interesting that Donne seems to
equate himself with the body rather than with the soul both in
this sermon and in 'Holy Sonnet VI', where he writes:

And gluttonous death will instantly unjoynt
My body and soule, and I shall sleepe a space,
But my' ever-waking part shall see that face,
Whose feare already shakes my every joint.

The 'ever-waking part' is of course the soul, but this means that
the 'I' who sleeps for a while is the body. It is clear, especially
since this is a revised draft and the earlier version is still extant,
that this is a conscious and deliberate statement of the poet's
own inclination towards the physical.

'A Valediction: forbidding mourning' compares the parting
of two lovers to the parting of a virtuous man's soul from his
body, and the whole point of the poem is to emphasize that
they will be reunited again. The reunion of the lovers in turn
becomes an implicit symbol of the eventual reunion of the body
and soul at the day of resurrection. Just as the souls of the two
lovers are one, so the body and soul together make up one
human being – not only in this world, but in the world to come.
Once again the experience of sexual love in this life points to and
symbolizes the experience of spiritual union in eternity. At the

most basic level, orgasm (the *petit mort* which is the source of so
many sexual puns in Donne and elsewhere in the seventeenth
century) represents death, and the re-arousal of the male organ
represents resurrection. 'The Extasie', on the other hand, seems
to be about the souls of the two lovers having an ecstatic
spiritual experience (going to heaven after death?) before being
reunited with their bodies again (on the day of resurrection?). In
fact, the last seven verses are perhaps Donne's most sustained
defence in his poetry of the importance of the body:

> But O alas, so long, so farre
>> Our bodies why do wee forbeare?
> They are ours, though they are not wee, Wee are
>> The intelligences, they the spheare.
>
> We owe them thankes, because they thus,
>> Did us, to us, at first convay,
> Yeelded their forces, sense, to us
>> Nor are drosse to us, but allay.
>
> On man heaven's influence workes not so,
>> But that it first imprints the ayre,
> So soule into the soule may flow,
>> Though it to body first repaire.
>
> As our blood labours to beget
>> Spirits, as like soules as it can,
> Because such fingers need to knit
>> That subtile knot, which makes us man:
>
> So must pure lovers soules descend
>> T'affections, and to faculties,
> Which sense may reach and apprehend,
>> Else a great Prince in prison lies.
>
> To our bodies turne wee then, that so
>> Weake men on love reveal'd may looke;
> Loves mysteries in soules doe grow,
>> But yet the body is his booke.
>
> And if some lover, such as wee,
>> Have heard this dialogue of one,
> Let him still marke us, he shall see
>> Small change, when we're to bodies gone.

If this is poetry of seduction, as Legouis (1928: 68–9) and
Kermode (1957: 12) suggest, it is seduction of an unusually

spiritual kind: the impulse to sexual union is not driven by lust, but simply by the impossibility of finding any other way of expressing their spiritual love. Without the body, the soul, like 'a great Prince in prison', is impotent, incapable of achieving fulfilment. As one would expect in a divine design, the combination of body and soul is a well-balanced one: the souls of lovers 'descend' to the body because they need its emotions ('affections') and physical functions ('faculties'), but the purpose of sexual activity is to create something spiritual ('our blood labours to beget spirits'). Just as God is revealed in the person of Jesus, and just as the truth of the resurrection was brought home to doubting Thomas when he was able to touch the wounded hands and side of the risen Lord, so those whose faith in love is uncertain need the body to convince them of its truth. 'But yet the body is his book' recalls the description of women in 'Elegy XIX' as 'mystick books', but what the line is saying is that the body is the book through which the spiritual mysteries of love are revealed. We can only understand love through the body, and ultimately there is little difference ('small change') between physical and spiritual love (cf. Osmond 1990: 116). This is precisely the message of incarnation theology.

Conclusion

In this chapter I have argued two things: more generally, the importance of the insights which a theological approach to literature may bring, and more specifically, the claims that the theology of incarnation is a major strand in Donne's religious writing (which is in fact the *whole* of his writing) and that it helps us to make sense of the disparate elements which other critics have found puzzling or unsatisfactory.

Throughout the chapter I have argued that in Donne's poetry the physical dimension points to and symbolizes the more important spiritual dimension of life, that it is in the body and through the body that the divine is revealed to us. I have argued further that though Donne presents a fairly conventional view of the soul in 'The First Anniversary' and 'The Second Anniversary' as a separate entity imprisoned in the flesh until its release at death, he goes beyond this in many of his other writings and sees soul and body as interdependent and mutually supportive. In a sense, Donne has already undermined the dualist philosophy of human nature which Descartes was to articulate most influentially a few years after the poet's death.

One final example will serve to summarize the various ways in which incarnation theology helps us to understand Donne's thinking. Tears are a significant minor theme in the poetry of Donne as in that of most other Metaphysical poets, and the approach Donne adopts to this theme illustrates the three main techniques he uses for describing the spiritual through the physical:

1 Sexuality becomes an image of the spiritual life. In the case of tears, Donne retains the conventional Petrarchan imagery of the lover's tears (for example, in 'Twicknam Garden' and 'Lovers Infinitenesse') and combines it with, or uses it to illustrate, the Christian idea of tears of repentance (as in 'Holy Sonnet IX'): one wins the mistress's love, the other God's.

2 We can only understand the soul through the body. The physical action of shedding tears provides a window to the soul, a tangible, physical way of coming to understand abstract spiritual emotions such as fear, repentance or 'holy discontent' ('Holy Sonnet III').

3 The human life of Jesus helps us to understand what God himself is like. In his important sermon on the shortest verse in the Bible (John 11:35), Donne explores the nature of Jesus's tears (Simpson 1967b: 157–77). They show his humanity, certainly, but also show something of the nature of God, who is able to understand and share our grief and suffering (cf. Young 1977: 36–7).

In each of these instances, the movement is inductive, from the physical to the spiritual: our understanding of the human and the familiar helps us to understand the spiritual and the divine. The physical world is a mirror which reflects an image of spiritual reality. All this implies a didactic purpose, which is certainly present in the sermons, but also arguably in Donne's poetry.

I want to conclude with a fourth dimension of incarnational theology which is more controversial because it does not lead beyond the body at all. It involves the incarnation of the lover in his mistress, or vice versa. The theme of tears will again serve to introduce this idea. In 'Witchcraft by a Picture' the poet sees his own reflection in his mistress's eyes and then imagines himself drowned by her tears, and in 'A Valediction: of Weeping', he suggests that when he weeps, it is the reflection of his mistress's face in his tears which gives them worth. Other poems develop similar images. 'The Exstasie' speaks of the lovers 'propagating' themselves by means of pictures in each other's eyes. In one sense, when one sees oneself in the eyes or tears of one's lover or mistress, one *becomes* the other; thus towards the end of 'A Valediction: forbidding mourning' the lovers appear to take on each other's characteristics – it is the woman who 'grows erect' and who shows 'firmness', while the man completes the circle (which perhaps corresponds to the 'sphere' and the 'glorious nothing', both images of the woman in 'Aire and Angels'). In another sense, when one sees oneself in the eyes or tears of one's lover or mistress, it is the other who contributes to one's self-knowledge.[5]

Perhaps what I earlier called Donne's self-absorption needs to be understood in this light. 'Elegy XIX', like numerous other poems, has a tendency to treat woman as an object, and this dehumanization of woman is sometimes taken to be a sign of the poet's essential misogyny (cf. Davies 1994: ch. 2); but this feminist/psychoanalytical approach misses the point. Woman is a mirror in which the male poet sees himself reflected, a sounding board for sharpening his witticisms and bouncing back his ideas (cf. Belsey 1994: 135ff.). She is the 'glorious nothing', an empty space which acquires a meaning in the process of the projection of the speaker's masculinity into her. Equally, however, it is through her that he comes to know himself. In 'A Valediction: of my name in the window' the poet's mistress can see both her own reflection ('... and cleare reflects thee to thine eye') and his name engraved in the window ('here see you mee'): the result is both self-knowledge and knowledge of the other, and at the same time a merging of the two ('I am you') (cf. Davies 1994: 13–16). In both 'The Canonization' and 'An Epithalamion, Or mariage Song on the Lady Elizabeth, and Count Palatine being married on St Valentines Day', Donne writes about a perfect union between husband and wife which suggests the erasure of sexual difference. The man and woman are initially described as separate but not differentiated:

> Two Phoenixes, whose joyned breasts,
> Are unto one another mutuall nests   (ll. 23–4)

Towards the end of the poem, however, the man assumes the place of the woman and the woman the place of the man:

> Here lyes a shee Sunne, and a hee Moone here,
>   She gives the best light to his Spheare,
>   Or each is both ...   (ll. 85–7)

By taking over the traditional alchemical symbols of the other, each lover both possesses the other and becomes the other. 'So to one neutrall thing both sexes fit' ('The Canonization', l. 25). The hermaphrodite thus created is an important alchemical image,[6] representing a stage on the path to perfection (cf. Davies 1994: 46); sex is transcended to the extent that the lovers 'forget the Hee and Shee' ('The Undertaking', l. 29). This notion of merging is most complete in 'Sapho to Philaenis',[7] where the fusion of the two lovers is such that it is no longer clear when Sappho is responding to Philaenis and when she is responding to her own reflection in the mirror:

> My two lips, eyes, thighs, differ from thy two,
>   But so, as thine from one another doe;
> And, oh, no more; the likenesse being such
>   Why should they not alike in all parts touch?
> Hand to strange hand, lippe to lippe none denies;
>   Why should they brest to brest, or thighs to thighs?
> Likeness begets such strange selfe flatterie,
>   That touching my selfe, all seemes done to thee.
> My selfe I embrace, and mine owne hands I kisse,
>   And amorously thanke my selfe for this.
> Me, in my glasse, I call thee; But alas,
>   When I would kisse, teares dimme mine eyes, and glasse ...

We can take this on two levels. As Herbert says, 'A man that looks on glasse | On it may stay his eye; | Or if he pleaseth, through it passe, | And then the heav'n espie' ('The Elixir'). On the purely sexual level, Donne's poem indicates a perfect bodily union, in which the bodies of the lover and the beloved merge into a single identity;[8] she speaks to Philaenis, but it is her own reflection that she touches and kisses in the mirror, and the two melt into each other. Of course, this parallels the union of souls that takes place in 'The Exstasie', but it also speaks symbolically on the divine level of the virtuous soul losing itself in, and attaining perfect union with, God. Either way, it clearly belongs to what I have identified as incarnation theology. Seeing oneself in the other (and the other in oneself), learning about oneself through the other (and about the other through oneself), becoming the other, are all aspects of incarnational theology, which is by definition concerned with what the body reveals.

Notes

1. This chapter grew out of an undergraduate module offered at the University of Plymouth entitled 'Sexuality and spirituality in seventeenth century England'. My thanks are due to both students and guest speakers who contributed to the module, particularly Katarzyna Lewicka, Cosmo Corfield, Dr Robert Hole and Dr Sam Smiles, and to others who read the developing manuscript, particularly Dr Chris Ellis and Dr William Kay.
2. Many critics (for example, Davies 1994; Herz 1994; Oliver 1997) rightly warn of too straightforward an identification of the 'I' of the poems with Donne himself; in view of the existence of poems like 'Sapho to Philaenis' in which a feminine voice is constructed, this seems an obvious point (see Correll 1995: 503 n. 6). The 'I' is better understood as the persona through whom the poet chooses to explore a wide range of ideas and emotions. And, of course, when the poem is read aloud, the reader becomes the 'I' as well. However, there is such compulsive self-dramatization in so many of Donne's poems – Davies talks of his 'excitable narcissism' (1994: 14) – that it seems wholly appropriate to see their self-focus and self-absorption as pointing to the poet himself.
3. I have here accepted Gardner's repunctuation of line ten (Gardner 1952: 79).
4. This view is broadly in line with that expressed by Hobbes (1651) within twenty years of Donne's death (cf. Osmond 1990: 42–4).
5. This idea foreshadows the mirror stage theory popularized by Lacan and others in recent years. Lacan suggests that the concept of the mirror is helpful in understanding 'the formation of the "I" as we experience it' (1977; cf. Williams 1995); the young child looking in the mirror begins to establish a relation between the body and its external reality. This relationship is marked by what Lacan calls 'the lack', which refers to an imaginary assumption that there had once been a state of wholeness with the (m)other which has now been lost and which the mirror image compensates for, offering the anticipation of a future self-control over the body which is taken to reflect the self-completeness of the ego. This state of frustration resulting from the discrepancy between what is felt 'inside' and what is experienced on the 'outside' is, according to Lacan, fundamental to the pursuit of one's identity and the mythical state of completeness of the 'I'. The human subject imagines that this completeness is achievable only in exchange with the other. Bakhtin (1990) argues that because one can never see from outside one's body, one always depends on the perception and the recognition of the other to see and construct one's own views of it, and further to supply an emotional dimension to one's self-conception which would otherwise be impossible to experience. Bakhtin suggests that when one gazes into a mirror one does not see an accurate reflection because mirrors are two-dimensional and show merely the reflection of one's exterior, the body, and never penetrate the inner self, the soul. Therefore one needs

the response of the other to shape one's own response. Hence the other, though not physically present in the mirror, makes his or her presence significant through one's own expressions. In the context of Donne's love poetry, when the male speaker treats the other as the mirror, the illusion is that the perception of the self that he receives is a most complete and accurate one, because it contains both the inner and the outer view of the self, being both responsive and informative.

6. Jung (1953; 1963) discusses in detail the central place in alchemy of the *coniunctio oppositorum* in the guise of the male Sol and the female Luna (elsewhere the opposites are represented by King/Queen, brother/sister, dry/moist, hot/cold, gold/silver, spiritual/physical, volatile/solid – and perhaps air/angels). In an alchemical allegory within the *Rosarium Philosophorum* of 1550 the king's son Gabricus dies as a result of his complete disappearance into the body of Beya (the maternal sea) during coitus. She embraces him with so much love that she absorbs him completely into her own nature and dissolves him into atoms: 'White-skinned lady, lovingly joined to her ruddy-limbed husband, | Wrapped in each other's arms in the bliss of connubial union, | Merge and dissolve as they come to the goal of perfection: | They that were two are made one, as though of one body.'

   Jung (*ibid.*) further discusses a series of pictures contained in the *Rosarium Philosophorum* in which the union of the King and Queen, Sol and his sister Luna, takes place. Figure 5, in this series, which depicts the actual union, is accompanied by this verse: 'O Luna, folded in my sweet embrace, | Be you as strong as I, as fair of face. | O Sol, brightest of all lights known to men, | And yet you need me, as the cock the hen.'

   Figure 6 shows the couple after the union, when they have become a two-headed hermaphrodite. The royal 'marriage' occupies such an important place in alchemy, Jung suggests, because it symbolizes the supreme and ultimate union of opposites at which the alchemist is aiming. Yet it is important to note that there is a third party to the union. The Queen (representing the body, Venus, the feminine) is united with the King (representing the spirit, Mercury, the masculine) so that they become an hermaphroditic being, but this hermaphrodite is incomplete without a soul. In the figures, the soul is symbolized by the dove, and, as Jung points out, if no unifying bond of love exists, they have no soul (*'spiritus est qui vivificat'*). Love is thus equated with the activity of the Holy Spirit. It is debatable how far this alchemical thinking had been absorbed into mainstream philosophy, science and theology in the age of Donne, but he certainly seems to be aware of it (as indicated by the extensive alchemical imagery he uses), and this awareness would have been reinforced for educated people by illustrations in copies of the Authorized Version of the Bible published in Donne's lifetime in which pictures of Adam and Eve in the Garden of Eden included symbols of sun and moon as well as the Holy Spirit in the form of a dove.

7. The reading here follows Benet (1994: 22–5). For an alternative (and very insightful) reading of this poem, see Correll (1995).

8. One reason why this poem is so important is that its lesbian orientation absolves it from the typical feminist critique of 'perfect union', that the merging of two heterosexual lovers usually implies the *submerging* of the woman. Barker (1981: 12–13) reminds us that this view of the virtual obliteration of the woman in marriage has a long history, by quoting the writer known only as T. E., the author of *The Lawes Resolution of Womens Rights* (1632): 'In this consolidation which we call wedlock is a locking together. It is true, that man and wife are one person; but understand in what manner. When a small brooke or little river incorporateth with Rhodanus, Humber or Thames, the poor rivulet looseth her name; it is carried and recarried with the new associate; it beareth no sway ...'

References

All references to John Donne's poems quoted in this chapter are taken from Patrides (1985); references to other metaphysical poets come from Gardner (1972).

Bakhtin, M. M. (1990) 'Author and hero in aesthetic activity' in M. Holquist and V. Liapuntov (eds), *Art and Answerability* (Austin: University of Texas)

Barker, F. (1981), 'The tremulous private body' in F. Barker *et al.* (eds) *1642: Literature and Power in the Seventeenth Century* (Colchester: University of Essex)

Barth, K. (1936), *Church Dogmatics*, I: *The Doctrine of the Word of God*, 2 (Edinburgh: T. and T. Clark)

Barth, K. (1962), *Church Dogmatics*, IV: *The Doctrine of Reconciliation*, 1 (Edinburgh: T. and T. Clark)

Belsey, C. (1994), *Desire* (Oxford: Blackwell)

Benet, D. T. (1994), 'Sexual transgression in Donne's Elegies', *Modern Philology*, 92/1, pp. 14–35

Brunner, E. (1952), *Dogmatics*, II: *The Christian Doctrine of Creation and Redemption* (London: Lutterworth)

Carey, J. (1981), *John Donne: Life, Mind and Art* (London: Faber and Faber)

Correll, B. (1995), 'Symbolic economies and zero-sum erotics: Donne's "Sapho to Philaenis"', *ELH* 62, pp. 487–507 (Johns Hopkins University Press)

Davies, S. (1994), *John Donne* (Plymouth: Northcote House)

Gardner, H. (ed.) (1952), *John Donne: The Divine Poems* (Oxford: Clarendon)

Gardner, H. (ed.) (1972), *The Metaphysical Poets* (Harmondsworth: Penguin)

Gibb, E. J. W. (n.d.) *Ottoman Literature: The Poets and Poetry of Turkey* (London: L. Beling Tetens)

Grenander, M. E. (1975), 'Holy Sonnets VIII and XVII: John Donne' in J. R. Roberts (ed.), *Essential Articles for the Study of John Donne's Poetry* (Hamden, Conn.: Shoe String Press)

Herz, J. S. (1994), 'Reading (out) biography in "A Valediction Forbidding Mourning"', *John Donne Journal* 13/1–2, pp. 137–42.

Hick, J. (ed.) (1977), *The Myth of God Incarnate* (London: SCM)

Hobbes, T. (1918), *Leviathan* (first published 1651) (London: J. M. Dent and Sons)

Hull, J. (1984), *Studies in Religion and Education* (London: Falmer)

Jung, C. G. (1953), *Psychology and Alchemy* (London: Routledge and Kegan Paul)

Jung, C. G. (1963), *Mysterium Coniunctionis* (London: Routledge and Kegan Paul)

Kermode, F. (1957), *John Donne*, Writers and their Work, 86 (London: Longmans, Green and Co. for British Council)

Lacan, J. (1977) 'The mirror stage' in *Ecrits: A Selection*, trans. A Sheridan (London: Tavistock)

Legouis, P. (1928), *Donne the Craftsman: An Essay upon the Structure of the Songs and Sonnets* (Paris: Henri Didier)

Macquarrie, J. (1966), *Principles of Christian Theology* (London: SCM)

Martz, L. L. (1954), *The Poetry of Meditation: A Study in English Religious Literature of the Seventeenth Century* (New Haven Conn.: Yale University Press)

Martz, L. L. (1970), 'The action of the self: devotional poetry in the seventeenth century' in M. Bradbury and D. Palmer (eds), *Metaphysical Poetry*, Stratford-upon-Avon Studies, 11 (London: Edward Arnold)

Oliver, P. M. (1997), *Donne's Religious Writings: A Discourse in Feigned Devotion* (London: Longman)

Osmond, R. (1990), *Mutual Accusation: Seventeenth-Century Body and Soul Dialogues in their Literary and Theological Context* (Toronto: University of Toronto Press)

Patrides, C. A, (ed.) (1985), *The Complete English Poems of John Donne* (London: Everyman)

J. Mark Halstead

Rosarium Philosophorum, Seconda pars Alchemiae de Lapide Philosophico (1550) (Frankfurt)

Simpson, E. M. (1967a), *John Donne: Selected Prose* (Oxford: Clarendon)

Simpson, E. M. (ed.) (1967b), *John Donne's Sermons on the Psalms and Gospels* (Berkeley, Calif.: University of California Press)

Wilcox, H. (1994), 'Squaring the circle: metaphors of the divine in the work of Donne and his contemporaries', *John Donne Journal* 13/1–2, pp. 61–79

Wiles, M. (1977), 'Christianity without incarnation?' in J. Hick (ed.), *The Myth of God Incarnate* (London: SCM)

Williams, L. (1995), *Critical Desire: Psychoanalysis and the Literary Subject* (London: Edward Arnold)

Young, F. (1977) 'A cloud of witnesses' in J. Hick (ed.) *The Myth of God Incarnate* (London: SCM)

11

Johnson's Cosmology: Vacuity and Ramification

Philip Davis

M any readers will know what Mrs Thrale said was the key to understanding Johnson: 'The vacuity of life had at some early period of his life struck so forcibly on the mind of Mr. Johnson, that it became by repeated impression his favourite hypothesis.' In this chapter I am interested in why Johnson's writing does not look like that – why it seems so full and dense, and not thin or empty, even when its subject is vanity or vacuity. There is a frightening asymmetry, a disturbing disproportionateness, I suggest, between Johnson's sense of an ultimate vacuity and that fullness of mentality in his writing which I'll call Johnson's ramifications.

I'll start with those rich ramifications. I've taken the term from Johnson's account, in his *Preface to the English Dictionary*, of the difficulties of clear verbal definition. Ideally, says Johnson, one ought to be able to mark the progress of the meaning of a word, showing 'by what gradations of intermediate sense it has passed from its primitive to its remote and accidental signification'. Thus, with each distinct explanation following from the preceding one, there might be formed a demarcated series 'regularly concatenated from the first notion to the last'. Linguistic life, however, is not reducible to that Enlightenment chain of orderly links, that line of rational succession – any more than is creation itself: for in his review of Soame Jenyns's *Free Inquiry into the Nature and Origin of Evil*

Johnson denies that the universe may be organized in terms of one great chain of being. To Johnson here as elsewhere, human history is not reducible to logic, any more than human meaning is simply subject to human explanation. The difficulties in the *Dictionary* are another model of the difficulties of life itself – of the struggles of thought in relation to the ever-burgeoning accidents and meanings of time.

Thus, in terms of the shape of thinking, Dictionary Johnson finds, instead of a clear ideal *line* of sequential development reaching backwards and forwards in *time*, a sense of intervolved and overlapping *areas* of being existing almost simultaneously in *space*:

> Kindred senses may be so interwoven, that the perplexity cannot be disentangled, nor any reason be assigned why one should be ranged before the other. When the radical idea branches out into parallel ramifications, how can a consecutive series be formed of senses in their nature collateral? The shades of meaning sometimes pass imperceptibly into each other; so that though on one side they apparently differ, yet it is impossible to mark the point of contact. Ideas of the same race, though not exactly alike, are sometimes so little different, that no words can express the dissimilitude, though the mind easily perceives it, when they are exhibited together; and sometimes there is such a confusion of acceptations, that discernment is wearied, and distinction puzzled, and perseverance herself hurries to an end, by crouding together what she cannot separate. (Preface to *English Dictionary*)

You can see there the last vestiges of an almost prelapsarian linguistic blueprint, before the fall of Babel. As Johnson's *Dictionary* itself shows, the word 'ramification' has within its Latinate etymological roots the idea of branching, first natural, then by metaphorical extension mental. The word 'kindred' has within it the radical memory of 'kin' and 'kind', related meanings which, as in 'ideas of the same race', unfold and spread as the life-principle itself does through its branching forms. Yet what we might call the poet's dream of a natural genetic pattern in language does not remain stable for long here: what begins with the idea of 'kindredness', of relations arising from or branching out of the same original, swiftly falls into being a matter of confused perplexity and entanglement. 'The dreams of the poet doomed at last to wake a lexicographer' (*Preface to English Dictionary*). Thus the straightforwardly 'consecutive' must give way to the 'collateral'. So it is with that great disciple of the school of Johnson, Edmund Burke, in his account of the history and practice of political society in contrast to rationally ideal theory:

> Metaphysical rights entering into common life, like rays of light which pierce into a dense medium, are, by the laws of nature, refracted from their straight line. Indeed in the gross and complicated mass of human passions and concerns, the primitive rights of men undergo such a variety of refractions, that it becomes absurd to talk of them as if they continued in the simplicity of the original direction ... The rights of men are in a sort of middle, incapable of definition, but not impossible to be discerned. (*Reflections*, pp. 152–3)

The primal straight lines of life are refracted and diffused in a fallen medium of complexity. In the middle and the midst of history, post-lapsarian society is like experience itself, something that evolves beyond simple starting points, making definition for Johnson not impossible, but no longer absolute and certain: now possible only as approximative and provisional. In the same way, the cure for the greatest part of human miseries, says Johnson (*Rambler* 32) 'is not radical but palliative'. We can never get back to the very root of a problem; we can only live with its spreading growth. Original absolutes become relative and ramify.

When you read Johnson, you feel the presence of a single and definite personality, speaking with the force of a seemingly unified but somehow deeply implicit set of principles. But you cannot quite define him or those principles. There is somewhere in him a lost or buried root, an original simplicity long since complicated by experience. Yet if you try to put your finger on it, you begin to feel a little like Mrs Thrale: so aware of Johnson as a man frighteningly made up of implicit rules and laws, which at any moment you might break or misapply without knowing it, because there's something you do not know from the inside as he did. Indeed, Johnson writes to Mrs Thrale on 27 October 1777, that only very seldom, in letters of unbuttoned confidence, do you see traces of the naked original soul of the writer, reduced to its first principles – 'nothing inverted, nothing distorted, you see systems in their elements, actions in their motives':

> The original Idea is laid down in its simple purity, and all the supervenient conceptions, are spread over it stratum super stratum, as they happen to be formed.

Normally, however, we live lost in the middle of life, first principles half-forgotten or half-compromised, radical simplicities entangled and overlaid within a complicating medium. Johnson wrote no one great work as a permanent expression of a unified philosophy worthy of his talents: he is above all the writer of occasional essays, including *Rasselas*, filling in the holes or following out the entanglements that have emerged out of life's original texture.

In a fallen world of refracted middles rather than final ends or simple origins, a saving intelligence, thought Johnson, lay in the powers of distinguishing. The definitive act of mind, when in danger of being insensibly lost and overwhelmed amidst the chaos of a crowding mass of similar phenomena, was to make out minute but crucial differences. So, when Soame Jenyns supported the general proposition that this is the best of all possible worlds – by arguing that the poor are generally compensated by having more hopes and fewer fears than those who possess riches – Dictionary Johnson is swift to pounce on Jenyns's definition of poverty:

> *Poverty* is very gently paraphrased by *want of riches*. In that sense almost every man may in his own opinion be poor. But there is another poverty which is *want of competence,* of all that can soften the miseries of life, of all that can diversify attention, or delight imagination. There is yet another poverty which is want of *necessaries* ... ('Review of a *Free Inquiry into the Nature and Origin of Evil*')

Formally, in language, there are three distinct areas to steer by here: want of riches, want of competence, want of necessaries. And when, more informally in life, you reach the point at which want of competence shades into want of necessaries, then though 'the milder degrees of poverty are sometimes supported by hope, the more severe often sink down in motionless despondence' (ibid.). Where Soame Jenyns in his *Free Inquiry* all too freely crowds together what he should have separated, Johnson goes the other way to work. Jenyns argues that in this fallen world knowledge often only increases consciousness without effecting remedies; ignorance may be an opiate which enables the poor the better to bear their lot. With the general proposition practical Johnson agrees: 'Whatever knowledge is superfluous, in irremediable poverty, is hurtful' (ibid.); but, says Dictionary Johnson: 'the difficulty is to determine *when* poverty is irremediable, and *at what point* superfluity begins' (ibid.).

Exactly *when*, precisely at what *point*; where is the line drawn between the ending of one thing and the beginnings of another; what is the limit? If all earthly things are, as Jenyns says, an inevitable *mixture* of good and evil, still, says Johnson, 'as far as human eyes can judge, the *degree* of evil might have been less without any impediment to good' (ibid.). Johnson uses the forensic tools of precision precisely to establish how, 'as far as human eyes can judge', precision itself is impossible. And thus a precise sense of impreciseness must be part of the equation. Err on the side of caution in matters speculative, on the side of generosity in matters human. 'The balance is put into our own hands,' says Johnson in *Rambler* 7, 'and we have power to transfer the weight to either side.' 'I am always afraid of determining on the side of envy or cruelty,' he says finally to Jenyns, 'The privileges of education may sometimes be improperly bestowed, but I shall always fear to with-hold them, lest I should be yielding to the suggestions of pride, whilst I persuade myself that I am following the maxims of policy' ('Review of a *Free Inquiry into the Nature and Origin of Evil*'). You understand: it's only the morally brave who have respect for fear.

For Johnson, then, the great Augustan act of distinction makes one all the more aware, on second thought, of the equivocal areas, the black holes, in between those distinctly defined. Again, it is like Johnson on the great chain of being in which he sees the constant possibility of missing links:

> In the scale, wherever it begins or ends, are infinite vacuities. At whatever distance we suppose the next order of beings to be above man, there is room for an intermediate order of beings between them; and if for one order then for infinite orders; since everything that admits of more or less, and consequently all the parts of that which admits them, may be infinitely divided. So that, as far as we can judge, there may be room in the vacuity between any two steps of the scale ... for infinite exertion of infinite power. (ibid.)

There is infinite possibility for God, but man is finite. He is not all or nothing but, in the midst, the creature of a world of 'more or less' – of degrees, shades, gradations. And the more he makes conceptual distinctions and divisions, the more a second mind, a second-order layer or level of intelligence in him, sees the intermediate points of remaining indistinctness, and thus the increasingly microscopic space for infinitely more subdivisions, reaching to the very vanishing points of human sanity. In the structure of daily life, says Johnson in *Rambler* 108, there are always those 'interstitial vacancies which intervene in the most crouded variety of diversion or employment' – he does not believe that every gap in life is filled by the principle of plenitude; life's lacunae appear like sudden depressive black holes for Johnson. And that gives you too much arbitrary time in which to think, too much indeterminate space in which to imagine. Thus:

> It was said of the learned Bishop Sanderson, that, when he was preparing his lectures, he hesitated so much, and rejected so often, that, at the time of reading, he was often forced to produce, not what was best, but what happened to be at hand. This will be the state of every man, who, in the choice of his employment, balances all the arguments on every side; the complication is so intricate, the motives and objections so numerous, there is so much play for the imagination, and so much remains in the power of others, that reason is forced at last to rest in neutrality, the decision devolves into the hands of chance, and after a great part of life spent in inquiries which can never be resolved, the rest must often pass in repenting the unnecessary delay, and can be useful to few other purposes than to warn others against the same folly, and to show, that of two states of life equally consistent with religion and virtue, he who chuses earliest chuses best. (*Rambler* 19)

This is how, for better and for worse, 'collateral' replaces 'consecutive': what one finds in hesitating are 'all the arguments *on every side*', blocking simple forward movement. That long final sentence itself both includes and pushes against its own sympathy with intricate complication and perplexity. For as Johnson puts it again in *Rambler* 185, 'we are on every side in danger of error and of guilt'. These then are Johnson's ramifications: at crucial nodal points in the act of thinking it occurs to the distinguishing mind that the argument could plausibly proceed in several different directions simultaneously, in several consecutively parallel mental universes of possibility, in several different individual lives. How, without losing yourself, can you produce a sentence that whilst following each competing thought and its offshoots through to their separate ends, still holds together the binding relation of all those separating considerations? Our limited minds naturally prefer one thought, single-mindedly. In his long periods, Johnson syntactically forces the mind beyond one thought, beyond even two simply opposing ones, into the uncomfortable realm of a third or fourth or fifth consideration (for we can probably manage no more). But that third or fourth ramification offers the mind, still within its limitations, an image of unlimited further thoughts – all plausible in the vacuum, none grounded in utter certainty – spinning into the realm where one begins to know just how much one does not know, till for survival's sake one has to pull back and return to earth. So it is in the conclusion to *Rambler* 19:

> and after a great part of life spent in inquiries which can never be resolved, the rest must often pass in repenting the unnecessary delay, and can be useful to few other purposes than to warn others against the same folly, and to show, that of two states of life equally consistent with religion and virtue, he who chuses earliest chuses best.

– for at the end of the day Johnson refuses what he calls neutrality and returns instead – by that characteristic mental twist of 'few other.../... than' – to the common world of compromised practicality. Thus this *Rambler* publicly *comes out* at the end just as the answer to a mathematical problem comes out, but in applied not pure calculation – arriving finally at the idea of starting early. 'Men more often require to be reminded than informed' (*Rambler* 2). Solutions are not original or radical but matters of recall and adjustment.

Or take this sentence, again from the 'Review of a *Free Inquiry*':

> In our passage through the boundless ocean of disquisition we often take fogs for land, and after having toiled to approach them find, instead of repose and harbours, new storms of objection and fluctuations of uncertainty.

This time the moralist's final clause is taken back into the sentence it comes out of and reinserted inside as the penultimate clause instead. That is to say: think how inferior the sentence would be if it read 'and after having toiled to approach them find new storms of objection and fluctuations of uncertainty, instead of repose and harbours'. That would be too merely linear, too consecutive a shape: to put the 'instead' clause in *earlier* adds a dimension from another 'side' to the now quickened horizontal sentence: it incorporates the failure of fond expectation *within* the emotional experience of finding disappointment and disorientation instead.

Or again this, frighteningly, from near the end of the *Life of Savage*:

> He proceeded throughout his life to tread the same steps on the same circle; always applauding his past conduct, or at least forgetting it, to amuse himself with phantoms of happiness which were dancing before him; and willingly turned his eyes from the light of reason, when it would have discovered the illusion and shown him, what he never wished to see, his real self.

One good way of starting to do Johnson might be to try to count the number of different single thoughts there are in any one long ramifying sentence of his: that way at least, you would discover what you thought a thought *was*, and it would let you see how even so one thought still shades into or contains another. So here: it is that little but devastatingly inserted parenthesis, 'what he never wished to see', that incorporates a sort of vertical dimension within what is otherwise the horizontal line of the sentence's thought, bringing *down* within the life of Savage the judgement Savage could never bear to bring down upon himself. Filling the vacuity Savage willingly left, that integrated parenthesis bespeaks Johnson's implicit first principles, used in passing in the middle of life, but deriving from the original judicial meaning of 'sentencing'.

To hold collateral thoughts within that consecutive medium called the linear sentences of temporal prose: that is the achievement of the Johnsonian sentence, densely defying the mere present tense of easy reading, left to right, like time's arrow, by bringing to it the extra time-dimensions of experience and thought. 'Whatever makes the past, the distant or the future predominate over the present,' says Johnson in his *Journey to the Western Islands*, 'advances us in the dignity of thinking beings' ('Inch Kenneth'). Johnson is the great writer of sentences as paradigms of thoughtful life. He says himself in *Rambler* 175:

> He may therefore be justly numbered among the benefactors of mankind, who contracts the great rules of life into short sentences, that may be easily impressed on the memory, and taught by frequent recollection to recur habitually to mind.

But, for all his concern for both the importance of reminding and the survival-value of small portable truths, Johnson's own sentences are themselves, of course, not usually short, not beautiful epigraphs or elegant maxims. What does this mean for his view of life? I return to this matter of the sheer shape of Johnson's thinking.

Samuel Beckett's sense of kinship with Samuel Johnson is well known. 'It's Johnson, always Johnson, who is with me;' wrote Beckett, 'And if I follow any tradition, it is his' (quoted in Doherty, *Samuel Beckett*, p. 120). But Beckett's writing is in its style as emptied of meaning, as pared down, as is his philosophy; whereas something in Johnson defies the vacuity he fearfully believes in. That said, nonetheless here is Beckett the modernist non-believer writing to Harold Hobson about an author, St Augustine, who does indeed belong to Johnson's Christian tradition. The reference is to the crucifixion, for in the words of the Gospel, 'Then were there two thieves crucified with him, one on the right hand, and another on the left.'

> I am interested in the shape of ideas, even if I do not believe in them. There is a wonderful sentence in Augustine: I wish I could remember the Latin. It is even finer in Latin than in English. 'Do not despair; one of the thieves was saved. Do not presume; one of the thieves was damned.' That sentence has a wonderful shape. It is the shape that matters. (quoted in Doherty, p. 88)

Of course what aesthetic Beckett offers here is really *two* sentences: it is the mental space that we inhabit in between them – in between despair and presumption, in probation between salvation and damnation – that is the shape to which Beckett refers, like the Grecian urn that emerges, you remember, between two facing profiles. It is true that Johnson knew all about that mental area. Thus Johnson to Mrs Thrale, on cautiously occupying that narrow line, trying to go through the eye of a needle: 'It is good to speak dubiously about futurity. It is likewise not amiss to hope' (Boswell, *Life of Johnson*, entry for December 1784) Not to presume; not to despair. In *Rambler* 67, on hope itself, Johnson says at the beginning of the second paragraph: 'Hope is necessary in every condition. The miseries of poverty, of sickness, of captivity, would, without this comfort, be insupportable ...' and then begins the next paragraph by also saying 'Hope is, indeed, very fallacious, and promises what it seldom gives ...'

This is like an original version of Johnson's dilemma before supervenient thoughts cover it, stratum over stratum. For hope is necessary; hope is fallacious. But Johnson is not like Beckett's Augustine; he is not usually content to leave that frightening vacant space or silence between those sentences but rather wants to know how those two sentences are to be joined in a mind, in a life. We know from Mrs Thrale Johnson's obsession with his sense of the 'vacuity of life', of how human nature's horror of life's vacuum leads us to do almost anything to fill up our time in order to distract ourselves from the thought of emptiness. Johnson hated the natural desert wildernesses of the Western Isles: they gave him nothing to hold onto in the created world, no place for man, but opened chasms in his very mind. The old Aristotelian maxim that nature abhors a vacuum is quoted by Johnson in *Rambler* 85 (and Charles Hinnant's *Samuel Johnson: An Analysis* is admirable here). In the *Dictionary* he cites Boyle under the word 'vacant' on air rushing impetuously into a cavity precisely because there is vacant room to require and receive it; but he also quotes Bentley insisting that nonetheless 'a vacuity is interspersed amidst the particles of nature'. To Johnson, that is to say, the abhorrence of a vacuum is a principle that applies more to human nature than to nature itself: 'So few of the hours of life are filled up with objects adequate to the mind of man, and so frequently are we in want of present pleasure or employment,' as he puts it in *Rambler* 41, 'that we are forced to have recourse every moment to the past and future for supplemental satisfactions, and relieve the vacuities of our being ...' That is why hope is necessary even if fallacious: it gives to the present some sense of a future even if that future never itself comes to be.

Life leaves open holes that the human mind struggles to fill, be it with physical distractions or mental explanations. In saying 'Do not despair. Do not presume,' Augustine left the mind in the hole between them. Gigantick and stupendous intelligences, says Johnson in *Rambler* 108 – great intelligences such as Augustine's in thought or Shakespeare's in poetry – may proceed by sheer intuition, leaping from one proposition to another, 'without regular steps through intermediate propositions'. But a common man in what Burke called 'a sort of middle' could feel abandoned, to fall between Augustine's two great negative imperatives, if the silent positive linkage between them were not spelt out. Under the word 'vacancy' in his *Dictionary*, Johnson cites Isaac Watts's commonsensical work on *Logick*: 'The reader finds a wide vacancy, and knows not how to transport his thoughts to the next particular, for want of some connecting idea.' That is why Johnson, like an intermediary filling the gap between the old giants and the present commonality, will always seek to turn two sentences into one, and if not find the connecting answer at least hold together the terms of the dilemma.

Thus in *Rambler* 184: 'for it is necessary to act, but impossible to know the consequences of action'; or thus in *Rambler* 32: 'It seems to me reasonable to enjoy blessings with confidence as well as to resign them with submission ...'; or even more magnificently in *Rambler* 29: 'Evil is uncertain in the same degree as good, and for the reason that we ought not to hope too securely, we ought not to fear with too much dejection.' In a medium in which rays of light no longer shine straightforwardly, this is the thing done back-to-front – life defined by its very lack of definition: two things (hope and fear, loss and gain, evil and good) held together only by an acknowledgement of their equal *un*certainty. 'For the reason that we ought not to hope too securely, we ought not to fear with too much dejection': we sense through inference in such formulations what Johnson told Boswell was 'the system of life' – don't hope too much, nor fear too much *for the same reason*; even if in the midst of that system we can give no higher primary rationale *for* that reason.

Why should evil be as uncertain as good? is still an unanswered primary question for Johnson, the greatest second-rater in the history of our literature. Second-rater –

yes, if only in this sense that he knew he had no answer to the primary question and himself felt diminished by that incapacity. But still downright Johnson will not flatter himself like Soame Jenyns by thinking that there is any provable difference 'between him that gives no reason, and him that gives a reason, which by his own confession cannot be conceived' ('Review of a *Free Inquiry into the Nature and Origin of Evil*'). 'If by excluding joy we could shut out grief ...' says Johnson beginning a sentence in *Rambler* 47; but we cannot be exclusive; grief is the price we must always be liable to pay for joy and hope and love. 'Is it not like advice, not to walk lest we should stumble?' he says in the great *Rambler* 32. You can't exclude the disadvantages. That is why in Burke's refracting medium of life one of Johnson's great inclusive words is the word 'without' as a paradoxical connective. A naive youth, says Johnson in *Rambler* 196, never imagines 'that there may be greatness without safety, affluence without content, jollity without friendship, and solitude without peace'. Or again as Johnson notes in Sermon 15, thinking not least of himself: 'Day rises after day, and one year follows another, and produces nothing but resolutions without effect and self-reproach without reformation.' And if that is so, there is also thus, in the 'Life of Collins', 'that depression of mind which enchains the faculties *without* destroying them, and leaves reason the knowledge of right *without* the power of pursuing it' ('Life of Collins' in *Lives of the Poets*). Yet still these sentences hold onto the terms of the trouble within them. 'Without' goes against the grain of apparently natural assumptions, filling us with the memory of painful vacuities. It is a recaller of those things that shouldn't belong together and yet do in this world and, equally, the things that don't come together but would do so in a better universe.

Yet as he forms these compound sentences, somewhere in the back of Johnson's mind is, I think, a simple, original analogical paradigm of construction:

> for, as the chemists tell us, that all bodies are resolvable into the same elements, and that the boundless variety of things arises from the different proportions of very few ingredients; so a few pains, and a few pleasures are all the materials of human life. (*Rambler* 68)

The basic elements are finite, but their compounds, mixtures and combinations are almost infinite. So it is in chemistry, so it is in psychology, so it is in language: basically the world still mirrors itself at all levels. Thus you can see Johnson putting together his simpler definitions out of the basic building-blocks of nouns:

> As cruelty looks upon misery without partaking pain, so envy beholds encrease of happiness without partaking joy. (Sermon 11)

For it is as if language were for Johnson a memory of the basic human disposition which antedates the action of our individual lives within it. That is to say: lives are spelt out, as it were, from the general vocabulary and grammar of human being, with only individual distinctions of formulation and tone. And yet there comes a point – a point which no human being can precisely put his finger on – when what is made out of what is simple itself becomes complex. Then life's sentences become longer and more self-modifying.

What Johnson can point to is where that complexity is followed too far, and that is with the metaphysical poets, with Donne and Cowley. 'The fault of Cowley, and perhaps of all the writers of the metaphysical race,' says Johnson, 'is that of pursuing his thoughts to their last ramifications' ('Life of Cowley' in *Lives of the Poets*).' In the metaphysical poets, the branches seem to have lost touch with their own roots. Cowley 'loses the grandeur of generality', becoming increasingly singular or individual in himself, and too idiosyncratic and minutely particular in his poetic concerns, as if the distinguishing power of mind has gone too far in Cowley. By *discordia concors* the metaphysicals were creating their own strange new world rather than recalling the common old one, using mind to bring different things unnaturally together, rather than to see the vital differences in things given as 'more or less' alike.

What Johnson, like Dryden, admired were those four lines from Denham's 'Cooper's Hill' on the river Thames:

> O could I flow like thee, and make thy stream
> My great example as it is my theme.
> Though deep, yet clear; though gentle, yet not dull;
> Strong without rage, without o'erflowing full.

In this metaphor the mind is *not*, as Johnson notes with regard to the wilder conceits of the metaphysical poets, 'turned more upon the original than the secondary sense' ('Life of Cowley' in *Lives of the Poets*): that is to say, it is not turned more upon that from which the illustration is drawn – the Thames – than that to which it is applied: the human mind or soul. The new ingenious sense gives way to the old natural meaning now freshly recalled. In contrast, the intellect of the metaphysicals forces connections upon their material: the sheer surprise at their imagery on the one side does not give way to renewed memory on the other. Cowley is, like all who pride themselves upon absolute rather than relative individualism, one-sided:

> He forgot, in the vehemence of desire, that solitude and quiet owe their pleasures to those miseries, which he was so solicitous to obviate; for such are the vicissitudes of the world, through all its parts, that day and night, labour and rest, hurry and retirement, endear each other; such are the changes that keep the mind in action.   (*Rambler* 6)

Cowley needed to be reminded that in a relative world those apparently absolute opposites, restlessness and peace, ironically owe their very existence to each other. In that sort of world the mind is not, like the Thames, ideally steady whilst also changing: the mutual links between the opposites of labour and rest are experienced successively not simultaneously and are only ironic versions of the lost harmony of opposites. No light without dark, no dark without light, yet no reason known as to why the dark could not be shorter or lighter.

> O could I flow like thee, and make thy stream
> My great example as it is my theme.

Even in Denham himself this is but the *wish* for the radical idea, the lost natural language, the lost correspondence, in contrast to those more unhappy 'withouts' or 'yet-nots' in Johnson. So: if you are Johnson, you cannot have Denham's language but you won't have Cowley's. You won't accept Soame Jenyns's rationalizations, but you won't give up on Watts's *Logick*. In Johnson's fallen, broken and second-order world where 'everything admits of more or less', everything does something, and nothing does enough. So you have to try to find the *degree* to which reason is useful, the *degree* to which language can help to show the general blueprint of human life. And even the degree will be relatively rough, not absolutely precise. Yet even that roughness must be very carefully pursued:

> Patience and submission are very carefully to be distinguished from cowardice and indolence. We are not to repine, but we may lawfully struggle ... (*Rambler* 32)

And furthermore not only must you carefully see those differences on the page, but also, across the biggest difference of all, you must think how to lift into *life* those differences which the distinction of words recalls on the *page*. Johnson always adds a further dimension, labouring for another bridge, and, in doing so, always does his corrections and makes his modifications across the realms of being: thus he constantly works to and fro, steering by language's compass towards life, and returning from his experience of life to correct the verbal course, accepting the need to create the balance he cannot otherwise find.

That is why Johnson is *the* occasional writer *par excellence*, only temporarily attached to writing, taking what he calls intermissions or retreats from its dominion, as temporarily empty spaces in which to remind himself that the reality which writing seeks to encapture lies elsewhere – *before* he then returns to write again, to fill up the gap or remake the join. Modern philosophers, he says in *Rambler* 8, say that the universe is made up of dispersed matter which if concentrated could be contained in the shape of a cube of a few feet. When Johnson does return to writing, he does so in a massy language which seeks to concentrate in its sheer sentences just such cubes of being, *pulling together* the life he had dispersed in time and vacuity.

And he writes in this general language, because that is what language is to him – always general, always a common code, always the root-story or memory or blueprint of the race as a whole. Only on the other side of language, as on the other side of Denham's figure of the River Thames, are the particular resonances of the common words evoked as tacit memories in the private mind of writer and reader. Where the common language ends, silence and in that silence individual memory begin. When in *Rambler* 14 Johnson says that 'a man proposes his schemes of life in a state of abstraction and disengagement, exempt from the enticements of hope, the solicitations of affection, the importunities of appetite', Johnson is not that sort of 'exempted man', not the sort of writer to treat language and writing as sites for autonomous abstractions. Instead we feel made up of these nouns 'the enticements of hope, the solicitations of affection, the importunities of appetite' – words you can look up outside in a dictionary, which nonetheless are registered by us *inside* as our feelings. Johnson, himself the most silently autobiographical of all writers, works through a language which finds its power in simultaneously *recalling and repressing* personal meanings on the other side of itself.

Cowley in his intellectual individualism, Soame Jenyns in his ambition for enlightened explanation, alike went too far beyond the point of silence. What Johnson as an anti-metaphysical writer does is stop short, embody silently in himself the thoughts he cannot quite think in the world – given his self-imposed rule that there is no provable difference 'between him that gives no reason, and him that gives a reason, which by his own confession cannot be conceived' ('Review of a *Free Inquiry into the Nature and Origin of Evil*'). And he ends his review of Soame Jenyns by reminding himself how easy it is merely to criticize: 'the hand which cannot build a hovel may demolish a temple' (ibid.). Johnson could demolish the hovel, he couldn't build the temple instead. And that is where he leaves it. For that is in Johnson, I believe, the tacit definition of a person – a person, an individual or particular human being, is that which is *left* to embody, to incarnate silently and incompletely all that cannot be spoken generally or solved neutrally. Under the word 'vacuity' Johnson cites Glanville thus: 'The soul is seen, like other things, in the mirror of its effects: but if they'll run behind the glass to catch at it, their expectations will meet with vacuity and emptiness.' You cannot quite get behind to that private other side, that soul of Johnson, though you sense it all the time in his tacit autobiography. The person in him is one who sees more than he can do, knows more than he can solve, and having to live with less than he would want, *makes* a life even so – filling what gaps he can, keeping silent in those he cannot, like a man who himself cannot even quite get to his own soul.

In such a life, a sentence for Johnson is a holdfast. Here is a final Johnsonian sentence, to end on – written in his last year of life to an old friend:

O! my friend, the approach of death is very dreadful. I am afraid to think on that which I know I cannot avoid.
(To Revd Dr Taylor, 12 April 1784; in Boswell, *Life of Johnson*)

What that second sentence holds together in one is the man of emotion – 'I am *afraid* to think' – with the man of impersonal knowledge – 'to *think* on that which I *know*'. And it holds them both together in the recogniton of a mortal man that he is mortal whatever he feels or thinks about it – 'that which I know/I cannot *avoid*'. Johnson keeps these different *levels* steadily on one *line*, the ramifying clauses incorporated still within one holding sentence, like different thoughts held still within one mind.

I conclude therefore that *The Rambler* is in its defiant density Johnson's holding-ground – against the silent, the empty, the dark. It is not that Johnson allows himself to fill his sense of a vacuum with compensating fantasies or fictions; rather he occupies with thought the fact that life is too little for us – and that that is felt as almost too much for us to bear. Johnson had to think and to care too much about what was too little and live with that imbalance, making some adjustments to the scale. There was never simply enough; there was only a tough holding-ground instead. Yet within and behind that practicality of Johnson's, converting the smallness of it into resistant density, lay a massive but tacit theological cosmology.

Select Bibliography

For Johnson the standard text is *The Yale Edition of the Works of Samuel Johnson*. Donald Greene's Oxford Authors *Samuel Johnson* (Oxford: Oxford University Press, 1984) is the most conveniently available selection.

Boswell, James, *Life of Samuel Johnson* (1791), and *Journal of a Tour to the Hebrides with Samuel Johnson* (1785), published together in G. B. Hill's great volume of the *Life*, rev. L. F. Powell (Oxford: Clarendon, 1934–64).
Burke, Edmund, *Reflections on the Revolution in France* (1790), ed. C. C. O'Brien (Harmondsworth: Penguin, 1968)
Davis, Philip, *In Mind of Johnson* (London: Athlone, 1989)
Doherty, Frank *Samuel Beckett* (London: Hutchinson, 1971)
Hinnant, Charles H., *Samuel Johnson: An Analysis* (London: Macmillan, 1988).
McGilchrist, Iain, *Against Criticism* (London: Faber, 1982).
Piozzi, Hester Lynch [Thrale], *Anecdotes of the Late Samuel Johnson* (London: 1786).

12

Ruskin's Christian Theory of Art

Michael Wheeler

... the mighty pyramids stood calmly – in the very heart of the high heaven – a celestial city with walls of amethyst and gates of gold – filled with the light and clothed with the Peace of God. Cancelled passage from *Modern Painters* II (*Works* IV, p. 364)

I

The sight of the Aiguilles standing quietly above the storm like the heavenly Jerusalem (Revelation 21) had, Ruskin claimed, first taught him 'the real meaning of the word Beautiful' – the subject of *Modern Painters* volume II.[1] Yet the substantial passage in the manuscript describing the inspirational moment 'before, and in the Presence of, the manifested Deity' at his beloved Chamonix in July 1842 (*Diaries*, p. 230), from which this epigraph is taken, was not incorporated in the printed text.[2] Ruskin (1819–1900) may have felt that its youthful effusiveness and its confessional quality would have been more in tune with the 'young-mannishness' of volume I (first edition 1843, second edition 1844), in which he had written of 'adorable manifestations of God's working' in mountain rock and heather (*Works* III, p. 198), than with the 'serious, quiet, earnest, and simple' manner he strove for in volume II, published in April 1846 (*ibid*. III, p. 668). Furthermore, the Italian tour of 1845 – the first made without his parents – changed the whole direction of the project, so that instead of continuing the discussion of landscape from volume I, as envisaged by Ruskin, his father, his publisher George Murray Smith, his 'literary master' W. H. Harrison and, interestingly, an engraver John Cousen in January 1844 (*Works*, IV, p. xxi), it became a theoretical study, without plates which focused upon the religious art of the Italian old masters. Thus the omission of the passage on the Aiguilles may also reflect Ruskin's new aim of bringing the reader before and in the presence of a quite different kind of revelation of the 'Peace of God': namely, the divine 'manifested' in art.

Ruskin's feverish 'gathering together' of a 'mass of evidence from a number of subjects' which he described to his mother in a letter from Florence dated 26 June 1845 (*Works* IV, p. xxxiii), and which provided rich material for the new volume, followed two years – based mainly at Denmark Hill – of picture research, drafting, and desultory reading, including the art criticism of Alexis François Rio and Gustav Friedrich Waagen, the philosophy of Aristotle and Plato, and the Anglican writings of Richard Hooker, Jeremy Taylor and George Herbert. It was in September 1845, however, that Ruskin's overwhelming encounter with Tintoretto's huge religious paintings in the Scuola di S. Rocco in Venice – then neglected and little valued – finally provided the focus that the book needed, and material with which to illustrate 'Ideas of Beauty' and theories of the imagination which had been incubating ever since an earlier visit to Venice in 1841 (*Works* I, p. 451). This chapter examines the way in which Ruskin's interpretation of both 'Tintoret' – the artist who temporarily displaces Turner as his chief focus of attention in his critical writing – and Fra Angelico is shaped by a theology which emphasizes divine attributes such as symmetry and repose, and a Christian aesthetic which celebrates beauty rather than the sublime as the true manifestation of divine wisdom and sign of the hope of heaven. It demonstrates that in *Modern Painters* II Ruskin comes closer to a mainstream Anglican position than ever before or after, while remaining an Evangelical in doctrine and a Dissenter in independence of mind;[3] that his concepts of Theoria and the Imagination Penetrative enabled him to publish Protestant readings of Catholic art which even his Evangelical English readers could accept; and that already

Ruskin's religious beliefs – unusually, perhaps, for a man in his twenties – centre upon the God of peace.[4] Although his religious position was to change dramatically over time, this particular emphasis was to remain.

II

Ruskin declares early in *Modern Painters* II that 'Man's use and function ... are to be the witness of the glory of God and to advance that glory by his reasonable and resultant happiness' (*Works* IV, pp. 28–9).[5] Characteristically, however, the writing gains energy and momentum as an enraged Ruskin sets against this eternal ideal the present reality of a time when neglect and 'restoration' are destroying the monuments of Europe, and when 'the honour of God is thought to consist in the poverty of His temple' (*Works* IV, pp. 31–2). In arguing in the first edition that God did not teach men of old how to 'build for glory and for beauty' that 'we, *foul and sensual as we are*, might give the work of their poured-out spirit to the axe and the hammer' (*Works* IV, p. 32), Ruskin is carried to extremes of impassioned pulpit oratory, as the removal in the second edition of the words italicized here indicates. Although the phrase 'the axe and the hammer' is to be taken up later in the work, where Ruskin relates a Tintoretto to the ideal architecture of Solomon's temple, for the moment his invective against the restorers is set aside until his next book, *The Seven Lamps of Architecture*, as he turns to a discussion of 'the Christian Theoria' (*Works* IV, pp. 42–50) – later approvingly explained by Ruskin himself, in the language of seventeenth-century Protestant divines, as being ' "Contemplation" – seeing within the temple of the heart' (*Works* XXIX, p. 576).

In print, Ruskin answers his Oxford tutor's query about the 'cultivation of taste' being a fit life's work for a person on the Revd Osborne Gordon's own ground, through an argument which underpins all his later art teaching:

> true taste is for ever growing, learning, reading, worshipping, laying its hand upon its mouth because it is astonished, lamenting over itself, and testing itself by the way that it fits things. And it finds whereof to feed, and whereby to grow, in all things. The complaint so often heard from young artists, that

they have not within their reach materials or subjects enough for their fancy, is utterly groundless, and the sign only of their own blindness and inefficiency; for there is that to be seen in every street and lane of every city, – that to be felt and found in every human heart and countenance, – that to be loved in every roadside weed and moss-grown wall which, in the hands of faithful men, may convey emotions of glory and sublimity continual and exalted. (*Works* IV, p. 60)[6]

A statement which would have appealed to Charles Kingsley's Alton Locke, as further evidence of the democratization of Victorian culture,[7] also offered comfort to Tory High-Churchmen like Osborne, in its emphasis upon 'faithful men', and in the subsequent reference to George Herbert, that moderate Anglican poet who in *The Temple* finds his divine analogies in commonplace experience:

Let therefore the young artist beware of the spirit of Choice;* it is an insolent spirit at the best, and commonly a base and blind one too, checking all progress and blasting all power, encouraging weaknesses, pampering partialities, and teaching us to look to accidents of nature for the help and the joy which should come from our own hearts.

* 'Nothing comes amiss,
A good digestion turneth all to health.' – G. HERBERT.
(*Works* IV, p. 60)

Ruskin had used the metaphor of digestion himself, in correspondence with his mother on the tour of 1845. She packed Bunyan's *Grace Abounding* for him to read, when in fact he preferred Herbert – just as vigorous in his 'imagination' and 'communings', but having a 'well bridled & disciplined mind'; taught by God, not 'through his liver', like Bunyan, but 'through his brains'; and 'full of faith & love, regardless of himself'.[8] The 'Author of *Modern Painters*' is often sarcastic in his analysis of certain features of his early manhood that he wishes to leave behind, including the self-centred introspection that can characterize ultra-Protestant belief and practice.[9] Similarly, in volume II he expresses his embarrassment at having in volume I attributed 'too much community and authority' to his own taste for 'scenery inducing emotions of wild, impetuous, and enthusiastic characters, and too little to those which I perceive in others for things *peaceful*, humble, meditative, and solemn' (*Works* IV, p. 75; our emphasis). Whereas the youth sympathizes more with the 'gladness, fulness, and magnificence of things', he continues, 'grey hairs' sympathizes with their 'completion, sufficiency, and repose'. The 'signature of God' is 'upon His works', but we 'see not all'.

In turning to what he considers to be the six most significant kinds of Typical Beauty, Ruskin seems to align himself with the wisdom of 'grey hairs', several years before the appearance of his first, literal grey hair,[10] while at the same time asking the reader to 'enter upon the subject with [him], as far as may be, as a little child' (*Works* IV, p. 77), like those who wish to enter the kingdom of God (Mark 10.15). In the mid-1840s, a period in which he often expresses a sense of profound weariness,[11] Ruskin's God is the God of wisdom and of peace, whose home is in heaven and in the temple of the pure heart. The Typical Beauty of 'Moderation, or the Type of Government by Law', is strongly reminiscent of Hooker. 'Infinity, or the Type of Divine Incomprehensibility', is exemplified in the 'calm and luminous distance', and the 'still small voice of the level twilight behind purple hills' (*Works* IV, p. 80; 1 Kings 19.12). In defining 'Unity, or the Type of the Divine Comprehensiveness', Ruskin turns to Hooker's statement that 'All things, God only excepted, besides the nature which they have in themselves, receive externally some perfection from other things' (*Works* IV, p. 92),[12] and to Christ's farewell discourses in John's Gospel:

> the only unity which by any means can become grateful or an object of hope to men, and whose types therefore in material things can be beautiful, is that on which turned the last words and prayer of Christ before His crossing of the Kedron brook, 'Neither pray I for these alone, but for them also which shall believe on Me through their word; that they all may be one, as Thou, Father, art in Me, and I in Thee.'
>
> (*Works* IV, p. 92; John 17.20)

A natural progression from Christ's last words to his disciples is to Stephen's 'apology' before his martyrdom, echoed when Ruskin argues that 'the unity of matter is, in its noblest form, the organization of it which builds it up into temples for the spirit' (*Works* IV, p. 93; cf. Acts 7.48); the unity of 'earthly creatures' is 'their power and their peace'. 'Symmetry, or the

Type of Divine Justice' is swiftly dealt with, and exemplified in Tintoretto's *Crucifixion*, 'where not only the grouping, but the arrangement of light, is absolutely symmetrical': 'When there is no symmetry, the effects of passion and violence are increased, and many very sublime pictures derive their sublimity from the want of it, but they lose proportionally in the diviner quality of beauty' (*Works* IV, p. 127). In discussing 'Purity, or the Type of Divine Energy', Ruskin reminds the reader that the 'ocular delight in purity is mingled ... with the love of the mere element of light, as a type of wisdom and of truth' (*Works* IV, p. 130); in colour, 'pureness is made to us desirable, because expressive of that constant presence and energizing of the Deity by which all things live and move, and have their being' (*Works* IV, p. 133; Acts 17.28); in the 'Apocalyptic descriptions' it is the 'purity of every substance that fits it for its place in heaven' (*Works* IV, p. 134). Whereas the eschatological endings of so many chapters in later works by Ruskin emphasize divine judgement, 'Of purity' is characteristic of *Modern Painters* II in its closing emphasis upon the hope of heavenly peace, as described in the book of Revelation.

It is in the chapter entitled 'Of Repose, or the Type of Divine Permanence', however, that Ruskin's emphasis upon divine peace is most clearly revealed. First, the theological groundwork is carefully laid, with references to the ' "I am" of the Creator opposed to the "I become" of all creatures', to the divine wisdom ('the supreme knowledge which is incapable of surprise'), and to the 'labour' inflicted upon mankind at the Fall, from which a profound longing for rest originates: 'Hence the great call of Christ to men, that call on which St. Augustine fixed as the essential expression of Christian hope, is accompanied by the promise of rest [Matthew 11.28]; and the death bequest of Christ to men is peace [John 14.27]' (*Works* IV, p. 114).[13] In subsequent paragraphs, which Ruskin was later to regard as some of his best, he argues that repose 'demands for its expression the implied capability of its opposite, Energy', and cites as an example the faithful 'standing still' of the Israelites on the Red Sea shore – 'the quietness of action determined, of spirit unalarmed, of expectation unimpatient' (*Works* IV, p. 116; Exodus 14.13). Here is the Old Testament type of Christ's peace before 'crossing the Kedron brook', cited in the chapter on 'Unity' – a peace which in Ruskin's view is to be consummated in the crucifixion, as we will see in his discussion of Tintoretto. For the moment it is the wisdom attributed to Solomon in Proverbs – itself the type of Christ's teaching in Matthew – to which Ruskin refers in his comment that the 'paths of wisdom are all peace' (*Works* IV, p. 118; Proverbs 3.17, cf. Matthew 11.29–30).[14]

Turning to examples in art, Ruskin compares 'the convulsions of the Laocoon with the calmness of the Elgin Theseus' (*Works* IV, p. 119) – the result of research carried out in the British Museum when, in the autumn of 1844, he found himself 'necessarily thrown on the human figure' for many of his illustrations (*Works* IV, p. xxiii). The chapter concludes, however, with the fruits of a visit to the cathedral at Lucca the following year. In a famous passage he chooses the monument by Jacopo della Quercia to Ilaria di Caretto as 'furnishing an instance of the exact and right mean between the rigidity and rudeness of the earlier monumental effigies, and the morbid imitation of life, sleep, or death, of which the fashion has taken place in modern times' (*Works* IV, pp. 122–3). Many of Ruskin's later histories of architecture, sculpture and painting are to turn upon such moments of equipoise, which are always explained with reference to the moral and religious climate in which the work was produced. Here, however, another kind of equipoise is emphasized, for about the lips there is 'something which is not death nor sleep, but the pure image of both' (*Works* IV, p. 123). Writing at a time when poets and novelists were interested in the deathbed as an ambiguous site of interpretation – is this sleep or death? is death itself a 'sleep' from which there will be an awakening?[15] – Ruskin's own meditation on Ilaria is at once aesthetic and moral: 'If any of us, after staying for a time beside this tomb, could see, through his tears, one of the vain and unkind encumbrances of the grave, which, in these hollow and heartless days, feigned sorrow builds to foolish pride, he would, I believe, receive such a lesson of love as no coldness could refuse, no fatuity forget, and no insolence disobey' (*Works* IV, p. 124). Whereas at the end of Gray's *Elegy* the reader participates in the act of reading an imagined epitaph, Ruskin concludes his chapter with an imagined act of seeing, distorted through tears, which teaches the difference between the peace of God and man's foolish pride – for Ruskin the root cause of the 'fall' in the

Renaissance. Poised between sleep and death, the effigy of Ilaria exhibits that power of repose that comes from a sense of former life and movement, but which for Ruskin remains, like the 'forms of the limbs', safely 'concealed'. Shunning studio life drawings, he makes his own private studies – written and graphic – in peace, from the draped figure of the classical and medieval sculptor.

In the last chapters of section I, 'Of the Theoretic Faculty', where Ruskin defines varieties of 'Vital Beauty', he adumbrates a number of themes – redemption, the ministry of angels, the wisdom of Solomon – which are to be developed in his interpretation of Tintoretto and Fra Angelico later in the volume. Vital beauty in man is discussed in the light of the Fall (*Works* IV, p. 177) – the subject of a sermon by the Revd Henry Melvill on Ash Wednesday 1844 that Ruskin found 'valuable' (*Diaries*, p. 266). The results of the 'Adamite curse', Ruskin argues, can be seen not only in the human frame and face, but also in the 'suffering of Christ himself' and the 'uncomprehended pain' of the angels, as they 'try and try again in vain, whether they may not warm hard hearts with the brooding of their kind wings' (*Works* IV, p. 186). Solomon, whom Thomas Scott describes in the famous commentary that we know Ruskin used as being 'deeply versed in all the branches of natural philosophy', and who 'discoursed in an admirable manner upon the nature, properties, and uses of the several species of plants and animals',[16] is identified as the type of Christ in his writing on the lower creatures:

> And so what lesson we might receive for our earthly conduct from the creeping and laborious things, was taught us by that earthly King who made silver to be in Jerusalem as stones [1 Kings 10.27] (yet thereafter was less rich toward God). But from the lips of a heavenly King, who had not where to lay His head [Matthew 8.20], we were taught what lesson we have to learn from those higher creatures who sow not, nor reap, nor gather into barns, for their Heavenly Father feedeth them [Matthew 6.26]. (*Works* IV, pp. 156–7)

Towards the end of chapter 14, 'Of Vital Beauty in Man', however, Ruskin quotes Hooker on the penetrative nature of the wisdom of Solomon: he was 'eminent above others, for he gave good heed, and *pierced* everything to the very ground'

(*Works* IV, p. 206; our emphasis). The section ends with a resonant piece of apocalyptic where the final emphasis is upon the promise that his servants shall see God:

> but this we know, that there will come a time when the service of God shall be the beholding of Him; and though in these stormy seas where we are now driven up and down, His Spirit is dimly seen on the face of the waters [Genesis 1.2], and we are left to cast anchors out of the stern, and wish for the day [Acts 27.29], that day will come, when, with the evangelists on the crystal and stable sea, all the creatures of God shall be full of eyes within [Revelation 4.6,8], and there shall be 'no more curse, but His servants shall serve Him, and shall see His face [Revelation 22.3–4].' (*Works* IV, p. 218)

In closing section I, Ruskin opens up ideas and metaphors with which he is going to work in that echo chamber of a chapter entitled 'Of Imagination Penetrative' – the longest and the most remarkable in section II, and indeed in the book.

III

Ruskin's reference at the beginning of the chapter to Milton's Leviathan in Book I of *Paradise Lost* (*Works* IV, pp. 249–50) not only echoes the nautical biblical references at the end of section I but also, through its whaling associations, prepares for the metaphor of 'piercing' through which the Imagination Penetrative – 'the highest intellectual power of man' – is to be described and illustrated. First the (startling) description: 'There is no reasoning in it; it works not by algebra, nor by integral calculus; it is a piercing pholas-like[17] mind's tongue, that works and tastes into the very rock heart; no matter what be the subject submitted to it, substance or spirit; all is alike divided asunder, joint and marrow, whatever utmost truth, life, principle it has, laid bare' (*Works* IV, p. 251). Following a number of literary examples of fancy and imagination, Ruskin invites the reader to compare a passage from 'Solomon's Song, where the imagination stays not at the outside, but dwells on the fearful emotion itself': 'Who is she that looketh forth as the morning; fair as the moon, clear as the sun, and terrible as an army with banners?' (*Works* IV, p. 257; Song of Solomon 6.10). The Authorized Version gives as a running head to this chapter,

'The church professeth her faith in Christ'; and Bishop Christopher Wordsworth, who finds in the enigmatic qualities of the Song 'a striking resemblance to its Christian counterpart, the Book of Revelation', comments that the question 'seems to be asked by a chorus of faithful friends, who behold the Bride coming': 'The question denotes wonder and admiration ... at her glorious appearance, after the ill-treatment to which she had been exposed in searching for Christ'; her banner is 'the blood of the Lamb (Rev.xii.11), shed on the cross'.[18]

The pacific nature of Ruskin's Christian aesthetic is then brought to bear upon the contrast between fancy and imagination, which he figures as 'being at the heart of things' as she 'poises herself there, and is still, quiet, and brooding, comprehending all around her with her fixed look' (*Works* IV, p. 258). Yet the things comprehended by that fixed look are often violent. Whereas in Retsch's fanciful illustrations to Schiller's *Kampf mit dem Drachen* we have the dragon 'from the beginning of his career to the end' and yet 'have never got into the dragon heart', in Turner's 'Jason' in the *Liber Studiorum* we 'have the dragon, like everything else, by the middle', through a kind of *ars negativa*: 'No far forest country, no secret path, nor cloven hills ... No flaunting plumes nor brandished lances, but stern purpose in the turn of the crestless helmet, visible victory in the drawing back of the prepared right arm behind the steady point' (*Works* IV, p. 259–60). In this, the first of a series of interpretations in which Ruskin employs in his descriptive prose the same Imagination Penetrative that he is analysing in a picture, the series of negatives and the synecdochic 'steady point' represent linguistically the engraving's absences – the former balanced by the trunks of the trees on the right in which Turner is said to address 'that morbid and fearful condition of mind which he has endeavoured to excite in the spectator, and which in reality would have seen in every trunk and bough, as it penetrated into the deeper thicket, the object of its terror'.

Tintoretto's *Annunciation* is also first described through a series of negatives, in this case in contrast with Fra Angelico's *Annunciation* in the convent of St Mark's. The Virgin is portrayed 'not in the quiet loggia, not by the green pasture of the restored soul' as in Fra Angelico's 'pure vision', but 'houseless, under the shelter of a palace vestibule ruined and abandoned, with the noise of the axe and the hammer in her ears' (*Works* IV, p. 264). The biblical echo suggests a further contrast between this ruin and Solomon's temple, 'built of stone made ready before it was brought thither: so that there was neither hammer nor axe nor any tool of iron heard in the house, while it was in building' (1 Kings 6.7),[19] which in turn prepares for the clinching evidence of Tintoretto's Imagination Penetrative in the foreground detail: the 'stone which the builders refused is become the Headstone of the Corner' (Psalm 118.22), a text which Christ quotes in his teaching to his disciples (Mark 12.10, etc.).

Tintoretto's 'wild thought' might seem, then, to be the perfect demonstration of Ruskin's earlier observation that 'the Theoretic faculty takes out of everything that which is beautiful, while the Imaginative faculty takes hold of the very imperfections which the Theoretic rejects; and, by means of these angles and roughnesses, it joints and bolts the separate stones into a mighty temple, wherein the Theoretic faculty, in its turn, does deepest homage' (*Works* IV, p. 241). Yet the 'force of the thought hardly atones for the painfulness of the scene and the turbulence of the feelings' (*Works* IV, p. 265), and the picture is set aside in favour of the *Baptism of Christ*. But the most 'exquisite instance of this imaginative power', Ruskin argues, occurs in an incident in the background of the *Crucifixion* (*Works* IV, p. 270). Even when, in the first flush of enthusiasm, Ruskin had described the work in its own dynamic terms when writing home in September 1845 – Tintoretto 'lashes out like a leviathan, and heaven and earth come together' – he felt that the true 'master's stroke' was his 'touch of quiet thought': 'there is an *ass* in the distance, feeding on the remains of strewed palm leaves'.[20] In the text the emphasis falls even more heavily upon two touches of quiet thought. Having first eschewed his own powers of rhetoric – 'I will not insult this marvellous picture by an effort at a verbal account of it' – he approaches the core of his subject by establishing what it is not ('the common and most Catholic treatment of the subject'), and then dramatizing in his prose the painter's use of the Imagination Penetrative in the displacement of muscular exertion from the crucified to the crucifying:

> penetrating into the root and deep places of his subject,
> despising all outward and bodily appearances of pain, and

seeking for some means of expressing, not the rack of nerve or sinew, but the fainting of the deserted Son of God before His Eloi cry, and yet feeling himself utterly unequal to the expression of this by the countenance, has, on the one hand, filled his picture with such various and impetuous muscular exertion, that the body of the Crucified is, by comparison, in perfect repose, and, on the other, has cast the countenance altogether into shade. But the Agony is told by this, and by this only; that, though there yet remains a chasm of light on the mountain horizon where the earthquake darkness closes upon the day, the broad and sunlike glory about the head of the Redeemer has become wan, *and of the colour of ashes.* (*Works* IV, pp. 270–1)[21]

Here is the 'manifested Deity' in the 'perfect repose' of the Atonement. At the heart of his chapter on the Imagination Penetrative, defined as that which pierces to the middle of a subject, dividing asunder, 'joint and marrow', Ruskin focuses upon the restraint and moderation of Tintoretto's treatment of the crucified Christ before he is pierced by the spear, where divine power and glory are signified, not through the coming earthquake darkness, but through a divine repose which also figures its harrowing 'opposite, Energy' in the saving agony of the cross.

A sudden rhetorical turn then draws our attention to 'something more' the 'great painter' felt he had to do yet, as Ruskin again uses negative constructions: 'Not only that Agony of the Crucified, but the tumult of the people ... Not only the brutality of the soldier ... but the fury of His own people, the noise against Him of those for whom He died, were to be set before the eye of the understanding, if the power of the picture was to be complete.' After the rhetorical fire, a still small voice, as the reader, already reflecting on the penitential colour of ashes, is directed to the palm-leaves which the 'multitude' – common humanity – had strewed in Christ's path on his entry to Jerusalem:

In the shadow behind the cross, a man, riding on an ass colt, looks back to the multitude, while he points with a rod to the Christ crucified. The ass is feeding on the *remnants* of *withered palm-leaves.*

With this 'master's stroke' – also privately recorded in a careful copy of the original – Ruskin believes he may 'terminate all illustration of the peculiar power of the imagination over the feelings of the spectator'. He has not, however, 'sufficiently dwelt on the fact from which this power arises, the absolute truth of statement of the central fact as it was, or must have been' (*Works* IV, p. 272). Thus in the *Massacre of the Innocents* there is 'no blood, no stabbing or cutting, but there is an awful substitute for these in the chiaroscuro': 'It is a woman, sitting quiet, – quite quiet, – still as any stone; she looks down steadfastly on her dead child, laid along on the floor before her, and her hand is pressed softly upon her brow' (*Works* IV, p. 273). And only in Tintoretto's *Last Judgment* has this 'unimaginable event been grappled with in its Verity; not typically nor symbolically, but as they may see it who shall not sleep, but be changed' (*Works* IV, p. 277; 1 Corinthians 15.51) – a power also evident in Michelangelo, who in the Sistine Chapel would 'pierce deeper yet' and 'see the indwelling angels' (*Works* IV, pp. 280–1).

Angels are also Ruskin's subject in the final chapter of *Modern Painters* II, 'Of the Superhuman Ideal', in which he defines four ways in which 'Beings supernatural may be conceived as manifesting themselves to human sense' – always in the 'form of some creature to us known' (*Works* IV, pp. 314–15). Fra Angelico is valued for his 'reserve and subjection' (*Works* IV, p. 317) and for his 'purity of colour almost shadow less' in painting angel forms (*Works* IV, p. 323). And it is with his angels that the final paragraph concludes:

> With what comparison shall we compare the types of the martyr saints; the St. Stephen of Fra Bartolomeo, with his calm forehead crowned by the stony diadem, or the St. Catherine of Raffaelle looking up to heaven in the dawn of the eternal day, with her lips parted in the resting from her pain; or with what the Madonnas of Francia and Pinturicchio, in whom the hues of the morning and the solemnity of eve, the gladness in accomplished promise, and sorrow of the sword-pierced heart, are gathered into one human Lamp of ineffable love? or with what the angel choirs of Angelico, with the flames on their white foreheads waving brighter as they move, and the sparkles streaming from their purple wings like the glitter of many suns upon a sounding sea, listening in the pauses of alternate song, for the prolonging of the trumpet blast, and the answering of psaltery and cymbal, throughout the endless deep, and from all the star shores of heaven? (*Works* IV, pp. 331–2)

Ruskin was later to be embarrassed by this 'honest canticle', which read 'more like a piece of Mrs Jameson' than of him (*Works* IV, p. 331). It is true that celebratory comparisons between a number of artists in their representations of one subject are frequent in *Sacred and Legendary Art* by Anna Jameson, whose *Early Italian Painters* had appeared in 1845.[22] Unlike her, however, Ruskin has prepared for his Dantesque evocation of heavenly peace – '*calm* forehead', '*resting* from her pain', '*solemnity* of eve', '*pauses* of alternate song' – through the painstaking writing of a Christian aesthetic and detailed analysis of religious art in the main body of his text. And even in this last canticle, the power of the Penetrative Imagination is suggested in what Ruskin would call the 'central fact' of the Madonna's 'sword-*pierced* heart'.

Furthermore, Ruskin's remarkable knowledge of the Bible, and his already long experience of hearing biblical exegesis delivered from a variety of pulpits in South London, the fashionable West End, and Oxford, equipped him with critical tools which were far more sophisticated that Anna Jameson's, and which were now applied to religious art that repaid his attention, in that they actually emulated the richness of the Bible.[23] Thus it was that Ruskin could justify his work on Italian Catholic art, not only to his father and to himself, but also to his Protestant English readers. Whereas the 'turbulence' of Tintoretto might prove to be too strong for English tastes, one of the master's 'quiet thoughts' could speak clearly of the peace of God which passes all understanding. For, crucial as the glory and the power are to Ruskin's understanding of the nature of God, and of his signature upon the creation, throughout *Modern Painters*, it is the peace of God – 'the death bequest of Christ to men' – and the hope of heaven – in which Fra Angelico's paintings strengthened his belief[24] – that inform the theology of *Modern Painters* II, and much of what followed in later years.

Notes

1. The volume contains Part III of *Modern Painters* – 'Of Ideas of Beauty'.
2. For a detailed analysis of the passage and its omission see C. Stephen Finley, *Nature's Covenant: Figures of Landscape in Ruskin* (University Park, Pa.: Pennsylvania State University Press, 1992), pp.177–9.
3. The specifically Evangelical content of a work which describes humanity as

'creatures in probation' (*Works* IV, p. 61) was to embarrass Ruskin later in life, although the harshness of some of the self-deprecating notes on his youthful 'insolence' which he added to the 'rearranged' edition of 1883 also reflects the effect upon his judgement of several major mental breakdowns from 1878. One reviewer of the first edition detected a 'serious spirituality about it; a *wresting*, if we may be permitted the expression, of all things in Nature to the glory of Nature's God, which would win for it the title of *Religio Pictoris* – for it is in very truth the religion of painting': '*Modern Painters*. Vol.II', *The Church of England Quarterly Review* 20 (July 1846), pp. 205–14 (p. 206). Another went further, saying that in volume II Ruskin 'still assumes art to be nothing but an auxiliary to the Church and to the Religious Tract Society': '*Modern Painters*, Second edition, and Vol. II', *The Foreign Quarterly Review* 37 (July 1846), pp. 380–416 (p. 403). This last reference to 'the Church', however, gives the clue to what is in fact a broader Anglican background to Ruskin's Evangelicalism in *Modern Painters* than has previously been recognized.

4. For a more detailed treatment of the subject, including discussion of the influence of Hooker upon *Modern Painters* II, see Michael Wheeler, *Ruskin's God* (Cambridge: Cambridge University Press, 1999), ch. 3.

5. In Finley's view, Ruskin 'became perhaps the nineteenth century's foremost "theologian" of the *Deus gloriosus*, practicing the *theologia gloriae* with lavish gifts of heart and hand and eye' (*Nature's Convent*, p. 44).

6. Cook and Wedderburn miss the hyperbolic variant reading in the first edition: 'astonished, casting its shoes from off its feet because it finds all ground holy, lamenting' (omitted in the second edition).

7. See *Alton Locke: Tailor and Poet* (1850), ch. 9, 'Poetry and poets'.

8. See *Ruskin in Italy: Letters to His Parents, 1845*, ed. Harold I. Shapiro (Oxford: Clarendon, 1972), pp.17–18, 33; see also Ruskin's comment on a view of religion as a 'particular phase of indigestion', p. 34. Cf. *Works* XXXV, pp. 344–5. John Brown wrote of 'repose' in volume II, 'The theology, natural and revealed, as well as the poetry of this, we have in George Herbert', quoting 'The Pulley': '*Modern Painters*. 2 vols.', *The North British Review* 6 (February 1847), pp. 401–30 (p. 424).

9. In *Praeterita* Ruskin states that he 'received' his religion from Bunyan and Isaac Ambrose, the Puritan divine (*Works* XXXV, p. 490).

10. On the morning of 2 September 1850 – his mother's birthday: Lancaster MS 5c, Diaries, fols 151–2; cf. *Diaries*, p. 466.

11. See, for example, *Works* IV, p. 134 n. and *Diaries*, p. 258. Symptoms akin to those of manic depression, or bipolar disorder, are present from Ruskin's adolescence onwards, including the period following the completion of *Modern Painters* I.

12. See *The Works of that Learned and Judicious Divine Mr. Richard Hooker: With an Account of his Life and Death by Isaac Walton*, ed. John Keble, 3 vols (Oxford: Oxford University Press, 1836), I, p. 317.

13. Cf. the commentary which Ruskin used: 'Our Lord being about to die, and leave his disciples, bequeathed to them "his peace" as a legacy': *The Holy Bible*, with explanatory notes, practical observations, and copious marginal references by Thomas Scott, 9th edn, 6 vols (London: Seeley, 1825), V, John 14.27. The last words of Ruskin's pamphlet, *Notes on the Construction of Sheepfolds* (1851) are those of Christ to his Church: 'My peace I leave with you' (*Works* XII, p. 558).

14. Thomas Scott offers the cross-reference in his marginal notes: see Scott, *Holy Bible* III, Proverbs 3.17. Not until 1853 did Ruskin notice that Solomon meant 'peaceable' (*Diaries*, p. 481).

15. See Michael Wheeler, *Death and the Future Life in Victorian Literature and Theology* (Cambridge: Cambridge University Press, 1990), pp. 35–41.

16. Scott, *Holy Bible* II, 1 Kings 4.30–4.

17. Like a sea mollusc that makes holes in stones.

18. *The Holy Bible*, with Notes and Introductions by Chr[istopher] Wordsworth, 6 vols (London: Rivingtons, 1864–70), IV, pt III, pp. 125, 148.
19. Cf. 'No hammer's clang, nor axe's pond'rous din, | Disturbs the Temple's majesty within, | In silent dignity the grand design | Starts into beauty, from deep wisdom's mine . . .': Charles J. Champneys, *The Temple of Solomon, and Poems on Scriptural and other Subjects* (Glasgow: Smith, 1848), p. 3.
20. Shapiro, *Ruskin in Italy*, p. 212.
21. The capitalized '*His* Eloi cry' was not substituted for 'his' until 1883, in the edition 're-arranged in two volumes, and revised by the author'.
22. Having met her in Venice in September 1845, Ruskin tells his father that Anna Jameson 'has some tact & cleverness, & knows as much of art as the cat': Shapiro, *Ruskin in Italy*, pp. 215–16.
23. Ruskin sensed this when he wrote to his father from Pisa on 15 May 1845: 'I have been drawing from Benozzo's life of Abraham, which is as full & abundant as the scripture itself – *nothing* missed, though a good deal added': Shapiro, *Ruskin in Italy*, p. 65.
24. Ruskin wrote to his mother from Florence on 9 June 1845: 'the fact is, I really *am* getting more pious than I was, owing primarily to George Herbert, who is the only religious person I ever could understand or agree with, and secondarily to Fra Angelico & Benozzo Gozzoli, who make one believe everything they paint, be it ever so out of the way' (Shapiro, *Ruskin in Italy*, p. 108).

References

Cook, E. T. and Wedderburn, Alexander (eds), *The Works of John Ruskin*, Library Edition, 39 vols (London: Allen; New York: Longmans, Green, 1903–12). Cited as *Works* in the text.

Evans, Joan and Whitehouse, John Howard (eds), *The Diaries of John Ruskin*, 3 vols. (Oxford: Clarendon, 1956–59). Cited as *Diaries* in the text.

Anon., 'Modern Painters. Vol. II', *The Church of England Quarterly Review* 20 (July 1846), pp. 205–14

Anon., 'Modern Painters, Second edition, and Vol. II', *The Foreign Quarterly Review* 37 (July 1846), pp. 380–416

[Brown, John], 'Modern Painters. 2 vols.', *The North British Review* 6 (February 1847), pp. 401–30

Champneys, Charles J., *The Temple of Solomon, and Poems on Scriptural and other Subjects* (Glasgow: Smith, 1848)

Finley, Stephen, *Nature's Covenant: Figures of Landscape in Ruskin* (University Park, Pa.: Pennsylvania State University Press, 1992)

Hooker, Richard, *The Works of that Learned and Judicious Divine Mr. Richard Hooker: With an Account of his Life and Death by Isaac Walton*, ed. John Keble, 3 vols (Oxford: Oxford University Press, 1836)

Ruskin, John, Lancaster MS 5c, Diaries. Ruskin Foundation, Ruskin Library (Lancaster University)

Scott, Thomas, *The Holy Bible*, with explanatory notes, practical observations, and copious marginal references by Thomas Scott, 9th edn, 6 vols (London: Seeley, 1825)

Shapiro, Harold I. (ed.), *Ruskin in Italy: Letters to His Parents, 1845* (Oxford: Clarendon, 1972)

Wheeler, Michael, *Death and the Future Life in Victorian Literature and Theology* (Cambridge: Cambridge University Press, 1990)

Wheeler, Michael, *Ruskin's God* (Cambridge: Cambridge University Press, 1999)

Wordsworth, Christopher, *The Holy Bible*, with Notes and Introductions by Chr[istopher] Wordsworth, 6 vols (London: Rivingtons, 1864–70)

13

'Naming Our Host': Eucharist and Apocalypse in *The Time Machine*

Kevin Mills

... a myth is always, openly or implicitly, connected with religion, and the religion of the modern city is precise science.[1]

Introduction

In *The Time Machine* (1895), H. G. Wells describes the world in the year 802,701, as seen by a time traveller. The latter discovers that the human race has evolved into two separate species, one of which (the Morlocks) preys upon the other (the Eloi).[2] Both of these names have biblical resonances. The 'Morlocks' seem to have been named after Moloch (or Molech) – the god of the Ammonites – to whom, the Bible tells us, children were sacrificed by fire (see, for example, Leviticus 18.21, 2 Kings 23.10). The name 'Eloi' recalls Christ's words on the cross: 'Eloi, Eloi, lama sabachthani' ('My God, my God, why have you forsaken me'?). At the most basic level, these biblical connections alert the reader to the God-forsakenness of the Eloi, and to the predatory character of the Morlocks, implying that the relationship between the two species is one of blood-sacrifice. But, far from constituting a religious or soteriological system, the sacrifice of the Eloi takes place in a time when any redemptive possibilities have long since become obsolete. The post-religious slaughter of the sub-human innocents in 802,701 emphasizes the message that evolutionary theory, by removing the teleological imperative from human

development, has denied the world any apocalyptic consummation. When the Time Traveller voyages to the end of the world,
after leaving 802,701, this important anti-apocalyptic aspect of
the novella appears even more clearly. There he encounters a
world too cold to support life, dying in a 'remote and awful
twilight' (p. 76). The then-new science of thermodynamics gave
grounds for just this kind of scientific eschatology: its
formulation of the law of entropy predicted that the universe
would eventually reach an inhospitable mean temperature, and
that, consequently, all life would be extinguished.

The novella's allusive nomenclature demythologizes the
world's end, and, simultaneously, replaces the substitutionary
death of Christ with an evolutionary version of sacrifice. Peter
Kemp points out that Wells often draws attention in his work to
'the fact that life consists in battening, that in order for one
organism to survive another must be sacrificed'.[3] As sacrificial
victims of the struggle for survival, the strategically named Eloi
embody the contrast between sacrifice as an evolutionary
principle and as a religious value, and their plight subordinates
one of Christianity's central themes to the Darwinian principle
of the survival of the fittest. While Jesus taught that 'the meek
shall inherit the earth', natural selection – the cumulative effect
of infinitesimal beneficial adaptations in organisms – can be seen
as determining a very different outcome. T. H. Huxley argued
that 'the followers of the "golden rule" ['Do as you would be
done by'] may indulge in hopes of heaven, but they must reckon
with the certainty that other people will be masters of the earth.'[4]
The sacrifice of the Eloi to the nutritional needs of the Morlocks
clearly reflects this Huxleyan challenge to Christ's teaching.
Wells, who studied under Huxley for a short time, envisaged an
epoch in the distant future during which the subterranean,
darkness-loving Morlocks would inherit the earth by brute force,
subjugating the physically weaker Eloi. In this formulation, the
Christian, biblical account of human history, the axial point of
which is the crucifixion of Jesus, is sacrificed to the anti-
apocalyptic evolutionary narrative.

The twin facts that the Eloi are named in memory of the
broken body of Christ, and that they exist only to be eaten,
should alert the reader to the eucharistic tone in certain
passages of Wells's novella. Working this eucharistic element
into an eschatological story, *The Time Machine* recalls the

profoundly futural character of Christianity's central ritual. Jesus's words at the Last Supper (the model for later eucharistic celebrations) establish this tone: 'I will not drink henceforth of this fruit of the vine, *until that day* when I drink it new with you in my Father's kingdom' (Matthew 26.29 – my emphasis). Christian tradition has, since the earliest times, viewed the crucifixion as an eschatological event, one which guaranteed the eventual establishment of God's kingdom on earth. The writer to the Hebrews asserts: 'once *in the end of the world* hath he appeared to put away sin by the sacrifice of himself' (Hebrews 9.26b – my emphasis). That the act of remembering the crucifixion in the eucharist is also an anticipatory gesture is evident from Paul's first letter to the Corinthian church: 'For as often as ye eat this bread, and drink this cup, ye do show the Lord's death *till he come*' (1 Corinthians 11.26 – my emphasis).

In exploring these biblical themes in *The Time Machine*, I aim to show that despite Wells's supplanting of the Bible's temporal horizon with a non-apocalyptic vision of the world's end (based on evolutionary theory and thermodynamics), his (ironic) deployment of eucharistic and apocalyptic motifs disrupts this vision, turning it back towards a biblical end.

The Time Traveller's Last Supper

That Wells was obsessed with eating and drinking (as well as with the shape of future kingdoms), has been shown by Peter Kemp, with great zest and with more than a little scholarly stamina. In *H. G. Wells and the Culminating Ape*, he offers nearly seventy pages of examples, from an impressive array of Wellsian sources, depicting a vast textual larder of 'memorable meals and toothsome moments garnished with odd eatables'.[5] At one point in this extended literary menu, he notes Wells's dislike of what the latter referred to as Christianity's ceremonial 'God-eating', and 'symbolical cannibalism'.[6] But he also provides abundant evidence of Wells's abiding fascination with human edibility to a variety of predators. Wells's qualms about Christianity's prandial rite may well be reflected in the approximation of cannibalism in *The Time Machine* (one post-human species preys upon another), as well as in the fact that those consumed bear the name 'Eloi'.

Kemp, for all his dogged persistence in exposing Wells's food fetishism (including his squeamish response to Holy Communion, and his contrasting relish of predatory instincts), does not point out the eucharistic undertones of *The Time Machine*. The novella begins in an 'after-dinner atmosphere' (p. 3), with a group of men sitting around a fire in the house of the Time Traveller. The following Thursday, over another dinner at the same house, tales of the year 802,701, and of the final setting of the sun are recounted. On this latter occasion, the guests have to begin their meal in the absence of the host: ' "It's half-past seven now," said the Medical Man. "I suppose we'd better have dinner?" "Where's – ?" said I, naming our host' (pp. 11–12). By virtue of its paradoxical character – not naming the host while referring to the act of naming him – the phrase draws attention to itself as a strategy of evasion, applying the name-avoiding word 'host' to its subject for the first and only time. The rhetorical gesture, which both names and fails to name the host, raises the linked questions of his identity and of the significance of his absence. Since the appellation 'host' marks both an absence with which the guests are preoccupied, and an expectation of imminent return, it allows the reader to hear a eucharistic tone in the description of this all-male supper, so that 'naming our host' may be a matter of identifying the Time Traveller with Christ.

The eucharistic meaning of the word 'host' (i.e. the bread or wafer which represents the broken body of Christ) may be no more than a faint echo here, but its resonance is strengthened by elements of the description of the Time Traveller when he eventually arrives: 'His face was ghastly pale; his chin had a brown cut on it – a cut half healed; his expression was haggard and drawn as by intense suffering ... I saw his feet as he went out. He had nothing on them but a pair of tattered, bloodstained socks' (pp. 12–13). The registering of intense suffering in the host's face, and the reference to his bloodied feet, contribute to the paschal tone of the meal. As he sits at the dinner table, his consumption of wine and meat are stressed, recalling the bread (symbolically, the *body* of Christ) and wine consumed in the eucharist. That there is some kind of sacramental aspect to the all-male dinner party is suggested by the gradual change in the Time Traveller's appearance as the meal progresses. His initial battered, bruised and bloodstained form recovers in phases. The change begins with the first glass of wine: 'He drained it, and it seemed to do him good: for he looked around the table, and the ghost of his old smile flickered across his face' (p. 12). His second glass enhances this effect: 'His eyes grew brighter, and a faint colour came into his cheeks' (p. 13). The final moment of restoration comes after he has been 'to wash and dress': 'He was dressed in ordinary evening clothes, and nothing save his haggard look remained of the change that had startled me' (p. 14). Washing and reclothing, of course, are extremely important metaphors in Christian soteriology; the book of Revelation associates both with Christ's death: 'These ... have washed their robes, and made them white in the blood of the lamb' (Revelation 7.14),

The 'ghost of his old smile' (along with two other 'ghost' references in the brief opening section of the framing narrative), and his generally altered visage, combine to give the Time Traveller something of the look of a revenant. With these passional and eucharistic parallels in mind, it is not difficult to understand the symbolism of his temporal exit from 802,701, made from the interior of a suggestively *cruciform* structure. The Morlocks have hidden his time machine inside the pedestal of a great White Sphinx which he has earlier described thus: 'the wings, instead of being carried vertically at the sides, were spread so that it seemed to hover' (p. 19). Alongside these eucharistic memorials of the crucifixion and resurrection of Christ, several incidents in the Johannine account of Jesus's post-resurrection appearances are also evoked by the description of the Time Traveller's return. His demand for meat, parallels Jesus's question to Peter and Thomas on the shore of the Sea of Tiberias: 'Children, have ye any meat?' (John 21.5). The distant air of the Time Traveller, as he refuses to answer any questions until he has eaten, might be compared with Jesus's strange insistence, on the morning of the resurrection, that he should not be touched (John 20.17). Again, the altered appearance of the returned Time Traveller, which shocks the narrator, and which gives rise to vaguely comic suggestions that he may be playing the 'Amateur Cadger', or moonlighting as a crossing sweeper (p. 13), bears comparison with the post-resurrection change in Jesus, marked by Mary Magdalene's failure to recognize him and by her mistaking him for a gardener (John 20.15). The Time Traveller's promise to make a

revelatory return, contributes an extra detail to the effect: '...
I'll come down and explain things' (p. 13).

The eucharistic affinities of Time Traveller's last supper (we
know from the end of the novella that it was the last of his
Thursday-night gatherings) are not a matter of straightforward
allusion. Some features of the story suggest that the Christic
parallels are parodic. Clearly, his longing for meat aligns the
Time Traveller (and, by association, the risen Christ?) with the
flesh-eating Morlocks, *against* whom he has fought on the side
of the vegetarian Eloi. This seemingly unconscious affinity with
his elective enemies is emphasized by his being 'dazzled by the
light' as he enters the dining room (p. 12): the Morlocks, who
only emerge from their underground lair at night, are similarly
dazzled both by daylight and by the Time Traveller's matches.
Furthermore, the latter responds in kind to the violence of the
Morlocks, even admitting, at one point, that he 'longed very
much to kill a Morlock or so' (p. 60). A little later he confesses
that he would not have been averse to attacking a few more of
them with his rod of iron: 'I threw my iron bar away, almost
sorry not to use it' (p. 70). John Huntington writes: 'Even when
he meets the Eloi, the Time Traveller's first thoughts are
violent: "They looked so frail that I could fancy flinging the
whole dozen of them about like nine-pins." '[7] On the other
hand, the Eloi, while they conform to a Christian image of the
'gentle Jesus', are completely unable to save themselves. It is
only by replicating the Morlocks' aggression, and by exceeding
their predatory violence, that the Time Traveller can hope to
escape being identified with the Eloi in their death.

The Time Traveller's Christic qualities, and his defence of
the helpless Eloi, combine with his Morlock-like belligerence
and hunger for meat, to produce a range of characteristics
which confront Christian values (such as meekness, charity and
a belief in divine providence), with 'Nature red in tooth and
claw'.[8] But, while this might be understood as a critique of
Christianity, inspired by Huxleyan evolutionism, it also reflects
the Gospels' own depiction of Christ: on the one hand, he
appears as a compassionate healer and as a teacher of
forgiveness; on the other hand, he is described as the outraged
scourge of temple-defiling money-changers.[9] The division of his
actions, between aid and aggression, is matched by the double
rhetoric in which he proclaims the coming kingdom of God – a

rhetoric which combines pacific with violent figures, sometimes in the same discourse:

> Think not that I am come to send peace on earth: I came not to send peace, but a sword. For I am come to set a man at variance against his father, and the daughter against her mother ... whosoever shall give to drink unto one of these little ones a cup of cold water only in the name of a disciple ... he shall in no wise lose his reward.   (Matthew 10.34–42)

This duality is encoded in Revelation's vision of the Lion and the Lamb – images of Christ as both predator and prey: 'And one of the elders saith unto me, Weep not: behold the Lion of the tribe of Juda ... And I beheld ... a Lamb as it had been slain ...'(Revelation 5.5–6).

The Time Traveller's Apocalypse

Although *The Time Machine* employs little overt biblical allusion, Bernard Bergonzi sees in it various mythical elements, some of which are drawn from Christian lore. The Time Traveller's descent into the unlit, underground domain of the Morlocks, he says, 'suggests a parody of the Harrowing of Hell, where it is not the souls of the just that are released but the demonic Morlocks, for it is they who dominate the subsequent narrative'.[10] But it may be that there is another, more specifically apocalyptic, layer of allusion here. The opening up of the underworld, and the release of the creatures of the darkness has a parallel in Revelation 9.1–3:

> I saw a star fall from heaven unto the earth: and to him was given the key of the bottomless pit. And he opened the bottomless pit; and there arose a smoke out of the pit, as the smoke of a great furnace; and the sun and the air were darkened by reason of the smoke of the pit. And there came out of the smoke locusts upon the earth; and unto them was given power, as the scorpions of the earth have power.

A number of details in this passage have echoes in events which the Time Traveller describes as taking place subsequent to his venturing below the surface. As a direct result of the emergence of the Morlocks, a forest is engulfed by fire and by 'masses of black smoke' (p. 68). Eventually, having moved further into the future, the Time Traveller also witnesses the darkening of the sun and the air, at the end of time: '. . . the pale stars alone were visible. All else was rayless obscurity. The sky was absolutely black' (p. 75)

If such resonances are faint and need to be teased out. *The Time Machine*'s one explicit reference to the Bible has a clearly apocalyptic tone. It occurs early on, when one of the Time Traveller's guests, pondering his host's dishevelled appearance, wonders if he has 'his Nebuchadnezzar phases' (p. 13). The reference is to the book of Daniel – the one example of a fully apocalyptic text included in the Old Testament. As Patrick Parrinder has pointed out, the figure of Nebuchadnezzar's sojourn amongst the beasts of the field can be read as 'a prophetic parable of human destiny', foreshadowing the evolutionary decline of humanity, and implying the possibility that another species will eventually upsurp our dominant place.[11] This association of the Time Traveller with Neb-uchadnezzar neatly summarizes Wells's project of rewriting the End. In his essay 'Zoological regression' (1891), he refers to the 'Coming Beast' as a creature who may 'rise in the fulness of time and sweep *homo* away into the darkness from which his universe arose.'[12] The phrase 'the fulness of time' (borrowed from the New Testament's repertoire of messianic language) suggests that Wells viewed the overthrow of humanity as an almost teleological principle – one which could replace the Bible's apocalyptic end with an alternative form of narrative closure.

In his visions of the Eloi, the Morlocks and the non-human creatures which inhabit the earth in its twilight age, Wells was rewriting Darwin's vision of the end as well as that predicted in the Bible. In *The Origin of Species* (1859), Darwin suggested that the evolutionary process could produce infinite refinement: 'as natural selection works solely by and for the good of each being, all corporeal and mental endowments will tend to progress towards perfection'.[13] T. H. Huxley, in his 1893 lecture on evolution and ethics, took a rather different view: the process, he claimed, would eventually begin to work back-wards: 'The theory of evolution encourages no millennial anticipations. If, for millions of years, our globe has taken the upward road, yet, some time, the summit will be reached and the downward route will be commenced.'[14] Wells envisaged just such a decline, using the division between the 'Capitalists' who lived at ease and the 'Labourers' who worked in the dark Victorian factories, mills, mines and service tunnels, as the model for a foreseeable, retrograde, evolutionary split in humankind (p. 43). The Morlocks, begotten of labouring-class ancestors, are compared with sloths, apes, spiders, lemurs and rats, in a vocabulary which stresses not only the Darwinian continuum of all forms of animate life, but also the evolutionary demise of humanity.

Yet, despite this post-Darwinian vision of humanity's animal origins and destiny, the Morlocks are also called 'damned souls' (p. 68): creatures of an older cosmogony. This phrase is an indication of the way in which Wells's text encodes an ambivalence about its own replacement of apocalypse with evolutionary and entropic decline. The designation of the Morlocks as 'damned souls' occurs during a curiously Dantean episode. Pursued through a forest by Morlocks, the Time Traveller has set a fire which spreads rapidly. At the centre of the blazing forest, the fugitive arsonist comes across 'a hillock or tumulus' (p. 67):

> Upon the hill-side were some thirty or forty Morlocks, dazzled by the light and heat, and blundering hither and thither against each other in their bewilderment ...
>
> At last I sat down on the summit of the hillock, and watched this strange incredible company of blind things groping to and fro, and making uncanny noises to each other, as the glare of the fire beat on them ...
>
> For the most part of that night I was persuaded it was a nightmare. I bit myself and screamed in a passionate desire to awake. I beat the ground with my hands, and got up and sat down again, and wandered here and there, and again sat down. Then I would fall to rubbing my eyes and calling upon God to let me awake. Thrice I saw Morlocks put their heads down in a kind of agony and rush into the flames.   (pp. 67–8)

The Time Traveller refers to the hillock as 'a kind of island in the forest' (p. 68). Dante, we may recall, described purgatory as an island mountain, and it is in ascending the purgatory-like mount that the Time Traveller looks down upon the Morlocks caught in the blaze as upon a nightmare vision of hell: 'these damned souls going hither and thither and moaning ...' (p. 68). Evolution, it seems, enacts some kind of eschatological judgement: some 'souls' are 'damned' by natural selection.

Furthermore, the fiery torment with which the Morlocks are punished is meted out by the fire-starting Time Traveller himself. Consonant with this act of judgement, his violent confrontation with the Morlocks casts him in the apocalyptic role of a messianic figure who rules with 'a rod of iron' (Revelation 2.27; 19.15). Having broken a lever from a machine, discovered in a derelict museum, he carries it with him as a weapon: 'I rolled over, and as I did so my hand came against my iron lever ... holding the bar short, I thrust where I judged their faces might be. I could feel the succulent giving of flesh and bone under my blows ...' (p. 66). Revelation 2.27 conjures a similarly gruesome image: 'And he shall rule them with a rod of iron; as the vessels of a potter shall they be broken to shivers.'

At the beginning of the chapter which follows the Time Traveller's purgatorial night, his narratorial tone, if not exactly penitent, is certainly somewhat chastened by his experience. He returns to the point of his first, naively optimistic view of the far-future landscape, and casts over it a colder eye: 'I thought of my hasty conclusions upon that evening and could not refrain from laughing bitterly at my confidence ... I understood now what all the beauty of the Upperworld people covered' (p. 69). Climbing above the flames and escaping the infernal fate of the Morlocks, the Time Traveller has gained a new perspective – a perspective which might be called 'apocalyptic' in that he now sees *beneath the cover* of Upperworld beauty.[15] But his revelation is an inverse apocalypse. While apocalyptic literature sought to explain the dark affairs of the 'lower', earthly world in terms of events in the 'world above', the Time Traveller discovers the truth about the Upperworld by uncovering a sinister lower region.

In John's Apocalypse, it is Christ who uncovers Upperworld mysteries to the visionary. He is characterized as the master of time, as 'the Alpha and Omega, the beginning and the ending' (Revelation 1.8, 11), holding sway over past, present and future, and able to reveal 'the things which are, and the things which shall be hereafter' (1.19). Such texts have produced, within Christianity, a vision of Christ as a kind of magnificent time-lord, as one well-known nineteenth-century hymn makes clear: 'Crown him the Lord of years, | The Potentate of time'.[16] Given this time-overcoming potency, there is a degree of irony in the acknowledgement that his return is deferred; nevertheless, the postponement of Parousia (return) was written into the New Testament itself, as Christ's lateness in coming back began to be noted by the early Christians. The writers of the canonical epistles were occasionally forced to excuse his delay to impatient believers: 'The Lord is not slack concerning his promise, as some men count slackness ... the day of the Lord will come ...' (2 Peter 3.9–10). The importance to Christian faith of Christ's ever-imminent return is evident in a passage from Paul's first letter to the Corinthians, which I have already quoted: 'For as often as ye eat this bread, and drink this cup, ye do show the Lord's death *till he come*' (1 Corinthians 11.26 – my emphasis). The eucharist is thus the focus of both the memorial and the proleptic aspects of Christian faith: it recalls Jesus's 'Last Supper', and looks forward to the 'marriage supper of the Lamb' (Revelation 19.9). But it also serves to mark the deferral of the promised return: every time it is celebrated, the believer tacitly acknowledges Christ's lateness, the fact that he has not yet come.

In Revelation, the 'marriage supper of the Lamb' follows the consummation of the world age. Like the apocalyptic Lamb, Wells's Time Traveller also appears at a meal, fresh from the end of the world. He comes to his last supper after having observed the entropic demise of the sun and the earth. Repeating the irony of Christ's delay, he is *late* for this meal as a result of travelling through time, and his lateness is what prompts the Christ-evoking phrase: ' "Where's – ?", said I, naming our host.' Not only is this ironic lateness an important Christological, apocalyptic moment, but it also draws attention to a related eucharistic parallel. Since the laboratory which contains the time machine is located in his house, the host is spatially present while being temporally absent. This strange logic of time travel repeats the paradox of the host's presence/ absence in the eucharist: the 'real presence' of Christ in the elements (the bread and the wine) is, as we have seen, also the mark of his continuing absence, of the fact that he has yet to come back.

However parodic they may be, the Christic parallels ultimately compromise the novella's anti-apocalyptic vision. *The Time Machine* ends with the speaker of the framing narrative (into which the Time Traveller's own account is set) worrying over his friend's delayed return, and fearing infinite postponement: 'I am beginning now to fear that I must wait a lifetime. The Time Traveller vanished three years ago. And, as everybody knows now, he has never returned' (p. 81). The universalizing of the sense of deferral ('everybody knows') recalls the delayed Parousia, while the time-laden phrases 'a lifetime', 'three years', 'never', reinforce the irony of that lateness. In the opening sentence of the epilogue, still musing on the whereabouts of the vanished host, the narrator asks: 'Will he ever return?' The end, it seems, it still in doubt. His wondering continues:

> I, for my own part cannot think that these latter days of weak experiment, fragmentary theory, and mutual discord are indeed man's culminating time! I say, for my own part. He, I know ... saw in the growing pile of civilization only a foolish heaping that must inevitably fall back upon and destroy its makers in the end. (p. 83)

Just as it shows us a double image of Christ, as Lion and Lamb, the text of Revelation also encodes both of these possible futures, depicting the collapse of 'the growing pile of civilisation' in the fall of Babylon, and envisaging a more glorious 'culminating time' in its depiction of the Millennium and of the New Jerusalem.

Recreating Abolished Horizons

Wells's Darwinian, or, more accurately Huxleyan, education led him away from the eschatological certainties of his evangelical upbringing. Armageddon, the last judgement and the triumphant return of Christ, the consummation of the world as described in Revelation, vanished in the open-ended, unimaginable timescale of geological formations and of the infinitely slow processes of natural selection, to be replaced by a 'blackness and a vagueness about the endless vista of years ahead, that was tremendous – that terrified'.[17] Wells's terror is understandable. As Frank Kermode has said: 'tracts of time unpunctuated by meaning derived from the end are not to be borne'.[18] Paul Ricoeur's extended analysis of the reciprocity of time and narrative uncovers the depth of our need to implicate time in the diegetic structures of emplotment: '... time becomes human time to the extent that it is organised after the manner of a narrative; narrative, in turn, is meaningful to the extent that it portrays the features of temporal experience'.[19] Darwin and Huxley, each in his own way, imposed a narrative of human temporality upon the measureless expanse of evolutionary time. Darwin did so by means of expressions of belief in the ability of science to throw light upon 'the origin of man and his history', and in natural selection as tending to produce perfection.[20] Huxley's humanizing emplotment involved asserting the opposite: the human story would ultimately be one of rise and fall, of gaining an evolutionary 'summit' and of descending once more into sub-humanity. It is worth noting, here, that Northrop Frye has described the biblical account of history as the archetypal form of this kind of undulating narrative pattern.[21]

In telling a story about the end of the world, Wells was bound by the sheer force of cultural imperatives – the weight of both the will-to-narrative and the Western, Christian biblical tradition – to construe his anti-apocalyptic tale as rewriting of biblical eschatology, and of its central event, the death of Christ. Just as the book of Revelation projects Christ into the age of human fulfilment and world-consummation, the Time Traveller humanizes the vast expanses of non-human, post-theological time by visiting its future extremity, and by reporting its non-apocalyptic end to his late-nineteenth-century (*fin de siècle*) audience of bourgeois males. In doing so, he necessarily returns geologico-evolutionary time to a narrative structure, creating an anthropocentric story with a beginning, a middle and an end.

In *The Sense of an Ending*, Kermode claims that, despite oft-repeated disconfirmations of apocalyptic prediction and counter-prediction, our drive to impose plots upon human experience remains undefeated. Even a plot as apparently counter-diegetic as that of *Ulysses*, he insists, contains a good deal of end-imposing emplotment.[22] While, on the one hand, we banish our teleological expectations by disconfirming our prognoses, on the other hand, 'we recreate the horizons we have abolished, the structures that have collapsed; and we do so in terms of the old patterns, adapting them to our new worlds'.[23] If Wells was intimidated by time's expansion, his first published work of fiction, *The Time Machine*, might be seen as an ambivalent response to that shock. Ambivalent because it both transgresses apocalyptic expectations and, simultaneously, 'recreates the horizons' which it thus abolishes. It does so precisely 'in terms of the old patterns' of Christian eucharistic and eschatological thought, 'adapting them to ... new worlds'.

Notes

1. Y. Zamyatin, *H. G. Wells*, reprinted in *A Soviet Heretic*, trans. M. Ginsburg (Chicago: University of Chicago Press, 1922), pp. 260–1.
2. H. G. Wells, *The Time Machine* (1895). In preparing this essay I have used the Everyman centennial edition (London: J. M. Dent, 1995). Page references for this edition are given in the text.
3. P. Kemp, *H. G. Wells and the Culminating Ape: Biological Themes and Imaginative Obsessions* (London: Macmillan, 1982), p. 34.
4. T. G Huxley, Prolegomena to 'Evolution and ethics' (1894) in T. H. Huxley and Julian Huxley *Evolution and Ethics, 1893–1943* (London: Pilot Press, 1947), pp. 33–60, 52.
5. Kemp, *Wells and the Culminating Ape*, p. 7.
6. Ibid., p. 39.
7. J. Huntington, *The Logic of Fantasy: H. G. Wells and Science Fiction* (New York: Columbia University Press, 1982), p. 177 n. 6.
8. A. Tennyson, *In Memoriam*, LVI, xv. That nineteenth-century thinkers saw a moral or ethical conflict between the violence of the natural world and the values of Christian faith is evident from many texts. The difficulty was summed up succinctly by Charles Darwin in 1860: 'I cannot persuade myself that a beneficent and omnipotent God would have designedly created the Ichneumonidae with the express intention of their feeding within the living bodies of Caterpillars.' Letter to Asa Gray (22 May 1860) in F. Darwin (ed.), *The Life and Letters of Charles Darwin*, vol. II, rev. edn (London: John Murray, 1888), pp. 310–12, p. 312.
9. The story of Jesus's purging of the temple can be found in all four Gospels: Matthew 21.12–13; Mark 11.15–17; Luke 19.45–6; John 2.13–16.
10. B. Bergonzi, '*The Time Machine*: an ironic myth' in B. Bergonzi (ed.), *H. G. Wells: A Collection of Critical Essays* (Englewood Cliffs, N.J.: Prentice-Hall, 1976), pp. 39–55, p. 48.
11. P. Parrinder, *Shadows of the Future: H. G. Wells, Science Fiction and Prophecy* (Liverpool: Liverpool University Press, 1995), p. 49. The story of Nebuchadnezzar's metamorphosis into a 'beast of the field' can be found in the book of Daniel, chapter 4.
12. H. G. Wells, 'Zoological regression', *The Gentleman's Magazine* 271 (September 1891), p. 253.
13. C. Darwin, *The Origin of Species* (1859), ed. Gillian Beer (Oxford and New York: Oxford University Press, 1996), p. 395.
14. T. H. Huxley, 'Evolution and ethics' in Huxley and Huxley, *Evolution and Ethics*, pp. 60–102, p. 83. On the subject of evolutionary degeneration in *The Time Machine*, see Parrinder, *Shadows of the Future*, pp. 49–64; see also, R. M. Philmus, 'The logic of "prophecy" in *The Time Machine*' in Bergonzi, *H.G. Wells: A Collection of Critical Essays*, pp. 56–68.
15. The word 'apocalypse' in an Anglicization of Greek *apokalypsis*, 'uncovering'. Apocalyptic literature flourished in Judaic culture from about 200 BCE to 100 CE. It is characterized by visionary descriptions of the 'world above', offered as

explanations for earthly events. The biblical books of Daniel and Revelation are acknowledged examples of the genre. On apocalyptic literature see N. Cohn, *Cosmos, Chaos and the World to Come: The Ancient Roots of Apocalyptic Faith* (New Haven and London: Yale University Press, 1993); J. J. Collins, *The Apocalyptic Imagination: An Introduction to the Jewish Matrix of Christianity* (New York: Crossroad, 1989); Christopher Rowland, *The Open Heaven: A Study of Apocalyptic in Judaism and Early Christianity* (London: SPCK, 1982).

16. The hymn is 'Crown him with many crowns', by M. Bridges (1800–94), revised by G. Thring (1823–1903).
17. H. G. Wells, *The Future in America: A Search after Realities* (London: Chapman & Hall, 1906), p. 10.
18. F. Kermode, *The Sense of an Ending: Studies in the Theory of Fiction* (London, Oxford, New York: Oxford University Press, 1967), p. 162.
19. P. Ricoeur, *Time and Narrative* I, trans. K. McLaughlin and D. Pellauer (Chicago and London: University of Chicago Press, 1984), p. 3.
20. Darwin, *Origin of Species*, p. 394.
21. N. Frye, *The Great Code* (London: Routledge & Kegan Paul, 1982), p. 171.
22. Kermode, *Sense of an Ending*, p. 45.
23. Ibid., p. 58.

14

Reconsidering Phlebas: Faith in the Life and Work of T. S. Eliot

Christopher Southgate

D avid Jasper's opening chapter to this volume focused on the Bible, which occupies so many roles in educational institutions, from literary- and historico-critical laboratory to devotional manual to fundamentalist proof-text. Here I shall be arguing the significance of a particular set of twentieth-century texts, a set which raises in a particularly sharp way questions about education as though the spiritual search mattered – namely the poetry and drama of T. S. Eliot. I will illustrate the importance of studying the hermeneutics of Eliot criticism – how the texts have been and continue to be received and appropriated – and give an example of how different presuppositions lead to different evaluations of the texts' significance. I will also suggest that *Four Quartets* in particular is an important resource for the Christian educator as contemplative.

It is now generally agreed that the most influential poet writing in English in this century spent the whole of his adult life on a spiritual search. At the age of 38 he identified himself explicitly with a particular religious tradition. Eliot has been 'claimed' both by the Christian establishment and by those readers of *The Waste Land* grateful for the decline of Christendom. It must therefore be of considerable interest to investigate not only how Eliot's search influenced his writings but how the preconceptions of his critics have influenced reception of the religious elements in his work.[1]

In discussion lately it has emerged just how difficult many recent generations of students have found Eliot – it has as Anne Stevenson has recently written 'become a gleeful pastime among Eliot's detractors to sabotage his hegemony in the realm of letters by opening fire on the man himself; on, that is, his elitism, his old-fashioned monarchism, his High Church Anglicanism, his putative anti-feminism and especially on what appears to have been an unappealing and today, of course, a politically damaging anti-Semitism'.[2] He is seen to be, in shorthand, profoundly 'incorrect'. This adds an extra dimension to the interest in studying Eliot studies: will TSE begin to disappear off 'correct' curricula, or will teachers take the braver step of exploring all the ambiguities thrown up by someone who wrote so eloquently about the Christian search for God, and yet evinced attitudes now found not just unpalatable, but repellent?

The ethos of much literary criticism in recent years has been that religious belief is at best a mere curiosity, an individual idiosyncrasy, at worst an outworn way in which an establishment dominates the hearts and minds of a people. To borrow Adrian Thatcher's borrowing of John Milbank,[3] the sublime has been very effectively policed. Thatcher goes on in the same paper to use language stemming originally from the philosopher of science Thomas Kuhn,[4] talking of 'incommensurable differences' between world-views which presuppose God and those which do not. The borrowing is a helpful one. When, however, Thatcher goes on to say that 'coping with incommensurability demands attentiveness to each rival position', he dilutes the force of Kuhn's point, which is that adherents of incommensurable paradigms cannot understand each other, because not only can they not agree on their metaphysics, *they cannot even agree on the basic data by which they develop their subject*. A famous example is the inability of pre-Copernican Western astronomers to observe sunspots, which the Chinese had been seeing for centuries. Kuhn also gives another fascinating example from eighteenth-century chemistry: at the time when what we now know to be mixtures were taken to be compounds, it was impossible to understand the properties which only compounds show.

All this may seem some way from Thomas Stearns Eliot Poet. But not so. Eliot's early career, culminating in *The Waste*

Land, wanders far in the territory of decay, disillusion and fragmentation. Later in his life he writes *Four Quartets*, which is for very many Christians a work almost scriptural in its importance. So here at once we can see potential for incommensurability: those who seek to 'police the sublime' may well see the Eliot oeuvre as startlingly original poetry of the modern crisis which then trailed off into dogmatic irrelevance. Those for whom religious poetry can disclose truths about the relations of humans to God will tend to see Eliot as someone who came through a phase of disillusion into an extremely rich relationship with the Christian tradition. The whole view of the subject will be different, and the gathering of the data itself will be different: at what phase is Eliot's poetry at its finest? Is the great poetry the disorientation of Prufrock, the disdain of the quatrain poems, the disconnections of *The Waste Land*, or the dignified musings of the *Quartets*?

So if we want to look at this question of incommensurability, Eliot studies offer us a fertile field, because the *same poet* seems to give currency to both paradigms.

Of course, the philosophy of science did not stop with Kuhn, but was developed along less starkly polarized lines by Imre Lakatos,[5] and later by Larry Laudan.[6] Both of these thinkers allow the possibility of a *number* of competing research programmes (Lakatos) or research traditions (Laudan). And there are of course other stances in Eliot studies besides the ones I have just sketched – in particular those which see Eliot as someone who only dominated modern poetry because he himself set the criteria for its assessment, or those who see Eliot as an artist so riddled with anti-Semitism, or misogyny, or political conservatism, as to be all but unusable except as a curiosity of his age. These points of view are, however, beyond the scope of this chapter, though I touched on questions of anti-Semitism in my recent book.[7]

David Moody has recently levelled a further important charge against Eliot, at the end of this essay 'Being in fear of women':

> What sort of soul is it which fears what is other and therefore to be loved, and which loves only its own nothingness? What sort of being is it that lives only in its death, and in the end of all things? Eliot of course gave his own answers, the answers of the

absolute. But we do not live in the realm of the absolutes. We have our being in all our contingent relations with other beings. And in its relations with others his elected being is disposed to act so very badly, so immaturely. To demand unconditional love and service while violently refusing any claims on oneself is the behaviour of a personality still cocooned in its own selfhood. Fear of the other is the natural reaction of the self in that condition; and with it goes a natural wanting to be freed not only from the threatening other but from one's own fearful self. That freedom may be found in the love that casts out fear – in loving another who loves you. But that way is not taken in Eliot's life and work unless near the end, in his last play and his second marriage. Most of his career is dedicated to saving the fearful self from others and for its own perfection. It never comes to love in the ordinary human way. *And I find it hard to credit a love of God which is not first of all a love of other beings. I must suspect its God of being only an absolute of the self.*

I am sceptical about the suggestion that Eliot's poetry discloses the permanent substratum of our being; and even more sceptical about its disclosing the nature of Being. What it discloses is certainly the truth of his own being – the verification is in the originality and power of the writing.[8]

Moody suggests not that Eliot never believed in God, but that he never truly *loved* God, the proof being his failure consistently to love the other human beings closest to him. Therefore, Moody claims, Eliot's spiritual explorations do not disclose to us anything fundamental about the nature of Being in general, as opposed to his own particular, strange way of being (which his work so powerfully explores).

This is a fascinating suggestion in the light of the idea of incommensurability. Moody complains in effect that Eliot's poetry does not teach him anything about the God he, Moody, doesn't believe in. He himself, as he goes on to imply, would rather learn from Ezra Pound. Again, for all Moody's sensitive critical attentiveness, two world-views are simply not communicating.

But Moody raises a serious point: how *can* the *Quartets* be revelatory of God when Eliot's own life did not manifest the love that 'casts out fear', when it did not in a reliable way, free of coldness, 'fructify' in the lives of those closest to him.

This flattens out the ambiguities of spirituality and art into something altogether too tidy and convenient. A research programme admitting of the authenticity both of the essence of Christianity, and of Eliot's efforts to convey something of it, will wrestle with a much more complex set of dimensions, and with two in particular: first that the life set upon God is not exempt from weakness and failure; second, that art is not a pale copy of an individual's spiritual state but something altogether more Promethean – it says more, in beauty and ugliness, than the artist could say in any other way. Religious art can be revelatory of God, but it is not censored by God; the revelation will therefore be interwoven with all sorts of other motifs.[9] It will contain prejudice as well as the understanding of prejudice,[10] human insecurities and blind-spots as well as 'odd angles of heaven'.[11]

David Daiches suggests five strategies for the religious poet.[12] He/she may: address God, tell the reader about God, recount a visionary experience, find God through the workings of nature, or lastly agonize about God's existence. The *Divina Commedia*, in Daiches' opinion, alternates 'in a most remarkable way between the visionary and the almost pedantically explanatory'. And so too *Four Quartets*, though being written in the age of Russell and Wittgenstein rather than that of Aquinas, Eliot's sequence approaches its religious task in a profoundly oblique way. The word 'God', in any sense that could refer to the Christian God, occurs only twice in the work's 876 lines; Krishna is mentioned as often. The *Quartets'* meditations on 'the intersection of the timeless with time' (which is the essence of revelation, of providence and of redemption) win through only very gradually to any sustained use of Christian language. The many-layered tracings have the effect of drawing the reader down into a state where, at last, in the final sections of 'Little Gidding', the method of Dante can be followed – we can hear the visionary conclusions of Julian and the author of *The Cloud of Unknowing* cast into the inexorability of sin and the ambiguity of history, and accept that for all their fragility these conclusions will prevail.

It seems particularly appropriate, in considering *Four Quartets*, to draw a musical parallel to its spiritual struggles. James Macmillan's percussion concerto *Veni, Veni, Emmanuel* wanders far in many musical lands, full of stops and starts and self-quotations, also of strange allusive character sketches (including one of Eliot himself). Yet when the final four-note motif, which will become the great Advent prayer, softly takes hold, the musical logic of the piece is finally revealed and seen as a whole. *Veni, Veni* ends with prayer, 'hardly prayable prayer' at that, certainly not with proclamation, but who could doubt the deeply Christian movement behind its struggles?

Moody's verdict on Eliot's spiritual state is an exaggeration. Granted, Eliot was tremendously aware not only of fear (on which Moody dwells in his essay) but of guilt in respect of women and of God. His faith, falling short of that of a saint, was much concerned with the search for absolution from such guilt and with the continual sense of failure which is so integral a part of the penitential tradition in Christianity. Perhaps Moody is right that only at the end of his life did Eliot experience in himself or others a perfect love casting out fear. But in his later poetry he nevertheless succeeds in showing us true and false directions in which to search for the source of that love. The poetry *is*, therefore, revelatory, both positively and negatively, of the object of the search. The best of the 'fruit' of Eliot's spiritual life, 'by which we may know' him, and hence, however indirectly, something of his God, was first of all in the poetry; also, over time, in his service to the Anglican Church, in personal and professional kindnesses, and finally – this is not to be belittled – in his marital love with Valerie. She has declared him to have been, at that stage of his life, 'made for marriage'.[13] The very considerable strains of the enormous age-gap between them seem never to have been an issue. He gave her a gift of 'six days short of eight years',[14] a gift of great happiness enormously treasured.

The Christian is entitled to ask where authentic happiness is deemed to come *from*, if not from God. Eliot's spiritual life was not principally about *attainment*, about a saintly state directly revelatory of the divine love. It was about a striving for a certain orientation ('marking channels for others'[15]), which striving was ultimately rewarded by a gift of love, given and received, so improbable as to be near miraculous. This gift was *not* accompanied by the making of great poetry – the time of searching, and of fruit expressed in the artistic struggle, was over. But the eight-year marriage, like the underlying movement of *Four Quartets*, is a profound sign of a sustained belief in love, and love as deriving from, and vindicated by, God.

I have endeavoured to show that Eliot's life and work survives recent efforts to reduce its importance for a spiritually informed curriculum. This is not to deny that problems remain, in particular in respect of his expressions of anti-Semitism, and, as the passage from Moody implies, in his apparently callous distancing of himself from some of those closest to him.

The epitaph Thomas Stearns Eliot drafted for himself is understated and seems to imply uncompleted search.[16] But he had written a more fitting one when he wrote these phrases about Paul Elmer More (a man to whom Eliot claimed uncannily similar spiritual experience[17]):

> One is always aware of the sincerity, and in the later works the Christian humanity ... of the concentrated mind seeking God; still with restless curiosity analyzing the disease and the aberrations of humanity.[18]

To apply this to Eliot at his best is not to deny the times when he failed his Lord and God. It *is* to affirm the genius of *Four Quartets* in catching up the universal human sadness at the relentless flux of time into a universal hope of consummation in the Spirit. The *Quartets* are also, incidentally, a remarkable example of how insights from Buddhist and Hindu thought can be included in a Christian affirmation. Eliot's work is therefore not only a crucible in which the world-views of contemporary criticism may be assayed against one another; it is also one in which innovative fusions of spiritualities are explored. It is thus a particularly appropriate example of an opportunity for a programme 'dedicated to recovering ... religious, ethical and spiritual dimensions'[19] to engage with curricula of literary studies.

I end by considering a recent challenge posed by Mary Grey: 'how can the educational experience of teachers and students include space for contemplation, for exploration into space and silence, into what humans can never adequately express but have in almost every age and culture needed to acknowledge – a sense of the divine other?'[20] *Four Quartets*, by its reflective tone and its use of parallelism and paradox, enters a contemplative world almost comparable in profundity to the late Beethoven that was Eliot's model. And the poet makes remarkable use of silence, as at the climax of 'Little Gidding' where there is a most extraordinary effect generated by the use of a single half-sentence from *The Cloud of Unknowing*: 'With the drawing of this Love and the voice of this Calling'. This is a line on its own, with space and silence before and after. Education as if the spiritual search mattered will allow such space and silence to interweave our learning, and admit always a measure of unknowing within it.

'Consider' once again 'Phlebas, who was once handsome and tall as you.' Consider Eliot, if you look to windward to catch the breath of God's Spirit working in hearts and minds.

Notes

1. A recent example of an attempt to address the dynamics of the reception of Eliot's Christian work is J. X. Cooper, *T. S. Eliot and the Ideology of 'Four Quartets'* (Cambridge: Cambridge University Press, 1995).
2. In the Foreword to my own recent book – Christopher Southgate, *A Love and Its Sounding: Explorations of T. S. Eliot* (Salzburg: University of Salzburg, 1997).
3. In *Journal of Further and Higher Education* 19/3 (Autumn 1995).
4. Kuhn introduced this terminology in his famous book, T. S. Kuhn, *The Structure of Scientific Revolutions* (Chicago: University of Chicago Press, 1961).
5. In, for instance, his essay in I. Lakatos and A. Musgrave (eds), *Criticism and the Growth of Knowledge* (Cambridge: Cambridge University Press, 1970).
6. In L. Laudan, *Progress and its Problems* (Berkeley: University of California Press, 1978).
7. *A Love and Its Sounding*, pp. 75–80. Some of the material for this chapter is to be found on pp. 90–4.
8. A. D. Moody, 'Being in fear of women' in A. D. Moody, *Tracing T. S. Eliot's Spirit* (Cambridge: Cambridge University Press, 1996), ch. 10, p. 194 – my emphasis.
9. This is especially true of the sort of poetry with which Eliot was particularly concerned, that of search, as opposed to devotional verse as such (see his letter to W. F. Stead, quoted in H. Gardner, *The Composition of 'Four Quartets'* (London: Faber & Faber, 1978), p. 29.
10. See C. Ricks, *T. S. Eliot and Prejudice* (London: Faber & Faber, 1988).
11. The phrase is from the title of an anthology of 'contemporary poetry by people of faith' – D. Craig and J. McCann (eds), *Odd Angles of Heaven* (Wheaton, Ill.: Harold Shaw, 1994).
12. D. Daiches, *God and the Poets* (Oxford: Oxford University Press, 1985), ch. 4.
13. Interview in *The Independent on Sunday*, 24 April 1994.
14. Mrs Eliot's own description, quoted by L. Gordon in J. Meyers (ed.), *The Craft of Literary Biography* (London: Macmillan, 1985), pp. 173–85.
15. The poem 'A Love and Its Sounding', section VI (see n. 2 above).
16. In the Church of St Michael and All Angels, East Coker, hangs a simple tablet reading: 'Pray for the repose of the soul of Thomas Stearns Eliot Poet'.
17. In his last letter to More in January 1937 (quoted in B. A. Harries, 'The rare contact', *Theology* 75 (1972), pp. 136–44).
18. *Princeton Alumni Weekly*, 5 February 1937.
19. I. Markham in *Engaging the Curriculum Bulletin* 5 (Spring 1997), p. 3.
20. 'Christian theology: spirituality and the curriculum' delivered at the Spirituality and Moral Development Forum of 'Engaging the Curriculum', 13–14 December 1996. The theme of 'Educators as contemplatives' was taken up in D. Nixon's paper to that Forum.

15

Chesterton and Father Brown: Demystification and Deconstruction

Thomas Woodman

G eneralizations about crime fiction are liable to multiple exceptions since the very nature of the genre means that even the most formulaic writers are addicted to tricks and surprises. Yet a typical pattern or archetype of traditional detective fiction can be discerned, as critics have often pointed out. In the most basic form a small safe community is disrupted by a crime. A great detective solves the whodunit by the superb application of reason and deduction. The scapegoat (either an outsider or, more threateningly, a treacherous insider) is punished and cast out and the purified community resumes its utopian life.[1]

G. K. Chesterton is a remarkable pioneer of modern cultural studies in his fascination with popular modes. He regarded popular literature as the real heart of the human literary impulse in its imaginative wish-fulfilment. Howard Haycraft has commented that Chesterton's own distinction in the history of detective fiction lies in his introduction of metaphysical elements.[2] It would be more accurate to say that Chesterton saw himself as drawing out the theological implications that were inherent in detective fiction as in all popular modes. This involves much more than the religious propaganda of which Chesterton has often been accused. Going deeper we might surmise that Chesterton attempts to ground detective fiction on a metaphysical basis by reminding us that the human justice and society that we find affirmed in this fiction must have its roots and ultimate meaning in God. Several of his interesting early essays on detective fiction certainly seem to present it as a way of defending systems of human order. He writes, for example, in a much quoted passage that the special virtue of detective fiction as an 'agent of the public weal' lies in the way it shows that civilization itself has a genuine element of romance to it and that the 'whole noiseless and unnoticeable police management by which we are ruled and protected is only a successful knight errantry'.[3] The allegorical import of Chesterton's choice of a priest as his detective would thus seem to be that human justice and civilization needs the Church as its ultimate support.

The matter is far more complicated than that, however. Chesterton is passionately anti-establishment in his politics and he also has a profound sense of the spiritual radicality of the Christian gospel and its invitation to live life to the full. These convictions inform his detective stories and enable them to transcend propaganda and comforting ideology. His work amounts to a full-scale examination and interrogation of all the implications of conventional detective fiction. In his view the traditional formulas may sometimes produce genuinely suggestive metaphysical analogies, but any religious implications may equally well be used for trite and complacent ideological ends. On the other hand conventional detective fiction may illegitimately seek to exclude metaphysics altogether in the interests either of scientism and rationalism or of a purely secular bourgeois social order.

In developing the tendencies he approves of and countering those he dislikes Chesterton is able to combine excellent detective fiction with rich fables of religious truth. In their brevity, excitement and pointedness these stories can provide brilliant paradigms of the relationship between theology and literature and impressive parables of the paradoxical workings of grace. He demonstrates affinities and analogies, for example, between the search for truth, justice and solutions in this fiction and in the wider universe. In 'The Insoluble Problem' Father Brown and Flambeau the reformed thief are deliberately distracted from a theft they are meant to prevent by an artificially set up 'murder' full of nonsensical clues. The priest manages to unmask the deception and Chesterton comments at the end that some are convinced that the 'enigma' of the universe 'also is an Insoluble Problem. And others have equal certitude that it has but one solution.'[4] He pushes the genre, in other words, towards allegory, but true allegory, where the literal sense and the dynamics of the story are convincing in their own right, whilst also pointing to deeper truths.[5] But Chesterton is equally aware of the *differences* between detective fiction and universal truth. If he believes that God lies behind all legitimate systems of the human order that detective fiction privileges he also highlights various paradoxes of crime and guilt and in particular the disjunction between human and divine justice. He thus both provides and fails to provide the comforts of closure in his work. He both uses and at the same time deconstructs the whole traditional pattern of detective fiction.[6] It is this sophistication and complexity that gives the best of these stories their remarkable theological pointedness.

As W. W. Robson points out, 'Father Brown remains true both to traditional theology, and to the genre of the detective story, in never decrying reason.'[7] This is one claim that Chesterton indeed makes with an almost tiresome insistence, the affirmation that Catholicism is the most genuine friend of reason. One of the clues that leads Father Brown to suspect that his brother priest in the first published story 'The Blue Cross' is really Flambeau in disguise is 'You attacked reason ... It's bad theology' (p. 23). 'Reason is from God,' the priest says in 'The Red Moon of Meru', 'and when things are unreasonable there is something the matter' (p. 565). Father Brown's detective abilities depend on reason, common sense, observation, not mysticism. This is both a literal presentation of the way a Catholic is supposed to work and, as noted above, an analogy with the way theology uses reason in its quest for the meaning of the universe.

Contrary to the popular stereotypes of Catholicism, therefore, Father Brown likes nothing better than debunking false mysticism and false mysteries. In 'The Oracle of the Dog', for example, there is the ominous howling of the victim's dog some way off from the place of the crime yet apparently at the very moment of the murder. It later transpires that the dog howls because the stick that is thrown into the sea for it to chase sinks because it is actually a swordstick used by the murderer. The priest comments:

> 'It's the first effect of not believing in God that you lose your common sense and can't see things as they are. Anything that anybody talks about, and says there is a good deal in it, extends itself indefinitely like a vista in nightmare. And a dog is an omen, and a cat is a mystery, and a pig is a mascot and a beetle is a scarab, calling up all the menagerie of polytheism from Egypt and old India ...' (p. 368)

Chesterton's thinking here is analogous to Karl Barth's idea of Christianity as the religion beyond religion; as Robson explains, it implies a distinction between man-made attempts to reach God and revelation as such. (This has a special relevance perhaps for us in a time of renewed esotericism and new-age thinking strikingly parallel to the craze for occultism in Chesterton's own age.) Time and again Chesterton sets up a pseudo-mystery, frightening and inexplicable, and proceeds to show that it has a perfectly natural explanation – human trickery, for example, or human obtuseness of the no-one-ever-notices-a-postman kind. Far from being credulous as most of those around seem to expect the priest is very sceptical. He believes some things, and this gives him a very good foundation for disbelieving others.

One grouping of these stories, for example, involves the idea of the Gothic curse on an aristocratic family, 'The Doom of the Darnaways', 'The Perishing of the Pendragons'. Chesterton enjoys himself hugely in building up the atmosphere of suspense and anticipation only to deconstruct the curse and show it as a mask for some much more mundane crime. Another group plays with the exoticism of the East, only to deconstruct it in similar fashion. 'The Red Moon of Meru', for example, tells how an Eastern guru is accused of the theft of a famous jewel. Father Brown persuades the real thief to put it back, but the guru is pleased to have the apparent disappearance and reappearance put down to his mystical powers. Gothic and sensationalist elements like these have always leaked into detective fiction proper. But Chesterton is working with the real grain of the genre in deconstructing false mysteries, as Sherlock Holmes does in *The Hound of the Baskervilles*, for example. He does so, of course, however, not from the perspective of scientific rationalism but by using the traditional Christian humanist reason he promulgates.

Consequently we find that Father Brown's kind of reason has to be distinguished carefully from false reason as well as from false mysteries. The great detective Valentin who appears in the first two stories is portrayed as the epitome of French free-thinking rationalism, and it is no accident that he is also revealed as the murderer at the end of the brilliant story 'The Secret Garden'. Sherlock Holmes is both the prototype of Father Brown and the great antitype, and he is referred to in intertextual fashion at various points in these stories. In 'The Absence of Mr Glass' the portrayal of Dr Orion Hood amounts to a parody of Holmes and his methods. In this revealing but very improbable story a young Catholic girl comes to ask the priest's help because she believes her fiancé has been drugged and tied up by a mysterious 'Mr Glass' to whom the apparent victim keeps referring. Dr Hood deduces various points about Mr Glass whilst omitting to untie the victim, a piece of practical help that is left to the suggestion of the priest:

> [Dr Hood] 'The hair of human beings falls out in varying degrees, but almost always falls out slightly, and with the lens I should see the tiny hairs in a hat recently worn. It has none, which leads me to guess that Mr. Glass is bald ... I should think we may deduce some advance in years. Nevertheless, he was probably vigorous and he was almost certainly tall. I might rely in some degree on the story of his previous appearance at the window, as a tall man in a silk hat, but I think I have more exact indication. This wine-glass has been smashed all over the place, but one of its splinters lies on the high bracket over the mantel-piece. No such fragment could have fallen there if the vessel had been smashed in the hand of a comparatively short man like Mr. Todhunter.'
> 'By the way,' said Father Brown, 'might it not be as well to untie Mr. Todhunter?' (p. 177)

In one of the most blatant examples of the deconstruction of a detective story in all of these volumes the priest works out that there is no crime, no criminal and no victim here at all: Todhunter has simply been practising conjuring tricks, juggling and escapology for a stage act and his references to 'Mr Glass' are in fact exasperated comments on his failing to catch the glasses he has been using to juggle with.

For the 'reason' Father Brown espouses is practical rather than purely deductive, commonsensical rather than theoretical and scientific. Unlike Holmes the priest is totally inconspicuous. His cerebral gifts do not draw attention to themselves, and he is constantly underestimated by those around him. He values reason, but does not overvalue it. He sees a place for something like intuition, although this is not a matter of psychic or spiritual powers as such but rather of psychological knowledge gained by experience, moral knowledge. Father Brown solves crimes by this faculty as much as by reason, although Chesterton would obviously regard the two as linked.

In 'The Eye of Apollo' Kalon calls the Church a spy or policeman who convicts man of guilt. He is right, though not in the way he intends it.[8] Clearly Father Brown's experience in the confessional enables him to fulfil here the function Chesterton attributes to the Church. He has gained a vast knowledge of the human heart and indeed of crime as such as he points out at the end of 'The Blue Cross'. But as he also explains in 'The Eye of Apollo', 'I am a man ... and therefore have all devils in my heart' (p. 130). This is not a case of the saintly priest discerning evil in others; this priest's sanctity comes from the humility of recognizing the evil in his own heart. The doctrine of original sin forces a deconstruction of the black-and-white morality of the traditional detective story (itself deconstructed, of course, by other writers in the more nuanced examples of the genre) and prevents the scapegoating of the criminal that often occurs. This theme of the priest's acknowledgement of his own potential evil grows as these volumes progress, and it is presented at times as the whole 'Secret of Father Brown' and his success. In the volume with that title he specifically recommends empathy with the criminal as a humbling spiritual exercise, although it will have the secondary consequence of helping to find out who committed the crime.

In another well-known comment Chesterton calls Browning's *The Ring and the Book* 'essentially a detective story. Its difference from the ordinary detective story is that it seeks to establish, not the centre of criminal guilt, but the centre of spiritual guilt.'[9] Legal guilt and spiritual guilt may overlap, of course. Human life is sacred to Chesterton, and therefore murder is a horrible crime. Many of these stories follow the traditional pattern and there is the conventional relief at the close and reaffirmation of established moral order. But Chesterton is equally aware that spiritual guilt and criminal guilt are not the same thing, as the very phrasing of the comment on Browning indicates. Murder is not always the worst of crimes or, at least, not always the worst of sins. On the other hand, no matter how bad a murder is it is still important to recognize that it is forgivable in the eyes of God ('The Chief Mourner of Marne'). Earthly justice is far from perfect. In 'The Sins of Prince Saradine' the priest says that we are on 'the wrong side of the tapestry ... Somewhere else retribution will come on the real offender. Here it often seems to fall on the wrong person' (p. 110). Had it not been for the priest's intervention a white lie would have got a man hanged in 'The Strange Crime of John Boulnois'. Other writers have been tempted, for the sake of sheer surprise, to infringe Monsignor Ronald Knox's decalogue of rules for detective story writers and make the detective the criminal. Chesterton's anti-establishment politics give a special pointedness to his use of this device. Another story uses a similar anti-establishment technique in making the criminal the prosecuting consul at the trial of an apparent murderer ('The Mirror of the Magistrate').

The concern with spiritual rather than legal guilt means that the whole emphasis is redemptive rather than retributive. In that the priest is a spiritual detective he both is and is not concerned with criminal guilt. In a very striking image that Evelyn Waugh has Julia Brideshead refer to at a crisis point in *Brideshead Revisited*, Father Brown compares the way God's grace pursues a man with the detective's pursuit of a criminal but also differentiates the two:

> 'Did you catch this man?' asked the colonel, frowning.
> Father Brown looked him full in his frowning face. 'Yes', he said, 'I caught him, with an unseen hook and an invisible line which is long enough to let him wander to the ends of the world, and still bring him back with a twitch upon the thread.' (p. 50)

In another self-conscious twist to the tradition the convention of the criminal being forced to confess to the crime turns into the linked but also very different concept of confessing the sin. When Flambeau repents in 'The Queer Feet' and returns the knives and forks then that is the end of the matter for the priest. At the end of 'The Hammer of God' the priest hears the murderer declare his guilt but leaves it entirely up to him whether he gives himself up to the police or not. At the end of 'The Eye of Apollo' Flambeau asks whether he should detain the murderer but Father Brown says, ' "No; let him pass" ... with a strange deep sigh that seemed to come from the depths of the universe. "Let Cain pass by, for he belongs to God" ' (p. 141).

Of course Chesterton is notorious for his addiction to paradox. Yet the paradoxes described here go far deeper than the purely verbal level. What is most distinctive about these stories is the way that Chesterton uses, expands, tests and breaks the genre to demonstrate explicit radical paradoxes about crime, sin, forgiveness and redemption. Politically Chesterton is anti-bourgeois, anti-commercial and anti-capitalist. He continually indicates that the crimes of the respectable may be much worse than more blatant crimes:

> The worldly man, who really lives only for this world and believes in no other, whose worldly success and pleasure are all he can snatch out of nothingness – that is the man who will really do anything, when he is in danger of losing the whole world and saving nothing. It is not the revolutionary man but the respectable man who would commit any crime – to save his respectability. Think what exposure would mean to a man like that fashionable barrister ...   (p. 585)

In 'The Crime of the Communist' the convention of the least likely suspect is turned to brilliant ideological use when two millionaires are murdered in a university college and they prove to have been killed not by the communist don who has railed against them but by the bursar:

> 'Do you recall what you were all saying in the Common Room, about life being only a scramble, and nature demanding the survival of the fittest, and how it doesn't matter whether the poor are paid justly or not? Why that is the heresy that you have grown accustomed to, my friends, and it is every bit as much a heresy as Communism. That's the anti-Christian morality or immorality that you take quite naturally. And that's the immorality that has made a man a murderer today.'   (p. 672)

Similar motifs have an almost allegorical significance in 'The Paradise of Thieves', another example of the deconstruction of a crime. An English banker who has embezzled money attempts to cover up the missing funds by paying an actor to impersonate a brigand, pretend to kidnap him in an area of Sicily called 'The Paradise of Thieves' and demand a ransom. Once again Father Brown sees through the deception. The actor announces at the end that he is going to 'Manchester, Liverpool, Leeds, Hull, Huddersfield, Glasgow, Chicago, – in short, to enlightened, energetic civilised society!' A poet has the last word in the story by rejoining, 'In short ... to the real Paradise of Thieves' (p. 195).

At the end of 'The Red Moon of Meru' the idea that the sins of apparently respectable society are far greater than those of more obvious criminals is given a specifically Catholic bias from history. After a story concerning the theft of a jewel in the aristocratic house of Mallowood Abbey the priest cannot resist pointing out that it was a far greater theft when such abbeys were taken away from the Church in the first place. But the boldest development of the motif comes with 'The Curse of the Golden Cross', where an archaeologist is the victim of an elaborate plot because he has gained possession of an early Christian cross. The criminal actually escapes and will never be found. The ending therefore appears amazingly relaxed, even slapdash, but what Chesterton wants to point to in one of the most radical deconstructions in any of his stories is the recognition the archaeologist himself eventually comes to: the plot against him, the persecution he has undergone, is as nothing compared with the persecution experienced by the early Christians and operated by the whole civilized society of the time, a 'destroyer' who 'owned all the earth and commanded all the armies and the crowds ... What was it like to deal with murder on that scale? The world has forgotten these things' (p. 407).

So the political and social paradoxes of crime and guilt that Chesterton explores fuse with and in part originate from religious paradoxes, the whole paradoxical New Testament emphasis on the radicality of grace and the invitation to a new fullness of life. The respectable Pharisee is condemned, the tax collector justified; Jesus spends time with prostitutes and sinners; those who are forgiven most have most reason for love; and Christ came to call sinners not the righteous. These motifs are at the heart of Chesterton's paradoxical development of a genre that concerns justice and retribution. Naturally enough he is especially keen on the traditional paradox of the good thief. If one of his detectives becomes a murderer then his first major criminal, the thief Flambeau, becomes a detective and more importantly a penitent:

> 'Odd, isn't it ... that a thief and a vagabond should repent, when so many who are rich and secure remain hard and frivolous, and without fruit for God or man.'   (p. 50)

'The Man with Two Beards' contains another impressive example. The story depends on a burglar disguising himself as a well-known thief who has just died so that the thief will get the blame for the crime. Father Brown is the only one that knows that the thief has become a kind of saint through his penitence, and that in dying to himself he has passed 'out of the judgement of this world' even before his physical death. The accusations that the world try to lay upon him are thus defeated even before their literal defeat in the denouement of the story.

In all the best stories these various motifs, disentangled here for the purpose of analysis, fuse together to remarkable effect. 'The Queer Feet' is perhaps the best example of all, as several critics have recognized in recent years, and I would propose it in conclusion as an excellent teaching text not only for detective fiction courses but also for courses exploring the relationship between literature and theology.[10] Flambeau here steals the silver cutlery of an upper-class dining club, 'The Twelve True Fishermen', by pretending to be a waiter to the diners and a gentleman diner to the other waiters, playing on the fact that both wear similar outfits. This both is a detective story, since a crime is committed and solved, and not a detective story in that the criminal is persuaded to repent as we have seen and no further action is taken. Moreover the story has an allegorical core that relates very precisely to its self-conscious deconstruction: thieves may be readier to repent than plutocrats and the whole mechanics of the crime depend on the fact that there is such a huge social gap between gentlemen and waiters and yet it is so easy for the same man to represent both. The wealthy club is itself an obvious parody of the apostles, and this in turn relates to Father Brown as a 'fisher of men' rather than a conventional detective (although he also fulfils the latter role). As in all Chesterton's best work in this genre, he provides here in remarkably brief compass the genuine rewards of detective fiction – puzzlement, suspense, a kind of closure – and yet also succeeds in illuminating the rich blend of social and religious paradox at the heart of the Christian gospel.

Notes

1. For a useful summary see Julian Symons, *Bloody Murder: From the Detective Story to the Crime Novel: A History* (Harmondsworth: Penguin, 1974), pp. 13–15.
2. Howard Haycraft, *Murder for Pleasure: The Life and Times of the Detective Story* (London: Macmillan, 1942), p. 76.
3. 'A defence of detective stories' (1900) in *The Defendant* (London: J. M. Dent, 1918), pp. 161–2.
4. *The Penguin Complete Father Brown Stories* (Harmondsworth, 1981), p. 704.
5. On the whole topic see Lynette Hunter, *G. K. Chesterton: Explorations in Allegory* (London: Macmillan, 1979).
6. For a wider discussion of Chesterton and deconstruction see Janet Blumberg Knedlik, 'Derrida meets Father Brown: Chestertonian "deconstruction" and that harlequin "joy" ', Michael H. Macdonald and Andrew A. Tadie (eds), *G. K. Chesterton and C. S. Lewis: The Riddle of Joy* (Grand Rapids, Mich.: Eerdmans, 1989), pp. 273–89.
7. W. Robson, 'Father Brown and others' in John Sullivan (ed.), *G. K. Chesterton: A Centenary Appraisal* (London, Paul Elek, 1974), pp. 58–72, p. 67. I am indebted to this discussion for several subsequent points.
8. *Penguin Complete Father Brown*, p. 137.
9. *Robert Browning* (London: Macmillan, 1903), p. 168, cited in Hunter, *Chesterton*, p. 136.
10. See, for example, Robson, 'Father Brown and others', above, and Martin Priestman, *Detective Fiction and Literature: The Figure on the Carpet* (London: Macmillan, 1990), pp. 130–3.

16

Spirituality and the Pleasure of the Text: C. S. Lewis and the Act of Reading

William Gray

T he character in C. S. Lewis's fiction who has the most developed interest in 'spirituality' is Edward Weston, the mad, bad scientist of *Perelandra*. In a bizarre encounter which takes place on the planet Perelandra, Weston engages Ransom, the hero of Lewis's science fiction trilogy, in a philosophical argument more suited to 'a Cambridge combination room' than such 'conditions of inconceivable strangeness' (*Cosmic Trilogy*, p. 223). Weston tells Ransom that during his convalescence after the exertions of his journeys to and from Malacandra (or Mars), where he had last encountered Ransom, he has developed an interest in 'spirituality'. This new stage in Weston's personal development has taken him beyond what Lewis calls (though not in the trilogy itself) 'Westonism': that is, the quasi-religious faith that humankind can achieve some kind of immortality by constantly colonizing other planets. For Weston, however, this project of interplanetary colonization has in principle been achieved, and he now feels led beyond 'mere Westonism'. He has become disillusioned with the traditional dualism of 'Man' and 'Nature', and thinks that this binary opposition (as we might call it nowadays) breaks down when we contemplate 'the unfolding of the cosmic process' (*Cosmic Trilogy*, p. 224). He is now 'a convinced believer in emergent evolution' (ibid.), that is, in a mishmash of Bergson and other Life-philosophies, with perhaps a hint of Teilhard de Chardin. For him 'the forward movements of Life – growing spirituality – is everything' (p. 225). Weston's mission henceforth is no longer to spread the human race (via interplanetary travel), but 'to spread spirituality' (ibid.).

The spirituality to which Weston has dedicated his life has led him to penetrate the crust of 'outworn theological technicalities' which surrounds organized religion (ibid.). The underlying 'Meaning' and the 'essential truth of the religious view of life' is 'pure Spirit', 'a great, inscrutable Force' that has chosen Weston as its instrument (ibid.). At this point the Lewis persona of the bluff defender of 'mere Christianity' appears in the figure of Ransom, who replies, 'wrinkling his brow': 'I don't know much about what people call the religious view of life.... You see, I'm a Christian' (ibid.). He continues, as a chap would: 'Look here, one wants to be careful about this sort of thing. There are spirits and spirits, you know.... There's nothing especially fine about simply being a spirit. The Devil is a spirit' (*Cosmic Trilogy*, p. 227). But from the perspective of Weston's vulgar Hegelianism, which might be seen as anticipating some of what passes for (post)modern spirituality in at least some Cambridge combination rooms, such binary opposites as God and the Devil, or heaven and hell, are 'pure mythology', 'doublets [which] are really portraits of Spirit, of cosmic energy' (ibid.). 'Your heaven', Weston continues, 'is a picture of the perfect spirituality ahead: your hell a picture of the urge or *nisus* which is driving us on to it from behind' (ibid.). Ransom's obtuseness and timidity in clinging to 'the old accursed dualism', 'the miserable framework of your old jargon about self and self-sacrifice', leads Weston into a paroxysm of indignation in which he cries: 'I *am* the Universe. I, Weston, am your God and your Devil. I call that Force into me completely ...' (p. 230). There follows an object lesson illustrating Ransom's earlier remark that not all spirits are good for you. It begins when 'a spasm like that preceding a deadly vomit twisted Weston's face out of recognition' (ibid.). In a melodramatic transformation scene reminiscent of film versions of *Dr Jekyll and Mr Hyde*, Weston is turned into the hideous 'Un-man', the Devil Incarnate of Perelandra.

The Devil's interest in spirituality is also evident in *The Screwtape Letters*, published the year before *Perelandra*. In this correspondence between a senior and a junior devil, Screwtape says that 'Our Father Below' has never forgiven 'the Enemy' for producing creatures which are not, like devils, pure spirit, but a 'revolting hybrid', 'half-spirit and half animal' (*Screwtape Letters*, p. 44). It was this adulteration of spirit that originally caused 'Our Father' to 'withdraw his support' from 'the Enemy' – a withdrawal whose rapidity gave rise to the ridiculous story of some kind of ejection or fall from heaven (p. 98). 'The Enemy' has in Screwtape's view degraded 'the whole spiritual world by unnatural liaisons with the two-legged animals' (p. 17). But the humans do possess an element of spirituality which it will take a long time to remove; in the meantime the tactic is to *corrupt* it (p. 116, author's emphasis). Spirituality, or rather, false spirituality, is always to be encouraged, says Screwtape; it disarms prayer by deflecting attention from the body, for whose needs 'the Enemy', in his 'commonplace, uninteresting way', has commanded the 'little vermin' to pray (p. 137).

Spirituality is also an indispensable defence against one of the most potent weapons in 'the Enemy's' arsenal – pleasure. As Screwtape reminds Wormwood, 'the Enemy' is 'a hedonist at heart' (*Screwtape Letters*, pp. 112, 127). Beneath the façade of 'fast and vigils and stakes and crosses', 'the Enemy' offers 'pleasure, and more pleasure ... pleasures for evermore' (p. 112). At all costs Wormwood's 'patient' must be protected from '*real* pleasure', as opposed to the 'vanity, bustle ... and expensive tedium' which Wormwood can palm off on him as pleasures (p. 67, author's emphasis). *Real* pleasure, which is a true and disinterested enjoyment of something for its own sake, and not for the sake of convention or fashion, can produce in the humans 'a sort of innocence and humility and self-forgetfulness' (p. 69). Such humility and self-forgetfulness is a step on the road to the kind of loss of self which 'the Enemy' sees as the humans' highest good. The first blunder for which Screwtape chastises Wormwood was to allow his patient one of the most dangerous of pleasures – 'to read a book he really enjoyed, because he enjoyed it and not in order to make clever remarks about it to his new friends' (pp. 66f.). Wormwood's second blunder was to allow his patient the pleasure of a walk through country he really likes; but it is significant that priority is given to 'the pleasure of the text'. For Lewis, as we shall see, a human being is practically constituted by the act of reading. While any genuine pleasure would in principle do to set a human being on the road to self-transcendence, for Lewis it is above all the pleasure of the text that can lead to the saving 'annihilation of the self', as he will later put it in *An Experiment in Criticism*.

The primacy that Lewis gives to the act of reading, the sense that his fundamental way of being is 'intertextual', can be seen even in his teenage years. At the age of sixteen he wrote to his life-long friend Arthur Greeves:

> You ask whether I have ever been in love: fool as I am, I am not quite such a fool as that. But if one is only to talk from first hand experience on any subject, conversation would be a very poor business. But though I have no personal experience of the thing they call love, I have what is better – the experience of Sappho, of Euripides, of Catullus, of Shakespeare, of Spenser, of Austen, of Bronte, of, of, – anyone else I have read. We see through their eyes. (*They Stand Together*, p. 85)

The idea that in reading literature 'we see through their [the writers'] eyes' re-emerges twenty years later in Lewis's essay *The Personal Heresy*. In this attack on what Wimsatt and Beardsley would, a decade later, call 'the Intentional Fallacy', Lewis declares that we should look with the poet's eyes, and not *at* him. In order 'to see things as the poet sees them I must share his consciousness and not attend to it', whatever philosophical difficulties this may entail (*The Personal Heresy*, pp. 11f.). Lewis's resistance to any undue attention to the author and his 'personality' derives from his conviction that the act of reading offers an escape from 'personality'. Although he does not acknowledge his closeness to T. S. Eliot on this point, Lewis does in fact share Eliot's suspicion of 'personality', and the latter's deep fear of solipsism (a suspicion and a fear that may reflect the Idealist philosophical background that Lewis and Eliot had in common). Literature can enable 'a voyage beyond the limits of his [the reader's as well as the writer's] personal point of view, an annihilation of the brute fact of his own particular psychology rather that its assertion' (*The Personal Heresy*, pp. 26f.). Although 'admittedly we can never quite get out of our own skins', as Lewis was to put it 25 years later in *An Experiment in Criticism*, the reading of literature does seem to offer 'a way out'. At the very least it can enable one to 'eliminate the grosser illusions of perspective.... If I can't get out of the dungeon I shall at least look out through the bars. It is better than sinking back on the straw in the darkest corner' (*Experiment*, pp. 101f.).

If Lewis in *The Personal Heresy* seems to anticipate critics who, from Wimsatt and Beardsley to Roland Barthes, have gunned for the author, in *An Experiment in Criticism* Lewis heralds the return of the reader. The experiment he proposes is to fix critical attention on 'the act of reading' (*Experiment*, p. 104). Books on the shelf are merely 'potential literature', since literature only exists *in actu*, in the 'transient experience' of good readers reading (ibid.). Lewis is closer to those 'reader-response' critics (such as Louise Rosenblatt and Wolfgang Iser) who emphasize the primacy of the text in the text–reader relationship. There is an element of self-surrender in good reading, which Lewis calls 'receiving' the work (p. 19). The opposite of 'receiving' a work of art is 'using' it. More 'subjective' reader-response critics such as David Bleich and the later Norman Holland could be seen in Lewis's terms as 'using' rather than 'receiving' works of literature. Lewis has an almost sacramental understanding of good reading. Of serious readers he writes:

> the first reading of some literary work is often ... an experience so momentous that only experiences of love, religion or bereavement can furnish a standard of comparison. Their whole consciousness is changed. They have become what they were not before. (*Experiment*, p. 3)

Such literary readers live, one might say, 'intertextually': 'Scenes and characters from books provide them with a sort of iconography by which they interpret or sum up their own experience' (ibid.). An obvious weakness of Lewis's approach is his over-confident conviction that it is possible to draw a clear line between the life-enhancing 'reception' of good literature by 'the few', and the self-gratifying 'use' of bad literature by 'the many'. It would have been interesting in this regard to hear what Lewis had to say about the cunning ambiguities of, for example, *Madame Bovary*, or the Gerty MacDowell chapter in *Ulysses*; but these were not Lewis's kind of books.

Whatever reservations we may have about his over-prescriptive demarcations between the 'reception' of good literature by the few and the 'use' of bad literature by the many, at least Lewis is not seeking to impose some monolithic canon after the fashion of F. R. Leavis. Although Leavis is not mentioned by name, *An Experiment in Criticism* is among other things a sustained attack on the Leavis school on its own Cambridge turf. It is easy perhaps to underestimate the boldness of Lewis in attacking what he calls 'the Viligant school' in 1961, when Leavis and his followers were still dominant in Cambridge. Whether or not the 'literary Puritans' mentioned by Lewis early in *An Experiment in Criticism* are entirely to be identified with the 'evaluative' or 'Vigilant' critics discussed later, the former certainly have the potential to become the latter. The 'literary Puritans' are in their way deeply 'spiritual'. For them 'the Puritan conscience works on without the Puritan theology – like millstones grinding nothing' (*Experiment*, p. 10). The literary Puritan 'applies to literature all the scruples, the rigorism, the self-examination, the distrust of pleasure, which his forebears applied to the spiritual life; and perhaps soon all the intolerance and self-righteousness' (ibid.). Such a literary temperament would find itself particularly drawn to the high spiritual calling of the Vigilant school, which Lewis describes thus:

> They are entirely honest, and wholly in earnest. They believe they are smelling out and checking a very great evil. They could sincerely say like St Paul, 'Woe to me if I preach not the gospel': Woe to me if I do not seek out vulgarity, superficiality, and false sentiment, and expose them wherever they lie hidden. A sincere inquisitor or a sincere witch-finder can hardly do his work with mildness. (*Experiment*, p. 125)

It is perhaps as well that Lewis did not name his opponents more specifically. The Leavisites may be long gone, but as a type 'the Vigilant critic' lives on, though the evils requiring exposure would now be different – the 'usual suspects' of more recent years would probably include 'monologism', '(phal)logocentrism' and 'humanism'.

But as Screwtape long ago pointed out, such fashion-dependent literary (or perhaps 'cultural') scrupulosity is hardly compatible with *real* (as opposed to merely *theorized*) pleasure, and especially the pleasure of the text. As Lewis puts it in *An Experiment in Criticism*:

> Vigilance must already have prevented many happy unions of a good reader with a good book.... The all-important conjunction (Reader Meets Text) never seems to have been allowed to occur of itself and develop spontaneously. Here, plainly, are young people drenched, dizzied, and bedevilled by criticism to a point at which primary literary experience is no longer possible. (*Experiment*, pp. 127ff.)

Or as A. D. Nuttall, an admirer of C. S. Lewis, more colourfully expresses it: 'The final result may be a kind of literary teaching which crushes literary enjoyment, the natural *coitus* of reader and work endlessly *interruptus*' (*A New Mimesis*, p. 84).

Like 'the Enemy' in *The Screwtape Letters*, Lewis the reader is 'a hedonist at heart'. He has no problems with founding his theory of literature on pleasure. It is just that 'pleasure' is an empty abstraction; the real work of defining the *particular* pleasure of reading still has to be done by a hedonistic theory of literature. Lewis resists locating the pleasure of the text in the 'shape' or 'form' of the *poiema* ('the something made' as opposed to the *logos*, 'the something said'). Without explicitly mentioning the 'Well-Wrought Urn' of Cleanth Brooks, Lewis nevertheless calls in question the adequacy of the metaphor of 'shape' to the phenomenon of literature. 'The parts of the Poiema are things we ourselves *do* ... in an order, and at a tempo prescribed by the poet', he says (*Experiment*, p. 133, my emphasis). And 'this is less like looking at a vase than like "doing exercises" under an expert's direction or taking part in a choric dance invented by a good choreographer' (p. 134). One wonders what Lewis would have made of Iser's phenomenological account of 'the act of reading', which Lewis's approach seems in part to anticipate (Iser does mention some of Lewis's books, but I can find no reference by Iser to *An Experiment in Criticism*). What Lewis calls the distinctive literary pleasure of 'obedience to what seems worth obeying and is not quite easily obeyed' (ibid.) is an end in itself, not a means to some further end, such as a view or philosophy of life, or a comment on life (p. 135). While Lewis rejects the literary theories of Aristotle and I. A. Richards, he thinks that they offer the right *sort* of theory; that is, 'they place the goodness (where we actually feel it to be) in what has *happened* to us while we read' (ibid., my emphasis).

The nearest Lewis gets to labelling what actually happens to us while we read is the phrase 'an enlargement of our being'

(*Experiment*, p. 137). 'We want to be more than ourselves', he says; 'we want to escape the illusions of perspective' (ibid.). By this Lewis does not mean that we aspire to some perspectiveless view, some objective 'view from nowhere'. Rather, 'we want to see with other eyes, to imagine with other imaginations, to feel with other hearts, as well as our own' (ibid.). Here Lewis seems very close to the hermeneutical tradition, particularly perhaps to Gadamer; the latter says of the hermeneutical experience, paradigmatically the experience of reading, that it is experienced not 'as a loss of self-possession, but rather as an *enrichment* of our self' (*Philosophical Hermeneutics*, p. 57, author's emphasis). The resonance should not surprise us too much, since Lewis retained the imprint of his youthful Hegelianism long after most British philosophers had discarded such unfashionable views. And behind this quasi-Hegelian aesthetic is a Platonic impulse, of the kind expressed in modern times by Simone Weil and Iris Murdoch. Thus Lewis writes:

> The primary impulse of each is to maintain and aggrandize himself. The secondary impulse is to go out of the self, to correct its provincialism and heal its loneliness. In love, in virtue, in the pursuit of knowledge, and in the reception of the arts, we are doing this. Obviously this process can be described either as an enlargement or as a temporary annihilation of the self. But that is an old paradox; 'he that loseth his life shall save it'. (*Experiment*, p. 138)

A key term in the above passage is 'reception', which here means the good reading of good art and literature, rather than the mere 'use' of bad art and literature 'to maintain and aggrandize' the self (here Lewis is close to Iris Murdoch, especially in *The Fire and the Sun*).

Lewis's residual Hegelianism is ultimately a form of Christian Platonism. The *stirb und werde* (die and become) motif runs through literary experience, love, moral action, and religion. There is no infinite qualitative difference, no absolute breach, between these central human experiences and Christian faith. Rather, there is a continuum from ordinary (but 'real') pleasures to the bliss of the beatific vision. Lewis talks elsewhere of the 'secret doctrine' that '*pleasures* are shafts of the glory as it strikes our sensibility' (*Letters to Malcolm*, p. 90, author's emphasis). Of such pleasures he writes: 'Adoration says: "What must be the quality of that Being whose far-off and momentary coruscations are like this!" One's mind runs back up the sunbeam to the sun (p. 91f.). Such a 'lived dialectic' is in effect a version of the ontological argument, as Lewis recognized when discussing 'the dialectic of Desire' in the Preface to the third edition of *The Pilgrim's Regress* (p. 15). In this 'lived dialectic', Sweet Desire, which 'pierces us like a rapier at the smell of a bonfire, the sound of wild ducks flying overhead, the title of *The Well at the World's End*, the opening lines of *Kubla Khan*, the morning cobwebs in late summer, or the noise of falling waves', will, if diligently followed, lead in the end to the *real* object of desire, that is, to God (ibid.).

While the pleasures which can lead us back to their divine source are by no means all literary, it is remarkable how many *are* literary, or have literary associations. One can see why Screwtape thinks that Wormwood has made a blunder of the first order by allowing his patient 'to read a book he really enjoyed'. But Wormwood's blunder pales into insignificance beside the incompetence of whatever devil was sent to acquire the soul of C. S. Lewis. For we discover that: 'a fortnight before his death, he [Lewis] was reading *Les Liaisons Dangereuses* and writing to a colleague at Magdalene, Cambridge – "Wow, what a book!"' (Wilson, *C. S. Lewis*, p. 292).

References

Gadamer, H.-G., *Philosophical Hermeneutics* (Berkeley: University of California Press, 1977)

Lewis C. S., *The Pilgrim's Regress* (1933; 3rd edn with Preface 1943) (London: Collins Fount, 1977)

Lewis C. S., *The Personal Heresy: A Controversy* (with E. M. W. Tillyard) (London: Oxford University Press, 1939)

Lewis C. S., *The Screwtape Letters* (1942) (London: Collins Fontana, 1955)

Lewis C. S., *Perelandra* (1943) in *The Cosmic Trilogy* (London: Pan Books in association with The Bodley Head, 1989)

Lewis C. S., *An Experiment in Criticism* (1961) (Cambridge: Cambridge University Press, 1965)

Lewis C. S., *Letters to Malcolm: Chiefly on Prayer* (1964) (London: Collins Fount, 1977)

Lewis C. S., *They Stand Together: The Letters of C. S. Lewis to Arthur Greeves 1914–1963*, ed. Walter Hooper (London: Collins, 1979)

Nuttall, A. D., *A New Mimesis* (London: Methuen, 1983)

Wilson, A. N., *C. S. Lewis: A Biography* (London: Collins, 1990)

17

'Gentle Jesus Meek and Mild': Religious Themes in the Novels of William Golding

Kevin McCarron

For God is a fire, that consumeth, devoureth, rageth; verily He is your undoing, as fire consumeth a house and maketh it dust and ashes.

Luther, *De Servo Arbitrio*

A lthough religion is a central issue in William Golding's fiction, it rarely manifests itself as conventional, contemporary Christianity. Golding's Christianity is an integration of the harshness of the Old Testament and the redemptive possibilities suggested by the New Testament. Overall, while his representation of religion often incorporates traditional Christian imagery, it is considerably less morally focused than most contemporary understandings of Christianity. Religion, in Golding's work, is often depicted as a force, morally neutral and even capricious. In *The Idea of the Holy*, Rudolph Otto uses the phrase *mysterium tremendum* to describe any powerful religious energy. He notes that while this can be apprehended in states of serenity and tranquillity this *mysterium tremendum* also has its darker side:

It may burst in sudden eruption up from the depths of the soul with spasms and convulsions, or lead to the strangest excitements, to intoxicated frenzy, to transport, and to ecstasy. It has its wild and demonic forms and can sink to an almost grisly horror and shuddering. It has its crude, barbaric antecedents and early manifestations ...[1]

The language of religion is constantly metaphorical, and Otto notes of the 'life within the spirit': 'It gives the peace that passes understanding, and of which the tongue can only stammer brokenly. Only from afar by metaphors and analogies, do we come to apprehend what it is in itself, and even so our notion is but inadequate and confused.'[2] Golding, too, attempts to depict the 'life of the spirit', from afar, by metaphor and analogy.

Golding's literary career is clearly divisible into three distinct phases. The first of these begins with *Lord of the Flies* in 1945 and ends with the publication of *The Spire* in 1964. The second phase incorporates the volume of essays *The Hot Gates* (1965), the novel *The Pyramid* (1967) and the three short stories collected as *The Scorpion God* (1971). With the exception of the collection of essays *A Moving Target* (1982) and the travel book *An Egyptian Journal* (1985), the third phase comprises novels alone, beginning with the publication of *Darkness Visible* in 1979; following this were *Rites of Passage* (1980), *The Paper Men* (1984), *Close Quarters* (1987), and *Fire Down Below* (1989), and then the posthumously published *The Double Tongue* (1995).

Golding's primary religious concern is the nature of evil, and while the earlier fiction often suggests that humanity is composed equally of good and evil, the later fiction implies that existence itself is similarly constructed. Golding's fictional modalities move from fable to fantasy, and his emphasis shifts from psychology to ontology.

In *Lord of the Flies*, Golding's ability to employ language which both provides narrative impetus and also evokes profounder, more theological implications is demonstrated immediately: 'Taking their cue from the innocent Johnny, they sat down on the fallen palm tree and waited.'[3] The novel is spare, deliberate in its intentions; and certainly Golding himself has little hesitation in referring to it as a 'fable'. In his essay 'Fable', Golding writes: 'It is worth looking for a moment at the great original of boys on an island. This is *The Coral Island*, published a century ago, at the height of Victorian smugness, ignorance and prosperity.'[4] Ballantyne's book is optimistic in an imperialist, Victorian manner. Evil lies firmly outside the English schoolboys in this book and is made manifest by savage, black cannibals. Throughout *Lord of the Flies*, Golding overturns Ballantyne's optimistic portrait, which equates

English with good and foreign with evil, and suggests that evil is more likely to reside within humanity and that external evil is a projection of an inner evil. Golding uses the same names for his central characters as Ballantyne does for his trio of brave, clean, young Englishmen, which assists the comparison and eventual subversion of the beliefs central to Ballantyne's book. Golding's characters are essentially used to portray sharply differing points of view on the nature of evil, and the means of placating this powerful force. For Piggy, there is no such thing as evil — it is just people behaving irrationally; for Jack, evil resides outside humanity and must be placated by various forms of sacrifice; and for Simon, evil expresses itself in the words of the Lord of the Flies: evil is inside humanity. Conversely, the depiction of evil in *The Coral Island* is strikingly simplistic, revolving about a specifically Christian/pagan dichotomy. Ballantyne offers a solution to the problem of evil at the end of *The Coral Island* that Golding has introduced at the beginning of his novel, and it is, significantly, no solution at all. *The Coral Island* insistently suggests that the cruelty and savagery of the pagans are due to their unfortunate ignorance of Christianity, and it is precisely this optimistic view that Golding seeks to subvert in *Lord of the Flies*.

Golding informs his readers immediately that the context of his characters' lives is specifically Christian: ' "I ought to be chief," said Jack, "because I'm chapter chorister and head boy." '[5] The choir is a specifically religious institution and yet it is Jack and his hunters who become the most cruel and violent of all the boys on the island. In *Lord of the Flies*, therefore, we find an adumbration of the disturbing connection between religion, violence and blood sacrifice that Golding examines in close detail throughout the first phase of his career, and which is realized most powerfully in *The Spire*. As Golding's first novel moves toward its grim conclusion, the reader must wonder if Jack and his choir become hunters and sacrificers of other human beings despite their obvious Christian origins, or because of them.

The plot of *The Inheritors* (1955) is as straightforward as that of *Lord of the Flies*, and indeed is similar to it: a small group of Neanderthalers is systematically killed by a larger group of 'New Men', *Homo sapiens*. From the novel's beginning, the New Men are associated with disruption,

violence and death. The title contains a sombre pun on 'Blessed
are the meek: for they shall inherit the earth' (Matthew 5.5) as
throughout the course of this novel we realize that here the
meek do not 'inherit' the earth, rather we, *Homo sapiens*, do –
and the meek are completely destroyed. One of Golding's
principal interests in his early fiction is examining the ways in
which humanity projects an inner evil onto something, or
someone, external. It is this issue of 'projection' which accounts
for the stress Golding lays in these early novels upon the
scapegoat, human sacrifice, and, in *The Inheritors*, upon
cannibalism. The acts of sacrifice and propitiation which are so
important in *Lord of the Flies* are equally important in *The
Inheritors*, and for many of the same reasons. They are a way
of projecting, and then attempting to appease, an evil which is
represented as actually internal. Golding's central characters,
Lok and Fa, for example, find 'presents' which have been left
for them by the New Men. These gifts are an act of propitiation
similar to the one which is made in *Lord of the Flies* when
Jack's hunters leave out their gift for 'the beast'. To the New
Men, Lok and Fa are devils and must be placated, even to the
extent of offering the child Tanakil as a blood sacrifice. *The
Inheritors* is a novel as deeply concerned as its predecessor with
humanity's persistent attempt to locate evil outside itself, and
then to offer it blood, in the doomed hope that then ' "it won't
bother us, maybe" '.[6]

While the religion of the New Men is patriarchal and is as
inevitably aggressive as its practioners, the religion of Golding's
Neanderthalers is strikingly matriarchal. Throughout the
novel, and particularly in the opening chapters, Golding depicts
the innocent life of the People. Their lives are hard, mundane,
and brutal, but we see their sense of tribal communion, their
gentleness, their physicality and love of play, and their worship
of a female deity who abhors bloodshed. Oa is fecund and
protective; she inspires joy, not fear. Oa is clearly the opposite
of the rutting, bellowing Stag God of the New Men, and yet the
reader is forced to accept that any culture based on Christianity
has more in common with this violent being than it does with
the gentle Oa. Another clear distinction is drawn when we see
that among the People it is the women who control the tribe's
religious life. When Lok follows the women into the cave of ice
where Oa is worshipped, he is so terrified by the religious

power he senses that Fa is forced to comfort him. The life-affirming vision of the People embodies a set of values which cannot comprehend human sacrifice, an action which is, as is revealed while Lok and Fa observe the New Men from the vantage point of a dead tree, itself a 'realistic' theological symbol, central to the New Men's religious practice. However, the fundamentally religious nature of human sacrifice is stressed by numerous writers. Hubert and Mauss write:

> But if sacrifice is so complex, whence comes its unity? Because, fundamentally, beneath the diverse forms it takes, it always consists in the same procedure, which may be used for the most widely differing purposes. *This procedure consists in establishing a means of communication between the sacred and the profane worlds through the mediation of a victim, that is, of a thing that in the course of the ceremony is destroyed.*[7]

Nigel Davis similarly notes: 'In essence, human sacrifice was an act of piety. Both sacrificer and victim knew that the act was required to save the people from calamity and the cosmos from collapse. Their object, therefore, was more to preserve than destroy life.'[8]

As noted above, Golding's primary religious concern is the nature of evil and, in particular, its often ambivalent causes and manifestations. For Hegel, whose views here on original sin are reminiscent of those suggested in *Lord of the Flies*, evil is rooted in particularity:

> My particularity and finitude are precisely the factors which constitute my lack of identity with God. This is the meaning of the doctrine that man is by nature evil, a far profounder truth than the modern shallow view that man is by nature good. For evil is simply particularity. I do evil when I persist in my particularity.[9]

Augustine's conception of evil is clearly anti-Manichaean: 'Augustine came to believe that evil originates not from some substance, but from perverseness of will.'[10] Golding's fiction, however, consistently suggests that any understanding of evil that sees it as simply opposed to good is severely limited. His fiction endorses the view expressed by David Parkin: 'It [evil] fits the ontological description of inexplicably human, inhuman monsters, and so is not simply a term opposed to "good".'[11] Golding's depiction of evil is not grounded in this conventional understanding of evil as the second part of the good/evil dichotomy. William Ray cites Derrida: 'an opposition of metaphysical concepts (eg: speech/writing, presence/absence etc) is NEVER the confrontation of two terms, but a hierarchy and the order of a subordination'.[12] Golding rejects the depiction of good and evil as a 'hierarchy and the order of a subordination'; instead he invariably illustrates the ways in which these two concepts are interwoven, not at all in opposition.

While both *Lord of the Flies* and *The Inheritors* consider the notion of the projection of evil on a grand scale, and assess its implications for humanity and for history, Golding's third novel, *Pincher Martin* (1956), reduces the scale of its concern and focuses on one unique individual, Christopher Martin, known as Pincher Martin. Again, the plot is extremely simple; the difficulty readers often experience with it is, as with *The Inheritors*, due to the complex form of expression. During World War II, Christopher Martin, a lieutenant in the navy, is thrown from the bridge of his ship when it is hit by a torpedo, and the novel opens with him struggling in the water. The novel describes him finding a small rock in the middle of the ocean and then recounts, in extraordinary detail, his grim struggle for survival on this rock. However, in the novel's extraordinary closing pages the reader discovers that Martin has been dead since the opening lines of the book. *Pincher Martin* investigates a greed so intense, a pride so enormous, that death becomes unthinkable. As Martin struggles in the sea we are told his thoughts:

> I won't die.
> I can't die.
> Not me.
> Precious.[13]

Just as the boys in *Lord of the Flies* project their fears and horrors onto 'the beast', and the New Men in *The Inheritors* turn the gentle Neanderthalers into demons, so Martin in this novel transforms an aching tooth in his own mouth into an island in the middle of the ocean, and creates from his egotistical and perverse refusal to die a heroic struggle for survival. Pincher Martin parodies the Genesis myth of creation and for six days and six nights Martin creates his world: the rock, the sea, the sky, night, day, the seaweed, the gulls, and the shell fish. Finally, on the sixth day, it seems that he creates God. The God he creates is in his own image, wearing an oilskin and seaboots, and it says to him ' "Have you had enough, Christopher?" '[14] But Martin refuses to admit he has had enough, and screams defiance to the end. Finally he is metonymically reduced to a pair of claws (pincers) and is annihilated by the black lightning which is the only conception of an afterlife which he possesses. Although the parallels with Genesis might prompt the reader to assume that the figure who speaks to Martin is God, it is also possible that this is the voice of the author. As Martin begins to disintegrate in the face of the black lightning, references which could clearly refer to the act of writing begin to appear: 'The sea stopped moving, froze, became paper, painted paper that was torn by a black line. The rock was painted on the same paper.'[15] *Pincher Martin* can also, therefore, be read as a metafictional text, openly commenting on its own fictional status, rather than as a purely theological fable. Golding's interest in the process of creation itself is further developed in his use of the painter Samuel Mountjoy, the protagonist of his next novel, *Free Fall* (1959).

A conflict between dual perspectives is anticipated in the novel's title. The phrase 'free fall' suggests an object obeying the law of gravity and falling through space, but it also has religious connotations, suggesting the theological fall of humanity, and it is possible that the title has been taken from Milton's *Paradise Lost* ('Sufficient to have stood | But free to fall'). The protagonist's name is one that also anticipates dualities. 'Samuel' is the name of an Old Testament prophet, while 'Mountjoy' clearly possesses sexual connotations. This tension between the religious and the carnal, the spirit and the flesh, provides the central dynamic of *Free Fall*. These two different perceptions of life are personified in the characters of Mountjoy's schoolteachers, Nick Shales and Rowena Pringle. Shales is a scientist, a rationalist; while Pringle teaches Scripture, and tells the children of a world in which a bush can catch fire and yet be unconsumed by the flames. Throughout the novel, Mountjoy tries to find a way to reconcile these two visions, to find a bridge between two worlds, and yet at the novel's conclusion he notes that Shales's world is real and so is Pringle's – there is no bridge. Mountjoy's failure, of course, is not Golding's. *Free Fall* can be seen as a book which is concerned not only with the attempt to find the truth, but also with the desire to communicate the truth. Early in the book, Mountjoy notes: 'To communicate is our passion and our despair.'[16] *Free Fall* ceaselessly investigates the ways in which we select the material we wish to communicate, and the nature of the language we use for this communication.

Golding's fifth novel, *The Spire* (1964), is also structured around the act of communication – in this case a vision and a command from God. Like *Free Fall*, *The Spire* is an investigation of the two differing worlds of the flesh and the spirit but unlike the earlier novel, *The Spire* moves toward an emphatic resolution. The novel has an omniscient narrator, but virtually every event within it is seen through Jocelin's eyes. This creates a perspective which is both uneasily ambivalent and brutally circumscribed, and this latter quality is paralleled in the claustrophobic, fourteenth-century setting of the novel. Similarly, the continuous blurring of the two narrative perspectives parallels the movement of the story toward the reconciliation of two worlds; an event most spectacularly realized in Jocelin's death-bed epiphany.

The Spire is like all of Golding's early fiction in that a simple story is told in a complicated manner. Jocelin, Dean of Barchester Cathedral, believes that he has been chosen by God to build a 400-foot-high spire on top of the cathedral. It quickly becomes apparent that the foundations under the cathedral will not support such a weight, and yet, against all sound practical advice, Jocelin persists with his dream. During the course of the novel the workmen murder Pangall, a deformed cathedral factotum, and Jocelin eventually realizes that Pangall has been sacrificed in an attempt to appease the dark powers which the workmen worship. Sacrifice is interwoven throughout *The Spire* with revelation and vision and as *The Spire* progresses we witness the appalling personal price Jocelin is prepared to pay, and the price he inflicts upon the innocent. In *The Inheritors*, too, we were made aware of cost – of the awesome price the New Men had to pay in order to surmount their origins. One of Golding's most persistent themes, and one as grimly embedded in the text of *The Spire* as Pangall himself is embedded in the foundations of the cathedral, is the necessity of acquiring knowledge. The results of Jocelin's actions, however, cannot change the intensity of the faith which he so obviously possesses, and it is the power of this faith which we are being asked to witness. Golding writes of a faith so strong that its destructive powers amount to what is virtually a blasphemous travesty of faith, yet still remains superior to its antithesis, reason. What appears to be a simple dichotomy between faith and reason, however, is complicated when it is seen that faith in this novel has two guises. The historical setting allows the proximity of Stonehenge to challenge the authority of the cathedral, and this allows Golding to depict a destructive collision between pagan beliefs and Christianity – and to suggest the deep and cruel similarities between them. At the novel's conclusion, when all the principal characters are dead or dying, the spire still stands. Disturbingly, the reader is asked to consider whether the spire stands despite the sacrifice of Pangall, or because it. The final moments are a technical triumph for Golding; the highly charged language and the splintered chronology brilliantly evoke the dying moments of Jocelin. In his last moment of life Jocelin discovers something of immense importance, and simultaneously discovers that what he understands cannot be communicated. Language is an ineffective medium for the communication of what Jocelin has to say, and he is reduced to simile:

> In the tide, flying like a bluebird, struggling, shouting, screaming to leave behind the words of magic and incomprehension – It's like the appletree![17]

In this final moment, Jocelin realizes that, like the spire itself, life is a miracle, rooted deeply in both innocence and guilt, in beauty and in blood.

Maggie Kilgour writes of Coleridge's 'The Rime of the Ancient Mariner', a work which has been seen by the majority of Golding's critics as central to his 'Sea Trilogy': *Rites of Passage*, *Close Quarters* and *Fire Down Below*: 'The world of the "Ancient Mariner" still could be considered sacramental in its assertion that the physical world has a spiritual meaning if one keeps in mind the fact that *sacer* is a primal word that unites the antithetical states of blessed and cursed.'[18] Although all of Golding's later fiction moves toward a state of synthesis, a denial of distinctions, which is achieved through the reconciliation of ostensibly antithetical positions, Golding's interest in specifically religious themes is most pronounced in *Darkness Visible* and *The Paper Men*. In *Darkness Visible*, good and evil, ostensibly represented by Matty and Sophy, are revealed as differing manifestations of a single ontological force, and in *The Paper Men* the belief that 'creative' writing, exemplified by Wilf Barclay, and 'critical' writing, represented by Rick Tucker, are antithetical is also emphatically refuted, as is the antithesis believed to exist between the holy and the unholy.

Darkness Visible is divided into three sections, each one of which is centred upon a specific character. The first section focuses upon Matty, who has emerged from the blazing ruins of London's docks after a bombing raid during World War II, and who acts throughout the novel like an Old Testament prophet. The second section focuses upon Sophy, who, because of her criminal behaviour, sexual excesses and general attitude to life, is usually seen as the antithesis to Matty, and therefore as a figure representing evil. The third section describes the convergence of these two characters. Sophy plans to kidnap a child for ransom from the school where Matty is working as a caretaker, but Matty sacrifices his life to stop this happening. The novel ends with the death of Mr Pedigree, a paedophile, who once taught Matty and who appears throughout the novel as both a tragic and a comic figure. In essence, *Darkness Visible* is a novel which illuminates the inseparably integrated nature of good and evil, not the polarized distinction between them. In *The Varieties of Religious Experience*, William James writes: 'In mystical literature such self-contradictory phrases as "dazzling obscurity", "whispering silence", "teeming desert", are continuously met with.'[19] The phrase 'darkness visible' could clearly be added to this list.

Critical consideration of the title to Golding's novel has been limited to announcing its probable source, and has focused exclusively upon Milton. Bernard F. Dick's comments may be seen as paradigmatic of the way in which this focusing upon *Paradise Lost* as the source for Golding's title structures subsequent responses to the novel. Dick writes that the title is 'taken from Milton's *Paradise Lost*; it comes from his description of hell (l.63) where, despite its fires, darkness alone is visible ... This, then, is hell: an unnatural state, a place of fiery darkness. *Darkness Visible* is about hell.'[20] However, *Paradise Lost* may be a misleading reference when it is used as a basis for assuming that *Darkness Visible* also presents an antithetical opposition between good and evil, in the respective forms of Matty and Sophy, parallel to that which is embodied by God and Satan in *Paradise Lost*. *Paradise Lost* is relevant to *Darkness Visible* only when the poem is viewed as the dramatization of a paradox, and not as a conflict between the separate and opposing forces of good and evil. Alan Macfarlane writes of *Paradise Lost*:

> This confusion at the heart of life is echoed in Milton's greatest poem. The central theme of *Paradise Lost* is the battle between good and evil. Yet the struggle is not between two opposed sides, but within the same principle. The poem is an attempt to state the paradox that good and evil are entirely separate, yet also entirely the same.[21]

This suggestion that good and evil 'are entirely separate, yet also entirely the same' is central to *Darkness Visible* and can be found in the work of a number of different writers. For example, within the notes he appends to Baudelaire's poem 'Les Litanies de Satan', C. F. MacIntyre quotes from Baudelaire's own work *Mon coeur mis a nu*: 'In every man, at the same time, there are two simultaneous postulations, the one toward God, the other toward Satan.'[22] Jean-Paul Sartre states specifically of these 'simultaneous postulations' suggested by Baudelaire: 'It must be understood that in actual fact these two postulations are not independent, are not two autonomous and opposing forces which are applied simultaneously at the same point, but that one is a function of the other.'[23]

Although Matty is invariably seen as good, a perspective which can offer the reader another way of regarding Matty may be suggested in the striking description of him as he emerges from the flames in the opening pages of the novel: 'The brightness on his left side was not an effect of light. The burn was even more visible on the left side of his head.'[24] Ronald Inden writes of Vena, 'the evil-souled one': 'He is the charred remains of a fire, not fire itself ... in a word, ugly. Appropriately, this dregs of a son was brought forth ... on the inauspicious (death-related) side of the body.'[25] Evil is seen here, not as a form of proud self-aggrandizement, as it is represented in *Paradise Lost*, but as a lack; as a manifestation of unfulfilment. David Parkin notes of Paul Ricoeur's book *The Symbolism of Evil*: 'Ricoeur's view of evil, as primordially that of defilement or staining what was clean or pure does not quite capture the more profound notion of physical imperfection.'[26] Although Golding's critics focus upon the possible biblical connotations of the name 'Matthew', the first book of the novel is called 'Matty', and this is the name he is known by throughout the novel. The name 'Matty' is similar to the word matter, the substance which in Manichaean cosmology is the very embodiment of evil: 'Manichaeism combined Christian and Zoroastrian elements, teaching that evil is a positive principle, embodied in matter, while the good principle is embodied in spirit.'[27] Stan Gooch similarly writes of Gnostic views on religious dualism: 'The world of matter (darkness) belongs to the Devil and he alone is its ruler.'[28] Sophy's name is of equal importance to *Darkness Visible*. Edwin M. Mosely notes of the central female character in Dostoevsky's *Crime and Punishment*: 'It has been pointed out that Sonia is a diminutive for Sophia, and that Sophia in the Greek-Orthodox religion is added to the Trinity as a kind of female principle suggesting both Wisdom and Love, almost in the sense of the Love that surpasseth Understanding.'[29]

Darkness Visible describes the counter-entropic activity generated by both Matty and Sophy. The central vision of unity that the novel conveys is in the depiction of Matty and Sophy as connected, not opposed; together, they *are* darkness visible. Like the two ostensible antithetical visions in Lipari and Rome which Wilf Barclay experiences in *The Paper Men*, Matty and Sophy embody the inseparable manifestations of religious power. Mircea Eliade writes of the violent Indian mother-goddesses Duraga and Kali: 'One understands that this conjunction of virtues and sins, of crimes and generosity, of creativity and destructiveness, is the great enigma of life itself.'[30] *Darkness Visible* depicts a world in which to choose damnation wilfully is to exist on a superior spiritual level to most of those who believe in salvation, and one in which human sacrifice may be pleasing to a God whom contemporary society erroneously envisages as 'Gentle Jesus, meek and mild'.

The Paper Men was very poorly received when it appeared in 1984, attracting the worst reviews of Golding's career. The novel describes the efforts of an elderly novelist, Wilf Barclay, to escape the predatory attempts of a young American academic, Rick Tucker, who wishes to write a biography of Barclay. Perhaps understandably, *The Paper Men* was seen as a rather cantankerous attack on academics by a famous author and, perhaps equally understandably, academics and reviewers were not particularly amused. However, the novel refutes any distinction between the critical and the creative, and in so doing it actively supports the literary theories which it appears to attack. Tucker introduces himself to Barclay as a professor, a claim which Barclay later discovers to be a lie. Nor is it the only one, and Tucker's subsequent lies, exaggerations and fantasies suggest that he lives by 'fictions'. Conversely, Barclay's primary gift is his ability to 'select' – he claims to 'invent' almost nothing. Patricia Waugh argues that no valid hierarchical order exists in the assignation of respective functions to product and process, but that instead: 'The two processes are held together in a formal tension which breaks down the distinctions between "creation" and "criticism" and merges them into the concepts of "interpretation" and "deconstruction".'[31] The attitude which post-structuralism adopts towards this ubiquitous antithesis is similarly one of vigorous denial: 'There is no clear division for post-structuralism between "criticism" and "creation": both modes are subsumed into "writing" as such.'[32] Eagleton also notes: 'deconstruction rejects the literary/non-literary opposition as any absolute distinction'.[33] Golding uses the conflict between Tucker and Barclay as a way of anticipating, then paralleling, the denial of an ontological antithesis.

On the Sicilian island of Lipari, Barclay, fleeing from Tucker, enters a cathedral and immediately realizes that it has a peculiar type of resonance:

> there was something about that cathedral, an atmosphere ... You could call it a complete absence of gentle Jesus meek and mild. I didn't like it and was in half a mind to leave but knew that if I did I should only find myself in an endless stream of time with nothing to help me forget it. I went on.[34]

Within the north transept Barclay discovers a silver statue of Christ, but he uneasily notes that the silver resembles steel somehow, and immediately he begins to wonder precisely who, or what, the statue really represents:

Perhaps it was Christ. Perhaps they had inherited it in these parts and just changed the name and it was Pluto, the god of the Underworld, Hades, striding forward. I stood there with my mouth open and the flesh crawling all over my body. I knew in one destroying instant that all my adult life I had believed in God and this knowledge was a vision of God. Fright entered the very marrow of my bones. Surrounded, swamped, confounded, all but destroyed, adrift in the universal intolerance, mouth open, screaming, bepissed and beshitten, I knew my maker and I fell down.[35]

The juxtaposition in the cathedral of Christ with Pluto, in an atmosphere that is terrifyingly empty of conventional religious reassurance, clearly constitutes a deeply ambiguous episode and one that many readers might describe as 'unholy'. However, it is precisely this antithesis that is commonly believed to exist between the holy and the unholy which is itself being assessed in this episode. Otto suggests that the conventional under-standing of the word 'holy' is itself often in error: 'We generally take "holy" as meaning "completely good"; it is the absolute moral attribute, denoting the consummation of moral goodness ... But this common usage of the term is inaccurate ...'[36]

The power in the cathedral that causes Barclay to faint is not good or evil. It can be seen as, in Nietzsche's famous phrase, *beyond* good and evil. The force that is revealed to Barclay in the cathedral is naked religious power, revealed in all its purity, stripped completely of its moral and ethical trappings. Eliade writes: 'In Yahweh, too, we find the benevolent creator combined with another, terrible, destructive, and jealous god, and that negative aspect of divinity makes it plain to us that God is *Everything*.'[37] Otto writes of that Old Testament phenomenon 'The wrath of God':

it is patent from many passages of the Old Testament that this 'wrath' has no concern whatever with moral qualities ... Anyone who is accustomed to think of deity only by its rational attributes must see in this 'wrath' mere caprice and wilful passion. But such a view would have been emphatically rejected by the religious men of the Old Covenant, for to them the Wrath of God, so far from being a diminution of His Godhead, appears as a natural expression of it, an element of 'holiness' itself, and a quite indispensable one. And in this they are entirely right.[38]

Barclay's initial response to the events in the cathedral is to assume, erroneously, that the wrathful power which over-whelms him is religious Truth in its entirety. In Rome, however, he has a vision which is beatific:

> There was sunlight everywhere, not the heavy light of Rome but a kind of radiance as if the sun were everywhere. I'd never noticed before, but now I saw, looking down, that the steps had the symmetrical curve of a musical instrument, guitar, cello, violin ... All the people were young and like flowers. I found that he was standing by me on the roof of his house after all and we went down together and stood among the people with the patterns of jewels and the heaps of flowers all blazing inside and out with the radiance. Then they made music of the steps.[39]

Just as the combination of Matty and Sophy begins to approach some representation of the nature of existence, so too the visions in Lipari and Rome, together, show Barclay the true nature of religious power, constructed equally of equal parts of terror and joy. Like virtually all the fiction which preceded it, *The Paper Men* is not concerned with concepts such as fairness and justice, but with the irrational, numinous force which Golding perceives at the centre of existence, and which can be apprehended as much, if not more, by outrage and violence as it can by conventional piety.

Golding's characters inhabit a religious universe because they are rarely helpless victims of socio-economic forces beyond their control. They live in a world touched by numinous forces, where tragedy is inscribed in the nature of things, a world in which one must choose and where the consequences of the wrong choice can be fatal. Golding's mythic and allegorical world is one where damnation and salvation are still possible and where the actions of a single individual have an effect on the world. For all its tragedy and pessimism, therefore, it can be seen as a world that has meaning; one which affirms and celebrates the unique humanity of every individual.

Notes

1. R. Otto, *The Idea of the Holy* trans. John Harvey (Oxford: Oxford University Press, 1970), p. 179.
2. Ibid., p. 34.

3. W. Golding, *Lord of the Flies* (London: Faber, 1954), p. 18.
4. W. Golding, *The Hot Gates* (London: Faber, 1965), p. 88.
5. *Lord of the Flies*, p. 23.
6. Ibid., p. 147.
7. H. Hubert and M. Mauss, *Sacrifice: Its Nature and Functions*, trans. E. E. Evans-Pritchard (Chicago: University of Chicago Press, 1964), p. 97.
8. N. Davis, *Human Sacrifice* (London: Faber, 1977), p. 13.
9. Cited in W. T. Stace, *The Philosophy of Hegel* (New York: Doubleday, 1955), pp. 512–13.
10. B. Russell, *History of Western Philosophy* (London: George Allen & Unwin, 1961), p.350.
11. D. Parkin (ed.), *The Anthropology of Evil* (Oxford: Blackwell, 1985), p. 13.
12. W. Ray, *Literary Meaning: From Phenomenology To Deconstruction* (Oxford: Blackwell, 1984), p. 173.
13. W. Golding, *Pincher Martin* (London: Faber, 1956), p. 18.
14. Ibid., p. 198.
15. Ibid., p. 204.
16. W. Golding, *Free Fall* (London: Faber, 1959), p. 8.
17. W. Golding, *The Spire* (London: Faber, 1964), p. 223.
18. M. Kilgour, *From Communion to Cannibalism: An Anatomy of Metaphors of Incorporation* (Princeton: Princeton University Press, 1990), p. 200.
19. William James, *The Varieties of Religious Experience* (1902; London: Collins, 1985), p. 405.
20. B. Dick, *William Golding* (New York: Twayne, 1987), p. 93.
21. A. Macfarlane, 'The root of all evil' in Parkin, *Anthropology of Evil*, p. 70.
22. C. Baudelaire, *Les Fleurs Du Mal*, trans. C. F. MacIntyre (Berkeley: University of California Press, 1947), p. 392.
23. J.- P.Sartre, *Baudelaire*, trans. Martin Turnell (London: Hamish Hamilton, 1964), pp. 69–70.
24. W. Golding, *Darkness Visible* (London: Faber, 1979), p. 14.
25. R. Inden, 'Hindu evil as unconquered lower self' in Parkin, *Anthropology of Evil*, p. 160.
26. Parkin, *Anthropology of Evil*, p. 7.
27. Russell, *History of Western Philosophy*, p. 325.
28. S. Gooch, *Total Man: Notes toward an Evolutionary Theory of Personality* (London: Abacus, 1975), p. 57.
29. E. Mosely, *Pseudonyms of Christ in the Modern Novel* (Pittsburgh: University of Pittsburgh Press, 1962), p. 44.
30. M. Eliade, *Ordeal by Labyrinth*, trans. Derek Coltman (Chicago: University of Chicago Press, 1984), pp. 53–4.
31. P. Waugh, *Metafiction* (London: Methuen, 1984), p. 6.
32. T. Eagleton, *Literary Theory* (Oxford: Blackwell, 1983), p. 139.
33. Ibid., p. 134.
34. W. Golding, *The Paper Men* (London: Faber, 1984), p. 122.
35. Ibid., p. 123.
36. Otto, *Idea of the Holy*, p. 5.
37. Eliade, *Ordeal by Labyrinth*, p. 125.
38. Otto, *Idea of the Holy*, p. 18.
39. Golding, *Paper Men*, p. 160.

18

His Word or Our Words? Postmodernity's Angelic Predicament in *The Satanic Verses*

Gavin D'Costa

I

S alman Rushdie's *The Satanic Verses* (1988) has received critical attention on three counts: as a catalyst for the 'free speech' versus 'religious rights' debate; for his portrayal of Islam – 'was it offensive or was it not?'; and for his postmodernist 'Third World Cosmopolitan' writing.[1] Now, some nearly ten years later, and two novels on, I want to return to *The Satanic Verses* to ask another question: does it present one of the most searching postmodernist critiques of 'religion', with special attention to Islam in particular? I want to suggest, in tension with my own earlier reading, that this book is far from a straightforward 'Orientalist' abuse of Islam (which it is, in part).[2] It is also a profound exploration of a major tenet of postmodernism: that all meaning is mediated through signs, and signs are forever shifting; they have no stable home, no pure meaning and they can be put to an infinite number of political uses (Derrida). There is no single overarching grand narrative that explains and stabilizes all signs, no foundational point from which to view the world (Lyotard). If these claims are true, then religions which claim that revelation has taken

265

place in history (Judaism, Christianity and Islam) – *they* say that God has spoken – have a lot more accounting to do for such a claim, given that all signs, all speaking is humanly mediated and subject to indeterminacy. In short, can one really distinguish the word of God from the word of man – and sometimes woman? I want to suggest that Rushdie is asking profoundly 'religious' questions with a keen nose for detecting easy idolatrous answers.

Ignore such questions, and terror is unleashed: 'From the beginning men used God to justify the unjustifiable. He moves in mysterious ways: men say' (p. 95).[3] The context of this quotation is the narrator's outraged amusement at Abraham being celebrated by the waters of 'Zamzam', even though this marks the site of his abandoning Hagar and Ishmael to die in the wilderness! Abraham's cruelty is occluded as a different story is celebrated. History is constantly rewritten, and as Rushdie writes in *Shame*, 'every story one chooses to tell is a kind of censorship, it prevents the telling of other tales'.[4] The unjustifiable justified in God's name finds expression in coercive power over others: 'personal', 'social', 'political' and 'religious'. There are of course no clear lines between any of these sites as each translates itself into the other, as can be seen, for instance, in Gibreel: a character in the novel, an actor who represents India's cinematic psyche, the angel in the Mahound/ Muhammad sequence, and thereby a figure who sanctions all sorts of power structures. The lack of demarcation also means that isolating 'religion' is methodologically flawed and the lack of such a clear focus is borne out in the writing of this chapter.

In 'real life' Rushdie seems to have forgotten that such divisions are inadmissible, when before the *fatwa* he said of the book:

> Actually one of my major themes is religion ... I have talked about the Islamic religion because that is what I know the most about. But the ideas about religious faith and the nature of religious experience and also the political implication of religious extremism are applicable with a few variations to just about any religion.[5]

Later, after the *fatwa*, he claimed that the book was not about Islam after all, but about 'migration, metamorphosis, divided selves, love, death'.[6] The book, of course, refuses such distinctions and it would be foolish to imagine that Rushdie has any special authority over his text, for this would be to commit the very fallacy the book explodes: that meaning is stable. If I am right in this, then my interpretation is certainly not exhaustive – and could not be.

Just as Rushdie cannot escape culture, so he cannot get away from religion. He had already employed Sufi traditions in his first book *Grimus* (1975), and *Midnight's Children* (1980) deconstructs both Hindu and Muslim myths to unravel the political mythology of Independent India, showing both to be forms of 'false consciousness'.[7] *Shame* (1984) shamelessly disarms the military government of General Zia al Haqq and his predecessor, Zulfikar Ali Bhutto through the characters of Ali Hyder and Iskandar Harappa respectively. Rushdie explores the way in which Islam in Pakistan constructed an edifice of power and control that kept political dictators comfortably in place. If *Shame* concerned the 'use' of Islam, *The Satanic Verses* pushes the question further: can Islam (or any religion) be understood apart from its many embodiments in history, apart from its many 'uses'? To those who would respond: 'but these are often misuses of religion', Rushdie would rightly reply: 'but signs in history are all we have'. There is no pure divine, unmediated message which is then misinterpreted, but a string of contested interpretations, no unpolluted Word, but endless sets of words claiming the unmediated authority of the Word. When signs are treated ahistorically (univocally), as if they were not semantically mediated, they deny history and our complex interrelated multi-layered omni-storied world. It is this theme that I wish to explore in this chapter.

Rushdie's next novel, *Haroun and the Sea of Stories* (1990), although a 'children's story', is about censorship and repression, about strangling alternative stories, which leads to two-dimensional life (hence the cartoon-character-like quality of so many of Rushdie's figures – holding a mirror to nature!). *East, West* (1994), his first collection of short stories, returns to the themes of the three big novels: cultural identity, power and the search for love.[8] *The Moor's Last Sigh* (1996), his most recent novel, is organized around the fluid metaphor of the palimpsest, a construction whereby one picture after another is painted on the same canvas, so that boundaries between time, people, inner and outer, private and personal are all erased: 'One universe, one dimension, one country, one dream, bumpo'ing into another, or being under, or on top of. Call it Palimpstine. And above it all, in the palace, you' (p. 226). The book takes its title from a painting by Moraes' (the Moor's) mother, Aurora Zogoiby, who faces up to the 'treatment of her only son' in the multi-layered painting which, with good Freudian timing, is stolen after (and by?) her death (p. 218). The relationship between the Moor and his mother and father is central to the book. 'Central' is metaphorically possible because the image of the palimpsest allows for three generations of parental relationships to come into view. The relationship between Saladin and his father and mother dominates *The Satanic Verses* and has its counterpart in Gibreel's orphan status.

As far as I am aware, the secondary critical material on Rushdie does not focus on this parental theme running through his major novels: the way our lives are shaped by our mothers and fathers – and subsequently our faith, and often our religion. Freud's analysis of totemic religion is always in the background.[9] However, this psychoanalysis is semiotically and culturally mediated, following writers like Jacques Lacan. There is an ambiguous relationship to feminist postmodern psychoanalytic concerns (as found in, for example, Luce Irigaray).[10]

This restless employment of a palimpsest of interpretative frameworks and narrative styles refuses closure of meaning defying any final act of reading the novel – or life itself. 'Magical realism' replaces the European realistic novel, marking the end of the colonial 'imperial view' and its genres, its sense of control and stable territory, and performs a transmutation of these idioms, a changing of its signs.[11] Rushdie's *style* shows that there are no pure signs, no unmediated 'realities', and therefore no constant pure meanings, and this includes ourselves (see Baal's description of his own writing: p. 370). The novel opens with two figures falling out of the heavens. Our descent down the birth canal (Saladin falls in 'the recommended position for babies entering the birth canal': p. 4) into the cold air of 'reality', and 'fall' into the life of signs, opens *The Satanic Verses*.

II

'To be born again,' sang Gibreel Farishta tumbling from the heavens, 'first you have to die. Ho ji! Ho ji! To land upon the bosomy earth, first one needs to fly. Tat-taa! Taka-thun! How to ever smile again, if first you won't cry? How to win the darling's love, mister, without a sigh? Baba, if you want to get born again ...' Just before dawn one winter's morning, New Year's Day or thereabouts, two real, full-grown, living men fell from a great height, twenty-nine thousand and two feet, towards the English Channel, without benefit of parachutes or wings, out of a clear sky. (p. 3)

I will comment on this passage in some detail to indicate how Rushdie's literary technique reflects precisely the postmodernist perspective constructed in the novel.

'To to be born again' echoes variously throughout the novel. This is the plight of the 'immigrant' who moves from one culture to another. Some like Salahuddin Chamchawala resist the father/land, Changez (his father) and his Bombay home, meticulously trying to reconstruct themselves, in Salahuddin's case, as English. Hence, while his name transmutes into the Anglicized Saladin Chamcha, he still ironically bears the name of the great medieval Saladin who also conquered a culture, defeating the Crusaders and restoring Sunni Islam to Egypt. Saladin tries to conquer England. He has to eat 'smoked fish full of spikes and bones', as his inauguration into the English public school system which takes him 90 minutes and a refusal to cry. 'The eaten kipper was his first victory, the first step in his conquest of England' (p. 44). A conquest which can never be won for it must confront 'the new empire within Britain': racism and class.[12] Saladin's accent changes because his classmates giggle at his Indian tones (which must now 'die'): 'he began to act, to find masks that these fellows would recognize, paleface masks, clown masks, until he fooled them into thinking he was *okay*, he was *people-like-us*' (p. 43). On his return to Bombay, Indian accents keep leaking out of his character, until finally he can speak in Urdu.

For Rushdie, like the Frankfurt-School, the personal is the political. He juggles the theme of being born again into cultural critique: people constantly construct and reconstruct themselves, religiously, politically, culturally, economically and every way they can. Saladin is a sign of his times, and signs, like people, use and are used in all sorts ways. Some try to construct impossible pure cultural selves such as the National Front, who must then necessarily efface both history and people. The Front's black counterpart is symbolized in Dr Uhuru Simba, who has changed his name from Sylvester Roberts and turns violent when his Africanness is called into question (p. 285). Pure culture, like pure identity or meaning, is a fictional construct, for signs constantly change according to the company they keep.

However, those who question cultural/ethnic identity are equally problematized, when, for example, Saladin attends a political meeting to free the arrested Dr Uhuru Simba and is told by 'a young black woman' wearing a lenticular badge showing two different messages, according to the viewing angle, 'Uhuru Simba'/'Freedom for the Lion':

> 'it's on account of the meaning of his chosen name,' she explained redundantly. 'In African.' Which language? Saladin wanted to know. She shrugged, and turned away to listen to the speakers. It was African: born by the sound of her, in Lewisham or Deptford or New Cross, that was all she needed to know ... Pamela hissed into his ear. 'I see that you finally found somebody to feel superior to.' She could read him like a book. (p. 413)

Saladin's desire to feel superior in noticing such cultural counterfeits, when he himself is one, is undermined by Pamela, while at the same time questioning such badge-wearing cultural identity that is skin deep. Saladin has the same annoyance at the meeting singing 'Nkosi Sikelel' iAfrica' (this time Afrikans, not Swahili): 'As if all causes were the same, all histories interchangeable' (p. 415). The same 'predictable stink' (p. 52) at questioning cultural identities is caused by Saladin's Bombay lover, Zeenat Vakil's book, *The Only Good Indian*. In it she 'questions the confining myth of authenticity, that folkloristic straitjacket which she sought to replace by an ethic of historically validated eclecticism, for was not the entire national culture based on the principle of borrowing what ever clothes seemed to fit, Aryan, Mughal, British, take-the-best-and-leave-the-rest?' (p. 52). As Zeeny puts it, ' "Why should there be a good, right way of being a wog? That's Hindu fundamentalism"' (p. 52). Further ironies are generated here: later Zeeny will tease Saladin that his Anglicized name, English accent, contempt for things Indian, are part of his loss of identity, and here she uses 'wog' quite differently: 'Your types got no culture. Just wogs now. Ain't it the truth?' (p. 54). What is also significant is that Zeeny, like the novel, makes no distinction between culture and religion, for 'both' are sign systems and Hindu fundamentalism is no different from the British National Front. Both groups try to control, monopolize and name reality univocally.

Hence, 'To be born again' further connotes a range of religious references. Hindu reincarnation theory, for example, is exemplified by Gibreel's 'unique [acting] career incarnating, with absolute conviction, the countless deities of the sub-continent in the popular genre movies known as "theologicals"' (p. 16). But straight after this sequence, Rushdie reminds us that there 'are secular reincarnations, too', typically beginning with Gibreel's birth name: Ismail Najmuddin (p. 17). Christians, Jews and Muslims are also born into and out of faith: Eugene Dumsday the Christian Creationist, Alleluia Cohen's Jewish family, and Gibreel and Saladin viz. Islam. Pure religious identity is, like pure cultural identity, undermined, for every sign by which we are constructed is mediated so that after the fall (into culture) meaning is never univocal. This applies to the 'pure' revelation of God (or was it Satan, or an angel, or both, or neither, or the Prophet himself?).

The Imam who resides in London, based on Khomeini's exile prior to the fall of the Shah, exemplifies the impossible forgery of religious purity and certainty. The Imam lives in Kensington surrounded by bodyguards. 'The curtains, thick golden velvet, are kept shut all day, because otherwise the evil thing might creep into the apartment: foreignness, Abroad, the alien nation' (p. 206). The irony is that the Imam cannot exist without foreignness: living in London; in his high theology of water whereby he has a glass every five minutes 'to keep himself clean', but 'the water itself is cleansed of impurities, before he sips, in an American filtration machine' (p. 209). The Iman's purity is also constructed upon his defeat of 'Ayesha', ruler of Desh, from where he is exiled, a woman who drinks wine. In this binary opposition, Rushdie elaborates upon the equivocal signifier, for the very name 'Ayesha' is semantically related to a myriad of characters within the novel: the Prophet's favourite wife (Ayesha), the whore who plays her part in a later sequence and adopts her name, and the prophetess (Ayesha) who leads the fantastical journey to the Arabian Sea and receives uninterrupted instructions from Gabriel sanctioning her authority. Ayesha of Desh is also pictorially and symbolically related via the signs of her depiction: her drinking wine relates to Hind, who also loves wine, the woman who opposes Mahound; and via the kali-like image of her drinking blood from skulls (p. 209) she is related to the Sikh hijacker, Taverleen ... the significations are endless. By this very technique, of palimpsest writing, which also recalls the incident of the Satanic Verses in Islam, Rushdie indicates that univocal signification is impossible, however much humans seek to control signs – and each other.

The Imam's attempt to destroy women as the founding act of his religious authority is related to Mahound's refusal of the three goddesses worshipped by Hind, and Gibreel's inability to mourn his mother's death and choose rather to compete with his father. The end of this competition is also the end of his religious faith (p. 30). In a humorous touch, the Imam's preaching of Islamic revelation, his mediation of the Word ('burn the books and trust the Book': p. 211), is via his own words being transmitted by another: 'the voice of the American convert Bilal is singing the Imam's holy song' (p. 210) – over pirate radio to Desh! Mediation in history is the condition of the Imam, which for his very self-image he must deny. In the account of Bilal's broadcast of the Imam's message, after his imprecations against Ayesha, this denial is unmasked:

> 'We will make a revolution,' the Imam proclaims through him, 'that is a revolt not only against a tyrant, but against history.' For there is an enemy beyond Ayesha, it is History herself. History is the blood-wine that must no longer be drunk. History the intoxicant, the creation of the lies – progress, science, rights – against which the Imam has set his face. History is a deviation from the Path, knowledge is a delusion, because the sum of knowledge was complete on the day Al-Lah finished his revelation to Mahound.   (p. 211)

The claim that 'The sum of knowledge was complete' is the outcome of univocal signification, a refusal to admit that signs are always mediated and in need of interpretation. But the denial of questions, doubts, plural interpretations, ambiguous significations, history, is not a perogative of any one religion or people. The American Christian creationist, Eugene Dumsday (eugenics, doomsday – modelled on Duane Gush of the Institute of Creation Research, California) is another such character (pp. 75ff.), like the Imam, and both are caricatures of features shared by many characters in the novel. It is not religion alone which is the target, but economics (see his equivalent portrayal of Hal Valance, the Thatcherite businessman), ethnic identity (Saladin's attempt at Englishness), any cultural construct that tries to preserve a single identity, a purity against history. Let me return to the opening paragraph. The next seven words are: 'sang Gibreel Farishta tumbling from the heavens'.

'Sang'. Singing is one cultural mode of production, and is a generic form that unites a number of formative semiotic configurations: the recitation of the Quran (we've already seen how the black American singer Bilal sings over the airwaves); popular Hindi musicals and theologicals (full of songs – 'Ho ji!' constitutes a musical refrain – and in which stars like Gibreel can cause the prime minister of India to cancel foreign visits, as did Indira Gandhi when the star Amitabh Bachan fell ill); jingles used in advertising (Saladin is the voice of garlic crisps and frozen peas, where reality and pastiche are indistinguishable); political black rap which mobilizes the angry crowd in the Club Hot Wax (p. 292); and high poetry (his mock allusion to Eliot in the 'Tat-taa! Taka-thun!' of line 3, opening paragraph).[13] Singing is also what angelic beings do in heaven; the same beings who are infernal, devilish after falling, which is why Saladin, also falling out of the sky, shouts 'to the devil with your tunes' at Gibreel (p. 3). The connection between angels and singing is made by the Urdu name 'Gibreel Farishta', which translates into 'Angel Gabriel' (who recites the Quran to Muhammad on Mount Hira), who is 'tumbling from the heavens'. The tumble suggests that he may in fact be a fallen angel. Hence, this tumble is what relates us to the angels: we, like they, fall into a world of unstable signs, such that one cannot always distinguish good from bad, angel from devil, being born from dying, smiling from crying, the divine from the human, and the human from the demonic. No wonder then, that Gibreel plays deities on screen and eventually off screen, and that Saladin turns into a huge goat with putrid breath, horns and a massive erection – they are both made up of many voices, songs and recitations.

Just as we are being sucked up into this vortex of fantastical images and associations, the (mock) voice of a realistic narrator enters, although this voice is really no different from that of the previous fantastical one. Precision and exactness calm our imaginations, a reporting of the facts: 'Just before dawn one winter's morning, New Year's Day'. Later, during the reporting of the facts by TV cameras at a 'race' riot (Brixton) we are reminded about how 'facts' are always constructed from points of view, and therefore obstruct from view other images and stories. A camera 'requires law, order, the thin blue line. Seeking to preserve itself, it remains behind the shielding wall, observing the shadow-lands from afar, and of course from above: that is, it chooses sides' (p. 455). But before we can grasp at any solidity, any realism, any 'truth' in the precision of 'Just before dawn one winter's morning, New Year's Day', authorial omniscience is deconstructed with the addition of 'or there-abouts'. To confound matters we are then given the exact height from which 'two real, full-grown, living men' fall: 'twenty nine thousand and two feet'. The Himalayas house the gods and Mount Everest (the symbol of European colonializa-tion of the East?) is precisely 29,002 feet high. With this allusion to holy mountains, Mount Hira is conjured up as is Mount Sinai. Hira is already established within the semantic field through Gabriel and the title of the novel, and soon we are to meet Gabriel's English lover: Allie Cone. Her name is a palimpsest for her 'real' name – Alleluia Cohen. Alleluia phonetically recalls 'Allah', and Hallelujah is the Jewish/ Hebrew term of praise to God. Cone is both an Anglicized form of Cohen (p. 297), for she is Jewish (hence Sinai, the site of another pure revelation), and puns upon 'kahin', the Arabic for soothsayer. In a comment on her Polish Jewish father who has changed all the family's names when they arrive in England, Rushdie writes: 'Echoes of the past distressed him; he read no Polish literature ... because for him the language was irredeemably polluted by history' (p. 297). His attempt to escape history ends when he 'jumped into an empty lift-shaft and died' (p. 298). Suicides litter the book.

A final comment, for one might read the entire novel

through its beginning, which indicates that it is not the 'beginning', but just one point within a complex interweaving narrative, signs mediating other signs, endlessly. We discover that Gibreel and Saladin are falling out of a blown-up hijacked jet: Bostan, Flight AI-420 (p. 4). This is based on an Air India jumbo jet blown up over Ireland in 1985, allegedly by Sikh terrorists (who also blow up the novel's jet). Two features are especially worth commenting upon. The fall from paradise into the babel of language is alluded to by the name of the jet: Bostan, one of the Islamic gardens of paradise. (Milton's *Paradise Lost* is also constantly alluded to in the novel.) It is significant too that Saladin is able to name the fruits and flowers of his own Bombay garden on return from England, something he could never do in childhood and something that establishes his distance and alienation from his parents: 'something had been lost which he would never be able to regain' (p. 45). Another significant garden is the house from which the Ayesha story develops, another of the gardens of paradise, 'Peristan' (p. 217). This is in contrast to Jihila (the place of ignorance) from which Muhammad comes and eventually conquers, where there are no gardens at all.

Second, the jet is blown up because the terrifying Sikh terrorist, Tavleen, will not compromise. This singularity, this unbending sense of her own righteous demand is metaphorically given a Durga-Kali image (the Hindu goddess of death and destruction) as she stands naked before the passengers 'so that they could all see the arsenal of her body, the grenades like extra breasts nestling in her cleavage, the gelignite taped around her thighs' (p. 81). And what does she demand which will cost the lives of all the passengers (but two)?: 'religious freedom' and 'justice' (p. 78). 'From the beginning men used God to justify the unjustifiable' (p. 95) – or did they?

I have spent so much time on the opening paragraph as form and content are inseparable, and complex multi-reading strategies are invited. Such analysis has also allowed me to pursue in a permissibly diffuse way (as the novel requires it) the question I have been pursuing: univocal signification leads to all sorts of spurious idols, obscuring a complex and even mysterious multivocal world of signs. In the next section, I wish to focus this exploration in two specific ways.

III

In this section, I want to develop my initial claim, that Rushdie's book is insufficiently analysed in purely 'Orientalist' terms, for it also poses a deeper more troubling question: if all signs are mediated, then the semiotic configurations called 'revelation' are inevitably ambiguous, as are all signs. The problem is, as I have argued elsewhere, that if doubt and ambiguity become credal statements, then a new faith, a new metanarrative is born: postmodern nihilism.[14] However, I want to suggest that at one level within the novel the 'religious sentiment' within postmodernism becomes apparent (as it has in the later work of Derrida) in the strategic resistance against the closure of meaning. This distinguishes nihilist postmodernism, which after all is yet another closed narrative, from religious postmodernism(s) which rigorously preserve transcendence, a Blochian openness to the future, in their resistance to closure. This resistance has an analogical similarity to a theological critique of idolatry. To imagine that we can adequately re-present God, by that which is not God, is idolatry and allows men to 'justify the unjustifiable' in the name of God, who is the unnameable (p. 95). St Thomas Aquinas is not the only one to point out that while all speech about God is analogous, and analogy works by similarity, it always operates within a greater dissimilarity, a greater unknowingness.[15]

Two avenues within the novel open up this kind of reading. The first regards the psychoanalytic, and the second, postmodern irony. Let me start with the second. There are a number of passages that question the narrator's clarity, his god-like point of view. Most obvious is Rushdie's own descent into the narrative in Gibreel's apparition (p. 318), where it is not clear whether he is Ooparvala, 'the fellow upstairs' or Neechayvala 'the guy from underneath' (p. 318). The description of the apparition matches Rushdie's face and is confirmed when in a later passage the authorial voice comments on this intervention: 'I'm saying nothing. Don't ask me to clear things up one way or the other; the time of revelations is long gone. ... Don't think I haven't wanted to butt in; I have, plenty of times. And once, it's true, I did. I sat on Alleluia Cone's bed and spoke to the superstar, Gibreel. *Ooparvala or Neechayvala*, he wanted to know, and I didn't enlighten him' (p. 409). It is this refusal to allow any final resolution that allows Rushdie possibly to escape secular fundamentalism or nihilistic post-modernism, both of which are resolved positions.

Another important example, as it touches on the question of religion, comes from an exchange between two characters. Swatilekha, a Bengali woman, criticizes Bhupen Gandi, the poet, for being ambiguous towards religion and not unmasking the ways in which it has been used by the elites in Asia to establish and consolidate power. In many respects her argument summarizes what others have said of Rushdie's own approach.[16] However, she is undermined by Bhupen's reply. It is worth quoting in full:

> Society was orchestrated by what she called *grand narratives*: history, economics, ethics. In India, the development of a corrupt and closed state apparatus had 'excluded the masses of the people from the ethical project'. As a result, they sought ethical satisfactions in the oldest of the grand narratives, that is, religious faith. 'But these narratives are being manipulated by the theocracy and various political elements in an entirely retrogressive way.' Bhupen said: 'We can't deny the ubiquity of faith. If we write in such a way as to pre-judge such beliefs as in some way deluded or false, then are we not guilty of elitism, of imposing our world-view on the masses?' Swatilekha was scornful. 'Battle lines are being drawn up in India today,' she cried. 'Secular versus religious, the light versus the dark. Better you choose which side you are on.'   (p. 537)

Secular fundamentalist Swatilekha (swastika, Tilak, tilaka?) mirrors the religious groups who try and draw equally clear battle lines between good and bad, secular and sacred, right and wrong, and if Rushdie is in danger of falling into such polarities himself, then one must acknowledge equally that he is painfully aware of their spuriousness. Bhupen, without romanticizing, keeps the questions open, whereas secular fundamentalism, in the person of Swatilekha, does not.[17] There are no real goodies or baddies in the novel, no secular or religious heroes or heroines, rather a canvas of complex, intricate, funny, telling and sometimes tragic stories: 'like life, nah?'.

The sense that Rushdie is questioning 'religion' (as he does with ethnic, economic and political identity) when it denies its historicity, and therefore its semiotic mediation, is made even more strongly in an earlier incident. Gibreel is losing his identity to the angel Gabriel, his namesake (an angel of death, or an angel of light?), and is floating above a London park trying frantically to block out the complex and unresolved stories of his frustrated love-affair with Allie Cone: 'he saw now that the choice was simple: the infernal love of the daughters of men, or the celestial adoration of God. He had found it possible to choose the latter; in the nick of time' (p. 321). I shall return to this shortly. Note the syntax at Gibreel's choice, his 'resolution':

> No more of these England-induced ambiguities, these Biblical–Satanic confusions! – Clarity, clarity, at all cost clarity! – This Shaitan was no fallen angel, – Forget those son-of-the-morning fictions; this was no good boy gone bad, but pure evil. Truth was, he wasn't an angel at all! – 'He was of the djinn, so he transgressed.' – Quran 18:50, there it was as plain as the day. – How much more straightforward this version was! How much more practical, down-to-earth, comprehensible! – Iblis/Shaitan standing for the darkness, Gibreel for the light. – Out, out with these sentimentalities: *joining, locking together, love*. Seek and destroy: that was all.   (p. 353)

To label, to keep the world in place, to divide good and evil, to deny the complex and multiple stories and voices that construct our lives, is 'more practical', but never the more truthful strategy. Clarity is a victory (always short-lived) attained by imagining that signs are univocal rather than multivocal, and our lives likewise. Rekha Merchant, who floats in and out of the novel on her flying carpet, the unexorcised guilt of Gibreel (?) who betrays her (so that she leaps off Everest, her high-rise apartment, to her death), refuses his clear-cut categories and mocks him: 'you played too many winged types for your own good' (p. 323). She suddenly becomes the voice of a comparative religion specialist, Gibreel realizing the 'real' Rekha incapable of such a speech, but a speech nevertheless that points to history and mediation and construction:

> 'This notion of separation of functions, light versus dark, evil versus good, may be straightforward enough in Islam – *O, children of Adam, let not the Devil seduce you, as he expelled your parents from the garden, pulling off from them their*

278

clothing that he might show them their shame – but go back a bit and you see that it's a pretty recent fabrication. Amos, eighth century BC, asks: 'Shall there be evil in a city and the Lord hath not done it?' Also Jahweh, quoted by Deutero-Isaiah two hundred years later, remarks: 'I form the light, and create darkness; I make peace and create evil; I the Lord do all these things.' It isn't until the Book of Chronicles, merely fourth century BC, that the word *shaitan* is used to mean a being, and not only an attribute of God' (p. 323)

The relentless postmodern point is that a closure of meaning, a settlement of signs, will always mask and construct tyrannical powers. Rushdie's narrative shows how falsely conceived certainties, be they religious, ethnic, economic, class, lead to denial, the loss of love, and the impossibility of forgiveness: 'Out, out with these sentimentalities: *joining, locking together, love.*' Gibreel's clarity is that of the Imam's: 'Seek and destroy.'

Such a reading suggests a profoundly 'religious searching', a refusal to bow to idols and a resistance to closure in created meanings. This, in tandem with Rushdie's exploration of evil, loss and love, his relation to his father and its analogue with faith, suggests other than secular fundamentalism and post-modernist nihilism. It is the possibility, suggested in the narrative, that love is the only way in which the story can be kept open – even if it is the most elusive of all realities, or perhaps precisely because it is!

I will focus on Saladin to explore this point, but one could equally focus on Mahound, his orphan status, his finding his 'mother' in his first wife (p. 118), and after her death, reproducing her in his harem through his two wives Ayesha and Hafsah. His desire to control women, signs and nature is seen in his distrust of whores and poets and is central to his defeat of the three goddesses – which precipitates the incident of the Satanic verses. His 'victory' is undermined on his death bed where he acknowledges the voice of Al-Lat, not Al-Lah (p. 394).[18] Or one could see Gibreel's refusal to cry at the death of his mother, his turning instead to competition with his father, and his subsequent self-construction as a constant attempt 'to blot out the tragic feeling of being endowed with a larger-than-usual capacity for love, without a single person on earth to offer it to' (p. 24). His loss of faith is linked with his 'anger with God', which after it has died, like God, leaves a 'terrible emptiness' (p. 30). Gibreel, with poetic justice destroys himself when Saladin finds his home/self (p. 546).

Saladin is constructed out of his desire 'to escape' his father, Changez Chamchawala, who constantly outwits and humiliates him (p, 37). Saladin's loss of faith confirms Freud's totemic thesis, but equally drives him into an alternative (binary opposite) construction. In a humiliating and hilarious incident where he carries a takeaway roast chicken (which will signify his heart) under his mackintosh in a hotel lift to his father (who has tricked him into paying for food), he comes to a moment of revelation:

> Chicken-breasted beneath the gaze of dowagers and liftwallahs he felt the birth of the implacable rage which would burn within him, undiminished, for over a quarter of a century; which would boil away his childhood father-worship and make him a secular man, who would do his best, thereafter, to live without a god of any type; which would fuel, perhaps his determination to become the thing his father was-not-could-never-be, that is, a goodandproper Englishman. (p. 43)

The novel follows him over this quarter century of 'implacable rage', not unlike Gibreel, trying to reconstruct himself endlessly. What they share in common is their inability to successfully find and give love, for it was not (perfectly) found or given in their being constructed by their partners. If God is displaced, they must now play God. 'A man who invents himself needs someone to believe in him, to prove he's managed it' (p. 49). Hence, Anglicized Saladin marries the perfect 'English woman', Pamela Lovelace, whose name is a cocktail of Samuel Richardson's (English realism) characters. Saladin is fixated by Pamela's 'Englishness' such that he never sees past her masks, like her upper-class smile, that 'brilliant counterfeit of joy' (p. 51). Her smile masks her own despair at not being loved by her parents, who had committed suicide (pp. 50–1). The fall from love, meaning and clarity at the beginning of our creation is seen in every character (not least in five suicidal jumps).

Saladin's self-constructions mirror the bizarre and multi-farious signs by which we create ourselves, and which we want others to affirm. Rushdie names Saladin's drive in his god-like self production: 'Not only the need to be believed in, but to believe in another. You've got it: Love' (p. 49). Of course, while Saladin cannot forgive and love his father, which he cannot without rage for what has happened, so too is he doomed to a restless denial of him – trying to endlessly construct himself as an opposite to Changez and being trapped in such binary logic, as is the Imam (denying foreignness), Ayesha the prophetess (denying ambivalence), Mahound (denying Al-Lat), Gibreel (denying women), Hal Valance (denying poverty), and, more or less, every character in the book. However, his inability to forgive contrasts with the easy forgiveness that Gibreel receives from the many women he sexually betrays, which only serves to further condemn him 'because their forgiveness made possible the deepest and sweetest corruption of all, namely the idea that he was doing nothing wrong' (p. 26). Denial and repression, it would seem, lead to univocality: a single story about who we are – which leads to personal and political tyrannies of all sorts.

Multiple forms of betrayal, 'the unforgiveable', run through the novel: political, sexual, personal, economic, religious. At one point, Rushdie seems to attain a rare singularity:

> What is the unforgiveable?
> What if not the shivering nakedness of being *wholly known* to a person one does not trust? .. in which the secrets of the self were utterly exposed? (p. 427)

However, this singularity is almost immediately deconstructed: 'an idea of the self as being (ideally) homogeneous, non-hybrid, "pure", – an utterly fantastic notion! – cannot, must not, suffice' (p. 427). Nevertheless, such an idea of the unforgivable indicates one way in which the novel can be read, and why it ends, as it does, at Saladin's father's home, at 'Scandal Point', a return to the garden of his childhood, even though Rushdie refuses any Eden-like, or other horticultural (Holly Wood), finishes.

To get back to Scandal Point Saladin must go through multiple mutations. His implacable rage turns into an infernal goat, not unlike Shaitan, in his slow recognition that he can never be 'English', not only because such an essence does not exist, but also because it denies his own past. He becomes dehumanized (a goat) because he wears rather than subverts the identities and constructions given him in Valayet (land of foreignness). Hence his ritual humiliation with the fish bones, and symbolically seen in his transformation into a goat in the back of a police van where he is beaten up. His rage at such namings will later save him. His marriage likewise fails, as it is based on his desire to affirm his Englishness, not on any real love of Pamela. While Saladin's transmutation operates on many levels within the novel, he is only returned to human form after he learns rage against the coercion of his many constructions, so that the image of his reconciliation to himself (which is a process, not a single image) is also an allusion to the image of his birth. He is found amidst the appalling devastation he has caused at the Club Hot Wax (where transmutations are the order of the day): 'mother-naked but of entirely human aspect and proportions, *humanized* – is there any option but to conclude? – by the fearsome concentration of his hate' (p. 294).

Saladin's reconciliation with his dying father, his ability to come to terms with him (and the word 'forgiveness' does not appear in this sequence) is a momentary meeting point between Rushdie's non-nihilist postmodernism and, for lack of a better term, an apophatic religious sensibility. That is, it is the point whereby Saladin realizes that love allows for the possibility of keeping stories, signs, our futures, open. Univocal signification is the choice of death in the middle of life; while equivocal significations celebrate the fecundity of love: keeping the future open, keeping meaning alive. The Imam, Eugene Dumsday, Ayesha and Mahound have all lived by closed stories, resisting equivocality. In a powerful passage, knowing that his father is dying, Saladin offers reconciliation, and in so doing, the image of the child is inverted, and makes possible the return of his father's love:

> Salahuddin suddenly longed to pick the old man up, to cradle him in his arms and sing soft, comforting songs. Instead, he blurted out, at this least appropriate of moments, an appeal for reconciliation. 'Abba, I came because I didn't want there to be trouble between us any more ...' *Fucking idiot. The Devil damn thee black, thou cream-fac'd loon. In the middle of the bloody night! And if he hasn't guessed he's dying, that little deathbed speech will certainly have let him know.* Changez continued to shuffle along; his grip on his son's arm tightened very slightly. 'That doesn't matter any more,' he said. 'It's forgotten, whatever it was.' (p. 526)

As he stays with his dying father, he finds even 'his Urdu returning to him after a long absence', so that he says to the dying Changez, of himself, his second mother, and his counterfeit first who are sitting at the bedside: '*We all love you very much*' (p. 530). In his new regeneration attained through his reconciliation, Saladin recognizes two things: 'love had shown that it could exert a humanizing power as great as that of hatred; that virtue could transform men as well as vice. But nothing was forever; no cure, it appeared, was complete' (p. 540).[19] In Rushdie's refusal to resolve the novel into a clear message, a clear narrative, a univocal reading of life, he preserves a more vital hope; that while no cure is ever complete, there is cure in love, for it keeps open the story, allows 'another chance', the possibility of a 'humanizing power' that is not defeated by hatred.

The close of the story is indicative of this theme. After 547 pages, Rushdie's story is to finish, although most readers who have survived it will return again to the start (as I did in section II of this chapter), rereading it with different significations. Saladin's story is not complete, but his 'Childhood was over', and in his reconciliation with his father he steps out of one narrative, into another: the search for love with Zeenat Vakil, a moving out of 'hell':

> 'Come along,' Zeenat Vakil's voice said at his shoulder. It seemed that in spite of all his wrong-doing, weakness, guilt – in spite of his humanity – he was getting another chance. There was no accounting for one's good fortune, that was plain. There it simply was, taking his elbow in its hand. 'My place,' Zeeny offered. 'Let's get the hell out of here.'
> 'I'm coming,' he answered her, and turned away from the view. (p. 547)

I have tried to suggest throughout this essay that to read Rushdie purely as an Orientalist (as I have done in the past) is to miss an important spirituality present in the book. This does not absolve him from the charge of Orientalism, but rather suggests that the book is also a profound postmodernist exploration of the dangers of univocal signification, a danger to which 'religions' are particularly prone, the danger of idolatry.[20]

Gavin D'Costa

Notes

1. For example in each category, see Richard Webster, *A Brief History of Blasphemy: Liberalism, Censorship and 'The Satanic Verses'* (Suffolk: Orwell Press, 1990) and *Free Speech* (London: Commission for Racial Equality, 1990); Shabbir Akhtar, *Be Careful with Muhammad: The Salman Rushdie Affair* (London: Bellew, 1989); Talal Asad, *Genealogies of Religion: Discipline and Reasons of Power in Christianity and Islam* (Baltimore: Johns Hopkins University Press, 1993); Timothy Brennan, *Salman Rushdie and the Third World* (London: Macmillan, 1989).

2. See Gavin D'Costa, 'Satanic disclosure and the clash of faiths: *The Satanic Verses* in British Society', *New Blackfriars* (October 1990), pp. 418–32.

3. All references to *The Satanic Verses* (1988) will be given in the text.

4. *Shame* (London: Jonathan Cape, 1983), p. 38.

5. Lisa Appignanesi and Sara Maitland (eds), *The Rushdie File* (London: Fourth Estate, 1989), p. 39; from *India Today*, 15 August 1988.

6. Malise Ruthven, *A Satanic Affair* (London: Chatto & Windus, 1990), p. 15, given without reference. The *fatwa* is reason enough for Rushdie's inconsistency.

7. Brennan, *Rushdie and the Third World*, p. 101.

8. 'The courter', pp. 173–211, closely and clearly overlaps with *The Satanic Verses*.

9. See S. Freud, *Totem and Taboo* (1913) and *Moses and Monotheism* (1939) in *The Penguin Freud Library*, vol. XIII: *The Origins of Religion* (London: Penguin, 1985).

10. Rushdie's recurrent 'feminist' theme in *Midnight's Children*, *Shame* and *The Satanic Verses* is how authoritarian religions/cultures always repress women more than men, even if women (Mrs Thatcher, Indira Gandhi, Hind, Ayesha) are running the show. Mahound's singularity is predicated upon his denial of the feminine (Al-Lat) and independent women (Hind) as well as poets (multiple voices). However, there is an ambiguous relationship to the Irigaraian critique of Freud as Rushdie tends to predicate religious development primarily in terms of relationship with the father. See Luce Irigaray, 'The power of discourse and the salvation of the feminine' in *This Sex Which is Not One*, trans. Catherine Porter with Carolyn Burke (Ithaca: Cornell University Press, 1993), pp. 68–85; and Jacques Lacan, *Ecrits: A Selection*, trans. Alan Sheridan (London: Tavistock Press, 1977).

11. See Brennan, *Rushdie and the Third World*, ch. 1; see also Gaytri Chakravorty Spivak, *In Other Worlds: Essays in Cultural Politics* (New York: Methuen, 1987); and Edward Said, *Orientalism: Western Conceptions of the Orient* (London: Routledge & Kegan Paul, 1978).

12. See Rushdie's essays, 'The new empire within Britain' and 'Outside the whale' in *Imaginary Homelands* (London: Granta, 1991), pp. 129–38 and 87–101 respectively.

13. This is an interesting reversal of colonial strategies. He is drawing from Eliot's use of Eastern wisdom in *The Waste Land* with the voice of thunder over 'Himavant', deriving from Sanskrit Upanishadic words: da-datta-da-dayadhvam-da-damyata. 'Tat' is Sanskrit from the Upanishadic saying 'tat tvam asi', thou art thou, and in cojoining it to taa, he turns high classic into low doggerel: ta-ta, goodbye. T. S. Eliot, *The Waste Land* in *Collected Poems 1909–62* (London: Faber & Faber, 1963), Bk V: 'What the thunder said', ll 397–420, pp. 78–9. Brennan is unnecessarily sanctimonious concerning Rushdie's use of dub/rap (Brennan, *Rushdie and the Third World*, p. 164), reading intentional parody as bad political faith.

14. See D'Costa, 'Satanic discourse', pp. 425–9.

15. *Summa Theologiae*, 1a. 2–11. Where postmodernity turns into religious sensibility

284

rather than nihilism, see for example, John Caputo, *The Prayers and Tears of Jacques Derrida: Religion without Religion* (Bloomington: Indiana University Press, 1997), esp. his comments on Rushdie and the problem of 'determinable' religions in section 4. Don Cupitt, who Rushdie actually refers to in 'Is nothing sacred?', p. 423, represents, to me at least, nihilistic postmodernism. It is worth pursuing the allusions to Moses on Sinai, in his being encountered by the unnameable ineffable 'God', and Allie Cone's experience at the top of Everest, where she faces death 'because it is not permitted to mortals to look more than once upon the face of the divine' (p. 303).

16. See for example: Brennan, *Rushdie and the Third World*; Wimal Dissanayake, 'Towards a decolonized English: South Asian creativity in fiction', *World Englishes* 2 (1985), pp. 233–42; A. D. Needham, 'The politics of post-colonial identity in Salman Rushdie', *The Massachusetts Review* 29 (1988/89), pp. 602–34.

17. Admittedly, immediately after the incident, Swatilekha's point of view is undermined by herself: 'Too much college education' she apologies to Bhupen (p. 537).

18. It is curious that this incident is not singled out as deeply offensive, for it is in terms of Islam's founding narrative and especially so in Ayesha's falsification to keep power.

19. In this respect, contrast Brennan's misreading of the book's 'triumphant conclusion' (Brennan, *Rushdie and the Third World*, p. 154) that 'evil is never total, that its victory, no matter how overwhelming, is never absolute' (p. 467). But the actual line that Brennan quotes is in fact qualified by the citation on p. 540 which I have just quoted and which recalls the incident of Saladin saving Gibreel from the fire, and its unedited version in the book reads: 'Is it possible that evil is never total, that its victory, no matter how overwhelming, is never absolute?' By neglecting the context of the quotation, Brennan actually misreads the book at this point.

20. This is also the central theme of Umberto Eco's remarkable *The Name of the Rose* (ET: London: Secker & Warburg, 1983) which like Rushdie's book, is concerned with 'names' and their relativity, which is why one monk will kill to hide Aristotle's treatise of laughter, which would undermine the stability of language. See Karl-Josef Kuschel's treatment of the book in *Laughter: A Theological Reflection* trans. John Bowden (London: SCM, 1994), pp. 22–31, 127–33.

I am indebted to Dr Gerard Loughlin for his helpful comments on an earlier draft of this paper and to three groups of undergraduate students at the University of Bristol who have helped me to constantly reread the novel.

19

The Writing of Catholic Worlds: Landscape and the Portrayal of Catholicism in the Novels of Brian Moore

Liam Gearon

The quest for a doctrine appropriate to the landscape may be taken as an image of the development of Catholic theology since Vatican II: it symbolises the way in which Catholic theology in the post-conciliar period is dependent upon the Council's readjustment of contemporary Catholic identity. In addition, it presents a theme that will become central to post-conciliar theology: the priority of the 'landscape' of lived experience in the articulation of theological doctrine. As the features of Catholic faith-experience were altered by the Council, the consequent theological reflection followed contours different from those that preceded it.

John McDade SJ (1991: 422)

Introduction

If the Second Vatican Council (1962–5) radically changed the public persona of Roman Catholicism, it is as fair to say that Brian Moore is one of the few novelists whose literary portrayal of Catholicism so effectively spans the period prior to and following this church council. Moore's novels represent a distinctive literary contribution to our understanding both of the portrayal of Catholicism in twentieth-century fiction in

English and of the changing theological face of Catholicism in the same period.[1] From the publication of *Judith Hearne* (1955) up to and including *The Magician's Wife* (1997), the religious and specifically Catholic themes of Brian Moore's major fictional work place him firmly on the interface of literature and theology.[2] The present task is to make explicit such a relationship within Moore's fiction; specifically, to demonstrate the ways in which Moore's portrayal of Catholicism in his novels reflects pre- and post-Vatican II models of Catholicism itself. For a religious tradition which prides itself on its universality, this literary reflection of Catholicism can be shown most strongly through the particularities of place. In the novels of Moore, geography is a key determinant of personal and cultural identity; and where the focus is upon Catholic personalities and Catholic cultural identity, as is invariably the case, narrative is plotted in a landscape which is both physical and theological.

The Writing of Catholic Worlds: Landscape and the Portrayal of Catholicism in the Novels of Brian Moore

There does exist a widespread, if somewhat diverse, critical literature to accompany Moore's fairly prodigious literary output (Studing 1975; McIlroy 1988; O'Donoghue 1990; Sullivan 1996; Sampson 1998). I want to focus on two strands of criticism which are central to an understanding of Moore's work – his representation of place and his portrayal of Catholicism – and, while highlighting the limitations of current approaches, demonstrate what critical possibilities might exist when both strands are more effectively integrated.

First, then, there is the issue of Moore's own migrations as crucial to an understanding of his work. Moore, Belfast born in 1921, emigrated to Canada in 1948 and achieved citizenship of that country soon before moving to the United States where he lived for many years until his death early in 1999. Critically, many have used Moore's migrations, particularly emigration from Ireland to North America, as a key to understanding Moore's fictional portrayal of 'Old World', especially but not exclusively Irish, migrants in the 'New World' (Dahlie 1969; 1981; Longley 1994; Sampson 1998) and some critics are thoroughly dependent upon the author's life as a key to his fiction (Flood 1974; Samspon 1998 but also O'Donoghue 1990, and to a much lesser extent Sullivan 1996). While fitting for his early Belfast novels (*The Lonely Passion of Judith Hearne*, *The Feast of Lupercal* and *The Emperor of Ice Cream*) or the early North American works (especially, *An Answer from Limbo* and *The Luck of Ginger Coffey*), analysis of place, migration and the author as exile being important, such a treatment is too limited in scope to provide a full appraisal, either of the latter novels or of his most recent fictions; and it is especially inadequate for an understanding of Moore's portrayal of Catholicism over the full span of his novels in which overtly autobiographical elements have become systematically sub-sumed by more universal, and thus inevitably less personal, religious and more widely ideological themes.

A second critical strand in the assessment of Moore's novels is the preoccupation with religious, especially Catholic, themes. Perhaps ironically, it is certainly less fully formed as a critical approach than discussions of place. Indeed, this is more surprising when one considers that one can barely have any understanding of Moore's work without some insight into his presentation of religion. While some have emphasized the theme more explicitly than others (for example, Brown 1988; Gallagher 1988), systematic possibilities have generally been neglected. Considerations of Catholicism have thus tended to be piecemeal. To cite more substantial and relatively recent studies, O'Donoghue suggests Moore is writing on Catholicism even when his themes are overtly secular; she deals in depth with many Catholic themes but neglects any detailed treatment of the historical nuances of a faith which is far from uniform over the period of Moore's writing. O'Donoghue even goes so far as to suggest that 'since he wrote *Catholics*, the direction taken by the Catholic Church as regards doctrine and ritual has concerned Moore no further ...' (1990: 143). This allows O'Donoghue to sidestep the issue of Moore's very detailed fictional portrayal of Catholicism, indeed *since Catholics* in an *increasingly* distinctive way. Similarly, Sullivan's study certainly deals with Catholic themes throughout his important work; but again he neglects entirely to address the significance of the changing face of Catholicism, there being no better way to indicate this than by his total omission of any reference to Vatican II in his index. Thus Sullivan attempts 'to show that, allied to personal quest for some form of certainty, Moore's work – especially *after Catholics* – becomes concerned in more complex ways (although such concern is present in Judy Hearne's demand for a "sign") with what could be called the semiotic of belief" (1996: xiii, my emphasis); but by the same token, taking a structuralist interpretation of Catholicism as a series of signs, Sullivan has ironically neglected that textuality, that system of signification, at the heart of modern Catholicism, the defining transformation of the contemporary Church subsequent to the Second Vatican Council, a transformation which is defined through its textuality in official conciliar and post-conciliar documentation.

While it would be difficult, and perhaps fruitless, to establish direct textual links between the author's novels and pre-conciliar church writing, the documentation of the Council itself and/or post-conciliar documents (though many such links may be hinted at), Moore's examination of Catholicism does very closely reflect pre- and post-Vatican II preoccupations within the Catholic Church. Significant, then, to this present examination is how important place is within the novelist's literary appraisal of pre- and post-Vatican II Catholicism. The task here then is to show *how* Moore's novels reflect these important developments. What becomes obvious is that two strands of criticism outlined above can form a coherent hermeneutical whole. Thus, those critical approaches which emphasize the importance of geography and place, simply put *landscape*, can be integrated with his portrayal of Catholicism, and as such represent a critical unity which can incorporate the full corpus of Moore's novels; and what is especially marked in Moore's fiction is the way in which presentation of what might be loosely termed a literary history of theological ideas almost invariably entails his use of landscape in an idealistic as much as physical sense. Place becomes representative of ideas, usually all-encompassing ones. Simplistically – and often the process is simplistically portrayed, especially in his early novels – a country comes to represent a world-view: Ireland, or at least Belfast, becomes associated with a narrow and repressive form of clerically dominated Catholicism; America comes to symbolize liberal and secular values. The process of fictional portrayal of Catholicism becomes more complex in a post-Vatican II era, as will become apparent.

The fictional realities within Moore's novels thus reflect a coinciding of created narrative, a diverse range of literary encounters with Catholicism, with the realities of an actually unfolding historical tradition of what Lyotard (1984) would term grandnarrative, and specifically the Catholic grand-narrative (the persistence of grandnarrative mitigating any expectations of its demise). Underlying this exploration, then, is the notion of intertextuality. However imprecisely, the novelist's texts, literally and metaphorically, encounter the metatext of a tradition. The written worlds created by Moore reflect 'real' places, 'real' and actual, historical Catholic realities refracted through the narrative prism of individual protagonists and other characters. This intertextual 'region', both physical and metaphysical, reflects an interface of the literary and theological. This critical approach, however preliminary here, may have something to contribute to our understanding of 'Catholic' writing, secular literature and theology, from both disciplinary positions. This can be best illustrated through further consideration of historical transformation within the Catholic Church and its literary reflection within the novels of Brian Moore.

The Fictional Portrayal of 'Pre-Vatican II Catholicism': Rejection, Retrospection and Replacement – The Early Irish and American Novels

Pre-Vatican II Catholicism

Theologically, pre-Vatican II Catholicism was well defined; and if its ecclesiological self-definition provided sharply set boundaries between itself and other churches, other faiths *and* the world at large, it was at least a world-view in which both laity and hierarchy knew their place. Thus Rausch comments authoritatively on the period immediately prior to the Second Vatican Council:

> When Pope Pius XII died in 1958, the Catholic Church was, to all casual observers, in excellent shape. In the first half of the twentieth century the Church had been led by a number of strong popes, particularly Pius XII himself, who guided the Church through the Second World War and focused its energies against the postwar threat of Communism. The Church was

continuing to grow in numbers and influence. Seminaries, convents and monasteries were filled to the bursting point ... Catholic theology, if not very creative, was very orthodox; there was almost no dissent, no public disagreement. Catholics knew who they were; they were proud of their Church and had a clear sense of their own identity.   (Rausch 1998: 259)

As Rausch goes on to comment, however, the surface situation barely concealed its authoritarianism, its hierarchical domination, and its fundamental insularity in the face of the modern world:

The Catholic Church in the middle of the twentieth century considered itself very much a Church under siege. Deeply suspicious of the modern world, the Church was on the defensive. Catholic scholarship had been crippled by the atmosphere of suspicion and mistrust that followed the Modernist crisis at the beginning of the twentieth century ... books by Catholic authors were rarely published without a review by ecclesiastical authorities, they had to obtain an *imprimatur* from the bishop or a *nihil obstat* from an official censor of books ... The Catholic Church was officially not interested in ecumenism ...   (Rausch 1998: 259–60)

There is clearly not room here for more extensive comment, but in brief, the major inheritance of Roman Catholicism in the first half of the twentieth century was from Vatican I (1870) in which the doctrine of papal infallibility was established. There is a degree of irony in that it was in that year in which political events in Italy curtailed this council when also in 1870 Garibaldi seized the Papal States and integrated them into the newly formed Italian nation, the loss of secular influence perhaps stimulating an authoritarian ecclesiastical backlash. The sense of siege which Rausch talks about and the boundaries which he thereby highlights in regard to the Church in the modern world was an inheritance of the Church's nineteenth-century self-definition in particular, but one which can be traced back to the Counter-Reformation and the sixteenth-century Council of Trent (1545–63). In many ways, the Catholic Church period prior to Vatican II was little different from that prior to Vatican I; and the sense of separation of church and world no better illustrated by Pius IX's publication of the *Syllabus of Errors* in 1863 which represented a systematic condemnation of the 'errors' of the modern world and which document rejected any notion of accommodation with 'progress, liberalism, and recent departures in civil society' (cited Rausch 1998: 262). It was a lack of accommodation which was certainly mirrored in the condemnation of Modernism in Pius X's encyclical *Pascendi* and the Holy Office's decree *Lamentabili* (both 1907).

The Early Irish Novels (Judith Hearne, 1955; The Feast of Lupercal, 1958; The Emperor of Ice Cream, 1965)

Such a Catholic world is largely portrayed by Brian Moore's first novel, set in the claustrophobic and morally repressive environment of 1940s Belfast. Judith Hearne is spiritually marginalized by her Catholic faith in a Protestant Ulster and physically ghettoized by her meagre, impecunious 'digs' existence. Alienation from the Church as well as any meaningful place in the social order is compounded by her alcoholism and her failings in love with the self-seeking James Madden (American and her false hope of Irish immigration), Hearne is certainly a victim of exclusion. In the final chapter of the novel, Hearne, in a spiralling decline, hospitalized and in the care of Catholic nuns and ministered to by a priest, close to despair, seeks a desperate renewal of faith in the words, 'I do not believe, O Lord, help my unbelief.' Realizing that her formal, if passionless, attachment to her faith is the one thing that provides some cultural anchor in her rootless life, Hearne ponders the existential difference that belief might make, if only it were true:

> If you do not believe, then how many things would seem different. Everything: lives, hopes, devotions, thoughts. If you do not believe, you are alone. But I was of Ireland, among my people, a member of my faith. Now I have no – and if no faith, then no people ... (1955: 252)

In Judith Hearne's Belfast, the geography of Ireland is as much a socio-cultural as physical landscape; in particular, Belfast represents theological as well as more obvious limits.

Such commentary, a fair précis of the main body of extant criticism, confirms an early trend of Moore's fiction in which a critical collective, 'early Belfast novels' (a very specifically defined landscape), is tied in with the representation of Catholicism, here a repressive Church at pains to keep the morally weak and wayward such as Judith Hearne in line. More 'rebellious' characters such as schoolmaster 'Diarmurd Devine, BA (Junior and Senior English)' in *The Feast of Lupercal* fare little better against the trinity of social forces which Sullivan has identified in this sequence as 'Home, School and Church' (Sullivan 1996; cf. Flood 1974). When the personal scorn of friends and eventual professional approbation of colleagues (inevitably) descend upon Devine for engaging in an impotent liaison with, of all people, a *Protestant* woman, the early impressions of Catholic Belfast presented through the figure of Judith Hearne are sufficiently confirmed, this time through a male protagonist. When Devine accepts the 'generous' mercy of his principal, the said forces of conformity have returned another to their fold. The model of a Vatican I Belfast Catholicism remains in place.

The appearance of the youthful academic failure, aspiring creative force, father-hater and ARP warden, Gavin Burke, in *The Emperor of Ice Cream* marks a fitful transition from the previous two portrayals of figures in a Catholic landscape. The Second World War setting of the latter novel provides Moore with an opportunity to highlight not only the usual conflicts of individual against overbearing religious and social forces. Further, and for the first time in the presentation of Belfast Catholicism, Gavin Burke's struggle is thus against the naiveties of both religious *and* political belief; Gavin's doctor father's German sympathies in a conflict against the long-time colonial enemy of Catholic Ireland, imperial Britain, identifies Irish nationalism with Roman Catholicism. The novel's late-Thirties/early-Forties setting and its appearance in 1965, just at the close and before any tangible effects of the Second Vatican Council, clearly confirm *The Emperor of Ice-Cream*'s place in a pre-Vatican II mould of Roman Catholicism. Gavin Burke's successful rebellion against an authoritarian father (cf. Flood 1974), a model of authority matched in a Vatican I Catholicism dominated by papal infallibility and the authority of clerical hierarchy over Catholic laity, is only part, though, of this character's success. His passing involvement with a group of decadent artists late in the novel is indicative of an alternative train of aesthetic and moral vision which had already been a feature of his first novel dominated by an American rather than Irish landscape, *An Answer from Limbo*. That such experimentation in life-style was Protestant, that it would have been an impossibility for Belfast Catholics, provides more than an ironic fictional backdrop to the fact that Moore, already of course an exile from Ireland since 1948, could only set forth and develop this theme of an alternative world-view to Belfast Catholicism not within its physical, social and theological confines but in physical distance from it.

*The Early American Novels (*The Luck of Ginger Coffey, *1960;* An Answer from Limbo, *1962;* I Am Mary Dunne, *1968;* Fergus, *1971)*

Rejection of and retrospection on Catholicism only gradually lead to the fictional development of the theme of finding a suitably all-encompassing replacement for it. In all of the novels in this phase the immigrant Irish characters seek various forms of replacement for an authoritative model of pre-Vatican II Catholicism with its unaccommodating stance against the modern world. Such differentiation between church and world allowed for Moore's fictional search for religious substitution to be equally well demarcated. In the pre-Vatican II phase of Catholicism and Moore's portrayal of the Church at this time, the limits between church and world are easily defined and indirectly allow Moore's characters the freedom to accentuate their rebellion in seeking other forms of meaning and world-view: economic success with Ginger Coffey; psychological/sexual definition with Mary Dunne; aesthetic endeavour with Brendan Tierney and Fergus. Space will only allow a brief consideration of the rest of Moore's novels here, but the ways in which the portrayal of landscape is integral to the portrayal of Catholicism should already be partly apparent: Ireland, at least Belfast, becomes the landscape which is synonymous with a narrow pre-Vatican II Catholicism; America, by contrast, becomes a secular antithesis, a landscape which represents both a physical and a theological move from Irish Catholicism.

Thus in *An Answer from Limbo*, which of Moore's first 'North American' novels must serve to illustrate the point for the rest of the novels in this phase, we see in Brendan and Jane Tierney a model of American liberalism, shown in their adoption of the secular materialist values of modern-day New York, this being contrasted with the arrival of Brendan's strictly traditional Catholic mother from Ireland. The encounter is, again, both one in which the author treats Catholicism as a theme, even in rejection/retrospection, but also one in which encounter is between different sets of values and contrasting world-views. Place/country/landscape take on idealistic as well as well physical contours. A Vatican I model of clearly defined Catholicism lends itself easily to limits of theological inclusion and exclusion, a matter modelled, as implied, by the facts (in a novelistic sense) of physical migration; here cultural interplay, the Irish Catholic mother visiting the Americanized liberal son, is highlighted by the transposition in geographical location.

The book marks an important stage in Moore's presentation of Catholicism. The physical shift to North American *An Answer from Limbo* is thus a distancing from that moral framework to a more secular and liberal notion of behaviour, again in the widest sense, including the freedom to develop world-view and life-style on an individual basis, within the framework of American law and constitution. But if the protagonist has wholeheartedly rejected the religion of his birth, the novel is to a much greater extent than *Judith Hearne* and *The Feast of Lupercal* concerned not simply with rejecting Catholicism but with providing an equally all-encompassing metaphysic by way of substitution, something which Gavin Burke could only hint at and unrealistically aspire to in his more restricted Belfast world. For Brendan Tierney it is writing – symbolized by his resignation from his post as journalist and his struggle to write and publish a literary masterpiece, his great first novel – which becomes his substitute for everything, and through which he aspires to transcendence without religion. Thus, for instance, after a late-night, drunken argument with his wife, before the eventual breakup, he talks with his mother in their New York apartment:

> 'Please,' I said. 'It's still early.'
> 'It's not early, it's late. And tomorrow I have to go to early Mass.'
> 'Ah, yes. Mass. If only Mass were the answer.'
> 'Mass *is* the answer.'
> 'Ah, Mamma, Mamma. There are far fewer things in heaven than are dreamt of in your philosophy.'

'How do you know?' she said. 'Who told you what there is in heaven?'
'Nobody. That's the trouble. That's why I've made writing my religion.'
She smiled. 'You call that a religion?'
'Well, it's an act of faith that by own efforts, some part of me will survive the undertaker.'
'Brendan, that's no religion, that's pure vanity.' (Moore 1962: 83)

But it is Brendan's preoccupation with literary survival that leads to the cruel and isolated death of his mother in a New York flat she is caretaking for an Irish-American relative. Meanwhile, as his mother dies alone, Brendan struggles towards the completion of his book. It is not simply the physical limit of an individual's life being marked by the physical limit of the text; the ritual burial of Brendan's Irish Catholic mother represents the symbolic death of a traditional (Irish) Catholicism on secular American soil (cf. Gearon 1998; 1998a). Just as importantly, though, the novelist's antipathy toward the naiveties of Catholic belief and practice show a degree of ambivalence at the funeral itself. The moment of death and the finality of the physical burial highlight the insecurities of an otherwise confident New York secular materialism. Brendan's relative literary success in writing his own book is at the end of the novel marked by moral failure. Rather bleakly, in the last lines of *An Answer from Limbo* Brendan Tierney is at the graveside of a literal and metaphorical Catholicism but left to confront the mortal weaknesses of his own selfishly individualistic, alternative aesthetic vision.

I Am Mary Dunne and *Fergus* were both published after the close of Vatican II, but the portrayal of Catholicism in both remains pre-Vatican II. *Mary Dunne*, for example, the story of a three-times married woman in psychological crisis, is framed from its opening with a representation of the eponymous Catholic convent schoolgirl, her secular American identity defined against an immigrant and pre-Vatican II Irish Catholicism. Not dissimilarly, the hallucinatory, psychological visitations on Fergus – again a naturalized American, a thoroughly secular screen writer living in California – are from a distinctly pre-Vatican II Irish Catholic past. In both novels, emerging, historical realities within the Catholic Church have not yet surfaced within Moore's novels, but such a fictional portrayal, particularly of Vatican II and its still unfolding theological aftermath, are not so distant; it would seem opportune then to outline the main features of transformation which were embodied by the Second Vatican Council.

Fictional Portrayals of 'Vatican II Catholicism' and Beyond: Ireland and America Revisited

Vatican II Catholicism

It is important to see the Second Vatican Council in the context of the preceding twenty centuries of Christian history as well as previous councils of the Church and to recognize that the post-Vatican II Church retains its notion of historical continuity, and that any attempts to draw distinctions which are too hard-and-fast would be inappropriate. Still, it is indeed difficult to overstate the transformation resulting from the council initially instigated by John XXIII, whom most observers expected to be merely a caretaker pope. When he called for the Council soon after his election in 1958 with a quest for renewal, *aggiorna-mento*, a 'bringing up to date' of the Church, it was a call to a Church which had largely atrophied in its insular response to massive changes in contemporary global society. By the time the Council had concluded its work in 1965, decrees of the Church's teaching authority, the *magisterium*, here the collegiality of bishops, indicated change on a scale probably never before seen in the Church's history. What distinguished this council from others was its foundational outlook as a pastoral rather than doctrinal council. Most, if not all, previous councils, from the early Church through to Trent and Vatican I, had arisen in response to supposed doctrinal or other perceived challenges either to the Church's teaching or to its authority. Vatican II simply recognized the need both to adhere to its long tradition but also re-present itself to the world in the light of changes which had occurred there; as such it was a reversal of tone as much as of doctrine established by Vatican I and the Church in the mid-nineteenth and early twentieth centuries.

Many of Vatican II's pronouncements, however, presented

so different an outlook that it might be easy to argue that its pastoral emphasis had doctrinal implications, and key areas of the Council's pronouncements are worth highlighting. The definition of the Church itself shifted from a hierarchical model to one in which it was defined not by its figure in authority but by its laity, the Church becoming the People of God (*Lumen Gentium*, see Flannery 1992: 350–426). The Latin form of much of the liturgy switched to the vernacular (*Sacrosanctum Concilium*, Flannery 1992: 1–36; also 37–282), and the removal of this universality in language signalled further massive democratization in the Church – distinct peoples and individual cultures achieved priority in terms of the medium of worship. In the study of Scripture, modern biblical methods were formally encouraged (*Dei Verbum*, Flannery 1992: 750–65), a move which itself paved the way for the other formal steps towards ecumenism (*Unitatis Redintegratio*, Flannery 1992: 452–70; also 471–563). Further, though, *Dignitatis Humanae* (Flannery 1992: 499–812) proclaimed the right to religious freedom for all, with *Nostra Aetate* (Flannery, 1992: 738–42) removing the traditional 'no salvation outside the Church' to present a model of universality for salvation, including those religious traditions beyond Christianity and (again *Lumen Gentium*, but specifically Flannery 1992: 367–8) those with no religious belief (also see, *Humanae Personae Dignatatem*, Flannery 1992: 1002–14). The Church also focused its attention beyond the theological to the political and the social and faced the plight of many societies in contemporary times; *Gaudium et Spes* (Flannery 1992: 903–1001) providing the momentum for the Church's wider social, cultural and political involvement. The separation of the Church from the world, so marked by the century of Church history preceding Vatican II, had ended, and the implications of this are, of course, still being worked out. Even so, we certainly see elements of the Church's new thinking reflected in the novels of Brian Moore.

Ireland Revisited (Catholics, *1972;* The Doctor's Wife, *1976;* The Temptation of Eileen Hughes, *1981;* Lies of Silence, *1990)*

If a key defining moment in twentieth-century Catholicism, then, was the period marking the Second Vatican Council between 1962 and 1965, the direction of Moore's fiction in the post-conciliar period can be said to be equally marked by his own consideration of changes which had taken place in the Church as the century drew to a close. Thus the 'futuristic' *Catholics* (1972) essentially charts the fictional progress of the Catholic Church after Vatican II. The radical changes in the Church's thinking, both in its view of itself and its mission of salvation in the modern world, become projected in *Catholics* on to the aftermath of fictional revolutions of an imagined Vatican IV. That Moore chose to portray such a revolution in Catholic thinking in the context of Ireland is significant. That the island was the main focus for Moore's fictional rejection of Catholicism in his early Belfast novels only adds to the significance of his less strident and even partially sympathetic presentation of religious tradition in this novella against the forces of institutional and doctrinal change within the ranks of the Church itself. Moore's fictional defence of Catholic tradition in Ireland heightens our awareness of a major development in his thinking not only about the Church but about the Church's role both within contemporary society and, given *Catholics*' futuristic setting, the society of the future. Centrally, the presentation of Ireland's landscape is integral to the portrayal of an encounter within Catholicism's own ranks: *Catholics* becomes the vehicle for the fictional analysis of change within the Catholic Church but just as importantly represents a development in Moore's fictional portrayal of Catholic religion in Ireland *vis-à-vis* the early Belfast novels. The sympathetic portrayal of the traditionalism of the Irish Catholic abbot over and against the less favourable presentation of Father Kinsella, the young and 'revolutionary' representative of a newly liberalized Rome, introduces a note of irony and surprise. One wonders if with the American nationality of Kinsella, Moore is indirectly perpetuating the notion of America's liberality; Catholicism's encounter with liberality becoming internalized while the old geographical stereotypes remain. Still, in this novella, many preoccupations of Vatican II are reflected directly: the renewal of liturgy (*Sacrosanctum Concilium*), the accommodation of Catholicism with other world faiths (*Nostra Aetate*) and the search for social justice (*Gaudium et Spes*, especially as this was taken up by the South American bishops at Medellín in 1968; see Dussell 1992).

Moore's later Irish novels deal in various ways with representations of post-Vatican II Catholicism in more indirect but no less interesting ways. Set for the most part in France, against the worsening Troubles in Belfast, Sheila Redden's affair with Tom Lowry in *The Doctor's Wife* illustrates an emerging political ascendancy and consequent decline in Catholic religiosity: Vatican II had liberalized the Church and weakened aspects of moral authority and, while Paul VI's contentious encyclical *Humanae Vitae* (1967) attempted to strengthen the moral side of this, ordinary Catholics, as evidenced by Sheila Redden, are no longer necessarily held in train by Catholic moral teaching. In this novel too, the Parisian priest Sheila Redden consults represents an accommodation between Catholicism and French existentialism (see again, *Humanae Personae Dignatatem*, Flannery 1992: 1002–14). *The Temptation of Eileen Hughes* and *Lies of Silence* too both represent ways in which a liberalized post-Vatican II Church has lost its hold on the lives of ordinary Catholics. Bernard McAuley's love for Eileen Hughes takes on a theological frame; his love is a replacement for the divine love which he feels has been denied him. In *Lies of Silence* Michael Dillon's moral dilemma is whether to inform the police of the bomb plot or keep silent and save his wife's life. It is, however, only part of the moral culture in this final Irish novel. Although the latter quandary complicates telling his wife about his affair with a young journalist, Dillon's easy lapse from Catholicism is a world away from the moral qualms suffered by Moore's earlier protagonists. Similar, though, to an earlier portrayal of Irish Catholicism, Moore's somewhat retrograde identification of the priest in *Lies of Silence* with IRA terrorism recalls Gavin Burke's Irish father's pro-German sympathies in *The Emperor of Ice Cream*. Moore has returned here to a simplistic identification between Irish Catholicism and Irish nationalism.

*America Revisited (*The Great Victorian Collection, *1974;* The Mangan Inheritance, *1979;* Cold Heaven, *1983;* Black Robe, *1985)*

Moore's fictional portrayal of Catholicism is clearly dependent upon the portrayal of place. Thus *Catholics* was the beginning of a period of writing in which Moore's reappraisal of

Catholicism coincided with a fictional return to the landscape of Ireland, a period concluding with *Lies of Silence*. In a largely overlapping period from *The Victorian Collection* to *Black Robe*, Moore's parallel preoccupation with America becomes evident. Moore's representation of uncertainties, in fictional encounter with a range of secular perspectives, will eventually allow for an increasingly sympathetic portrayal of Catholicism. Thus the novel which Sullivan has perhaps over-defined as Moore's masterplot, *The Great Victorian Collection* does reach to the heart of Moore's increasing dissatisfaction with the certainties of an empirically verifiable realism, even to the extent of undermining the fictional possibilities of a narrative re-presenting worldly realities (Sullivan 1996: 109–26). *The Mangan Inheritance*, which begins in North America, shifts its action for a large part of the novel to southern Ireland, and returns to conclude in the landscape in which its narrative began, continues to problematize the secular; and its fable-like qualities share something of *The Great Victorian Collection*'s questioning of 'realism' (Deane 1988: 74–82; cf. Cronin 1988: 24–37). James Mangan's travels to Ireland are more concerned with the examination of his secularized North American life-style than with the portrayal of Ireland. That *The Mangan Inheritance* places Catholicism fully to the periphery of the narrative demonstrates that Moore's characters have not fully abandoned the exploratory hope for the sort of religious surrogate typical of Brendan Tierney in *An Answer from Limbo*; for James Mangan there is too a seeking of literary and his case specifically poetic identity. That James Mangan seeks this in Ireland highlights the island's long literary history, but, in terms of the development of Moore's novels, also presents a new scenario: Ireland is no longer simply a Catholic place, inimical to the freedoms, literary and otherwise, of North America. The more extensive tradition of the poet *manqué*, an indigenous form of rebellion and licence, is as subject to critique as any supposed freedom of the North American liberal.

Cold Heaven, however, marks the beginning of the final stages of Moore's dissatisfaction with the secular. As the protagonist ironically but in the end successfully struggles to maintain her agnostic faith in the face of powerful religious experience, Moore signals America's place as a fundamentally *religious* landscape in which *secularity* has no right to automatic ascendancy. As evidenced by the mental efforts of Marie Davenport, secular agnosticism, acting against direct experience of the numinous, needs to *struggle* for predominance. In particular, though, the often all-too Catholic Marian visions amidst the well-defined beauty and purity of a Californian coastline present a new vision of a sacralized American landscape in which religious scepticism seems ill-conceived.

Serving to confirm Moore's re-valuation of America's fictional place as a sacred rather than secular world is his representation of a seventeenth-century, pre-colonial Canada. *Black Robe* is set in a sacralized North American landscape, a place wherein seemingly contrasting world-views encounter their differences, certainly, but in the meeting of Jesuit and Algonkin, Catholic and native American, differences in metaphysical detail which *conceal* initially ultimately *reveal* a considerable commonality in perceptions of divine presence in the physical world, however differently conceived. Certainly there is here a great shift in the presentation of a North American geography from earlier novels: the literary purification of the landscape is central: *Black Robe* is a pre-colonial but essentially also pre-industrial environment, a world before the urban corruption of any Canadian or American cityscape. Given such considerations, the world of Father Laforgue's encounter with the Algonkin and other Indian worlds, though vastly dissimilar, is marked by a fundamental metaphysical struggle in a 'pre-modern' world. The divine, the transcendent, in *Black Robe* is no longer played out in the midst of the secular materialist and narrowly reductionist world-views of a modernist scepticism. The challenges presented in *Black Robe* are in terms of the particular interpretations of the world, especially the physical landscape itself; but sacralized view of the world meets sacralized view of the world. The world of *Black Robe*, whatever its precise definition, and whatever its horrors, is one characterized by a sacralized presence. By contrast, Moore's early Irish and early North American novels define a world in which the forces of Enlightenment scepticism and 'reason' are still being played out: as we have seen, from *Judith Hearne* right through to *Fergus*.

There is one way at least, though, in which Moore's

portrayal of the Catholic world in *Black Robe* is thoroughly contemporary rather than historical. To some extent it presents an anachronistic portrayal of Catholicism which is considerably more in line with twentieth- than seventeenth-century Catholic thinking. Despite Jesuit letters of cultural analysis which form a supposedly historical context for the novel, Laforgue's final appreciation of the Indian world and its people is one which, of all Moore's novels, presents the most sophisticated treatment of contemporary Catholic thinking concerning the universality of salvation, perhaps the most significant defining doctrinal characteristic of Vatican II itself (*Nostra Aetate, Lumen Gentium* and *Humanae Personae Dignatatem* have already been cited); most importantly for our understanding *Black Robe* as a novel, Moore has thrown such questions back into a landscape and into a time before such questions could even have been theologically formulated. Given the history of political and religious colonization throughout the Americas (see Handy, 1976), through the pre-colonial wilderness encounter of world-views in the novel, Moore presents his most conclusive critiques both of subsequent north American 'civilization' and of the narrowness of Catholic (and broadly Christian evangelical) mission (cf. *Ad Gentes Divinis*, Flannery 1992: 813–56; also 857–62). As such, *Black Robe* is the proper context in which to view Moore's long literary experimentation with North America and appropriately indicates a closure of the novelist's preoccupation with the continent. *Black Robe* represents too a transition in Moore's treatment of Catholic theological landscape beyond which his drawing of key Vatican II themes is reflected in an increasing diversity of geographical settings.

The Church in the Modern World: Theological Universality and Geographical Particularity (*The Colour of Blood*, 1987; *No Other Life*, 1993; *The Statement*, 1995; *The Magician's Wife*, 1997)

The portrayal of Catholicism in Moore's most recent fiction, from *Black Robe* onwards, variously re-presents a world in which Catholicism has found new ways of involvement with, rather than, as in the pre-Vatican II days, separation from the world: so we see that the Church aligned itself against political forces in eastern Europe and was almost a rallying point against injustice, whether of Church or atheistic communism, with an almost mild soteriological accommodation for the good in both (*The Colour of Blood*); and the Church, particularly in Latin America and through its liberation theology, is seen to be on the side of the poor (*No Other Life*). It is not by any means always a positive portrayal, though. Thus Moore raises issues of significance for a post-Vatican II Church which needs to reflect very critically on its past: in *The Statement*, upon Catholic–Jewish relations, especially during and directly after the Holocaust in Europe; and more broadly in both *The Statement* and his final novel, *The Magician's Wife*, upon Catholic relations with other faiths, here respectively Judaism and Islam. The notion of landscape and encounter remains central to the portrayal of Catholicism in all of these novels. In a post-Vatican II Catholic world, especially through the notion of the Church as 'the People of God' (rather than simply a hierarchical entity of priests and bishops, see *Lumen Gentium*, Flannery 1992: 359–69), cultural differences have achieved a much greater significance, language being obviously as central to cultural definition as democratization was to ecclesiological redefinition. Liturgical shifts to the vernacular signalled by *Sacrosanctum Concilium* were as important here as statements in *Lumen Gentium* about the model of the Church as a People of God, though the Church's hierarchical nature is reaffirmed in chapter 3 of *Lumen Gentium*.) Importantly, then, this can account for Moore's use of such a wide variety of geographical locations in his fiction. There is no longer room for a stereotypical presentation of the forces of either secularism or Catholic religiosity which so dominated the vast majority of his early and middle periods of fiction in portrayals of Ireland and America. Thus each of these later novels focuses in one way or another on landscapes which had not received the author's attention before: eastern Europe (*The Colour of Blood*); Latin America/ the Caribbean (*No Other Life*); Algeria (*The Magician's Wife*); and even *The Statement*, which is unique in its focus solely upon France, has North Africa, again especially Algeria, in the background. Limited comment may illustrate the nature of encounter within each of these diverse landscapes.

Published in the final years of the Cold War, *The Colour of*

Blood portrays an ideological landscape of church–state conflict which has now passed into history. Moore's novel reflects a universalized conflict of political and religious interests which means that the novel's human themes transcend but are dependent on the particularity of the setting. The novel tells the story of Cardinal Bem who as the novel opens avoids assassination – is it the forces of state or, more worryingly, church, behind the attempt? The story continues with, and mainly constitutes, Bem's journey through an unnamed land and his attempts to reach the Rywald martyrdom commemoration. Here, radical Catholic forces are seeking to confront the state in more violent ways than the official Church under Bem's accommodating leadership can permit.

The particularities of the physical, religious and political landscape of *The Colour of Blood* certainly confirm the continuing importance of place in Moore's work and in his portrayal of Bem, perhaps his most sympathetic Catholic character. By ideological contrast with Bem, Urban, ex-Catholic, Jesuit-educated, communist leader, is a one-time schoolboy friend of the cardinal. The ideological and religious worlds of the two men are re-linked now through a notional 'politics' of social action, a connection between secular and ecclesiastical governance. Both wish for a (differently defined) common good, both are subject to authority beyond the physical, geographical space in which they operate; Cardinal Bem being ultimately answerable to Rome and the prime minister to Moscow. Yet, despite these links to an 'outside' world, ironically more defined than the unnamed (but distinctly east European) country where the action takes place, both men are also contained within these geographical limits, physical limits which are themselves imagined. Ironically, the ideological and theological limits are a lot more 'real' than the described physical realities (actual named places), a matter which like many of Moore's later novels gives them an allegorical significance; to see them as parables for our time (simple language, accessible characters, landscapes of experience) furthers the ironic proximity to the religious model of story found in the Christian tradition, a tradition from which his early fiction so avowedly distanced itself. The East-European sounding names of places (the Volya river, the Jasna mountain, the suburb of Praha, the towns of Gneisk and

Rywald) serve, then, to heighten the Soviet-bloc atmosphere while at the same time creating a world of fable. The hard edges of the real worlds of Rome and Moscow serve only to highlight this very unreality. Differences in ideological encounter, the atheistic communism of the ex-Jesuit schoolboy Urban and the 'conservative' Catholicism and church–state compromise of Bem, are well matched to the territory and the cardinal's passage in particular, his literal journey through the geo-political/ theological landscape.

No Other Life (1993) is set on a Caribbean island, another imagined place, but here reminiscent of Haiti in recent decades (cf. Griffiths 1997), and is the first-person narrative of a Catholic priest, Father Paul Michel, who reflects on the political rise and eventual demise of his protégé Jeannot to the office of president. Rome is again a strong background presence but its theological discussions are very much to the fore in the controversy following Jeannot's presidency:

> Let me explain. I know that Father Cantave and others like him sincerely believe that by improving the lot of the poor they are doing God's work. They also believe that Rome is hostile to change, that here in the Vatican we do not understand the modern world. They are wrong. We understand the world, as it was, as it is, and as it may become. We know that the Church is changing and will change. But if, by following the preachings of Father Cantave, the people of Ganae lose the Kingdom of God in the course of improving their lot here on earth, then you and I must remember our duty. Our duty, and Father Cantave's duty, is to remember always that, while it is a holy and wholesome thought to wish to improve the material lives of the poor, the primary task of the Church is, and always has been, to save their immortal souls. In this day and age, that task may not be uppermost in the minds of clerics such as Father Cantave. Sincere as he may be, he is still mortal, frail, capable of falling into heresy and leading his people away from the true faith. (1993: 96)

The cardinal's voice, while serving the dramatic needs of the novel, also clearly represents the conservative wing of the Catholic Church's critique of liberation theology. Decrees like *Gaudium et Spes* from Vatican II spawned a greater political consciousness in the Church; subsequent considerations of its applications especially from the 1968 Medellín conference of Latin American bishops onwards are evidence of this. The

Church to this day, though, continues to discuss the validity of the form of such involvement, and such tensions are mirrored in *No Other Life*.

In terms of the portrayal of Catholicism, *The Statement* is another important novel which focuses upon key theological issues for the Church, that of Catholic–Jewish relations, and more broadly Catholic theological understanding of religious plurality. The trans-historical dimension, which sets the narrative in a timescale from mid-1940s to late-1980s France, not only spans Moore's own career as a novelist but also marks developments from pre- to post-Vatican II Roman Catholic · thinking in the same period. *The Statement* certainly mirrors certain theological developments; and, much to the fore here, Moore's focus on France shows again how literary treatment of theological universals can be demonstrated by the particularities of encounter within a specific location.

The 'Statement' itself highlights the central anti-Semitic theme of the narrative while *The Statement*, the book itself, amplifies the unfolding historical context of the story, and its political, more broadly moral, and theological twists and turns:

> THE STATEMENT
> COMMITTEE FOR JUSTICE FOR THE
> JEWISH VICTIMS OF DOMBEY
> This man is Pierre Brossard, former Chief of the Second Section of the Marseille region of the milice, condemned to death in absentia by French courts, in 1944 and again in 1946, and further charged with a crime against humanity in the murder of fourteen Jews at Dombey, Alpes-Maritimes, June 15, 1944. After forty-four years of delays, legal prevarications, and the complicity of the Catholic Church in hiding Brossard from justice, the dead are now avenged. This case is closed.
>
> (1995: 7)

Shifts in landscape and setting as Brossard moves around France in search of an ever elusive security also mark, then, or present different maps of ideological and religious debate. The complexities of the story are greater for the fact that it is a trans-historical narrative. It is not simply that we are, as in chapter 1, taken back to Occupied France as a narrative reference point from the past, but that the events from that time surface continuously in Brossard's consciousness, and in what little of it might be termed conscience – notably, when the major elements of the Dombey massacre are recounted by Brossard, crucially at the close of the book itself. France becomes a prison for Brossard as, trapped by memory and politico-theological shifts in the Church culture, his demise becomes inevitable. Such long-overdue developments in Catholic thinking on Catholic–Jewish relations mirrored in specific encounters within *The Statement* are evident in Vatican II documents like *Nostra Aetate*, but the reception of more recent Church thinking in this area shows that a collective ecclesiastical conscience may be still found wanting, as recent commentary would seem to indicate (for example Hill, 1998; cf. Fry 1996).

Moore's most recent novel confirms the importance of physical geography in the representation of religious and ideological space. Landscape is central to the portrayal of belief in *The Magician's Wife* just as it has been in his other fictions, but here its explicitness is distinctive. Set in the mid-nineteenth century, the book is divided between two continents, a cross-cultural feature not unknown to his other novels, but unlike before this book's two geographical settings are stated as titles, openly linking both history and geography; the first being 'France, 1856' and the second, with Moore's first full, literary journey into Africa, 'Algeria, 1856'. The story is a simple one in outline. A French magician is enticed into the court of Napoleon III and his skills as a conjuror are to be employed in the process of colonial subjugation in nineteenth-century north Africa. Perhaps to a greater extent than in any of his other books, *because of this explicitness*, the landscape becomes one of direct encounter which is both literal – here Europe meets Africa – and metaphorical, where a waning, post-Enlightenment French Catholicism oddly combines with pseudo-scientific magic and meets a credulous, essentially pre-scientific, Muslim world. The historical context, despite a vastly different physical and ideological landscape, is reminiscent of *Black Robe*: it seems that Moore has again looked to the past for a physical place to experiment with the ambiguities of contrasting belief systems – in *Black Robe* between the French Jesuits and the native American Indians, and in *The Magician's Wife* between the modern scientific rationality of the French and the pre-modern faith of Islamic Algeria.

As in *Black Robe*, though, Moore is writing a fictional history of the past with the authorial hindsight of the future. Thus, the two sentences of italicized conclusion to *The Magician's Wife* contextualize the novel in events which give credence to the book's historicity while simultaneously provide a meta-fictional reading:

> *The following year, in the summer of 1857, French armies under the command of Maréchal Randon and Général MacMahon subdued the tribes of Kabylia, thus completing the conquest of Algeria by France.*
> *In the summer of 1962, Algeria officially declared its independence, ending the French presence in that country.*
>
> (1997: 215)

Thus, while the tensions of this encounter are certainly historical in nature, Moore's novel presents the events of 1856 as part of a wider history. As in *Black Robe* too, issues of colonization are both religious and secular, and this certainly adds to the complexities of the encounter in *The Magician's Wife*. If the political ramifications in the novel are religious and secular and centre around two distinct landscapes in one historical encounter, the conclusion highlights, however indirectly, shifts not only in colonial power but, given that 1962 also marks the opening of the Second Vatican Council, impending transformations in the official Catholic world-view. If, as Sullivan has pointed out, *Black Robe* represents a sort of 'comparative anthropology' (1996: 104), and, as argued here, also a reading of twentieth-century concerns of religious and cultural difference *into* historical context, then *The Magician's Wife* too represents an historical nineteenth-century religious conflict in the light of a theological accommodation which was only formulated a century later.

Throughout the work of Brian Moore, then, the physical and geographical contexts of narrative coincide with various levels of political and religious ideology. Landscape encompasses the confrontation in Moore's novels with Catholic 'realities' where the landscape is invariably a place of encounter between Catholicism and the 'other', a meeting of both cultures and continents, a literary environment where shifts in physical, metaphysical and cultural geography invariably push charac-ters' identities, especially Catholic identity, to the limit and, more often, to crisis. Concisely stated, it can be contended that landscape within the novels of Brian Moore is not simply a physical environment, but to a greater degree represents that metaphysical, religious and ideological space in which Catholic identity is variously formed and reformed, and not infrequently disintegrated.

Notes

1. These are wide issues. For a consideration of the developing of portrayal in British fiction, see Woodman (1991); cf. Sherry (1996). For selected historical and theological overviews of Catholicism, see MacBrien (1994); Hastings (1991); Alberigo, Jossua and Komanchak (1987); and Hayes and Gearon (1998).
2. With the exception of *I Am Mary Dunne*, *Lies of Silence* and *Catholics*, all of which were published in a Vintage edition, 1992, *The Statement* published in a Flamingo edition in 1996 and most recently *The Magician's Wife*, a Bloomsbury edition in 1997, all the novels of Brian Moore were reprinted by Flamingo in 1994. I have retained the original dates of publication to avoid confusion when referencing but page references in this chapter are to these most recent and easily available editions.

References

Alberigo, G., Jossua, J. P., and Komanchak, J. A. (eds), (1987), *The Reception of Vatican II* (Tunbridge Wells: Burns & Oates)

Brown, T. (1988), 'Show me a sign: the religious imagination of Brian Moore', *Irish University Review* 18/1, pp. 37–49.

Cronin, J. (1988), 'The resilient realism of Brian Moore', *Irish University Review* 18/1, pp. 24–36

Dahlie, H. (1969), *Brian Moore* (Toronto: Copp Clark)

Dahlie, H. (1981), *Brian Moore* (Boston: Twayne)

Deane, S. (1988) 'The real thing: Brian Moore in Disneyland', *Irish University Review* 18, pp. 74–82.

Dussell, E. (ed.) (1992), *The Church in Latin America 1492–1992* (Tunbridge Wells: Burns & Oates)

Flannery, A. (ed.) (1992), *Vatican Council II: The Conciliar and Post Conciliar Documents*, new rev. edn (Dublin: Dominican Publications)

Flood, J. M. (1974), *Brian Moore* (Lewisburg, Pa.: Bucknell University Press)

Fry, H. P. (ed.) (1996), *Christian–Jewish Dialogue: A Reader* (Exeter: Exeter University Press)

Gallagher, P. (1988), 'Religion as favourite metaphor: Moore's recent fiction', *Irish University Review* 18, pp. 50–8.

Gearon, L. (1998), 'No other life: death and Catholicism in the novels of Brian Moore', *Journal of Beliefs and Values* 19/1, pp. 33–46

Gearon, L. (1998a), 'Catholics: sex and death in the novels of Brian Moore' in Hayes, Porter and Tombs (1998)

Griffiths, L. (1997), *The Aristide Factor* (Oxford: Lion)

Handy, R. T. (1976), *A History of the Churches in the United States and Canada*, Oxford History of the Christian Church (Oxford: Clarendon)

Hastings, A. (ed.) (1991), *Modern Catholicism* (London: SPCK)

Hayes, M., and Gearon, L. (eds) (1998), *Contemporary Catholic Theology: A Reader* (Leominster: Fowler Wright Books/ Gracewing)

Hayes, M., Porter, W. and Tombs, D. (1998) *Religion and Sexuality* (Sheffield: Sheffield Academic Press)

Hill, Roland (1998), 'Christian and Jews: redeeming the past', *The Tablet*, 21 March

Longley, E. (1994), *The Living Stream: Literature and Revisionism in Ireland* (Newcastle-upon-Tyne: Bloodaxe)

Lyotard, J.- .F. (1984), *The Postmodern Condition* (Manchester: Manchester University Press)

McBrien, R. (1994), *Catholicism*, new edn, (San Francisco: Harper)

McDade, J. (1991), 'Catholic theology in the post-conciliar period' in Hastings (1991), pp. 422–43

McIlroy, B. (1988), 'A Brian Moore bibliography', *Irish University Review* 18/1, pp. 106–33.

Moore, B. (1955), *Judith Hearne* (London: Andre Deutsch; London: Flamingo, 1994)

Moore, B. (1957), *The Feast of Lupercal* (London: Flamingo, 1994)

Moore, B. (1962), *An Answer from Limbo* (London, Andre Deutsch; London: Flamingo, 1994)

Moore, B. (1965), *The Emperor of Ice-Cream* (London: Flamingo, 1994)

Moore, B. (1968), *I Am Mary Dunne* (London: Jonathan Cape; London: Vintage, 1992)

Moore, B. (1972), *Catholics* (London: Jonathan Cape; London: Vintage, 1992)

Moore, B. (1979), *The Mangan Inheritance* (London: Jonathan Cape; London: Flamingo, 1994)

Moore, B. (1983), *Cold Heaven* (London: Jonathan Cape; (London: Flamingo, 1994)

Moore, B. (1985), *Black Robe* (London: Jonathan Cape; London: Flamingo, 1994)

Moore, B. (1987), *The Colour of Blood* (London: Jonathan Cape; London: Flamingo, 1994)

Moore, B. (1990), *Lies of Silence* (London: Bloomsbury; London: Vintage, 1992)

Moore, B. (1993), *No Other Life* (London: Bloomsbury; London: Flamingo, 1994)

Moore, B. (1995), *The Statement* (London: Bloomsbury; London: Flamingo, 1996)

Moore, B. (1997), *The Magician's Wife* (London: Bloomsbury)

O'Donoghue, J. (1990), *Brian Moore: A Critical Study* (Dublin: Gill and Macmillan)

Rausch, T. (1998), 'The Church and the Council', in Hayes and Gearon (1998), pp. 259–78

Sampson, D. (1998) *Brian Moore: The Chameleon Novelist* (Dublin: Marino)

Sherry, P. (1996), 'The end of the Catholic novel?', *Literature and Theology* 9/2, pp. 165–78

Studing, R. (1975), 'A Brian Moore bibliography', *Eire-Ireland*, 10, pp. 89–105

Sullivan, R. (1996), *A Matter of Faith: The Fiction of Brian Moore* (London and Westport, Conn.: Greenwood)

Woodman, D. (1991), *Faithful Fictions: The Catholic Novel in British Literature* (Milton Keynes: Open University Press)

Part III: Curriculum Considerations

20

The Theologian as Artist: Exploring the Future of Religion

Beverley Clack

The Problem: Religion in a Secular Society

One of the most significant features of contemporary Western life is the secular nature of our society. The role of religion in our institutions and lives has steadily declined over the years. On a societal level, the rules and practices of our society are no longer determined by religious institutions or precepts. On a more personal level, the declining number of people who regularly attend church services provides a testimony to the reality of the process of secularization.[1] Even where people *do* hold religious beliefs, these are often held in an individualistic and flexible manner; they form part of the private life and experience of the individual. In many cases, spirituality is not tied to any formal religious institution. Rather, a person's religion is a 'private affair'. An individual chooses which beliefs and practices appeal to them in order to pursue their own personal spiritual quest. No longer bound by their cultural inheritance, an individual may draw upon a multiplicity of sources for their spiritual life; thus certain Christian beliefs may be combined with elements drawn from other religions, like Buddhism or neo-paganism.[2]

Against such a backdrop, it seems appropriate to consider the future for religion. The erosion of the social aspect of religious commitment raises particular problems, for in many senses the power of religion lies in its communal aspects.[3] Yet if a movement like contemporary paganism is considered, it seems that an individualistic approach to spirituality is in part a creative rendition of particular attitudes to the earth and to others. Religion, under this model, is seen to arise from the creative impulses of individuals. Feminist theologians such as Sharon Welch and Kathleen Sands have built upon such ideas by using literature to give shape to their respective theologies. So Welch uses the writings of black women to develop her 'feminist ethic of risk',[4] while Sands employs stories which portray 'elemental conflicts'[5] to develop a 'tragic heuristic'.[6] The aim of this paper is to focus on this common sense that personal creativity may offer the best way forward for a religion which is appropriate for the contemporary world. As such, I shall consider the conscious remodelling of the theologian as an artist. If the creative aspect of religion is taken seriously, what kind of religion might evolve into the next millennium?

A Solution?: The Theologian as Artist

Don Cupitt is arguably the best example of a theologian who has taken most seriously the ideas and possibilities open to us if we conceive of the theologian as an artist. At one point he writes:

> Think of yourself not as a soldier, but as an artist who has chosen to work mainly within a particular tradition. That is faith, the production of one's own life as a work of religious art.[7]

Cupitt's theology is characterized by a full-blooded acceptance of the process of secularization, and by its attempt to reframe the notion of divinity in a way which is appropriate to the contemporary milieu. He rejects the idea of an objectively existing, external God as outmoded, developing instead a 'non-realist' account of the divine. God is 'a symbol that represents to us everything that spirituality requires of us and promises to us'.[8] Central to such an understanding is a tacit acceptance of Nietzsche's claim that we must accept the full extent of 'the death of God'. Not only is the objective God dead; so are all objective and absolute moral values.[9] In the face of such nihilism, we are left with the task of creating our own meaning and our own values.

In one of his most recent works, *Solar Ethics*, Cupitt combines this need to create our own values with a thorough-going acceptance of the transitory nature of human life. He argues that the human self, like the world itself, is constantly moving towards nothingness. This is not a cause for alarm, but for celebration, for it means that the self is 'a miniature counterpart of the world. It too burns, pours out and passes away. We should burn brightly, all out.'[10] Rather than fear change and the inevitable death which awaits us all, we should seize the moment, live life to the full and glory in the transience of life.

Such an outlook leads Cupitt to rethink the shape of a future religion. Religion, under his schema, is not so much a set of coherent beliefs; it is not a quasi-scientific enterprise designed to obtain certain, objective knowledge of the nature of reality. Neither is it necessarily that which binds together a given society.[11] Rather, 'true' religion is best understood as the fruit of human self-expression. In rejecting the realist claims of theism, he establishes the centrality of human creativity for a contemporary account of religion. Religion becomes a matter of individual self-expression, rather than the acceptance of a core set of beliefs which are binding and authoritarian.[12]

If religion is equated with the development of human creativity, as Cupitt's thought suggests, it would seem that the artist is likely to have a significant role to play in the future shape that religion takes. While having a particular resonance with contemporary mores, this is not a new idea. The nineteenth-century liberal theologian Friedrich Schleiermacher offered a similar understanding in his *On Religion*.[13] Addressed to 'the cultured despisers of religion' who believe that the Enlightenment has shown religion to be false and pointless, Schleiermacher's argument is simple. He does not seek to convince them of the 'truth' of religion, or of the objective existence of God. Rather, he argues that in order to be fully human, in order to live the cultivated human life, they need religion. Religion is thus fundamentally associated with human creativity. This leads Schleiermacher to the following conclusion:

A man's special calling is the melody of his life, and it remains a simple, meagre series of notes unless religion, with its endlessly rich variety, accompany it with all notes, and raise the simple song to a full-voiced, glorious harmony.[14]

Far from limiting the extent of human creativity, religion is viewed as adding colour and vibrancy to human life. Writing some one hundred and fifty years later, the theologian Paul Tillich echoed this conclusion. Throughout his work, Tillich argues that religion deals with the 'depth experiences' of human life. Even God is to be redefined in relation to these experiences. As Tillich puts it:

The name of this infinite and inexhaustible depth and ground of all being is God. That depth is what the word God means. And if that word has not much meaning for you, translate it, and speak of the depths of your life, of the source of your being, of your ultimate concern, of what you take seriously without any reservation . . . He who knows about depth knows about God.[15]

It seems strange that such rich and evocative views of the meaning and purpose of religion should be viewed by many as 'reductionist'. For those theologians concerned with the creativity which stems from a religious appreciation of the world, such accounts of religion do not diminish human life; rather, they enrich it. Of course, the implicit optimism of such ideas should be questioned, particularly in the light of the twentieth-century phenomenon of genocide. Thus the remainder of this paper will explore the extent to which this notion of the theologian as artist is viable in an age such as ours. As a way of doing this, two specific strategies will be considered. First, attention will be paid to the way in which a literary approach might illuminate the beliefs and practices of a given religious tradition. Many of Graham Greene's novels grapple with his Catholic faith, and the concepts which arise from this tradition. If Greene's writings show the struggle with a particular religious tradition, the second model employs the novels of Iris Murdoch to explore what religion might involve if we take seriously the notion of the secular world as one in which the sense of the transcendent has been lost.

Model 1: Graham Greene and the Struggle with Tradition

In many ways, Graham Greene's work is the obvious place to

start when considering the way in which literature and theology might meet. Much of Greene's work involves a struggle with Catholicism, which, while reflecting his personal concerns, also explores the tensions between a given religious tradition and the secular society in which these beliefs are lived out. The way in which Greene develops such themes takes different forms. He might consider the way in which the transcendent can be shown to break into the secular world, a good example being provided by *The End of the Affair* (1951). Alternatively, his work can consider what it means to be religious or good, a theme which is explored most powerfully in *The Power and the Glory* (1940).

THE END OF THE AFFAIR

In this novel, Greene considers the way in which a supernatural divine enters the life of a human individual. The narrator is a sceptical, secular person, and this tension between the sacred and the secular enables Greene to confront the reader with the overwhelming strangeness of the transcendent God. Ostensibly, this is the story of a love affair between Maurice Bendrix, a jealous and embittered man, and Sarah, the married woman he loves. Their relationship has come, unaccountably, to an end. As the novel develops, the reader learns that the event which ruptured the relationship has an apparently supernatural cause. Set during the Second World War, Bendrix and Sarah are making love in his rented room when an air raid takes place. In an effort to avoid the discovery of their clandestine relationship, Bendrix goes downstairs to ascertain if anyone is in the air raid shelter. At that moment, a bomb explodes, and Bendrix is caught in the blast. Sarah finds him under a heap of rubble at the foot of the stairs. Believing him to be dead, she vows to the God in whom she has yet to believe, 'let him be alive and I will believe ... I'll give him up for ever, only let him be alive with a chance ...'.[16] Bendrix recovers; and Sarah takes her vow seriously. The novel tells of the aftermath of this event, and considers the relationship between love and hate, and the nature of belief. Sarah's diary forms a central part of the narrative. While maintaining her vow, she begins by hating this God who put the idea into her head, and who has separated her from the man she loves. Gradually, however, this hatred transforms itself into love.

When considering the interface between religion, literature and creativity, two themes stand out in this novel. First, Greene refutes the idea that religious belief is a reasoned response to the facts of existence. A common metaphor throughout the novel likens belief to a disease; it is something that has to be caught. Hence Sarah says that she has 'caught belief like a disease';[17] while her mother tells Bendrix of Sarah's secret childhood baptism, and comments: 'I always had a wish that it would "take". Like vaccination.'[18] Such an idea is in dramatic contrast to the claims of some parts of the tradition. Philosophers of religion, in particular, have focused on the rational basis of religious belief. According to such an approach, it is possible to provide logical or evidential arguments for the existence of God. Belief can be given a reasoned basis.[19] This may reflect an unconscious Protestantism. Protestant thought and theology has tended to suggest that right belief precedes right practice.[20] As a Catholic, Greene rejects such a vision of religion. For him, there is a randomness, an unpredictability about belief that mirrors the nature of God. By envisaging belief and God thus, Greene suggests that art captures a sense of that wildness, that unpredictability, in a way which reasoned argument cannot. Religion is primarily a phenomenon of the heart or emotions, not of reason or the head, and thus creativity, not scientific logic, takes centre stage.

The second significant theme in this novel concerns the way in which the transcendent breaks through the opacity of the secular world, illuminating the life experience of the key characters. Sarah is a woman given to extramarital relationships, a woman who describes herself as 'a phoney and a fake'.[21] She is not a 'good' woman in the conventional sense of the word. Yet Greene hints at her transformation into a saint. Two miracles are ascribed to her;[22] those who meet her are affected by her. And by the end of the book one is left feeling that through his relationship with her even the sceptical, twisted Bendrix is on the verge of belief. The reader, likewise, is left questioning their own understanding of the meaning and purpose of life. Does the secular ethos adequately capture the depths of existence? This strange and compelling novel suggests that it does not.

THE POWER AND THE GLORY

At the end of *Brighton Rock* (1938), the old priest to whom Rose has confessed comments that 'you can't conceive ... the appalling strangeness of the mercy of God'.[23] These words convey a further sense that religion is something odd; that God is an entity who does not conform easily to the dictates of reason, or scientific enquiry, or, indeed, logic. This notion is developed and exemplified by Greene's most successful novel, *The Power and the Glory*. Greene uses the historical reality of religious persecution in Mexico to tell the story of the last remaining priest in a state where to be a cleric is to court execution. But we are not presented with a heroic figure; rather Greene draws a picture of a 'bad' priest to explore the function of the priesthood. His central character is a 'whisky priest', the father of an illegitimate child. Yet through his commitment to the role he has been given – he can put God into people's mouths – he becomes both martyr and saint. Greene traces the way in which 'failure is transformed into sainthood'.[24] But this is no sickly sweet martyrdom drawn from the pages of the kind of pietistic literature that Greene portrays the boy Luis's mother reading to her family. Fear, self-doubt and a sense of inadequacy characterize the priest's approach to his own execution.[25]

It is perhaps this focus on the reality and frailty of human flesh that hints at Greene's particular concerns. If *The End of the Affair* suggests a God who breaks into the dullness of the secular world, *The Power and the Glory* reveals the seemingly absent God who is to be found in the physical. Love is seen as the way in which the divine can be found in human life: and this includes ordinary, fallible, *human* love. Indeed, the priest's passionate commitment to his seemingly damned daughter Brigitta is the catalyst for his salvation.[26] Likewise, when he hears the confession of a pious old woman, he becomes angry at her hard-hearted piety:

He said, 'Have you any love for anyone but yourself?'
'I love God, father,' she said haughtily ...
'How do you know? Loving God isn't any different from loving a man – or a child. It's wanting to be with Him, to be near him ... It's wanting to protect Him from yourself.'[27]

This immanent, vulnerable God seems rather different from the 'hound of heaven' who pursues and wins Sarah. Indeed, in one place the priest reflects on the implications of claiming humanity to be made 'in the image of God':

> God was the parent, but He was also the policeman, the criminal, the priest, the maniac, and the judge. Something resembling God dangled from the gibbet or went into odd attitudes before the bullets in a prison yard or contorted itself like a camel in the attitude of sex.[28]

This shift in emphasis from the transcendent God to the God in human form directs us to the second model to be explored in this paper. For Greene, the answer to the question of what meaning can be ascribed to life is located in the physical reality of the divine presence.[29] Catholicism, with its peculiar emphasis upon the body of the suffering Christ, is thus well-placed to reflect the God to be found in the human. Hence Greene is concerned to stress the real parallels between divine and human love.[30] Yet throughout, it is an awareness of the otherness of God which shapes his ideas. God is able to take a human life, shake it up and turn it around. God is able to influence the actions of those around him so that the whisky priest does not cross the border to freedom, but goes on to martyrdom. But what happens if one has lost that sense of the transcendent, if one does not speak out of any given religious tradition? Iris Murdoch's writings take on board the full force of this problem, suggesting that this sense of loss need not signal the end of religion, but may suggest a new shape for the religion of the future.

Model 2: Iris Murdoch and a Religion Without Transcendence

As a philosopher, Iris Murdoch is best known for her explorations of what it means to be good.[31] Influenced by Plato's writings, her concern is with the notion of 'the Good', rather than with the idea of an objective God. Her novels, which themselves have been critically acclaimed, also deal with these themes, and with what it means to be religious in a secular world. *The Time of the Angels* and *The Good Apprentice* provide good illustrations of the scope of her writing, giving an indication of the way in which the theologian might be an artist in the modern age.

THE TIME OF THE ANGELS

What happens when a religious man loses his faith in God? This is the question which dominates this early novel by Iris Murdoch. The central character is the rather mysterious and foreboding figure of Carel Fisher, an Anglican priest. An eccentric pastor, he has recently been moved from his last parish where he was given to delivering controversial sermons. In these sermons he would confront the congregation with questions like 'What if I told you there is no God?'.[32] His own response to this question is forthright: he has lost his own faith, and Murdoch's concern is to portray the bleakness of the attempt to live without God. Through the character of Carel she seems to be asking whether it is possible to be good without 'God'. The answer is by no means certain or positive. Carel is an unpleasant, manipulative character, whose malign influence affects the other characters, despite the rarity of his actual presence. Murdoch uses Carel as a catalyst for chaos and destruction. This is not surprising: Carel, like Nietzsche, has realized the true meaning of the death of God. It is not just that the concept of God as habitually framed is dead; rather, *all* forms of morality are now open to question. There is no transcendent guarantor for an objective moral code. Self-centredness seems the only response; at one point, Carel even claims that 'When I celebrate mass, I am God.'[33]

Contrary to what we might expect from a renewed account of the importance of spiritual creativity, Murdoch portrays this identification of the self with God as far from healthy: Carel's actions are at best amoral and at worst immoral. Indeed, it is the concern with morality which connects the diverse parts of the book. Carel's brother Marcus is writing a book on morality in a secular age. Unlike Carel, Marcus still believes that it is possible to construct a morality if the death of God is accepted. However, by the end of the book he is not sure that this exercise is profitable or possible:

> 'Carel's right about the absurd optimism of all philosophy up to the present, and he's right that people who pretend to dispense with the idea of God don't really do so. One's got to learn to live without the idea of the Good being somehow One. That's what's hard.'[34]

If it is difficult to visualize the shape of morality after the death of God, it is even more difficult to conceive of religion without the transcendent God. Minor characters pass judgement on the death of Christianity: 'All those stories are simply false, and the oftener it's said the better.'[35] Even a bishop whom Marcus meets shares his conviction that the old symbolism of the faith must die. Marcus finds this disturbing, for while he does not believe, 'he wanted other people to believe'.[36]

By the end of the book, the reader is left no clearer as to the way forward in a world without God. Carel has committed suicide, implying that it is not possible to live without some kind of belief in a transcendent deity or truth. Critics have complained that *The Time of the Angels* is not a successful piece of work;[37] yet there is in this dark, ominous work an almost barely perceptible hint of a possible way forward. Muriel, Carel's neglected daughter, is a poet who feels that 'the only salvation in this age is to be an artist'.[38] This certainly coheres with the argument of this chapter; it would, however, be an overstatement to claim that Murdoch herself is offering this idea as a positive message. In part it is a rather poignant reflection on the sorry state of Muriel's life: her poetry is rejected by her cousin Elizabeth as clichéd and over-long. Yet in her description of Muriel's commitment to poetry, Murdoch suggests something of the attention and commitment required for living the moral life:

> She was no longer a scribbler down of random inspiration. She knew how to work, steadily and for hours on end, like a carpenter or a shoemaker.[39]

The book may leave the reader with a sense of hopelessness, yet it is in these small indications of a possible way forward that the stage is set for a more positive analysis of the way in which one might live the good life after the death of the transcendent God.

THE GOOD APPRENTICE

If *The Time of the Angels* presents us with the vision of a world without God, *The Good Apprentice* offers a vision of the moral life as a quest for truth and goodness. The central character of the book, Edward, is suffering from a complete mental breakdown, caused by his sense of guilt following the death of his best friend, Mark. Edward gave Mark LSD without his knowledge, leaving him alone when he was called unexpectedly away. On his return, Edward discovers that Mark has jumped out of the window and is dead. Edward – one senses, rightly – feels responsible. Those around him, particularly his stepfather Harry, seek to show him that what happened was simply an accident, that he wasn't responsible, that he is ill and will recover.[40] Edward dismisses such rationalizations, and attempts to find atonement through finding his natural father, Jesse Baltram, an eccentric artist. The book follows his attempt – often thwarted – to find redemption for his 'crime'.

Edward's quest is paralleled by that undertaken by his stepbrother Stuart. Stuart is seeking a 'religion without God'.[41] The rejection of the objective God is central to Stuart's revised form of spirituality. In rejecting the God of Western theism, Stuart argues that the very concept of God is too small to accommodate the truth of the spiritual path:

> 'God' had always seemed to Stuart something hard and limited and small, identified as an idol, and certainly not the name of what he found within himself ... Christ was a pure essence, something which, as it were, he might have kissed, as one might kiss a holy stone, or the soil of a holy land, or the trunk of a holy tree: something which was everywhere, yet simple separate and alone. Something alive; and he himself was Christ.[42]

In many ways, the character of Stuart is a positive version of Carel. Like Carel, Stuart identifies self-knowledge with the knowledge of God. Likewise, Stuart acts as a catalyst for the events of the novel. His appearance often marks disturbing, sometimes destructive events. In this sense, it seems that Murdoch is making a point about the disturbing nature of goodness and the moral/spiritual life. So, Midge's quest for a useful life is initiated by her encounter with Stuart, which itself has ramifications for those about her. Most notably, it necessitates the end of her affair with Stuart's father Harry.

Throughout the book, Murdoch recognizes the difficult nature of finding the good life. For Edward, this is achieved through a process of gain and loss. At Seegard, the home of his natural father Jesse, his stepmother and stepsisters, Edward initially finds that work can form a framework for the 'good life'. However, this ideal is later shown to be false, for, just as the relationships between the protagonists at Seegard collapse, so the house itself deteriorates. Yet even this situation is far from clear: for Edward, the structured life seems to form the basis for his recovery. For Stuart, the gradual recognition of the difficulty of being good without the personal God is resolved in practical action: he eventually decides to become a teacher.

Murdoch's literary landscape is complex, and she does not offer a simple answer to the question of how one is to live in the religionless world. Rather, she presents the reader with a plethora of voices which suggest different responses to this question of how one is to live in a world which has lost its sense of the transcendent. In this we find the strength of the novel over works of theology. Literature allows for diverse accounts of the nature of God, and what constitutes the good life: so for Thomas, the psychotherapist, 'God is a belief that at our deepest level we are known and loved ...';[43] for Harry, 'abstract good and bad are just fictions';[44] and so on. A novel, unlike a consistent piece of philosophical theorizing offers the reader alternative approaches to key moral and spiritual issues. The emphasis is placed upon the individual's need to choose for themselves. Murdoch thus confronts the reality of a world which rejects the presence of God, but also presents the need for some sort of continued discussion concerning the Good/ God.

Conclusion: The Immanent Divine

This chapter has suggested two ways in which reframing the theologian as an artist might facilitate the possibility of a religion appropriate to life in the secular world. In considering the creative contribution of Graham Greene and Iris Murdoch, examples have been given as to the varied ways in which literature might challenge our understanding of what religion entails. Both writers offer different accounts of the future shape for religion in an age when confidence in the old transcendent truths is waning. While both come at this question from different perspectives, both suggest rather similar solutions. For Greene, it is in the human that one locates the divine; hence the importance of the Christian notion of incarnation. For Murdoch, it is through practical action and attention to the good or moral life that one attains a sense of place and purpose in the world. Both accounts suggest different understandings of religion from those habitually offered by Protestant-influenced Western ideals of right belief and factual truth. It is this expansion of our understanding of religion which signals the importance of engaging with literary works concerned with such issues. Religion does not simply offer a different paradigm for understanding the nature of reality; rather, religion involves a creative engagement with the world. As such, our secular world-view may not doom religion to irrelevance, but may force us to reconsider and perhaps to recapture the creative possibilities of the religious outlook. The playwright Dennis Potter captures brilliantly this invigorating sense of religion:

> I see God in us or with us, if I see at all, as some shreds and particles and rumours, some knowledge that we have, some feeling why we sing and dance and act, why we paint, why we love, why we make art.[45]

Such an approach offers an account of religion which makes it more than viable for the next millennium. By engaging with literature and art, the theologian can, perhaps, make this vision a reality.

Notes

1. See for example Philip Richter and Leslie J. Francis, *Gone but not Forgotten: Church Leaving and Returning* (London: DLT 1998), for analysis of the reasons for church leaving.
2. For an introduction to contemporary pagan movements, see Graham Harvey and Charlotte Hardman, *Paganism Today* (London: Thorsons, 1996).
3. See for example Emile Durkheim, *The Elementary Forms of the Religious Life* (1912; ET, London: George Allen and Unwin 1915), and D. Z. Phillips, *The Concept of Prayer* (London: Routledge & Kegan Paul, 1965). Both in different ways stress the importance of notions of community and society for understanding the nature of religion.
4. Sharon Welch, *A Feminist Ethic of Risk* (Minneapolis: Fortress Press, 1989).
5. Kathleen M. Sands, *Escape from Paradise: Evil and Tragedy in Feminist Theology* (Minneapolis: Fortress Press, 1994), p. 138.
6. Ibid., p. 137.
7. Don Cupitt, 'Free Christianity' in Colin Crowder (ed.), *God and Reality* (London: Mowbray, 1997), p. 15.
8. Don Cupitt, *Taking Leave of God* (London: SCM, 1980), p. 14.
9. Cf. Friedrich Nietzsche, *The Gay Science* (1887), §125.
10. Don Cupitt, *Solar Ethics* (London: SCM, 1995), p. 2.
11. Hence claims that the word 'religion' arises from the Latin *religare* ('to bind').
12. Hence Cupitt's damning comment on realism: 'The more firmly such a [realist]

God is believed in ("fundamentalism" being the extreme case) the more demonic and disastrously *ir*religious religion becomes; whereas in true religion people feel divine world-forming, value conferring life welling up in themselves and flowing out through their own eyes and their fingertips' (Cupitt, *Solar Ethics*, p. 50).

13. Friedrich Schleiermacher, *On Religion* (1799), trans. J. Oman (New York: Harper & Row, 1958).
14. Schleiermacher, *On Religion*, p. 87.
15. Paul Tillich, *The Shaking of the Foundations* (Harmondsworth: Penguin, 1962), pp. 63–4.
16. Graham Greene, *The End of the Affair* (Harmondsworth: Penguin, 1962), p. 95.
17. Ibid., p. 147.
18. Ibid., p. 164.
19. Cf. Richard Swinburne, *The Coherence of Theism* (Oxford: Clarendon Press, 1977), and Brian Davies, *An Introduction to the Philosophy of Religion*, 2nd edn (Oxford: Oxford University Press, 1993).
20. For detailed analysis of how this came about, see Keith Thomas, *Religion and the Decline of Magic* (Harmondsworth: Penguin, 1978).
21. Greene, *The End of the Affair*, p. 147.
22. Cf. ibid., pp. 178 and 185.
23. Graham Greene, *Brighton Rock* (Harmondsworth: Penguin, 1975), p. 246.
24. Roger Sharrock, *Saints, Sinners and Comedians* (Tunbridge Wells: Burns and Oates, 1984), p. 126.
25. Graham Greene, *The Power and the Glory* (Harmondsworth: Penguin, 1991), pp. 216–17.
26. Ibid., p. 82: 'Oh God, give me any kind of death – without contrition, in a state of sin – only save this child.'
27. Ibid., p. 173.
28. Ibid., p. 101.
29. Greene, *The End of the Affair*, pp. 109ff.
30. Cf. ibid., p. 47.
31. Cf. Iris Murdoch, *The Sovereignty of Good* (London: Ark, 1985); *Acastos* (London: Chatto & Windus, (1986); *Metaphysics as a Guide to Morals* (London: Chatto & Windus, 1992).
32. Iris Murdoch, *The Time of the Angels* (Harmondsworth: Penguin, 1968), p. 31.
33. Ibid., p. 174.
34. Ibid., p. 195.
35. Ibid., p. 19.
36. Ibid., p. 94.
37. Richard Todd, *Iris Murdoch* (London: Methuen, 1984), p. 59.
38. Murdoch, *The Time of the Angels*, p. 35.
39. Ibid., p. 97.
40. Cf. Iris Murdoch, *The Good Apprentice* (Harmondsworth: Penguin, 1985), p. 16.
41. Ibid., p. 31.
42. Ibid., p. 52.
43. Ibid., p. 77.
44. Ibid., p. 91.
45. Dennis Potter, *Seeing the Blossom* (London: Faber & Faber, 1994), p. 6.

21

'The Liberal in Crisis': or, Teaching Queer Theory in a Methodist College

Elisabeth Jay

Westminster College has recently been looking afresh at its 'mission statement'. Having had an upbringing where a child who dared confess to 'ennui on a Sunday' was swiftly directed to the bookshelf where missionary stories were kept, I have had a conceptual problem with this contemporary genre which seems to be spoken of and evaluated in secular terms but to appropriate as 'top-dressing' words such as 'vision', 'ethical', 'moral', 'concern for the community' that seem to belong to a different register.

The process was led by a recently recruited colleague, and virtually every premise he employed troubled me. Now since I had been the first to criticize the notion of 'customer *satisfaction*' as an academic criterion, I should also consistently have been the first to have welcomed the notion of being disturbed by the discussion at working parties whose deliberations were designed to draw up a fresh statement of the College's mission as a Methodist foundation. I found, however, that I was frequently irritated by the presumption of 'basic values' that I did not share and I will start by examining a few of these.

My first objection was to the use of 'Non-conformist' as a rallying cry. I retreated to a pedantic display of 'pseudo-

professional' expertise upon the connotations the word held
for anyone whose academic training had been largely in the
nineteenth century. I found myself engaged in a disquisition
which, when I thought about it afterwards, bore very close
resemblance to Matthew Arnold at his most obnoxious. I
claimed that 'Non-conformist' carried overtones of the
nineteenth-century Nonconformist conscience – a politically
malleable concept shading into the narrow, rancorous 'Mialism'
[*sic*], Arnold had been so happy to denounce. (As editor of the
Nonconformist, Miall had deployed to great effect that slogan
adopted from a speech by Burke: 'the dissidence of Dissent and
the Protestantism of the Protestant religion'.) In the chapter of
her book, *Victorian Poetry: Poetry, Poetics and Politics* (1993)
devoted to Arnold, from whose title, 'A liberal in crisis', I have
taken mine, Isobel Armstrong makes the astute remark that,

> The poet of wholeheartedness and centrality was never really
> certain where the centre was ... His terror of infiltration,
> contamination, and emasculation, from within – by effeminate
> poets, by women, by the masses or by his own troubled
> consciousness – and from without – by foreign trade, by
> European revolutionaries or by the alien hordes of non-
> European civilisations which come up from the sea like the
> rejected merman – was matched by his fascination with the
> sources of cultural dissolution.

Accustomed to taking an 'agin the government' position in
College politics I was perhaps resentful at being outflanked and
thus marginalized. Furthermore I was unhappy with the
frankly-aired notion that only 'radical Anglicans', whoever
they are, cut the Non-conformist mustard. As I unpeeled the
layers of my discontent I found ever more suspect reasons: here
I was, one of the longest-serving members of the academic staff,
suddenly feeling that my 'establishment' position was being
challenged. In fact I found that on the one hand I disliked the
thought that anyone, by nature of their religious convictions,
could usurp my chosen role as *agent provocateur*, and on the
other that I had begun to feel that mere seniority in experience
of the college should 'count for something'. But what exactly
was this cultural capital which I felt entitled me to 'pull rank'?

When I joined the college I was asked if working in a
Methodist foundation would cause me any problems, to which

I replied, with what I assume I must then have considered some kind of cultural trump card, 'Not at all: if it causes you no problems that I am an Anglican.' End of discussion. In the early Seventies it was pretty safe to assume that most academics were liberal humanists. My interlocutor was a historian and an eminent Methodist and I was an Anglican: that having been declared it would have been unbecoming for either of us to have pushed the other further for any confessional statement: we would 'agree to differ' without investigating the grounds of our difference – which had in any case recently been subjected to lengthy investigation by yet another inter-church initiative. Furthermore as long as I had not declared myself fundamentally out of sympathy with a Christian ethos it went 'without saying' that my private beliefs would not 'contaminate' my teaching. My doctoral work on Anglican evangelicalism and the nineteenth-century novel had, it is true, departed from the traditional liberal-humanist view as expressed in its most extreme form by E. M. Forster:

> We are to visualize the English novelists not as floating down that stream which bears all its sons away unless they are careful, but as seated together in a room, a circular room, a sort of British reading-room – all writing their novels simultaneously.
>
> (Jay 1979)

I had argued the case for an understanding of social, political and religious influences being a necessary prerequisite of literary criticism and I had even gone so far as to disclose my own cultural formation in the Preface when it was published (Jay 1979), but the entire exercise had, nevertheless, in part been designed to distance certain troubling features of the evangelical tradition in which I had been brought up; to cauterize these anxieties by placing them within the hermetically sealed discourse, the neutral area, suitable for 'academic study'. Since the 1970s, feminism, deconstruction and cultural materialism have all played a part in undermining a liberal-humanist consensus that all too often embodied essentialist attitudes and totalizing notions of a universal human nature transcending race and gender. Philosophical relativism, and postmodernist distrust of absolute truths or originating absolutes, in their turn achieved a fashionable consensus position, until quite recently the warning bells have begun to sound. Christopher Norris expressed the moral caveat to postmodernist orthodoxy by remarking that while he would not wish 'to defend the notion of Truth with a capital T', he did want to dispel the postmodernists' fear 'that if you believe in truth, you must be on the side of some ultimate, authoritarian, monological discourse of truth' (Norris 1996). He denounced as simply 'very bad' a 'fairly powerful poststructuralist orthodoxy', which marked students down for raising questions of authorial intention or historical veracity. Instead Norris argued for the re-admission of the Kantian standard, which he interpreted as implying 'not that everything is up for grabs because there is no final truth' or there are 'no standards' but that 'on the contrary, what it means is that those standards are always in principle open to question'.

This chapter is designed to illustrate by example some of the uneasy accommodations we may make as we strive, often with missionary zeal, to introduce students to the complexities of current critical theory. This year I designed and taught a fresh option entitled: 'Contemporary theory and Victorian women's writing' and I sought conscientiously to take my second-year students through the ideas and critical terminology of Marxist, feminist, psychoanalytic, new historicist, cultural materialist and post-colonial criticism as we applied these to a variety of nineteenth-century women's writing, ranging from the ever-popular and infinitely malleable *Jane Eyre* (1847) to Olive Schreiner's *Dreams* (1890). Unsurprisingly the students (a self-selecting bunch of twenty women, about a third of whom might have been described as 'non-traditional' students) found some of these theories more user-friendly than others: in particular they preferred using Marxist and feminist theory. Partly to destabilize any sense that feminist theory could be totalized into a simple check-list of questions (or applied prejudices) I decided that we should launch ourselves upon the world of 'queer theory'. Some of the class had become assiduous in finding cuttings, usually from the literary pages of newspapers, that reflected the issues and attitudes we had been dissecting. I therefore came armed with a cutting taken from that week's newspaper in which Jeanette Winterson alleged that at a less commercially successful stage of her career she had prostituted herself to wealthier women for Le Creuset saucepans. In groups the students duly deconstructed the assumptions lying behind the reporting: we discussed to what extent Jeanette Winterson had used the weapon of postmodernist irony to reveal precisely these attitudes in *The Times* newspaper, and whether the position of mimicking the dominant ideology, as advocated by Irigaray, could ever, in practice, be accounted a successful weapon, or whether it could only ever be an exotic pirouette performed for the pleasure of the feminist cognoscenti. From there we proceeded to examine 'queer theory', looking at the way that lesbian theory had arisen partly from a desire to return to feminism's radical origins, to challenge the complacency of creeping institutionalization, with its accompanying essentialist notions of female identity. We continued through the lesbian criticism that had detected in this politically driven animus a covert impulse to deny sexuality as lesbianism's defining difference and the resulting reconfigurations of lesbian/gay alliances and the fresh challenge offered to binary opposition as a controlling metaphor of identity offered by critics like Judith Butler. By the end of this theory session I was elated by the sense of how interested the students had been by these ideological permutations. In fact if I am to be honest I can remember a distinct tinge of self-righteous pleasure that I had raised such topics for academic discussion in a college such as ours. The hubris was short-lived. In my reading for this chapter I discovered I was certainly not the first to effect the introduction of gay theory to Methodism. Henry Abelove, author of *The Evangelist of Desire: John Wesley and the Methodists.* (1990), in which he argued that Wesley's pastoral arrangements for separate-sex worship and continuous exhortation to celibacy effectively drove Methodists into forming same-sex intimacies, three years later appeared as joint editor of *The Lesbian and Gay Studies Reader* (Abelove, Barale and Halperin 1993).

What I should instead have recognized is that, despite my opening gesture of using the contemporary article from *The Times,* I had, in effect, sanitized the subject and placed it firmly and squarely back in the hermetically sealed box of a neutral academic discourse. I had implicitly used the old liberal-humanist assumption that we were a homogeneous bunch of 'civilized' adults, none of whom were likely to express any embarrassing personal or moral dissent from a shared tolerance of any and every shifting sexual orientation. My only concession to 'a world of difference' had been to suggest, tentatively, that on the whole lesbianism seemed to me to meet with less overt hostility than homosexuality because it had traditionally been less associated with the taint of child-abuse and had been seen more as a private matter between consenting adults.

As my next trick I had invited a recently appointed male colleague, who had been working on the poetry of 'Michael Field', that composite writing identity adopted by the late Victorian lesbian couple, Katherine Bradley (1846–1914) and Edith Cooper (1862–1913), to speak to the next seminar. Like the students I read through the poems and a couple of recent articles on the poets' work. Seeing myself as in this case a student, I effectively abandoned my responsibilities as a teacher and gave little, if any, thought to the implications behind what I was doing. In the first place thirteen weeks of working closely together creates a certain complicity between the tutor and the group, so the tutor in acting as host should think very carefully about his/her duties as host. Is he/she there to effect an introduction and leave the relationship to develop or wither as it will: is she bound to influence that relationship as much by maintaining a silent presence as by taking an active role in the discussion? Do her duties and responsibilities lie equally with the students and her new colleague? Can she resist the position of adopting the role of the 'bright student', raising questions of genuine interest to herself, but questions that may serve to obliterate the voices of the paid-up students and embarrass her new colleague? All these are questions naturally raised by 'team teaching'. Worse still, I had not been imaginative about the group dynamic: here was a male colleague proposing to talk about a couple of lesbian poets to an all-female group. If I had been more on the ball I should have remarked upon this to him and then, with his permission, raised this in my introduction as something they might like to think about.

Let me describe to you, very briefly, what happened: he began by asking them what the term 'Sapphic poetry' meant to them. Silence. I found myself wondering whether, rather than introducing them to the last word in contemporary theory, I shouldn't be spending more of my time giving them the basic landmarks, the vocabulary and definitions, that often, by virtue of their 'non-traditional' student status, our students so conspicuously lack, but that academics of my generation tacitly assume, however often and however rudely this is challenged, to be a universal educational bedrock. He was able to use their comparative ignorance to introduce the question of what 'Sapphic' might have meant or not have meant to Victorian readers. He engaged them in discussion of the poetry, the techniques it employed, the literary conventions it both flirted with and challenged and briefly alluded to his own interest in the writing: the part that Robert Browning had played in 'editing', or offering amendments to, the pre-publication versions of 'Michael Field's' poems: a contribution that necessarily problematized the status and identity of these poems as 'lesbian writing'. This excursus necessarily took him into a brief description of the writing career of 'Michael Field' and the comparative failure of the work of the surviving partner in the literary enterprise. It was at this point, toward the very end of the seminar, that one of the mature students, a keen and lively single mother in her late twenties asked, 'When did the two women become lovers?' My colleague replied that he didn't know, nor was it of particular importance to him: what mattered was that they were self-declared and widely known to be a lesbian couple. 'On the contrary' replied the student, 'it matters very much: since the one was the other's aunt and in the role of guardian to her niece, the age of her niece when a lesbian relationship was first broached mattered a great deal.' My colleague replied that since Robert Browning was a friend of the couple and seemed untroubled by their relationship, what was good enough for Browning was good enough for him.

Students for the next class could already be seen milling around the door, so at that point I thanked my colleague and and wrapped up the seminar: as we walked off for our coffee, I remarked that I was pleased by the fact that the students had found their own voices sufficiently to make such a point, and that their willingness to enter into discussion was a further tribute to an interesting seminar. I do not have any easy answers to what I should have done, and the need to wrap up the proceedings relieved me of the immediate burden, but I would like now to suggest some of the issues raised by this incident. Since I imagine that I can safely assume that most teachers of English literature believe these days that it is part of our duty to raise the consciousness of students to the fact that all texts are ideological constructions, it follows that none of us should then be surprised if the discussion takes an ideogically challenging turn. I have always found it fairly easy to preface discussions of feminist theory and literature with the announcement that this is not merely a forum for airing grievances or prejudices, but this does not cover the case in hand, which raises in a legitimate academic framework the relation between literature and life. It would heve been easy to retreat to an explication of theories of 'authorship', expounding Foucault's theory of 'penal appropriation', or, by taking a Barthean approach, to point to the pernicious effect of imprisoning the text within an imagined individual consciousness and thus ignoring the web of textuality. In this case, however, either variant of this redirection from originating presence/s to cultural sites would have been an evasive tactic, since the concept of two women representing themselves under the jointly manufactured male title, 'Michael Field' raises legitimate questions of identity.

I could have started the discussion by taking exception to my colleague's view that 'what was good enough for Browning was good enough for him': either by unfairly implying that what the student was receiving was a double put-down of supposedly illegitimate anxieties from two patriarchal authoritative voices: his voice, as a male tutor, appealing to a canonical voice of nineteenth-century Dissent. (A version of 'don't worry your pretty little heads over a debate that weightier minds have foreclosed'.) This is of course monstrously unfair to my colleague, but I did find myself wondering whether he would really be prepared to take Browning as an authoritative reference point for all his views so happily – would he, for instance, appeal to Browning's moral authority on matters such as animal vivisection? Even if he did regard Browning as a moral touchstone of sorts does the evidence of Browning tinkering with this couple's poetry really serve as evidence for anything more than liberal tolerance of a relationship that the male poet did not find personally threatening? Was Browning in fact an exemplar of the kind of tolerance described by Ian Markham as a tolerance embedded in a position of power, which amounts to permitting the existence of 'differences of which we disapprove' as long as they put forward no claim for public legitimacy? (Markham 1994). In Browning's case the apparent divide between the public and private persona of the poet, so interestingly diagnosed by Henry James, complicates this matter still further (James 1963).

I could have started the discussion by asking the brave student who had raised the question to explore her own premises further. Was she in fact saying that lesbian relationships and their resulting expression, either literary or personal, were perfectly acceptable as long as they were practised between consenting adults, but any suspicion that they had been engaged in before an arbitrary age-limit would necessarily render any subsequent literary expression of that relationship obscene? Such a process of Socratic questioning, if played with a less experienced 'adversary', almost inevitably results in demanding that the student disclose her value systems, while the tutor maintains a mask of impartiality.

Perhaps, instead, I should have capitalized upon the collaborative spirit that we had built up as a group and asked how many of 'us' shared Rebecca's reaction, and to what extent? I think such a process might have enabled them and me to distinguish between various aspects of our reaction: as a mother I found I shared Rebecca's dislike and unease at the sense of manipulative power implied in the transition between the relationship of aunt–niece (an aunt who had in fact acted as mother, bringing the child up) turning at about the respective ages of 32 and 16 into a lesbian pact in the face of the world's disapproval (the version of their relationship given by Angela Leighton, (Leighton and Reynolds 1995)). As 'a Christian' I found my reaction harder to unpack – since it seemed compounded of a deep dislike of fundamentalist use of biblical prohibitions, and an equally deeply ingrained view that I did not think that the injunction to 'love one another' justified any and all expressions of love.

And yet … even if I theoretically endorse the strategy of unwrapping the complicated layers of cultural influence upon my often confused thinking in such areas, how far can this, in practice, deconstruct the authoritative position conferred upon me as the 'tutor'? By disclosing such thoughts and feelings am I in danger of appearing as someone likely to penalize a student who in the ensuing discussion declares herself as a lesbian? It is true that our students, who include Muslims and atheists, are, like the staff, formally aware that they have joined a Christian foundation, but this of course merely makes it easier for me to declare values that probably lie within the range of the broad swathe of Protestant conviction. If, on the other hand, I always endeavour to mask my own position, I have not only learned nothing from the critical theories I have taught, but may inadvertently contribute to an 'anything goes' morality that I in fact deprecate. When I began this chapter I thought that I would end up by endorsing wholeheartedly the position taken by The Bible and Cultural Collective, whose collective process of enquiry became their 'means to contest an epistemology and a set of disciplinary practices that privilege the autonomous self, an ideology that values private ownership, and a professional discursive practice that legitimates the production and discrimination of knowledge in one form at the expense of another' (Schwartz, Moore, Castellie and Phillips 1995). I liked their view of reading as 'an ethical act that involves an encounter between ideal and text, an encounter that is always situated within individual lives and institutional systems'. This means that it is possible to make the judgement that some readings are better than others. Better ideological readings are those that support and encourage positive social change, which affirm both difference and inclusion. There are also ethically mixed readings, such as a reading that improves the conditions of one oppressed group – for example, the status and power of heterosexual women in the Church through ordination – but which at the same time ignores the specific issues and conditions surrounding the ordination of lesbians.

Nevertheless, I do question how far undergraduate seminars can ever produce a genuinely collective process of enquiry. I like the notion of seminars as reading communities where dangerous topics can be negotiated in an atmosphere of courtesy and informed disagreement, but I also feel that the road from liberalism to postmodern collectivity may well be strewn with as yet unexploded minefields. Perhaps the most optimistic reflection with which I can end is the thought that what is learned in a seminar is not necessarily what we think we have taught, or, in the words of The Bible and Cultural Collective,

The power and privilege of the exegete and interpreter in part determines the ethical boundaries of reading, but the ethical is not reducible to the reading method or approach. Like meaning, the ethical exceeds the particular desire of the reader, the text, the context.   (Schwartz *et al.*, 1995)

References

Abelove, H. (1990), *The Evangelist of Desire: John Wesley and the Methodists* (Stanford: Stanford University Press)

Abelove, H., Barale, M. and Halperin, D.M. (eds) (1993), *The Lesbian and Gay Studies Reader* (New York and London: Routledge)

Armstrong, I. (1993), *Victorian Poetry: Poetry, Poetics and Politics* (London and New York: Routledge), p. 219

Forster, E. M. (1971), *Aspects of the Novel* (Harmondsworth: Penguin), p. 16

James, H. (1963), 'The private life' in *The Complete Tales of Henry James*, (London: Hart Davis), 8, pp. 189–228; also *Spectator*, 4 January 1891, pp. 11–12

Jay, E. (1979), *The Religion of the Heart: Anglican Evangelicalism and the Nineteeenth-Century Novel* (Oxford: Clarendon)

Leighton, A. and Reynolds, M. (1995), *Victorian Women Poets: An Anthology* (Oxford and Cambridge, Mass: Blackwell), pp. 487–9

Markham, I. (1994), *Plurality and Christian Ethics* (Cambridge: Cambridge University Press)

Norris, C. (1996), *The Messenger* 5/2 pp. 35–42

Schwartz, R. M., Moore, S., Castellie, C. A., and Phillips, G. A. (1995), *The Postmodern Bible* (New Haven: Yale University Press), pp. 302–4 *The Times* 4 January 1997, p. 3

22

Love Relations: Exploring the Intimacy between Women's Writing and Theology

Heather Walton

D avid Jasper has written in this volume of the creative tension between literature and theology. My particular interest is in women's literature and theology and I picture that tension as being like the one explored by Virginia Woolf in her last novel, *Between the Acts*. The play *Orlando* is being performed on the summer lawn. Women and men are confused. Loves are multiple and mirroring. The scene appears to be as peaceful as an English park but in fact Virginia Woolf is writing on her body the last chapters of a world at war. The novel ends with a coupling, a mating as night falls. It is a dark and fertile moment in the long conflict.

> The old people had gone to bed. Giles crumpled up the newspaper and turned out the light. Left alone for the first time that day they were silent. Alone enmity was bared; also love. Before they slept they must fight. And after they had fought they would embrace. Out of that another life might be born. But first they must fight as the dog fights with the vixen in the heart of darkness, in the fields of night. (Woolf 1990: 58)

This erotic image standing for a relation between the sacred tradition and the female imagination is not one which I conceived alone. Feminist novelists and poets have been engaging in *affairs* with the tradition, surreptitiously and openly, for many years. Hidden in deep cloaks we have seduced our fathers at the cross-roads or openly slept with our kinsmen at harvest suppers. I shall follow the work of four women who have engaged with the tradition in a flagrant way. They might collectively, if rather prosaically, be termed 'revisionist' thinkers. I begin with the poet HD, to whom I devote most attention, and continue my explorations through visiting the work of Adrienne Rich, Alicia Ostriker and Michele Roberts. But before doing so I must concede that the love play of revisionism is only one way in which feminists have constructed the relationship of women's literature to the theological tradition. Very influentially for religious feminists Carol Christ rejects the claims of the tradition entirely and replaces theology with women's writing as a source of spiritual sustenance. She sets a direction which many religious feminists have followed in declaring that

> The new stories that women tell each other in conversations with each other, in consciousness raising and in fiction, poetry and other literary forms are key sources for discovering the shape of women's spiritual quest. Indeed ... fictions and poetry written by women may come to be viewed as 'sacred texts' of a new spiritual consciousness ... This does not mean necessarily that women writers set out to create new sacred texts. What it does mean is that the telling of women's stories involves a new naming of the great powers and hence a new naming of the whole of women's experiences. (1980: 12)

From an alternative perspective others have also avoided the 'creative tension' between sacred texts and women's writing; the violent mating of dog and vixen in the heart of darkness, in the field of night. Some feminists seek, rather, to work directly at the reconstruction of the tradition. This is the process, instigated by Elisabeth Fiorenza (1983), which initially involved a painstaking historical quest for the missing woman within the biblical text. It has now evolved into a wider deconstructive movement which, by marking female absence, offers the promise of a female epiphany. Scripture, like a pregnant virgin, miraculously delivers a girl child who becomes redeemer. What begins in historical criticism transforms the tradition into fiction. Revisionism is thus but one option alongside rejection and reconstruction. It is a difficult option. It is a creative option ... a pleasurable one.

HD stands as the most prominent representative of this position in the feminist literary tradition. Her personal history has been taken as symbolic of the literary trajectory she represents. HD was famously bisexual and 'engaged' in various ways with the genius of women and men. One-time fiancée of Ezra Pound, a friend of D. H. Lawrence and analysand of Freud, she was also a lover of women. She has fascinated feminists precisely because of her willingness to enter fully into dialogue with the body/texts of men whilst never denying her love of women and her desire to consummate their veiled creativity. Such a position Liz Yorke describes as 'contrary' rather than oppositional (1991: 12). HD sought an amorous space in which multiplicity, ambiguity and heterogeneity confused the terms of engagement between the binary couple of compulsory heterosexuality.

In HD's poetry a delight in heterogeneity, multiplicity and amorous ambiguity govern the approach to the male-centred religious tradition. Her background, in Mennonite Christianity, is not rejected but reconceived. After experiencing a traumatic period which saw the breakdown of her marriage and the birth of a new relationship with life-partner Bryher she penned her poetic manifesto, 'Notes on thought and vision' (1988). In this essay, written long before *écriture féminine* but waiting many decades for publication, she attempts to write the female body in relation to poetry. The work opens with her acknowledgement that poetic vision is traditionally seen as intellectual activity, 'I first realised this state of consciousness in my head,' but she goes on to say, 'I visualise it just as well now, centred in the love region of the body or placed like a fetus in the body. The centre of consciousness is either the brain or the love region of the body. The brain and the womb are both centres of consciousness, equally important' (1988: 95). Elsewhere she speaks of her centre of consciousness as a jelly fish living in her womb with its streamers floating up toward the brain and calls it 'the vision of the womb' or 'love vision'.

I read this attempt to reconcile 'head consciousness' and 'womb vision' as one manifestation of HD's wider project in which she seeks to explore what intimacy with 'woman' generates – not only for herself as a poet but also for men, for the male tradition, for myth, wisdom and faith. The work from which I am quoting opens with her thoughts about sex and poetry. It ends with a hymn to the Galilean; but the Galilean is now pictured as united not with the father but with the female consort/sister/mother. These are the closing lines of the work.

> Christ and his father, or as the Eleusinian mystic would have said, his mother, were one. Christ was the grapes that hung against the sun lit walls of that mountain garden Nazareth. He was the white hyacinth of Sparta and the Narcissus of the islands. He was the conch shell and the purple-fish left by the late tides. He was the body of nature, the vine, the Dionysus, as he was the soul of nature.
>
> He was the gulls screaming at low tide and tearing the small crabs from amongst the knotted weeds. (1988: 109)

In her later writing this love vision is developed further. Christ is often pictured but not alone. He is accompanied by 'the lady'. She is a composite of Madonna and Magdalene. She has been known in many forms before but her visage has been erased and her shrines broken. Despite this violent sacrilege her trace remains. In a resonant image, which HD bequeaths to other revisionist writers, culture is described as a palimpsest. The slate on which we write, erase what we write and can never erase what we write completely. Within the male tradition signs of what has been obscured remain forever etched. In *Trilogy* the symbols of the lady and the palimpsest are given mature articulation in reflections upon the Blitz and the prospects of spiritual rebirth after the Second World War.

In the first poem, 'The walls do not fall', the palimpsest is figured by the walls of bombed-out houses and the hanging tatters of wallpaper. These ruins are blasted and yet still standing. They are testimony to a former habitation and its painful transfiguration: 'where poor utensils show, like rare objects in a museum' (1983: 510). The bomb-strewn rubble recalls other lost civilizations and sacred sites long forgotten but still haunted by a divine presence.

In the second poem, 'Tribute to the angels', HD sees in amidst the devastation of bombing the blossoming of a half-burnt apple tree. This signals for her the return of the lady. She is powerful and independent. Carrying a book which is both inscribed and blank. HD affirms that this book is our book and its empty pages offer us the opportunity to tell the story of 'the Galilean' in a new way, 'different yet the same as before' (1983: 571).

In the final poem this hope is consummated in the meeting of two multi-faceted male and female characters. They have taken many mythological forms in former epochs. The woman announces that she is Mary. Mary who has had many faces but her own integral identity. She requires from her male counter-part no authorization, no seal, sacrament or 'anything that you can offer me' (1983: 592). She carries her own scent. The male merchant/magi/Abraham/God (the one who gives Mary her perfume for the birth and the anointing in the old stories) acknowledges that it is the unseemly presence of the woman which has filled the house of history (whose walls stand still) with the mysterious fragrance of all things blossoming together (1983: 162).

The conclusion of *Trilogy* is powerfully evocative of a hope that the old walls are haunted. That inspiration stalks us through gloom; that even now the lady has appeared and is standing at the turn of the stair filling the whole house with perfume. She presents a love vision that the tale of the Galilean can become different yet the same as before through the return of this lady. Reading the work of Adrienne Rich presents a bleaker picture.

It is important to note that Rich is of Jewish descent and demonstrates little concern with the Christian tradition. She has also moved through a number of distinct phases in her own spiritual and feminist journey. Her concern with revision belongs to a certain epoch when, in the quest for a poetic relation to myths, culture and religion, she was still exploring the potential of androgyny. This was envisioned as a quest to create cultural forms which reflected the image of both sexes and allowed individuals to become reconciled to the lost twins of divided gender. This creation of a new future entails a painful rereading of the past. In the collection, *Diving Into the Wreck*, she writes in the title poem of the process of submerging herself in traditions which have denied female creativity. The woman poet/diver must descend into the depth in order to view the damage wrought by patriarchal culture and discover 'the treasures that prevail' (1973: 23).

In Rich's poem we are presented with another image of the meeting between male and female imaginations but it takes place in an underwater land witnessed only by the rotting dead. In what for me is the most powerful poem in this particular collection, Rich, who has been very influenced by HD, presents her own bleak version of the palimpsest. In 'Meditations for a savage child', she reflects upon the discovery of a child living in a forest. It bore the wounds of attempted infanticide overscored by the scars formed through living in the wilderness. This place beyond had offered a dangerous safety and a fearful refuge. The child cannot speak, language is impossible but the face is writing. 'These scars bear witness' Rich affirms but finds it difficult to decide whether it is the possibility of repair or the inevitability of destruction that they speak of (1973:58).

For Rich the business of rewriting culture is a forensic examination of agony conducted with blade and thorn. It entails painful attention to the wounds of violence and neglect. It is a process of drowning and dismemberment which may lead either to repair or to destruction. There is no word of promise that the wreck can be raised or that the red mouth slowly closing will ever speak its pain. Nevertheless, a minute attention to the tradition is required – if only in order to construct memorials to its victims.

Alicia Ostriker has been regarded as a prominent critical interpreter of feminist revisionism since writing 'Women poets and revisionist mythology', which appeared in her celebrated work, *Stealing the Language: The Emergence of Women's Poetry in America* (1987). Ostriker claims to have identified a political project in the work of American female poets to articulate a female position from within the mythology of culture. She has since written more explicitly of re-visioning within the Jewish and Christian traditions in *Feminist Revision and the Bible* (1993). Ostriker is also a Blake scholar, a poet – and she is Jewish.

Studies in romantic poetry have made Ostriker aware that revisionist myth-making is not a new strategy recently developed by women. Blake sought in his visionary writing to create an alternative mythological system to escape 'enslavement' to another man's. However, Ostriker interprets the work of women poets not as attempts to replace the male body of tradition with a female form. She argues, rather, that the poets she studies assume an erotic relation with the tradition in order that reconceptions might take place. She asserts the sacred stories women inherit from the common store are too precious, too desirable to be discarded and replaced by a new mythology

343

more friendly to women. The feminist revisionist is both seduced by her tradition and compels it to become generative of new possibilities for women. Ostriker is fascinated by HD and her bisexuality and draws on this to describe the process of revision as one of vulnerability and intimacy. 'To love is to enter and be entered both at once ... to penetrate the other and be penetrated by the other' (1993: 118–19).

Believing that the Bible both forbids and invites this revisionist work Ostriker asserts that whilst it has been necessary to register anger and resistance to the misogyny of the male tradition women have also born many illegitimate children to the urtexts of patriarchy. These labours have resulted in innumerable rereadings and revisions of sacred narratives and, just as Jasper puts his hope for the future on communities celebrating plural interpretations, Ostriker suggests:

> Human civilisation has a stake in plural readings ... Most people haven't caught on though. Most people need right answers just as they need superior races ... Still this is an activity we are undertaking on behalf of humanity, all of whom would be the happier were they to throw away their addiction to final solutions.   (1993: 123)

This vision is political, progressive, optimistic. Ostriker claims that the Jewish Midrashic tradition legitimates her revisionist work. She plays the part of the wife, the daughter, the mother and the mistress of tradition. It is clear that she feels at home in these roles. Her palimpsest is not the speaking wounds on the body of a child but the domestic collage of a family bulletin board. She inscribes her own message and pins it up alongside others. Although what she has written is ephemeral, it will be 'spattered with wine one night at a party' (1990: 83), it represents an invitation to the divine to find a new home in her kitchen.

Lastly, and briefly, I turn to the work of Michèle Roberts. Her novel *The Wild Girl* (1991), a 'Gospel' according to Mary Magdalene, is presented as an example of revisionist myth-making deeply rooted in historical study of gnostic texts. In many passages she employs the gnostic tradition of an erotic reconciliation between the sexes and proclaims its productive outcome. This is a typical example of the teachings of her gnostic Christ:

> What is this rebirth. How is it to be achieved? The image of this

rebirth is a marriage, as I have told you before, the marriage between the inner woman and the inner man. You must go down deep, down into the marriage chamber, and find the other part of yourself that has been lost and missing for so long. Those who are reunited in the marriage chamber will never be separated again. *This* is the restoration. *This* is the resurrection. (1991: 110–11)

Roberts's novel is a little too didactic for my taste but it does have an interesting symbolic sub text and it does portray with real tenderness and beauty the imagined love of Christ and Magdalene. However, although *The Wild Girl* nicely illustrates my subject of the erotic potential of a female 'relation' with male-centred tradition, it is not this particular work by Roberts that most intrigues me. I am much more interested in her fictional reflections upon her own history in other writings.

Roberts is not only familiar with ancient gnostic Gospels but also uses a symbolism which resonates with that contemporary code of secret knowledge – post-structuralist theory. She takes her personal history and it becomes transformed into literature exploring a similar terrain to that surveyed by Lacan and Kristeva. Roberts is of French descent. Her mother was 'foreign' and spoke a strange language. These personal circumstances generate a powerful symbolic through which Roberts is able to explore the disturbing presence of the mother on the threshold of culture. She forges images of the 'unspeakable maternal' whose presence on the edge of language and silence disrupts the paternal text of myth and culture – and revises it. This is the underlying dynamic of her most famous work to date, *Daughters of the House* (1992).

In this novel Therese's mother has died. The child constantly seeks her but she is irrevocably lost. Therese also fails to see a vision of the great 'Red and gold lady' her cousin Leonie witnesses in the sacred grotto in the woods. Jealous of this mysterious encounter Therese claims that she herself saw a vision of the Virgin 'dressed in blue' in the forest. She is believed by the priest and people of the village. Her cousin is not. Therese becomes a nun because she has 'found herself another mother, she'd been sold one ready made by the priests of her Church' (1992: 165). However, she is drawn back to the place of her supposed vision, her real blindness, in later life. There she has a re-vision.

The villagers have prepared a statue of Therese's 'Virgin' to be carried in procession to the grotto. Standing before it in the empty church she surrenders to a moment of madness which admits her aching loss. She lights a pyre beneath the plaster idol. As the figure burns she encounters beneath its false visage her true mother of flame who 'was outlined in gold. She held out her hands to her daughter, to pull her in, to teach her the steps of the dance' (1992: 196). In this moment Therese is both annihilated and restored. She leaps clear of the flames uttering as she does so the word she had repressed so long, 'Maman!'.

This burning encounter frees Therese to remember other things she has repressed. The submerged clues to her own identity, the war, the betrayal by Christian authorities of a Jewish family which had taken refuge in the village; other hidden truths. In the light of her re-vision this subterranean history is given representation at last. Her strange encounter in the chapel changes not only her life but the lives of those in her community living with silence and lies. This re-vision is a violent eruption of what has been repressed. It issues in a painful regeneration of social ties. There is an intense but renewing conflagration as a result of the forbidden encounter between paternal tradition and maternal power.

In conclusion, I refer to Roberts's poem, 'Restoration work at Palazzo Te'. It is her version of the palimpsest and is a self-assured, gently ironic work. It recalls HD's concerns with sex and poetry, faith and work (love-vision). The revisionist is represented as the female restorer of an ancient mural who, in turn, becomes a figure for Psyche exploring her sleeping lover:

> Return to that house of desire
> made flesh. Re-vision it.   (1995: 58)

She throws light upon the male body which slumbers below the surface of mythology. There is a frank acknowledgement of the 'phallic' nature of tradition and the way the female artist may both clinically survey its contours and 'arouse' its potential to meet her own. As the restorer works the figure of Eros re-emerges, naked and newly vulnerable to the female gaze.

> Her task is to rescue what she can
> from the fresco: not
> to smooth-talk; not to make him up . . .

Possibly she's absurd
Anyway it is the work that matters.   (1995: 58)

Re-visioning is a painstaking work. It entails tracing and teaching the unspeakable words deep below the surface of culture, tradition, language and memory. Examining the form of the male lover and recalling the obliteration of the female face. Engendering new children. Engaging the curriculum. Sleeping with the enemy. Her body is all covered in chalk dust and possibly the woman who does this work is absurd. But for the lover it is the work that matters.

References

Christ, C. (1980), *Diving Deep and Surfacing: Women Writers on the Spiritual Quest* (Boston: Beacon)

Fiorenza, E. (1983), *In Memory of Her: A Feminist Theological Reconstruction of Christian Origins* (London: SCM)

HD (1983), *Trilogy* in L. Martz (ed.) *HD: Collected Poems 1912–1944* (New York: New Directions Books), pp. 505–612

HD (1988), 'Notes on thought and vision' in B. K. Scott (ed.) *The Gender of Modernism* (Bloomington: Indiana University Press), pp. 93–109

Ostriker, A. (1987), *Stealing the Language: The Emergence of Women's Poetry in America* (London: The Women's Press)

Ostriker, A. (1990), 'The road of excess: my William Blake' in G. Rouff (ed.), *The Romantics and Us: Essays on Romantic and Modern Culture* (New Brunswick: Rutgers University Press)

Ostriker, A. (1993), *Feminist Revision and the Bible* (Oxford: Blackwell)

Rich, A. (1973), *Diving Into the Wreck: Poems 1971–1972* (London: Norton)

Roberts, M. (1991), *The Wild Girl* (London: Minerva)

Roberts, M. (1992), *Daughters of the House* (London: Virago)

Roberts, M. (1995), 'Restoration work at Palazzo Te' in *All the Selves I Was: New and Selected Poems* (London: Virago), p. 58

Woolf, V. (1990), *Between the Acts* (1941) (London: Grafton)

Yorke, L. (1991), *Impertinent Voices: Subversive Strategies in Contemporary Women's Poetry* (London: Routledge)

23

Post-colonial Literature and Metaphysics

Suman Gupta

Introduction

Post-colonial literature connotes an area of conceptual, critical and creative flux rather than the *terra firma* that is already mapped by literary cartographers. The air here has for the informed reader-writer and *litterateur* a whiff of a New World, a whiff of promise and prospects and academic spice which is reminiscent of that originative moment when the whole tumultuous business of colonialism began; and which releases the bitter reproaches of its distortions, injustices and failures; and which draws on a cathartic present when some quiet recompense or tranquil renewal is expected. Post-colonial literature denies any sort of closure. It is somewhere on the transitive fringe of a past world and an emergent world. It reflects on the black and white colonial world and its fantasies and realities, it reflects the past in the particoloured present and the *beyondness* of the present from any containment in the past: post-colonial literature necessarily embodies an ongoing and incomplete process. It speaks from the aftermath of the colonial experience, and it speaks as the aftermath that is still attached to the colonial experience. It is associated with civilizations (some ancient, some created, some no more than ghosts) that have been rebirthed into nascent nation-states, that have either still not entirely recovered from the birth pangs or come to grips with their fraught ancestry. Most importantly, post-colonial literature

348

inevitably reflects on its own location, and this is necessarily a subversive self-consciousness. It tries to defeat the past by understanding it, and overcome the present by exorcising the past. Post-colonial literature is by definition in process – presumably it reaches towards some sort of end when it will be reconciled to its past and at peace with its renamed and settled (no longer *post-colonial*) present. Arguably, though, the mark of the colonial cannot ever be wholly erased: that would only result in an omission in history. The colonial past can only be welded into the hypothetical no-longer-post-colonial present in some new and as yet unresolved fashion.

Let me emphasize that again: an area of conceptual, critical and creative flux. For this essay the creative and the critical and conceptual are not held asunder, even if the former is understood to emanate from the interstices of post-colonial societies, and the latter is often seen to recede into Western institutions. The geographical and cultural locations of, and distinctions between, post-colonial critics and writers may be of some political moment, but are unimportant in this overarching view of a composite *post-colonial literature*. As far as this essay goes that is a flux, of a self-conscious processive nature, into which all practitioners of post-colonial literature (whether critical or creative, and from wherever) make their specific transitive marks. The more individuated and distinctive and *placed* these marks become the more does the generalized designation of 'post-coloniality' recede into the background, and there is the beginning or renewal or simply clarification of another linguistic/national/cultural canon. This doesn't mean that colonial experiences have been the same in all colonial contexts (far from it): I merely mean that to understand the designation 'post-colonial literature' in its broadest sense the commonality of the different experiences have to be emphasized.

It is important for the purposes of this chapter to understand post-colonial literature in its broadest sense, and to apprehend its processive unstable transitive nature. This realization of the scope and nature of post-colonial literature allows me to insert the metaphysical (primarily that, but also in a loosely related fashion the 'spiritual' and the 'theological') therein. The insertion of the metaphysical in the flux of post-colonial literature cannot be a compendium of the spiritual recognitions and theological convictions that may be found there. That could be a useful thematic study in any literary formation (within an accepted canon, genre etc.), or in comparative literary studies, or perhaps in placing literary formations within a history of ideas. But if the focus is on post-colonial literature as such then the connection to the metaphysical (and spiritual or theological) would have to emerge more vitally, in a more contingent fashion, from its processive unstable transitive *post-colonial* consciousness. It is this connection of the metaphysical and post-colonial in literature that I labour in this chapter. Moreover, I maintain that this connection is traceable because metaphysical apprehensions can also be processive, can *contain* the anxieties and imperatives which impel post-colonial literature; and arguably slip in and out, reify gaps, provide channels and outlets.

Clearly it is a particular mode of metaphysical apprehension that I am referring to: otherwise spiritual recognitions and theological convictions would have to be more squarely faced here. To put it briefly, the model of metaphysical apprehension I have in mind is less related to the affirmative spiritual and theological recognitions/convictions that are available in Spinoza's, Descartes's, Kierkegaard's, Buber's, or even Riceour's writings, than to an encounter with the limits of enunciation (and therefore apprehension) and a reaching out towards a field beyond enunciation. In the latter the emphasis of models of metaphysical apprehension is on the *limits of enunciation*, and gestures towards a metaphysical and pregnant but unenunciable beyond are contingent but not necessarily affirmed. No affirmation is involved in the gestures towards the metaphysical in the latter, except to reiterate the limits of the enunciable. Suitable models for this kind of non-affirmative metaphysical understanding are legion. This is most likely to be reminiscent of, for instance, the general structure of Hegel's *Phenomenology of Spirit* (or *Mind*, depending on how *geist* is translated). This operates by apprehending and transcending each moment of self-understanding (where self-understanding connotes the entire breadth of a total consciousness of being conscious and stretches from individual consciousness to the holism of a human consciousness *per se*). Each step of apprehension is a step of synthesis, and each consequent step is one of transcendence to a further synthesis which effectively renders the previous step irrelevant. The end product is, for Hegel, an absolute knowledge (where consciousness itself becomes total or one, or where, in his words, 'I' = 'I'). The whole of Hegel's *Phenomenology* therefore represents a process of 'upward' steps moving towards a final knowledge in the course of which the previous step ceases to matter in-itself once it is bypassed. An absolute spiritual and religious affirmation occurs at the end of this, but this cannot be apprehended in any way other than as the end of the process which takes place – it is merely a collection of signifiers which mark the end of the process and mean nothing in themselves unless the process is apprehended:

> The *goal*, Absolute Knowing, or Spirit that knows itself as Spirit, has for its path the recollection of the organization of their realm. Their preservation, regarded from the side of their free existence appearing in the form of contingency, is History; but regarded from the side of their [philosophically] comprehended organization, it is the science of knowing in the sphere of appearance: the two together, comprehended History, form alike the inwardizing and the Calvary of absolute Spirit, the actuality, truth, and certainty of his throne, without which he would be lifeless and alone.[1]

For Hegel this processive apprehension of metaphysics provides the *raison d'être* of both his understanding of the teleological principle of universal history, and his placement of political and aesthetic conception within it. An analogous processive metaphysical apprehension, with even less of a spiritual or religious affirmation, and rather more of an emphasis of the limits of enunciation, is available in Wittgenstein's essentially positivist *Tractatus Logico-Philosophicus*. The early Wittgenstein's description of a monologically complete logic of language (i.e. charting out the mechanics of the sayable) leads to the point of reaching a complete apprehension of language, and therefore of the metaphysical space beyond the sayable. The latter, as Wittgenstein famously observed, is not a nullity but a realization which is conditional to apprehending the end of the process of monological construction – it will have to be posited if the process of philosophically apprehending the logic of language as set out in the *Tractatus* is to make sense:

> The sense of the world must lie outside the world. In the world everything is as it is, and everything happens as it does happen; in it no value exists – and if it did exist, it would have no value.

> If there is any value, it must lie outside the whole sphere of what happens and is the case. For all that happens and is the case is accidental.
>
> What makes it non-accidental cannot lie *within* the world, since if it did it would be accidental.
>
> It must lie outside the world.[2]

And therefore:

> My propositions serve as elucidations in the following way: anyone who understands me eventually recognises them as nonsensical, when he has used – as steps to climb beyond them . . .[3]

It is not ironical that the examples of models of processive metaphysics, which I feel can be inserted into the processive flux of post-colonial literature, derive from the context of such patently imperial cultures. There is little doubt that Hegel's idealistic and Wittgenstein's positivistic understanding of the process leading up to the unenunciable and metaphysical embody the peculiar discourse of Enlightenment rationalism – the politics and rituals of which are so ably described in Horkheimer's and Adorno's well-known *Dialectics of Enlightenment* (1947). It is precisely because these are so self-evidently evocative of Enlightenment rationalism that they appear here. It is precisely because of the lingering *colonial* in the process of post-colonial literature (and despite the optimism of its processive flux, perhaps this lingering predicate will never, and indeed shouldn't ever, be wholly abandoned) that these evocations of processive metaphysics are relevant to post-colonial literature.

I mark out below, in terms of practical examples, the manner in which the above-mentioned model of metaphysical apprehension has inserted itself into post-colonial literature. Instead of trying to do this with an ambitious overview on the entire area of post-colonial literature (that would be well outside the scope of the space allotted here), I do this in terms of three specific points of focus within the general flux. I believe that the three focused discussions presented here are indicative of the general direction in which post-colonial literature is flowing at present.

Oriental Mystique

The present academic vogue of post-colonial literature was indubitably given a definitive direction by Edward Said's *Orientalism* (1978).[4] Essentially, this involved the wedding of Foucault's mode of socio-historical analysis through discourse formations to existing colonial and post-colonial texts which were, till then, usually brought into the remit of academic discourse through methods associated with sociological, historical, anthropological, political and economic modes of enquiry. If what the student now normally encounters as post-colonial literature had existed as a putative academic discipline before that, it would have been in terms of its immediate sphere of sociological, political, historical, etc., relevance; it would probably not have appeared in terms of the commonality of the colonial experience in its broadest sense, nor in terms of the commonality of that experience in terms of its discursive practices (even within the confines of literature). If, for instance, a few books of Indian English literature shouldered their way into the usual canon of English literature in Indian schools and universities, it was more as a political and ideological statement than as a means of examining the nature of post-colonial discourses, or examining the presumptions of English literary studies from that perspective. It was more likely (sticking with the instance of India) that English studies in India would have asserted its nationalistic orientation by focusing on books on India by English writers (Kipling, Forster, Myers, Masters, Jhabvala, etc.) and subjecting these to well-worn liberal-humanistic or new-critical appraisals. There might have been the odd course on Indian or African or Caribbean literature in English or French in European and American universities (very rarely), but more as a recognition of their existence in accepted canonical terms than as a recognition of their existence as post-colonial literature.

The impact of Said's book, and the proliferation of post-colonial literary stars and *litterateurs* since, comprehends a two-fold displacement in the identification of areas of academic enquiry (or objects of academic enterprise). The first is a direct result of the kind of displacement performed by Foucault himself, which was happily in consonance with the linguistics-oriented project of critical theory as a meta-discipline that had already emerged in European academia. The identification of discourse formations as a kind of quanta of knowledge (analogous to Durkheim's 'social facts' or Weber's 'social acts' but without the determinative *social* object) – given its broadest import in *The Archaeology of Knowledge* (1969) – allows for the paradigms of all disciplines of knowledge (especially the *literae humaniores*) to be examined, instead of these paradigms determining the modes of examination. With a bit of help from a Barthes-like placement of the Text as a general object of analysis, and some Gramsci-like organic intellectual commitment, the methods of analysis offered by discourse formations easily flow into an increasingly more accommodative area of literature and critical theory. Said's book used these tendencies to displace the usual object of colonial and post-colonial studies from their usually allocated sociological, historical, anthropological, etc., disciplinary spaces, and identified instead the fluid and pervasive Oriental Text and its discourse formations. Post-colonial literature as we understand it now is largely a result of this displacement, and is given its universal import through these processes. The second displacement has already been mentioned: it occurs within the field of literary studies *per se*.

The first displacement is based on, I have mentioned, an ability to turn the academic gaze on the constitution of academic disciplines. Though most disciplines of knowledge noted, and some were even influenced by, the aspirations of the meta-discipline of critical theory they generally retained their paradigmatic integrity. Literary studies, however, (in all its diversity) is one of those disciplines which actually capitalized on, and transformed itself radically through, critical theory. In a sense it began to and continues to embody the meta-disciplinary aspirations of critical theory in itself – which allows a development like post-colonial literature (analogous to feminist literature or black literature), in the renewed terms made possible by Said's innovations, to acquire an air of social/political/cultural efficaciousness. Post-colonial literature displaces itself from being the arena simply of historist or formalist or cultural reflexiveness, to actually expecting such reflexiveness to be universally affective in social/political/cultural terms.

The issue of 'sayability' or 'limits of enunciation' described above is at the heart of this emergence of the flux of post-colonial literature as understood now. Said's *Orientalism* described, using the most ambitious field of reference, the following process:

1. The evolution of the Orient as a discursive space 'outside' Europe or 'other than' European, and yet enclosed by the European imagination and distilled into images, symbols and texts arraigned in a self-reflexive and self-centred fashion (the Orient as the 'other' enclosed in the culturally centred European 'us').

2. The homogenization of the 'otherness' of the Orient, thus merging together vastly culturally and socially distinct contexts merely on grounds of difference from the Occident.

3. The formalization of Oriental studies, made possible by and constructed in accordance with this homogenisation of the 'other', and designed to consolidate imperial conquest and the exertion of colonial power.

4. The introduction of empirical rigour and scientific methodology in Oriental studies, but only to maintain its ideological assumptions in a non-consensual fashion, and largely at the behest of colonial domination.

5. The naturalization of Orientalist attitudes, and their widespread persistence into our time, not just in academic institutes and archives but in the mass media and in 'our' *zeitgeist*, so to say – so that the East–West divide continues to be a socially, politically and culturally effective factor.

A formidable amount of scholarship has been devoted to examining these points in detail with reference to a vast variety of histories and cultures since; and more often than not Said's sweeping view has been found to be fraught with ambiguities and contradictions.[5] But the general point has been more or less retained: colonialism has engendered a complex and detailed method of enunciating or containing the colonized in (often apparently very different) discourses so that the latter's 'otherness' and subjugated-status are maintained; and post-colonialism is a gradual process (in diverse contexts) of apprehending the effectiveness of that endeavour in our time and of trying to contest it in different ways.

Since the flux of post-colonial literature appoints itself the arena both of apprehension of the processes and continuing power of colonial discourses and of combative critiques thereof, it often finds itself up against the philosophical limits of 'sayability' or 'enunciability' that derive from Enlightenment rationalism. Understandably the kind of processive metaphysics cited above seeps through – in differentiated terms, and more by similitude than actual reference. The emphasis on the common features of diverse discourses of colonialism, contained in the flux of post-colonial literature, repeatedly throws up, for instance, a mystical (or inscrutable, or inexplicable) factor in the Orient as encountered by the Occidental writer and scholar. This is a commonplace of post-colonial readings, and a large number of post-colonial readings are devoted to deciphering the negotiations which the mystical factor symbolized. The perception of the Oriental mystical (or inscrutable, inexplicable, etc.) factor is located within the social psyche, or field of imagination, of the early colonialists, often with a self-critical inflexion (critics are accustomed to placing the vogue of Oriental fantasies and the Oriental Gothic from the seventeenth to the early nineteenth centuries in this fashion). It becomes the subject of nineteenth-century empiricist subversion, and an index of the irrationality (and immorality) of colonized cultures. To be able to explain the magical and the baffling through the resources of science becomes a challenge to the integrity of non-Western (and generally colonized, or available to colonization) cultures. Thus students of colonial/post-colonial literature are able to comprehend the rationale at work in Kipling's stories (in *Kim* (1901), for example, the Lama's mystical attainment is no more than a submersion in a ditch, and Kim's ability to see through Lurgan Sahib's *jadoo* rests on his ability to chant the multiplication table in English – and the only hint of the mystical or divine in the native's world is the advent of the white man himself), or in those of Rider Haggard (all the myths of the Africans in *King Solomon's Mines* (1885) or *She* (1887) are debunked, and the mystical is reoriented in the 'natives'' view in a magical or god-like whiteness, ultimately personified in She). The subtle process of empiricist, and implicitly cultural, subversions of non-Western cultures (identified with the mystical factor) is possibly best exemplified in the most popular genre to emerge from the nineteenth century: the detective story. The mystery in Wilkie Collins's *The Moonstone* (1868), and a large number of Sherlock Holmes stories, told by the intrepid ex-colonial doctor, and indeed later in Chesterton's Father Brown stories and in Agatha Christie's Hercule Poirot stories (especially those set in Egypt), derive from the Oriental mystique and are resolved by Western science and its 'grey cells'. The mystical element of the Orient is reinstated to some extent in the early-twentieth-century liberal, and occasionally anti-colonial, writings: the inexplicable and all-subsuming *boum* of the caves in Forster's *A Passage to India* (1924) would, of course, come to mind; the spiritual affirmations of L. H. Myer's *The Near and The Far* (1929), or, on a quite different note, D. H. Lawrence's or Ezra Pound's or T. S. Eliot's spiritual poetic affirmations drawn in terms of symbols from south American and Asian cultures, could equally be evoked here. The mystical factor of the Orient, or the affirmative spiritual aspect of the Orient, after a few evocations in Western modernist self-critiques of spiritual sterility (Arthur Koestler, for instance), get absorbed into the New Left politics of the Sixties.

The different evocations of the Oriental mystical factor as apprehended in the Occidental gaze are easily linked to the kind of metaphysical process identified above in the retrospection of post-colonial literature. Whether this apprehension comes as the self-reflection of a social psyche, as a proto-scientific cultural subversion, as a liberal reaffirmation of cultural value in the non-Western and colonized world, or as an expression of the culture of the *id* (following broadly Marcuse's New Left formulation in the Sixties) which is potentially radical from a Western view-point, all these express the contingency of the limits of sayability. The insertion of the mystical factor in colonial/post-colonial discourses revolves around the assertion of the all-encompassing nature of rational and scientific explication, or the denial thereof. To assert it, writers extend the scope of sayability indefinitely; the logic of language subsumes the view. To deny it writers gesture towards the limits of the logic of language, and Forster's *boum* becomes the inexplicable signifier which counters all attempts at explication. Implicit in these evocations of the mystical are the different sorts of power-alignments which legitimize or subvert colonial/post-colonial discourse formations. These become clearly traceable and comprehensible as such only in the retrospection of the flux of post-colonial literature.

One of the significant outcomes of the above observations on post-colonial literary production from within the (ex-)colonies – the so-called 'New', Post-Colonial, Commonwealth, etc., literatures in English could be noted here. In different ways, the latter often begin their assertion of cultural coherence and their challenge to the Occidental view by *taking possession* of the mystical factor. What had been a liberal mode of cultural affirmation extended to non-Western, usually colonized, cultures is wrested from the dialectical opposition to European rationalism (for example, Forster's European order and India's mess) and, so to say, taken possession of by Indian, Nigerian, South African, Malaysian, etc., writers reflecting on colonialism/post-colonialism, especially when doing so in the 'language of the coloniser'. I do not mean that such writers thereby proudly profess mystical allegiances – they often do, but that is not the point. The point is that such writers have a more sympathetic and natural assimilation of the mystical or metaphysical, not as something odd, different, 'supernatural', but as something that is understandable even if not sayable, 'natural', and essentially human. When R. K. Narayan (the same could be said of Raja Rao, or Nissim Ezekiel, or Kolatkar) evokes the mystical in the fictional world of Malgudi – and he does so consistently, notably in books like *The English Teacher* (1945), *The Guide* (1958), *The World of Nagaraj* (1990), amongst others – it flows into the daily existence of Malgudi, and becomes an indelible part of its mundaneness and harmony. Similarly, when Chinua Achebe describes the tribal rituals and beliefs of the Ibo people in *Things Fall Apart* (1958) (or when Amos Tutuola, Ngugi wa Thiongo, Wole Soyinka, or Ama Ata Aidoo bring these up for the different tribal groups of their respective countries), these become part of an understandable and harmonious way of life to which colonial influx does violence. And yet again, in Wilson Harris's novels one finds the evocation of the spiritual as an aspect of the almost existential encounter (as he explains in *Tradition, the Writer and Society* (1967)) with the Caribbean colonial history of mind-boggling displacements and disappearances of whole populations.

The latter kind of accommodation of the metaphysical and the physical appears to hold promise: if the dialectics of physical/metaphysical is somehow dissolved into a homologous area, the processive model of metaphysical apprehension cited above (and the oppression of sayability) seems to be somehow discredited. Perhaps in this the flux of post-colonial literature may somehow perceive the reconciliation which it arguably reaches out to. But can the limits of enunciation be disregarded so easily? Is this a substantial ideological attitude with affective cultural, social and political repercussions? What are these, if these are indeed there? I cannot approach these questions without a significant departure from the theme of this chapter – a separate space would have to be reserved for that. Instead I move on to an analogous theoretical position which is pertinent to post-colonial literature and scrutinize that.

Third Space

In post-colonial theory an unenunciable but meaningful resolution of the dialectics implicit in a consideration of colonial/post-colonial discourses is potentially encountered in Homi Bhabha's now well-known notion of the 'third space'. This emerges from Bhabha's perception of the slippages and ambivalences which can be located and used to subversive effect – and perhaps lead to theoretically constructive spaces – in colonial/post-colonial discourses (in the frame of this chapter I, of course, include both within the flux of post-colonial literature). The interesting positing of the subversive effects and constructive spaces that may emerge through an examination of ambivalences is not unrelated to the attempt to reach a metaphysical beyond of enunciation. But the spirit in which Bhabha's metaphysical space (which is what, I think, his notion of the 'third space' ultimately amounts to) is conceived does not emulate the models of processive metaphysics I had outlined at the beginning of this chapter. Instead, analogous to the harmonizations of physical and metaphysical noted above in R. K. Narayan's and Chinua Achebe's works, Bhabha tries to derive the Third Space against the grain of a processive metaphysics, by seeking an alternative to the necessary dialectical reasoning involved in models of processive metaphysics. *It seems to me that Bhabha's attempt fails because his alternative is misconceived and inevitably refers him back to the sort of dialectical conception he wishes to leave behind; and because in its own terms it cannot possibly be a historically, culturally, and politically affective idea – it is no more than a blank in the flux of post-colonial literature.*

In this section I confine my comments on Bhabha's

description of the so-called Third Space and its shortcomings to the essay 'The commitment to theory'. The dialectically understood physical space which he hopes to circumvent is, of course, self-reflexively identified with his own location as post-colonial theorist and academic, and the universalized dialectic of theory/practice which is involved in that location. This is probably best put in Bhabha's own words:

> It is said that the place of the academic critic is inevitably within the Eurocentric archives of an imperialist or neo-colonial West.... Must we always polarize in order to polemicize? Are we trapped in a politics of struggle where the representation of social antagonisms and historical contradictions can take no other form than a binarism of theory vs politics? Can the aim of freedom of knowledge be the simple inversion of the relation of oppressor and oppressed, centre and periphery, negative image and positive image? Is our only way out of such dualism the espousal of an implacable oppositionality or the invention of an originary counter-myth of radical purity? Must the project of our liberationist aesthetics be forever part of a totalizing Utopian vision of Being and History that seeks to transcend the contradictions and ambivalences that constitute the very structure of human subjectivity and its systems of cultural representation?[6]

The rhetorical questions with which Homi Bhabha's 'Commitment to theory' commences are restated here as the matter of our scrutiny. This section is not the recipient of their address; this section interrogates the direction of their address. These questions are addressed to those who are not committed to theory in the same manner as the addressor of these questions. The addressee needs to be persuaded that the polarities which fix Bhabha's position (as a theoretician) 'within the Eurocentric archives of an imperialist or neo-colonial West' demand clarification, and that the ostensibly and self-reflexively Westernized form of address is not a linear and unproblematic transfer of political allegiances but also an interrogative and radical (though historically structured) discursive gesture. It is only in this sense that Bhabha's questions are rhetorical. The questions could be perceived as the beginnings of an answer to, say, Aijaz Ahmad's sort of critique of postmodern and concurrently post-colonial critical theory through the medium of a metatheoretical Marxist analysis which delineates the 'project' of critical thinking as ideologically dependant on its context – an amorphous assimilative European-American advanced-capitalist context. Within this project Homi Bhabha is fixed exactly as he doesn't wish to be.[7] In the argument that follows in 'Commitment to theory' Homi Bhabha's contention that 'the attention to rhetoric and writing reveals ... the discursive ambivalence that makes the "political" possible'[8] could be taken as an adequate counter to the Ahmad kind of analysis except, of course, that it isn't one. The two modes of enquiry (Bhabha's and Ahmad's) do not engage with each other except at cross-purposes. Whether to look at the 'rhetoric and writing' from which the political emerges, or whether to discern the superstructure through which 'rhetoric and writing' are insidiously and inevitably available is a bit like assailing the chicken-and-egg question. There is no dialectic involved here (in this Bhabha is misled by his rhetoric) – there are two consistent approaches at work here which don't overlap and don't negotiate with each other. When they appear to do so they simply reaffirm their discrete methodologies and convictions. However unpleasant their asseverations might be to each other Aijaz Ahmad can launch no attack which could impinge on Homi Bhabha, and the latter could set out no defence which would persuade Ahmad. Both attack and defence are unnecessary; an attempt at either leads to no resolution and can only exacerbate differences. There is a misconception behind even the basic understanding of the dialectics (it is not one) which impels Bhabha's desire for this sort of resolution.

What is more interesting given the focus of this chapter however, is that Homi Bhabha addresses himself as he does above, defensively, with an air of leading up to resolutions where no resolutions are possible or even (for those who understand Bhabha in his terms) required. The resolution that is offered depends on the ambivalence which purportedly escapes the dialectics, the so-called 'third space', and it is consistent with the tracing of ambivalence within difference which characterizes Bhabha's rereadings of Said and Fanon and sundry eclectically chosen colonial texts. A longish quotation delineates the notion of the 'third space':

> The linguistic difference that informs any cultural performance
> is dramatized in the common semiotic account of the

disjuncture between the subject of a proposition (*énoncé*) and the subject of enunciation, which is not represented in the statement but which is the acknowledgement of its discursive embeddedness and address, its cultural positionality, its reference to a present time and a specific space. The pact of interpretation is never simply an act of communication between the I and the You designated in the statement. The production of meaning requires that these two places be mobilized in the passage through a Third Space, which represents both the general conditions of language and the specific implication of the utterance in a performative and institutional strategy of which it cannot 'in itself' be conscious. What the unconscious relation introduces is an ambivalence in the act of interpretation. The pronominal I of the proposition cannot be made to address in its own words the subject of enunciation, for this is not personable, but remains a spatial relation within the schemata and strategies of discourse. The meaning of the utterance is quite literally neither the one nor the other. The ambivalence is emphasized when we realize that there is no way that the content of the proposition will reveal the structure of its positionality; no way that context can be mimetically read off from the content.[9]

The ineluctability of the 'third space' (its essentially unsayable but potent metaphysical character) as it is apparently elucidated here renders it a curiously ineffective concept, despite the use to which Bhabha goes on to put it. There is a certain sleight of hand involved in the exposition which seems to *transcend* the oppositionalities and dualities but only by being *dependent* on their relation as such: the 'third space' seems to be a resolution which doesn't accept either side of the dialectic by paradoxically affirming the dialectical relation as such. This is emphasized by the either/or, or neither/nor, relations which are used to present the 'third space'. This explanation is conditional to the clarity between *énoncé*/enunciation; I/you; one/other; first space/second space being disturbed, sunk into disjuncture and ambivalence, by the 'third space'. If, however, the rationale of the ineluctable third space is given its full import (a process not dissimilar to the mad philosopher dealing with induction, a kind of Humean sceptic), if its unconscious and performative intervention is given full effect, the language of dualities becomes meaningless. The 'third space' implies that none of the dualities can even be posited: one is caught in the endless discontinuities and disjunctures between I and I (rather than I and You), a space and a space (rather than first space and second space), one and one (rather than one and another), and so on. And, it is the condition of this rationale that 'third space' makes no distinct sense in being designated as such, and 'ambivalence' is a *condition* of statement-enunciation or the lack of it rather than the *actuating principle* thereof.

Homi Bhabha, as I have maintained above, needn't address dualities and oppositionalities because his understanding of these is false. He has no battle to fight because in his terms these battles can't exist and needn't be resolved. When he therefore goes on to extend the above to maintain that:

> [The 'third space's'] intervention quite properly challenges our sense of this historical identity of culture as a homogenizing, unifying force, authenticated by the originary Past, kept alive in the national tradition of the People;[10]

or:

> It is that Third Space, though unrepresentable in itself, which constitutes the discursive conditions of enunciation that ensure that the meaning and symbols of culture have no primordial unity or fixity; that even the same signs can be appropriated, translated, rehistoricized and read anew;[11]

it seems to me that he is actually begging the rhetorical questions with which he had begun. The 'third space' as theoretically constituted above doesn't merely subvert homogenizing, unifying, origin-attributing, and tradition-building processes, and open up appropriation, translation, rehistoricization and renewed-reading, it throws a question mark over the very apprehension of history and culture. History and culture cease to be enunciable as such when the condition of ambivalence is ceaselessly disjunctive; history and culture seem to be *non sequitur* in this context. I don't mean to suggest that Bhabha's is an implicitly nihilistic mode of theorization: my contention is that *the conceptual level at which notions like 'third space' are effective and the conceptual level at which historical identity and culture can be constituted and analysed are different.* There may be a continuous area of theorization which links these but Homi Bhabha doesn't provide it. What he does is pretend to provide it, while actually presenting a tenuous analogy between the two. The tenuousness extends to the programme that Homi Bhabha sets himself generally, and with occasional clarity, as in 'The post-colonial and the post-modern'.[12] This can be demonstrated in detail, but demands more effort than we can here expend on the issue. Needless to say, despite this, as a gesture of political conviction Bhabha's post-colonial programme is valuable, and insightful interventions with regard to specific *textual* details are legion in his work ('Signs taken for wonders'[13] is a case in point).

But, in a more general sense, the kind of alternative metaphysical intervention (outside the dialectics of processive metaphysics) that Bhabha attempts in post-colonial theory (or, in my terms, within the flux of post-colonial literature) is no more than insubstantial.

Cultural Essentialism

There is another strand of metaphysical expression to be found in the flux of post-colonial literature. And again this is not unrelated to models of processive metaphysics – though instead of simply apprehending the limits of enunciation and gesturing towards a beyond, it actually devolves into some sort of spiritual affirmation or religious conviction. Closer examination of these reveal no more than a regressive and unsecular cultural essentialism. As an example of this strand of metaphysical expression I briefly consider V. S. Naipaul's sustained and lengthy assault on colonial and post-colonial experiences, and the cultures of the so-called Third World.

Naipaul is much-revered, and occasionally condemned, for being a kind of witness against the Third World who is rooted in the Third World (there are many others – Nirad Chaudhury comes to mind). A series of early novels and stories written in the fifties, *Miguel Street* (1959), *The Mystic Masseur* (1957), *The Suffrage of Elvira* (1958), and *A House for Mr Biswas* (1961), set him up as a denouncer of the cultural vacuity, political sectarianism and psyche of despair with which his homeland Trinidad, and the Caribbean generally, was allegedly possessed. Naipaul's cultural and political critique of the Caribbean developed through a selective presentation of history in his fiction (notably his description of the 1948 and 1950 elections in Trinidad and Tobago in *The Mystic Masseur* and *The Suffrage of Elvira*), an ironical focus on the Hindu Trinidad context (with its own paradoxical reiteration of communalist attitudes), certain convenient narratorial strategies (particularly distanciation techniques in the placement of narrators and their language), and the reiteration of certain motifs (especially escape to England or the desire thereof, and the impotent potency of images of the West in the post-colonial mind – say, daffodils[14]). If one was left wondering whether this creation of a body of works of cultural and political critique was underlined by any affirmative cultural perspective or ideology suggestive hints began to emerge in Naipaul's books of the sixties. These consisted of both an analysis of the processes underlying the deplorable cultural hollowness Naipaul had depicted (primarily in the non-fiction), and the presentation of a clearer counterpoint between mimic cultures and peoples and mimicked cultures and peoples (largely in the fiction). His non-fictional overview of Caribbean and South American countries, *The Middle Passage* (1962); his account of his experiences of India, *An Area of Darkness* (1964); and his episodic historical account of events from the search for El Dorado by Spanish conquistadores to the first appearance of Chinese indentured labour in Trinidad, in *The Loss of El Dorado* (1969), are all, in different ways, explorations of the shifting and undermining of cultural identities, especially amongst those who had been colonized, in the process and aftermath of colonization. Images are constantly evoked in these to convey a sense of cultures – in the Caribbean, in India – which disjunctively hang on to the straws of their past heritage (often out of touch with the present) and look wistfully to the West and seek validity from the West at the same time: mimic cultures. In the sixties fiction the depiction of mimic cultures is put into counterpoint with the culture that is mimicked: this is seen in the arrangement of stories in the collection *A Flag on the Island* (1967), and in the clear Isabella-England juxtaposition in *The Mimic Men* (1967). More interestingly, a sustained treatment of England as often mimicked (especially from a Trinidadian-Indian perspective) receives some attention in the novel *Mr Stone and the Knights Companions* (1968). These counterpoints do not present the mimicked England (or the west generally) as an ideal culture – much of *Mimic Men* and

Mr Stone is devoted to demonstrating the deep-seated alienation and loneliness that lies at the heart of Englishness – but it is seen nevertheless as a self-contained, self-possessed and therefore 'authentic' culture. Naipaul's readers might have been forgiven for feeling that he was at this stage no more than a liberal humanist in a very traditional sense in his values, and though he didn't see these values necessarily exemplified in England he did see them located there, and he drew on them for his cultural and political critiques of the Third World.

Naipaul's modes of cultural appraisal appeared to be clear and complete after the sixties phase of fictional and non-fictional writing – he could have gone on applying them indefinitely to different cultural locations. In a sense that is what he set out to do from the seventies and has continued to do in the nineties: Africa came in for the Naipaul treatment in a series of fictional and non-fictional writings (including the novels *In a Free State* (1971), *Guerillas* (1975), and *A Bend in the River* (1979), some of the essays in *The Return of Eva Peron with the Killings in Trinidad* (1980), and the section entitled 'The crocodiles of Yamoussoukro' in *Finding the Centre* (1984)); India was re-examined critically again in *India: A Wounded Civilization* (1977) and more affirmatively later in *India: A Million Mutinies Now* (1990); the Islamic world (Iran, Pakistan, Malaysia, Indonesia) in *Among the Believers* (1981) and recently in *Beyond Belief* (1998); and the southern part of the United States of America received a brief incursion in *A Turn in the South* (1989). The presentation of the Caribbean-English counterpoint continues to get rewritten in thinly veiled autobiographies and carefully arranged fictions in *The Enigma of Arrival* (1987) and *A Way in the World* (1994). The patterns of cultural and political appraisal, and implicitly self-place-ment, established by Naipaul in the course of the fifties and sixties is constantly renovated with slightly different inflexions. Distanciation techniques in approaching the Third World proliferate: Africa is always seen through some sort of expatriate or outsider viewpoint; India and the Islamic world are not only given the outsider viewpoint, this viewpoint is brought to bear authoritatively on these subjects as reduced to a set of texts (interviews, newspaper reports, anecdotes) . . . and so on.

But this latter phase of writing is so self-consciously

reiterative of the sameness of Naipaul's perspective that it paradoxically begins to differ. In building on and testing the scope and extent of his area of sayability (textualization, scripting – however it is seen, it is a very self-conscious element of his writing), in traversing between his placement in the world and his cultural and political apprehension of the world, in constantly hopping across the mimic and the mimicked ... gradually, a sense of exhaustion begins to manifest itself in Naipaul ... a sense of having traversed, in a very material fashion, the field of sayability, and being left with nothing more to say, and no choice but to say the same things over and over again. Naipaul's denunciations of the Third World evidence more of a sense of impatience: his writings on Africa grow more disturbing, and are distastefully racist in connotation; his assessment of Islam in the two books express spiritual revulsion behind the careful distanciation techniques. His autobiographical movements between Trinidad and England exude the contentment of having 'arrived' from the former to the latter, and the disappointment of ending in the latter. Clearly some sort of transcendence (of both mimic and mimicked, of self and world) can be anticipated. Naipaul's controversial development in the flux of post-colonial literature gets sucked into the kind of processive metaphysics with which I had begun this essay.

I am not, therefore, surprised to find David Dabydeen's review of Naipaul's most recent book, *Beyond Belief*, expressing surprise at the manifestation of sympathy for the spiritual therein:

> The hopefulness in Naipaul's narrative lies in his accounts of individuals who resist such cleansing processes, and seek out the resources of pre-Islamic faiths (often a mixture of Animism, Hinduism and Jarvanism) in manifold ways. One such, the Indonesian scholar Dewi Anwar, believes passionately in the sacredness of place: a sacredness rooted in an awareness of the spirits of earth and of the animal kingdom. The ancient spirit world of nature has been denied by modern Islam, and by the financiers of Indonesia's skyscrapers: hence the possibility of the country's ecological and economic collapse.
>
> That Naipaul gives space to the expressions of ideas about the sacred is surprising to begin with. That he shows genuine sympathy for them is completely unexpected. The originality

for this travelogue lies not so much in its descriptions of societies gripped by fundamentalist beliefs as the autobiographical glimpses it offers to the reader.[15]

It might seem, as Dabydeen appears to imply here, that Naipaul himself (the autobiographical insight) has taken a new turn – has surveyed the scrutable with great care and reached out to the inscrutable, has viewed the physical and is beginning to apprehend the processive metaphysical. Another way of thinking about that may be that Naipaul is beginning to look beyond the mimic and the mimicked for some kind of transcendent and idealized spiritual culture.

I fear, however, that Naipaul's variety of processive metaphysics is the very reverse of transcendence: actually it is politically and culturally the most regressive stance that he could have adopted in the current *zeitgeist*. That this emerges (despite the veneer of liberal motivation, the call for intellectual development and self-awareness) from a familiar kind of Islamophobia, and that it devolves into sympathetic noises for 'sacredness of place', should have put Dabydeen on his guard. What Naipaul's processive metaphysical development amounts to is not simply an interesting biographical quirk, or another predictable reconciliatory moment in the flux of post-colonial literature, it has disturbing and all too concrete political repercussions. Naipaul has actually been systematically feeding these metaphysical reflections (ostensibly some as yet unresolved state of intellectual self-awareness *à la* Hegel) to the present-day physical world, and quite possibly with a full awareness of his metaphysical development (recent interviews suggest that he is quite satisfied with his own wisdom), from well before the appearance of *Beyond Belief*. This is amply evident if one examines the role Naipaul has (I hope unwittingly) played in the real-politics of India since the early nineties.

In a series of interviews and articles relating to India since the assault on Babri Masjid by Hindu communalists (with the support of the now in-power Bharatiya Janata Party (BJP)) in December 1992 in Ajodhya, Naipaul has offered himself as a defender of aggressive and ultra-conservative Hindu politics. Naipaul's search for an ideal culture beyond the mimic and the mimicked has clearly led him (at least in so far as he reflects on India and his *Indian* roots) to the notion of an essential Indian culture – easily conflated with the conservative fantasy of a pre-Islamic, homogeneous and nation-defining Hindu culture. This was there to be inferred from both *India: A Wounded Civilization* and *India: A Million Mutinies Now*, and he has made it as unambiguous as possible in recent articles. In articles written in the *Los Angeles Times* in 1996, and in the Independence Day issue of *India Today* in 1997,[16] Naipaul talks more pointedly of an India which was 'vandalized' and 'wounded' by an Islamic invasion (and to some extent regenerated by the British!) just as if India was a cohesive entity before that. These articles have been consistently used by the BJP in its Hindu communalist political propaganda (from which it is apparently now beginning to distance itself to some extent), and is a standard reference point of the literature of ultra-conservative Hindu organizations (like the VHP and RSS). These articles are easily appropriated to the logic of the founders of modern ultra-conservative Hindu politics, which calls for the creation of a homogeneous and harmonious Hindu India.[17] In an interview in July 1993,[18] Naipaul declared himself as favourably inclined to the assault on the Babri Masjid and saw in it a new historical awakening (the assault was followed by nation-wide communal violence). In an interview in January 1998,[19] he continues to maintain that position. He had also hailed in April 1995[20] the victory of the BJP and Shiv Sena in Maharashtra the latter is another political party which has established itself through aggressive Hindu communal politics. The effect of the end-result of Naipaul's processed metaphysics on politics in India could be summed up as follows:

1   He has promoted, along with and much to the delight of, established Hindu communalist organizations a notion of a culturally homogeneous and harmonious India of the past, and the need to return to some sort of cohesive intellectual self-identity in the future. This is not only historically dubious, it actually means defining the national status of India by trying to erase or reverse a thousand years of Indian history.

2   He has contributed to the sense of insecurity and alienation of the Muslim citizens of India – a minority of 110 million people and citizens of other religious denominations. In fact, he has actually condoned the violence that has been

369

perpetrated against them as a necessary facet in the 'rediscovery' of the above dubious historical and future purity, and as an aspect of democratic politics.

3 There is no getting away from it – Naipaul's metaphysical apprehensions have been translated into the most retrogressive cultural essentialism in the Indian context. It is fascist by appropriation. Fascist is not simply, as Naipaul would assert, a fashionable Western term. It might derive from the *fascio* of Mussolini's Italy but, as anyone minimally informed of the political connotations of that term knows, it has come to represent the description of nationhood in terms of racial, cultural and communal purity wherever that occurs.

Conclusions

I don't intend to do this elaborately. The above three points should speak for themselves. My final statement can be made in a single sentence: there are undoubtedly a few instances when a processive metaphysics has made promising contributions to the flux of post-colonial literature, but more often its appearance has been either insubstantial or retrogressive.

Notes

1. G. W. F. Hegel, *Phenomenology of Spirit*, trans. A. V. Miller (Oxford: Clarendon, 1977), p. 493.
2. Ludwig Wittgenstein, *Tractatus Logico-Philosophicus*, trans. D. F. Pears and B. F. McGuiness (London: Routledge and Kegan Paul, 1961), p. 71.
3. Ibid., p. 74.
4. Edward Said's *Orientalism* (London: Routledge and Kegan Paul, 1978) is accepted by most post-colonial theorists as being the starting point of post-colonial studies. Gayatri Chakravorty Spivak, for instance, describes it as the 'source book in our discipline' in the essay 'Marginality in the teaching machine' in *Outside in the Teaching Machine* (New York and London: Routledge, 1993), p. 56. Most surveys of post-colonial literary theory begin with an examination of Said: this is exemplified recently in Bart Moore-Gilbert's *Post-Colonial Theory: Contexts, Practices, Politics* (London and New York: Verso, 1997), which also stresses the initiatory significance of Said's book, pp. 34–5.
5. The most trenchant criticism of *Orientalism* is associated with Aijaz Ahmad's *In Theory: Classes, Nations, Literatures* (London and New York: Verso, 1992), especially in the chapter entitled '*Orientalism* and after: ambivalence and metropolitan location in the work of Edward Said', pp. 159–220. A comparatively early account of some of the problems to be encountered in Said's book is to be found in Robert Young, *White Mythologies: Writing History and the West* (London and New York: Routledge, 1990), pp. 126–40. A more recent view of the debates

around *Orientalism* is available in Bart Moore-Gilbert's *Post-Colonial Theory*, pp. 40–53.

6. Homi K. Bhabha, 'The commitment to theory' in *The Location of Culture* (London and New York: Routledge, 1994), p. 19.

7. Aijaz Ahmad, 'Literary theory and "Third World literature": some contexts' in *In Theory: Classes, Nations, Literatures* (London and New York: Verso, 1992), pp. 68–9.

8. Bhabha, 'Commitment to theory', p. 24.

9. Ibid., p. 36.

10. Ibid., p. 37.

11. Ibid.

12. Homi K. Bhabha, 'The post-colonial and the post-modern' in *The Location of Culture*, p. 175.

13. Homi K.Bhabha, 'Signs taken for wonders: questions of ambivalence and authority under a tree outside Delhi, May 1817' in *The Location of Culture*, pp. 102–22.

14. In an essay entitled 'Jasmine', first published in *The Times Literary Supplement*, 4 June 1964, and later included in the collection *The Overcrowded Barracoon and Other Articles* (London: Andre Deutsch, 1972), V. S. Naipaul makes the point about the dominance of Western images in the Caribbean neatly by noting that the daffodil is familiar in Trinidad *à la* Wordsworth (though it doesn't grow there) while the jasmine flower is considered exotic (though it does grow there).

15. David Dabydeen, 'In God's aeroplane', *Independent Saturday Magazine*, 10 May 1998, pp. 10–11. This is a review of V. S. Naipaul's most recent book *Beyond Belief: Islamic Excursions Among the Converted Peoples* (London: Little Brown, 1998).

16. Most of these are selectively quoted by the organs of Hindu organizations. An especially useful source is the internet site run by the Hindu Vivek Kendra from Mumbai (editor: Ashok Chowgule), which has an informative Archives section. Quotations from Naipaul's *Los Angeles Times* article were posted there on 23 June 1996. V. S. Naipaul, 'A million mutinies', *India Today*, 18 August 1997, pp. 36–9.

17. The historical insights and political repercussions are not too far, for instance, from the views of one of the founding fathers of modern Hindu nationalist politics. In his book on *Hindutva* (1923; Poona: Lokasangraha Press, 1942) V. D. Savarkar presents Indian national identity as based on a homogeneous Hindu culture which was destroyed by Muslim invasion – and therefore calls for a reinstatement of the description of India as Hindu, where Hindu is defined as an overlapping of race (*jati*), culture (*sanskriti*) and nation (*rashtra*) (p. 74).

18. Reported in *The Times of India*, 18 July 1993.

19. Interview with Rahul Singh in *The Times of India*, 23 January 1998.

20. Reported in *The Indian Express*, 2 April 1995.

24

Getting Someone to See

Colin Lyas

I hate everything that merely instructs me without augmenting
or directly invigorating my activity.

Goethe

A lthough my target is literature, theology and, indirectly,
ethics I can best draw attention to the phenomenon which
will centrally concern me, an understanding of which is a
prerequisite to any properly constructed curriculum in English
literature or religious studies, by taking an example from the
visual arts.

I

Richard Wollheim writes:

> A painting that I want to consider is one of Rothko's canvases
> from the Four Seasons series, now hanging in the Tate: to my
> mind one of the sublimest creations of our time.... The
> greatness of Rothko's painting lies ultimately, I am quite sure,
> in its expressive quality, and if we wanted to characterise this
> quality – it would be a crude characterisation – we would talk
> of a form of suffering and of sorrow, and somehow barely or
> fragilely contained. We would talk perhaps of some sentiment
> akin to that expressed in Shakespeare's *Tempest* – I don't mean,
> expressed in any one character, but in the play itself. (Wollheim
> 1973: 128)

Suppose, as I often have, I take someone not well versed in
the arts to see this painting, having first let her or him read the

passage from Wollheim, and that person reacts with incredulity that someone could speak as Wollheim does of what appears to be no more than one colour superimposed upon another.

That reveals the phenomenon with which we shall be concerned. For I and my companion both see, in one perfectly good sense of 'see', everything that there is to see. We can agree what colours are present, how they are configured, could even if we wished measure their properties scientifically and give such exact spatial co-ordinates as to allow that picture to be reconstructed were it to be destroyed. My sight is no better than that of my companion, nor is my state of scientific knowledge, nor even need I know more about artistic techniques and art history. Yet I, with Wollheim, say that this picture possesses a wondrous quality whereas my companion simply cannot see the quality I am attributing to it.

Consider now three other areas in which this phenomenon importantly exhibits itself, namely, literature, ethics and religion.

When I studied English literature A-level it was the custom for the student to be given two poems and to be asked to compare and contrast them, saying which was to be preferred. I always got the wrong answer. I did so, because, having at that time no grounds upon which to decide between the rival candidates, I merely settled for the one I liked (thereby nicely illustrating Kant's contention that there is a difference between the judgement of liking and the judgement of value). But although I was prepared to assent to my teacher's judgement that a Hardy poem was better than the Shelley poem with which it was bracketed, I could not *see* either that it was or why it was.

Consider next the case in which we read in Penelope Hall's *The Social Services of Modern England* (1965) that it is the duty of a social worker to establish a relationship of friendship with her [*sic*] clients; but that she must never forget that her first duty is to the policy of the agency by which she is employed. I simply see in this a debasement of the notion of friendship. Suppose another doesn't, thinking this an entirely proper and understandable way to think of the client–counsellor relationship. He or she, then, simply cannot see what I claim to see about the moral character of this attitude.

Third, I believe that there is a perfectly good sense of 'see' in which a religious person sees the world differently from the non-religious person. (And it is possible to say this whether or not one is religious oneself.) This is compatible with admitting an equally good sense in which both sorts of people see the same world, the same trees, clouds, skies, flora, fauna, actions, sufferings and so forth. But one claims, as Meister Eckhardt put it, to *see* God *in* these things.

In all these cases the situation is the same. We can be told that there is a perceptible difference between two things, and we can simply believe what we are told, perhaps because we trust the person who tells us, perhaps because we are encouraged to think that certain people are likely to be right simply by virtue of holding certain positions (schoolteachers, vicars and parents). But although we believe, we do not see, and in many cases we would like to see. For when we do not see we become shadows cast in a place by the opinions of others, and that sits ill with the wish to be autonomous from which, presumably, education gets its point.

II

Two main sorts of reactions are possible, given the situations that I have characterized. First, there are those who simply deny that there is anything to be seen such that one person can be right in saying that he or she sees the excellence of a poem and another wrong in denying that excellence to be present. That position generates subjectivism in aesthetics and ethics. 'That is a magnificent painting' boils down to 'I like that painting hugely', which is, of course, compatible with the truth of someone else's confession not to like it at all. Similarly 'That is a debased notion of friendship' which, again, is compatible with 'I've nothing against it' as said by another.

Some have tried the same tactic in religious contexts, so that 'There is (or isn't) a loving God' comes out as 'I take (or don't take) a certain sort of attitude to the world', which would entail that the atheistic assertion 'There is no loving God' and the theistic assertion 'There is a loving God' can both be true. That construction of religious utterances has not, however, had much appeal, if only because interchanges between atheists and believers seem absurdly mischaracterized when treated as analogous to differing but compatible preferences for ice cream. Atheists and theists take themselves genuinely to be in dispute, even though, as we shall see, the kind of dispute that is involved and the methods for settling it may have been misconceived.

But what goes for religion goes for literary and ethical judgements, too. We do not treat these as expressing compatible differences of taste. We argue about the merits and demerits of this or that view of friendship no less than we do about the merits and demerits of Hardy. The hard thing is to get a clear grasp of what is involved in those discussions. For there is a special temptation here. One begins, quite rightly, by assuming that if there is a genuine dispute between critics, ethical beings and believers and non-believers, then something had better be relevant to its resolution. Not understanding the nature of such disputes the wrong models are suggested as decision procedures (models which, as we shall see, can infect the curriculum). When those decision-procedures do not work, either that failure is disguised behind a mask of authority, or scepticism emerges as to whether there is any genuine dispute at all. For nothing seems so conducive to scepticism about whether there is or is not a truth about some matter as the failure of a prolonged attempt to find it.

III

I shall say no more about the first, subjectivist, reaction to the kinds of incomprehension that can arise when someone claims to see what another simply cannot see. Here my concern is a second reaction. This is to admit, what seems patent, that there is some kind of genuine dispute going on in criticism, in ethics and about religion and to ask what kinds of strategies are appropriate in the conduct of those disputes.

Here we immediately come to matters which have significantly to do with the construction of curricula. For I take it that an education in literature must have at its core the wish that those who have had it will understand what literary value is and be equipped to make their own judgements of that value. The curriculum then ought to be designed to meet that end. Similarly an ethical education must have as its core the wish that those who have had it will understand what an ethical judgement is and be able to make their own ethical judgements. And, finally, a religious education ought to equip those who have had it with a capacity to understand what religion is and to make their own responses to it. Failures to understand what it is to have these sorts of understandings and to be able to make these sorts of judgements will simply cripple the effort of designing such a curriculum.

I do not, incidentally, wish to deny that an education in literature, morality or religion is just to do with fostering a certain kind of insight into the values, if any, of literature, ethics and religion. Thus we may wish to study the history of religion, ethics or literature, the biographies of literary, ethical and religious figures, or we might seek explanations of why this or that form taken by literature (the novel), ethics (benevolence) or religion (Buddhism) arose where and when it did. But those activities are predicated upon the fact that there is something called literature, ethics, religion, which makes demands of us. Unless we understand those demands we do not understand what literature or ethics or religion is, and so have nothing, the origin or history or causes of which to study.

An example may help here.

Some years ago I was asked to teach eighteenth-century English literature in a university department. I asked my students in my first class what we would be asking about, for example, Alexander Pope. I got, as I expected answers like what history could tell us of the kinds of concerns that would have exercised Pope (for example, concern about activities forbidden to Catholics such as military service or university education). I was told, too, to look for influences on Pope and Pope's influences on others. But why *Pope*, I asked. And eventually, after much too-ing and fro-ing came the answer 'because he was a great poet'. And wherein, I asked, did his greatness as a poet lie? I even read parts of poems that seemed to be to have the stamp of greatness on them, and I asked what made that judgement appropriate. And no-one knew what to do. The odd one could venture 'his mastery of the couplet', though when asked for examples of that mastery and wherein it consisted could not proceed. But unless Pope was a great poet why bother with him? I shall study such things as what influenced him and what he influenced because I already can see from his work that he is a great poet (although I expect that the more I discover about him the more that understanding might be enhanced). By the same token, I can study why Methodism arose when and where it did or why the

Reformation took place. But any understanding of that as a contribution to the understanding of religion is parasitic on my understanding of religion as a form that life takes and of obtaining at least some comprehension of the power that religion exercises over those who are its followers.

I operate, then, with the assumption that a genuine debate goes on between those who claim, in literary, ethical and religious contexts, to see something and those who claim not to be able to do so. I operate with the further assumption that a literary, religious and ethical education seeks to produce insight. In the literary case this will be a matter of helping people to a capacity to see what is in literary works for themselves. I begin there. Later I shall ask what producing insight might amount to in a religious education.

IV

Let us return to the situation, characteristic, I take it, of the teaching situation, in which one person says of a work that it has a certain quality and another cannot see it. (Other cases, for example, where someone imputes a certain quality and another simply denies it is there, or where someone imputes one quality and someone else a different and incompatible one, will, I think, also be illuminated by the discussion of the teaching situation.) The teacher wishes to achieve two things. First, one wishes the learner to *see* the quality that one imputes to the work and not merely to learn to *say that*, or *believe without seeing*, that the work has that quality. Second, one wishes the act of getting the learner to see to be a part of an on-going process which will eventually terminate in the student's becoming possessed of the capacity to make such judgements unaided (or, in view of what is to follow, in a certain sense unaided).

There is a step that is now commonly made, and made for understandable, if not condonable reasons, that is quite disastrous. For the whole exercise is now commonly represented as one of first giving the learner a particular proof that the work does have the quality that the teacher imputes to it, and, second, teaching the student that this particular proof is an instance of a general proof procedure that, having now been learned, can be applied to settle any future cases in which doubt emerges. After all that is what one does when one proves to the student that the angles of a triangle add up to 180°.

To be sure, the student does want a proof in the sense of being shown that the work has the feature that is imputed to it. The trouble is that our notion of proof in academic life is now deeply dominated by what quite properly happens in mathematics or the natural science. That leads to the expectation that if there are to be proofs in criticism, ethics and religion, then they have to be the sorts of proofs that we find in mathematics and science. The prestige accruing to these disciplines has meant that nothing counts as a discipline with proof procedures unless it conforms to the models of proof to be found in those subjects.

Then two things have happened. First, attempts have been made to model the kinds of discussions appropriate to the arts, to ethics and to religion on the proof procedures thought characteristic of mathematics or physics. These give us the successful exemplars of knowledge-gaining subjects to which all others had better conform. But, as I shall show, all those attempts ended in nonsense. But then the second consequence occurred. For since the proof procedures of mathematics and physics are the model to which any well-founded discipline must aspire, and since the study of the arts, the practice of ethics and beliefs of the religious do not conform to those proof procedures, so those are lesser subjects than mathematics and science. Those who do not believe that this has been a consequence ought to ask themselves questions about the marginalization of certain subjects in the national curriculum, ought to ask why the arts have to fight more vigorously for their place in the curriculum than the sciences pure and applied. And those who point out that ethics does have a place allotted to it might reflect that those who allotted it that place (as opposed to already hard-pressed teachers who are imaginatively trying to use it) manifest not the slightest idea what the teaching of ethical insight might be, being, I suspect, motivated rather by the slender hope that a bit of ethical education might, somewhat more cheaply than proper provision for leisure and meaningful work, reduce the crime rate.

I wish now to do two things. I wish to show why modelling criticism, ethics and religion on the proof procedures of mathematics and the sciences is bound to be a useless undertaking. Second, I want to show that this is no reason to

378

demote these subjects in the league table of rationality. Other, more attractive models offer themselves upon which coherent curricula can be constructed.

V

What are the proof procedures envisaged by those who take mathematics and the natural sciences as their paradigms of rationality? One is clearly deduction, the kind of proof manifested in demonstrations that the angles of a triangle add up to 180°. That kind of proof has had a hypnotic effect on our thought. For if it is valid it is conclusive. If I can get someone to accept premises from which a conclusion deductively follows, then that person has no choice but to accept the conclusion that follows. The other kind of proof is induction, the kind that is often said to be typical of the natural sciences. Here the evidence gives me reason to believe something without forcing me on pain of contradiction to that conclusion. If, having observed 2,000 cars pass with one passenger I infer that the next one will probably have one passenger, I use induction. That kind of reasoning is persuasive in human life.

Those kinds of procedures are of no help when we are trying to get someone to see some quality of a poem or an ethical action. Our problem is that the other can agree with us about the poem – for example, that it has a certain rhyme scheme, certain metaphors and other figures of speech. Our problem is to get him or her from these features on which we agree to a state in which she or he can see what is embodied in these by way of poetic quality. How is deduction to help? For from the premise that a poem has a certain rhyme scheme, a certain pattern of stress, exhibits certain tropes it will not deductively follow that poetic quality is present. One could agree that all those features are present and not be inconsistent in refusing to admit that the work has poetic quality.

Induction is slightly more interesting. For one can make inductive inferences about poetic quality. For example, knowing that a poem is by Keats is a reason for concluding that it is probably good. This, indeed, is how some people proceed, those who are lost if they do not know by whom a poem is written. But note two things: first, the person doesn't *see* that the poem is good, but rather believes that it is, and that is not what we want. Second, how is the induction established? Presumably one looked at a poem and saw it to be good, then found it to be by Keats or Byron and so correlated goodness with being by Keats or Byron. But then the induction is not basic. What is basic is the judgement that the painting or poem was good. This was not an inductive judgement. Until it had been non-inductively made there was nothing inductively to correlate with anything.

Yet people often proceed in the teaching of literature and ethics and religion in ways that do involve deduction and induction. Notoriously in theism people are offered by theologians deductive and inductive proofs for the existence of God. Much is made of the fact that these proofs don't work. When this is shown, those who have been brought up to believe in God on the basis of them experience something of a let-down. More of interest to me is the fact that even if they worked they would not do what is wanted. For what is wanted is not that someone should *believe that* there is something or other, but that someone should *see and feel* what it is to be religious, just as one wants not that someone should *believe that* this is a good poem but should *see* wherein its goodness lies.

What we often have, also, is an appeal to authority. Sometimes this is perfectly legitimate and useful. If I can't see that a poem is a great one, being told that those who have spent time on such matters think it is gives me some reason to believe that it is and some motive for believing that if I go on trying I might come to see what appeals about it. Less legitimate is simply telling someone that Shakespeare is a great playwright and then forcing a study that delivers no insight.

Most pernicious is this fact. Some believe that only what can be empirically observed and quantified counts as objective. If, then, the study of poetry is to be objective, there had better be something one can count and observe. So one's attention is drawn to rhyme schemes, stress patterns, alliterations. But to see these is not to see the value of the work, which is emergent from these.

When I was a schoolteacher I had occasion to mark examination scripts which asked the candidate to analyse a poem. These would often list the features of the piece, using such fine-sounding phrases as iambic pentameter, onomatopoeia and oxymoron. At the end I was inclined to put 'So what?'. For the bearing of all that on the judgement of poetic quality was never shown.

Literary teaching too often degenerates into history or sociology. We are told what influenced someone, what caused certain revolutions in taste. This is because that exempts the teacher from having to say wherein the value of a work consists and from the task of getting someone to see that. And when the work is not already included in what is question-beggingly called 'the canon', the teacher may be entirely uncertain whether it has value. Much safer then to dwell on themes, history and quasi-sociology.

I need scarcely add that the teaching of ethics and religion fares no better. An ethical education, no less than a literary education, ought to be aimed at inducing a certain kind of insight, an awareness of a certain way of thinking about others and our relations with them (which is not, as we shall see, a matter of seeking some unanimity). When someone asks a teacher why it is wrong to keep a bundle of used five pound notes which has fallen off a lorry on its way to the incinerator, that person is asking for a certain kind of insight. He or she is puzzled because unable to see what is wrong with that action and is asking to be *shown* this. How many people would be confident of saying anything that would help that puzzlement? What we often get is the invocation of some moral injunction (it's wrong to steal), which simply reinforces the puzzlement, or some dubious speculation about what would happen if everyone did that. Likewise, someone who asks why a loving God countenances suffering can only be helped by being given some insight into the concept of God's love that eases the puzzlement. Usually what is offered is some reason why God should be excused for allowing suffering (it makes us better, it is a punishment) as if it made sense to call God to judgement. That I do not have to be a believer to find that bizarre is shown by the penetrating remark by Camus, himself no believer, that he who calls God to judgement kills him in his own heart (Camus 1965: 57). Here even a non-believer can glimpse the point of Simone Weil's remark in *Gravity and Grace*, that the problem is not to find an excuse for evil but a use for it.

VI

If induction and deduction worked in the arts, in ethics and in religion, one would have expected disputes there to have yielded to these long since. They have not. The temptation is then, as I have said, for someone to think that a discipline is well-founded if it has proof procedures, that induction and deduction are the only methods of proof, and then to conclude that the non-applicability of these to religion, ethics and the arts shows these to be not rationally well-founded.

But, of course, deduction and induction are not the only proof procedures, so that their absence from the disciplines we are discussing shows nothing about the non-rationality of those disciplines.

Let us begin by noting that although I can reason you into going to see something, Stonehenge perhaps, I cannot reason you into seeing it. You open your eyes and there it is. But although I cannot reason you into seeing it, you can nonetheless be entirely justified in saying that you see it, if you are standing before it and employing the operative visual apparatus. You can, moreover, be justified in saying that you perceive something even if others, including a majority of others, cannot perceive what you claim to be perceiving. A trained eye can see the difference between colours which the untrained cannot, just as a trained palate can discriminate between wines that to the majority are indistinguishable.

When seeing is in question, the proper proof procedure is looking. If you want a proof of my claim that it is raining outside, I can simply say that if you don't believe me, you should go and look. Since, as I have argued, what we are after in literary, ethical and religious education is ultimately an ability to see something, what we need is a training not in reasoning but in seeing. Reconceiving the curriculum to that end seems to me the most interesting challenge that now faces us.

I now wish to make some remarks about what might be involved in a training in seeing. What I say is schematic, but I know, from the experience of having teacher trainees devising curricula as exercises in the training of seeing, that the schema offers ample scope for the imagination of those who would fill it in.

VII

An essential first point is that in educating perception one is not giving someone a capacity which but for the education they would not have had. The skills we seek to develop in an education in the arts, in religion and in ethics are already there in the learner. Take first the arts: a child spontaneously reacts aesthetically. I quote:

> Everything we are to study rests on the bedrock of the spontaneous reactions we made, from earliest infancy, to nature and created things. A child hears a piece of music and reacts by marching up and down, swinging its arms: it listens enraptured to story tellings: it may begin by throwing paint, but soon takes an intense interest in the precise choice and positioning of colours; it delights in the movements of trees and clouds and the textures and fragrances of the world. These responses are a form our life takes, as natural to us as eating and sleeping. They are the beginning of what would issue, were education systems designed to reinforce rather than frustrate our aesthetic development in being moved by Jánacek, entranced by Kundera and fascinated by Kitaj. (Lyas 1997: 1)

As small children we simply marched up and down to music, or giggled at clever rhymes or sang along to bouncy rhythms. To develop aesthetically is, in part, to augment those responses with words and gestures that allow infinitely more complex and subtle ways of articulating our aesthetic reactions: words like 'too', 'trite', 'garnish', 'beautiful', 'ace', 'wicked', and countless others.

Now consider three lessons for those considering literary (aesthetic) and (as we shall see) ethical and religious education.

First, we learn to use the words of our language in the traffic of life. That is how we acquire words like 'believe', 'time', 'know', 'clock' and so forth. Only sustained immersion in the practices of time-telling, information-giving, counting and the like will give us a mastery. From that it follows that a mastery of a vocabulary with which to talk about literature can only come from an immersion in literature and in the communal activity of talking about literature during which our primitive reactions are refined. (Note how children who become fascinated by certain popular forms of music develop extremely sophisticated capacities for making comparative judgements between them simply by the fact of immersion). Without that stimulus all that will be in place will be the residuum of the primitive responses – the kinds of responses one is likely to get when asking someone deprived of aesthetic stimulus to talk about Chaucer. But far from that immersion being *de rigueur*, the arts are marginalized (as are ethics and religion). Yet those who marginalize them have the audacity to blame the teaching profession when adults seem aesthetically stunted. There is a sadness here. Children, I said, are naturally aesthetic. They love daubing. On that could be constructed a rich life. But, as I found in my own case, if one was not 'good at art' one was shunted sideways at the age of eleven to woodwork or domestic science and arrived at the age of twenty ignorant of what do to in front of the world's great artistic treasures.

Second, we learn by immersion. (Those who think mathematics is intrinsically difficult should watch those who gave up on it at school calculating at the pub dart board or the bookie's counter, skills learned by immersion.) But with that goes the fact that we develop, so that at different stages we are ready for only certain things (D. H. Lawrence being rather advanced for six-year-olds). Typically we start garish and refine (watch children using cosmetics). We learn the aesthetic vocabulary of colour and rhythm very early and very quickly. The conceptual content of art, and the ways in which it can be treated by great artists, wait upon our own conceptual development. Hence one has to match the literature to the things that interest the learner at the stage the learner is at. That does not stop one introducing such topics as bereavement, divorce and death, about which more and more children are becoming experts.

Third, there remains the question how one educates seeing. Here there are two answers. One is a general answer: seeing is educated by immersion. (How else are such things as wine appreciation and acute colour discrimination acquired?) The more interesting question is the more particular one: how does one get someone to see something one has seen in a work in a particular case?

Here I repeat that the problem is not how to get someone to believe that something has a certain sort of quality, which is easy enough given the intimidatory powers available to authority figures such as teachers, but to get that person to *see* it.

Here are some possibilities. First, one simply points out what one wants the other to see. 'Have you noticed the bouncy rhythm?' Second, one might try to connect up the work with something the other can see. So one makes comparisons: 'You remember when you made that witty remark? Well, that's the kind of wit here.' Or: 'Isn't it like that when the whole world loses its meaning?' Or: 'Doesn't it remind you of someone being soppy?' We can use metaphors. 'It's as if the words were straining under a heavy weight.' We use 'what ifs': 'What if the story had been given a happy ending?' We can use gestures of the hand and body, intonations of the voice in reading, so as to enact what we want someone to see. Such things are all we have, and they can be effective, although their effectiveness is not guaranteed. (Anyone interested in the development of curricula based on such models should address their enquiries to Nick MacAdoo of Goldsmith's College and the Open University.)

Two corollaries of this: first, one can do all this only if one can oneself see what there is to be seen. No teacher of English ought to pretend to see. Second, in teaching literature we have to put ourselves at risk in two ways. First, we may be dealing with something about the merit of which we are unsure. Then all we can do is, collectively with those we teach, *explore*, using the techniques I have suggested. (That is more fun, anyway.) Second, we run the risk that those we teach will get us to see that we have got something wrong. Of course this will be so. Those we teach are not empty vessels waiting to be filled with our superior knowledge. They bring a life and experience which is not ours, and which may in certain dimensions be richer than ours. All that is to say is that the teaching of those subjects which seek to impart insight cannot be authoritarian.

VIII

I wish now to say two final things, one about marginalization and one about the bearing of what I have had to say on the relation between literature and religion in the curriculum.

I have spoken critically of the marginalization of the arts, and I can imagine someone arguing that this occurs because the arts *are* marginal. Though women and men cannot live by bread alone, it is for sure that they cannot live without bread, so that those subjects which have to do with the production of bread – the sciences, pure and applied, and their matrix of mathematics – must have the base role. (That, by the way, is called into question by the interesting statistic that the majority of our jobs and earnings at home and abroad will be culture-related within the next twenty years). Moreover, it is said, the arts are an adornment, an icing on the cake, a matter of non-essential pleasure (a word likely to make them immediately suspect).

There *are* views of the arts that make them seem marginal, and there *are* engagements with the arts that have to do with relaxation after work is done, sheer pleasure and escapism. But that is not all that there is to it. For those who have had dealings with the arts – and I include all those who are fascinated by contemporary developments in popular music, cinema and television – are wont, from time to time, to say that the experiences they have had are the deepest and most meaningful of all their experiences, so that without them life would have been diminished.

That intuition is correct, although spelling it out is one of the central problems for the philosophy of art. My own suggestion invokes the notion of art as expression, although it is essential to understand the force of the term 'expression' here. For there is a sense of the term 'express' where that term refers to a venting of anger, say, in a boiling over. I contrast this with the case in which we feel there is something that we want to say which we cannot get clear. We struggle to find the words and then we find them and we feel that our inner lives have been clarified. What is mere art can be the midwife of this. I read a poem and I think 'that is how it is with me', and I feel illuminated.

I distinguish being in the grip of an emotion, anger or sorrow, say, and having that emotion in one's grip. I might feel overcome by an inarticulate sorrow and burdened by an inability to get it out. I then see *Four Weddings and a Funeral* and hear the magnificent rendering of Auden's poem about loss. I feel that has expressed how it is with me, and now I have the feeling in my grasp.

For many, many people I see around me I have the sense that they are in the grip of their feelings and that it would be better for them and for us if those feelings were in their grip. One thing a sympathetic teaching of literature can do is give people illumination and so bring their feelings into their grasp.

Merely to be at the mercy of feelings blindly occasioned in us is not to be self-possessed. When we can articulate them we make them ours. This is to say, however, that expression is rooted in, and will eventually only be understood when we have understood, the mechanisms of the mind's economy. Wollheim has it right when he relates expression to such psychic mechanisms and projection where 'over a widely varying range of conditions, from the benign to the pathological, the function of projection is to help the individual to achieve, or to restore, or to impose, internal order' (Wollheim 1993: 6–7). Could anyone seriously deny that helping people to bring that order to their lives is a central task of education?

IX

I believe that everything I have said about what an education in literature may be applies to religious education. First, that education simply has to start with the fact that certain experiences, experiences which can blossom into religion, are natural, theology being simply the elaboration of these. Someone not moved to awe by great mountains, the wide seas, the starry heavens above, majestic music, someone lacking any sense of wonder, of some love for things as they are, of some sense of contingency and dependency, is not educable about religion. Religious education has to be rooted there, and unless the learner eventually comes to see the world's great religions are rooted in such feelings which he or she has too, he or she will simply not understand religion.

That said we need now to note an ambiguity in the notion of religious education. For that education might be directed to securing an understanding of religion that would leave it optional whether the person being taught would or would not come to adhere to a religion. On the other hand the education might simply assume the truth of a religion and seek to induct the child into that truth. (Politicians who prate about the need for religious education in schools ought always to be asked which they espouse, the answer, I suspect, being an uneasy amalgam of the two approaches in which education of the first sort is reckoned likely to produce religious adherents, that, by some odd logic, being thought a short and cheap way to better social behaviour.)

What has to be done in either case conforms to the considerations I have earlier outlined. We have to start with what is innate by way of response to the world, those experiences of which I have just spoken. To *be* religious is to grow by immersion into a use of language which immensely refines and sophisticates the ways in which those experiences are articulated. To understand religion is to understand that at its root lie those sorts of experiences, experiences of wonder, awe, dependency and the like. The teaching will be adjusted to the conceptual development of the child. Discussion about the truth of religion will have to be conducted by trying to get someone to see something a certain way, to see, for example, what one wishes to do when speaking of the love of God. (By parity of reasoning, though I do not develop it here, ethical education will have to start with primitive reactions, like the propensity of every child to say 'it's not fair' in certain situations.)

It is a neat question how much understanding one can obtain without believing. (This is paralleled in the literary case: I can imaginatively understand Lawrence's world-view without in the end assenting to it.) In the end I am not sure that an understanding which stops short of believing is a full understanding. But we do not need that for the kind of understanding that a religious education in the secular state may require. Wittgenstein once remarked that although not religious, he had the possibility of religion in him (Malcolm, 1958: 72). That would mean, I think, one could understand such notions as awe, dependency, contingency, wonder at existence, without in the end being able to use religious language as a believer. And since I think everyone has the possibility of religion in her or him to that extent, we have all we need for religious education.

X

This is a book about literature and theology, and I conclude with two remarks that will summarize my contribution to that debate.

First, I have argued that religious education and literary education have this in common, that they both seek to produce a certain sort of insight, to get someone to see something. In both cases the way in which education must proceed is dictated first and foremost by innate propensities which are refined by immersion in the form of life that one wishes to bring to understanding. In both cases, moreover, simply telling someone something won't be enough to produce insight, so that education never can in these areas be authoritarian. The authority must be earned by delivering insights. In both cases, too, the stages by which the insight is deepened will depend on the conceptual and cognitive development of the individual, on which educational psychologists are better placed to deliver advice than I. But just as it is absurd to a teach a child by literature that eludes its conceptual state, so it is absurd to teach religion that way. Theology, like critical theory, must come late.

Second, the foregoing says that literary and religious education will run parallel courses. But there is more to it than that. For I have said that one of the points of literature, and the arts in general, is to bring to expression what is inchoate in us, and what may be inchoate in us is religious feelings of awe, wonder and dependency. But that is to say that one way in which to bring religion to clarity would be to treat, as part of an education in religious understanding, the great literary expressions of religion. That is why, when I lecture on religion, I use the first part of *The Wreck of the Deutschland* to give my students some sense of the experiences that underlie religion. That is why, too, if I wished to give someone a sense of what a believer is committed to when speaking of the relation between God and man, I would not use unhelpful analogies between powerful rulers and their subjects but the book of Job, which portrays a quite different relation. That is to say that literature might be essential to the task of bringing about religious understanding.

References

Camus, A. (1969) *The Rebel*, trans. A. Bower (London: Routledge)

Hall, P. (1965), *The Social Services of Modern England* (London: Routledge)

Lyas, C. (1997), *Aesthetics* (London: University College Press)

Malcolm, Norman (1958), *Wittgenstein: A Memoir* (Oxford: Oxford University Press)

Weil, Simone (1952) *Gravity and Grace*, trans. A. Willis (New York: Putnam)

Wollheim, R. (1973), *Of Art and the Mind* (Harmondsworth: Penguin)

Wollheim, R. (1993), *The Mind and its Depths* (Cambridge, Mass.: Harvard University Press)

Name Index

Name Index

Name Index

Subject Index

Subject Index

Subject Index

estates, medieval – analysis of *Canterbury Tales* in terms of 86–7, 88
ethics
  Chaucerian (in *Canterbury Tales*) 85–103
  Shakespearean (in *Much Ado About Nothing*) 136–48
  value judgements, establishing criteria for 372–89
  see also lesbianism; values
ethnic/cultural identity, relativity of 269–71
eucharistic themes in *The Time Machine* 208–12, 216
eutrapelia (wittiness), virtue of 139, 140–2
evil 250–2, 253–4, 258–60, 262, 273, 277–9
evolutionary theory, implications for apocalyptic 206–7, 211–12, 213–14, 217–18

faith, loss of 321–2
Faith in the City 112
Fall
  allusions to in *The Satanic Verses* 275
  Augustine's interpretation of 51–2, 56
  in novels of William Golding 255–6
  in religious thought of John Ruskin 197
fear 183, 223, 224, 226
Feast of Lupercal, The (Brian Moore, 1958) 288, 293, 295
feminism
  and the Bible 10, 14, 32
  feminist theologians 314, 338–47
  mystery plays, promotion of through 106, 111, 120
  see also lesbianism
fictional portrayals of Catholicism 286–311, 316–20
food, in novels of H.G. Wells 208–9
Four Quartets (T.S. Eliot, 1935–41) 221, 223, 224, 225, 226, 227
Free Fall (William Golding, 1959) 255, 256
Freudian analyses underlying novels of Salman Rushdie 268

General Prologue, *Canterbury Tales* 77, 86–91, 92–100
Germanic cultural traditions, Christianization of 63–84
Gnosticism 260
Golding, William – religious themes in novels of 249–64
'good' and 'bad' literature according to C.S. Lewis 244–5, 247
good and evil
  in novels of William Golding 250–2, 253–4, 258–60, 262
  in *Satanic Verses* 273, 277–9
  in thought of Samuel Johnson 183–4
Good Apprentice, The (Iris Murdoch, 1985) 320, 322–4
grace, paradox of in detective fiction of G.K. Chesterton 237
grandnarrative 1–3, 265, 290
Great Victorian Collection, The (Brian Moore, 1974) 301
Greene, Graham – novels of 316–20
guilt 226, 234–6

Hegelianism 247, 253
hell 241, 258–60
  see also evil
Hinduism, defence of by V.S. Naipaul 368–70
Hollywood, use of biblical images in 12
hope 182, 183
host, eucharistic undertones in *The Time Machine* 209
humanism, Renaissance 136, 137

I Am Mary Dunne (Brian Moore, 1968) 296–7
Idea of the Holy, The (R. Otto, 1970) 249–50, 262
idolatory, exploration of in *The Satanic Verses* 265–85
imagination
  contrasted with theoretic 197, 200
  Imagination Penetrative 191, 198, 199, 200, 201, 203
  importance of in engaging with texts 46–60, 86
  see also reading
immanence of God 319–20, 324–5
incarnation 149–72, 324
  see also mystery plays, contemporary productions of
incommensurable paradigms 222, 223, 224
individualization of spirituality 313–14
induction, limitations of in relation to the arts 379–80, 382
Inheritors, The (William Golding, 1955) 251–2, 254, 256
innovation, possibility of within Judaeo-Christian literary culture 38–9
interdisciplinary dialogue 9–60
interpretative communities 24, 25, 30
Irish novels of Brian Moore 292–4, 298–300

Subject Index

Subject Index

third space 359–64
postmodernism
  in dialogue with *The Cloud of Unknowing* 124–35
  exploration of in *The Satanic Verses* 265–85
  nihilism 276, 277, 315, 329–30
  postmodern irony, use of in *The Satanic Verses* 276–9
Power and the Glory, The (Graham Greene, 1940) 319–20
praise and adoration, place in religious poetry of John Donne 150–1
preconceptions, influence upon reading of texts 221–8
Preface to the English Dictionary (Samuel Johnson) 173, 174
pre-Vatican II Catholicism 290–7
  see also Vatican II
printing of Bible, role in facilitating internalization of Bible 39
processive metaphysics in post-colonial literature 348–71
Professional Correctness (Stanley Fish, 1995) 29
proof procedures, inadequacy of in relation to the arts 377–81

'queer theory', teaching of 330–7
Qur'an/Quran 38, 273
  see also The Satanic Verses

Rambler, The 175, 178, 179, 181, 182, 183, 184, 187, 189
ramifications of Samuel Johnson's insights into vacuity of life 173–89
reading
  approaches to Bible 27–34
  as doxology in St Augustine 44–61
  interrelationship with spirituality 35–43
  pleasure of 242–8
  relationship to spirituality in writings of C.S. Lewis 240–8
  religious reading, need for rediscovery of 9–26, 32
rebirth, recurrence of theme in *The Satanic Verses* 269–71
reductionism 316
religion
  future of in the light of secularization 313–26
  religious education 25, 327–37, 387–9
  religious postmodernism, aspects of in *The Satanic Verses* 276–83
  religious reading, need for rediscovery

of 9–26, 32
  religious themes in novels of Brian Moore, key critical strand 288–9
  religious value judgements, establishing criteria for 372–89
  religious verse of John Donne 149–72
Renaissance humanism 136, 137
resurrection, allusions to in *The Time Machine* 210–11
revelation, relativity of 265–7, 271, 272–3
'Review of a *Free Inquiry into the Nature and Origin of Evil*' (Samuel Johnson) 176, 177, 184, 188
revisionism, feminist 338–47
'Rime of the Ancient Mariner, The' (Samuel Taylor Coleridge) 257
Rushdie, Salman – exploration of postmodernism in *The Satanic Verses* 265–85
Ruskin, John – Christian theory of art 190–205

sacred and secular, tension between 317–18
sacred texts 10, 12, 14–17, 32–3, 265–85
  see also Bible
sacred, distinction from spiritual 40
sacrifice
  evolutionary and redemptive in *The Time Machine* 206–7
  in novels of William Golding 252, 253, 256, 257, 260
Satanic Verses, The (Salman Rushdie, 1988) 16–17, 265–85
Screwtape Letters, The (C.S. Lewis, 1942) 241–2, 246, 248
Scriptures *see* Bible
Seafarer, The 73–80, 81, 82
Second Vatican Council (1962–5) 286–7, 289, 290–2, 297–8
secularization
  impact on religion 313–14
  long-term implications for religion 324–5
  theological responses to 314–24
'seeing', levels of 372–89
self
  fulfilment through loss of sense of 242–4, 246–8, 315
  love of in theology of T.S. Eliot 223–4
  rediscovering through engagement with Bible 20
  relationship to ethics 90–2, 99
  self-expression, religion as 315–16
  self-reflexivity 93, 99, 100
  self-understanding 350–1

399

Subject Index

Subject Index